MONOPOLIES AND MERGERS COMMISSION

Mid Kent Holdings plc and General Utilities PLC and SAUR Water Services plc

A report on the proposed merger

Presented to Parliament by the Secretary of State for Trade and Industry by Command of Her Majesty
January 1997

Cm 3514 £28]

© Monopolies and Mergers Commission 1997

Members of the Monopolies and Mergers Commission as at 9 December 1996

Mr G D W Odgers *(Chairman)*
Mr P H Dean CBE *(Deputy Chairman)*
Mr D G Goyder CBE[1] *(Deputy Chairman)*
Dr D J Morris *(Deputy Chairman)*
Professor J Beatson
Professor M Cave
Mr A T Clothier
Mr R H F Croft CB
Mr R O Davies
Professor S Eilon
Mr J Evans CBE
Mr N H Finney OBE
Sir Archibald Forster
Sir Ronald Halstead CBE
Mr D B Hammond
Ms P A Hodgson CBE
Mr D J Jenkins MBE
Mr H H Liesner CB
Mr R Lyons
Mr N F Matthews[1]
Professor J S Metcalfe CBE
Mrs K M H Mortimer[1]
Mr R J Munson
Dr G F Owen
Professor J F Pickering
Mr L Priestley
Mr M R Prosser[1]
Dr A Robinson
Mr J K Roe
Dr L M Rouse
Mr G H Stacy CBE[1]
Mrs E C Tritton QC
Professor G Whittington

    Miss P A Boys *(Secretary)*

---

[1] These members formed the Group which was responsible for this report under the chairmanship of Mr D G Goyder.

Note by the Department of Trade and Industry

In accordance with section 83(3) and (3A) of the Fair Trading Act 1973, the Secretary of State has excluded from the copies of the report, as laid before Parliament and as published, certain matters, publication of which appears to the Secretary of State to be against the public interest, or which he considers would not be in the public interest to disclose and which, in his opinion, would seriously and prejudicially affect certain interests. The omissions are indicated by a note in the text.

Contents

Page

Part I—Summary and Conclusions

Chapter 1 Summary 3
2 Conclusions 6

Part II—Background and evidence

3 Background to the reference, the parties, their operations and financial performance 41
4 The regulatory framework and the role of comparators and competition 65
5 Water resources in the region 78
6 The views of General Utilities and SAUR Water Services 94
7 The views of Mid Kent Holdings 117
8 The views of the Director General of Water Services 133
9 The views of the Environment Agency 149
10 The views of other parties 159
List of signatories 185

Appendices (The numbering of the appendices indicates the chapters to which they relate.)

1.1 The reference and background 186
1.2 Statutory provisions governing (a) Mergers between water enterprises and (b) Bulk supply transfers 188
2.1 Synopsis of GU/SAUR proposals as finally presented to us 193
3.1 Chronology of main events involving GU, SAUR and Mid Kent 195
3.2 CGE financial information 197
3.3 The WaSCs and WoCs 199
3.4 FDWS financial information 200
3.5 SAUR Group financial information including the results of associated companies 201
3.6 SEW financial information 204
3.7 Significant interests in the share capital of MKH at 30 September 1996 .. 206
3.8 MKW financial information 207
3.9 Assets test 208
4.1 Legal framework for the water industry and for water resource management (BSTs and abstraction licensing): Note by the DoE 209
4.2 The operation of the current statutory regime: Note by OFWAT 212
4.3 Customer service levels 219
4.4 The DGWS's view of the status of water companies 222
4.5 The DGWS's approach to valuing the loss of a leading comparator 223
4.6 MKH's approach to valuing the loss of a comparator 227

Page

5.1	Key water resource schemes—Southern region	230
5.2	NRA Southern regional strategy—future resource balance	232
5.3	Local resource developments identified by the NRA Southern Region 1994	234
6.1	Extract from Martin Smith's affidavit in the course of proceedings before Mr Justice Knox in April 1996	235
6.2	Undertakings by GU to the Secretary of State for Trade and Industry	237
6.3	Notice of Annual General Meeting	239
8.1	The use of comparators in the water industry and effects of losing them: Note from the DGWS	243
9.1	The EA's specific longer-term demand management and other proposals	268
	Glossary	269
	Maps	273

Part I

Summary and Conclusions

1 Summary

1.1. On 21 December 1995 General Utilities PLC (GU) and SAUR Water Services plc (SAUR) announced their intention to make a bid for Mid Kent Holdings plc (MKH). MKH holds 99.9 per cent of the shares of Mid Kent Water plc (MKW). GU and SAUR currently have voting shareholdings of 19.45 per cent and 19.39 per cent respectively in MKH. GU also has shares in a number of other UK water companies, including Folkestone & Dover Water Services Limited (FDWS), whose area adjoins that of MKW, and where it has a 74.1 per cent shareholding. SAUR has two water subsidiaries in the UK: South East Water Services plc (SEW), which also adjoins MKW and is wholly owned, and Mid Southern Water plc, where SAUR owns 99.5 per cent.

1.2. MKW, SEW and FDWS supply water to a population of 1.3 million in most of Kent and East Sussex and part of West Sussex, one of the driest areas in England. The other main supplier of water in Kent and Sussex is Southern Water Services Ltd (SWS). We term the water supply areas of FDWS, SEW, MKW and SWS within Kent, East Sussex and West Sussex 'the region'. SWS is also a sewerage undertaker and provides sewerage services to the customers of FDWS, SEW and MKW.

1.3. GU and SAUR have formed a joint venture company to bid for MKH. Their proposals are complex. Under the terms of the Joint Venture Agreement (JVA) dated 20 December 1995 GU and SAUR agreed that once the share capital of MKH had been acquired at Stage 1, they would divide its principal operational area into two parts of approximately equal value (see Appendix 2.1). The western half (MKWest) would be merged with SEW and the eastern half (MKEast) would be merged with FDWS (Stage 2 of the proposals). Certain of MKW's water resource assets, chiefly abstraction licences and supply rights from third parties, would remain under the joint control of the enlarged SEW and FDWS. A Joint Resources Company (JRC) would be set up for this purpose.

1.4. Under our original terms of reference dated 23 May 1996 (see Appendix 1.1) we are required to decide whether arrangements are in progress which, if carried into effect, will result in the creation of one or more mergers of two or more enterprises as are required by section 32 of the Water Industry Act 1991 (the 1991 Act) to be the subject of a merger reference.

1.5. Our terms of reference were varied on 13 September 1996 (see Appendix 1.1), extending the scope of our inquiry to consider, in addition, whether there was an existing merger in place.

1.6. So far as any *existing merger* is concerned, we find that GU and SAUR have not been acting together to exercise control of MKH. However, we conclude that GU and SAUR are associated persons as defined in section 77(4) of the Fair Trading Act 1973 (the FTA) by virtue of the fact that they are acting together to secure control of MKH as a result of entering into the JVA. This means that for the purpose of section 65 of the FTA they should be regarded as one person. We find that their combined shareholding of almost 39 per cent confers the ability materially to influence the policy of MKH. However, in the very special circumstances of this case we conclude, using the discretion conferred upon us by section 65(3) of the FTA, that GU and SAUR should not be treated as having control of MKH for the purposes of sections 65(1) and 65(2) of the FTA.

1.7. We do not find that either GU or SAUR individually has the ability materially to influence the policy of MKH.

1.8. Accordingly, we conclude that there is no existing merger.

1.9. So far as the issue referred to in paragraph 1.4 relating to the *proposed arrangements* is concerned, we examined carefully the details of the proposed arrangements, the action taken by GU and SAUR to further the proposals and the value of the assets of the water enterprises controlled by GU, SAUR and MKH. We conclude that arrangements of the type described in paragraph 1.4 are in progress.

1.10. In considering whether the proposed arrangements may be expected to operate against the public interest we are required by section 34(3) of the 1991 Act to have regard to the desirability of giving effect to the principle (the comparator principle) that the Director General of Water Supply's (DGWS's) ability to make comparisons between different water enterprises should not be prejudiced. Comparative competition underlies the regulation of the water industry in England and Wales by the DGWS.

1.11. MKW is currently one of only five remaining independent water-only companies (WoCs) of a size that the DGWS finds useful for comparative purposes. MKW has improved its performance over recent years and does now seem to have the potential to reach the efficiency frontier in terms of operating costs. At Stage 1 of the proposals the loss of MKW as an independent comparator would materially affect the quality of comparative data available. At Stage 2, the complete loss of MKW would significantly reduce the amount of data available to the DGWS. We conclude, therefore, that the proposed arrangements would prejudice the ability of the DGWS to make comparisons between different water enterprises. This detriment, although difficult to quantify, is, in our view, substantial.

1.12. We also find that the proposed arrangements would lead to reduced prospects for competition within the region.

1.13. GU and SAUR argued that their proposals would have substantial benefits and would result in much improved management and use of water resources in the areas of the three companies. Their plans included new infrastructure which they argued would improve security of supply by facilitating the transfer of water from areas in surplus to those in deficit, better conjunctive use of water sources and new programmes for metering, leakage reduction and customer education. We recognize that there is a problem for FDWS and SEW over the availability of water resources in the region.

1.14. Section 34(3)(b) of the 1991 Act requires us to have regard to the desirability of achieving any 'other purpose' so far only as we are satisfied:

(a) that it can be achieved without conflict with the comparator principle; or

(b) that the achievement of that 'other purpose' is of 'substantially greater significance in relation to the public interest than that principle and cannot be brought about except in a manner that conflicts with that principle'.

1.15. We consider that the benefits that will derive from the proposed arrangements are not as great as was claimed by GU and SAUR, especially since most of the surplus water in the region is controlled by SWS, not MKW. Moreover, the bidders have been reluctant to negotiate bulk supply transfers (BSTs) and have not made use of the existing powers of the DGWS to order supplies and settle terms where negotiations have failed. We conclude that, even taking all of the benefits into account (whether or not they can be achieved otherwise than by a merger), the achievement of those benefits is not of substantially greater significance than the comparator principle.

1.16. We conclude that the proposed acquisition of MKH by GU and SAUR may be expected to operate against the public interest, with the particular adverse effects of prejudice to the DGWS's ability to make comparisons between different water enterprises and reduced prospects for competition in the region. Even if we were to take into account all the benefits of the merger the detriments would not be outweighed by these benefits.

1.17. We are required under section 72(2) of the FTA to consider what action should be taken to remedy or prevent those adverse effects.

1.18. The DGWS told us that the detriment of prejudice to his ability to make comparisons might be remedied through a package of measures designed to compel the newly-merged companies (MKWest and SEW and MKEast and FDWS) to become exemplary comparators, coupled with immediate price reductions.

1.19. MKH argued that the merger should be prohibited outright.

1.20. GU and SAUR argued that there would be no major detriment to comparative competition. Price cuts were an inappropriate remedy in view of the amount they were proposing to spend to achieve the benefits of the merger.

1.21. It was clear to us that the efficiency gains achievable through the proposed arrangements were small. In view of this, large price reductions would not be sustainable in terms of long-term cost reductions and were therefore an inappropriate remedy. The benefits would last only until the next Periodic Review, whereas the damage to the comparator regime arising from the loss of an independent WoC would be permanent.

1.22. We consider, therefore, that in this case the proposed merger should be prohibited.

1.23. Finally, we recognize the water resource difficulties FDWS and SEW face. If all the water undertakers in the region were prepared to co-operate one with another and with the two regulators we have no doubt that satisfactory long-term solutions could be found which would benefit the consumer. The DGWS and the Environment Agency (EA) have between them the necessary powers and influence to help develop such solutions. They should make every effort to do so.

2 Conclusions

Contents

	Paragraph
The region	2.1
The parties to the merger	2.4
Background to the reference	2.9
Subsequent developments	2.17
Terms of reference	2.20
The existing situation	2.22

Associated persons
- Acting together to secure control ... 2.25
- Acting together to exercise control ... 2.29
- Material influence as associated persons ... 2.35
- Section 65(3) of the Fair Trading Act 1973 ... 2.37
- Individual material influence ... 2.42
- Conclusions on an existing merger ... 2.44

The proposed merger ... 2.45
- Arrangements in progress ... 2.55
- Assets test ... 2.59
- Conclusion on the first question of our terms of reference ... 2.60

The public interest ... 2.61
Structure and regulation of the water industry in England and Wales ... 2.62
The use of comparators ... 2.68
Prejudice to the DGWS's ability to make comparisons
- Section 34(3)(a) of the 1991 Act ... 2.78
  - Independence ... 2.81
  - Reduction in the number of comparators ... 2.86
  - Valuing the loss of a comparator ... 2.99
- Minor issues affecting the comparator regime ... 2.105
  - Loss of a Stock Exchange listing ... 2.106
  - Disruptions in the collection and analysis of comparative data ... 2.107
  - The creation of the Joint Resources Company ... 2.108
- Finding under section 34(3)(a) ... 2.113

Other purposes
- Section 34(3)(b) ... 2.114
- Finding under section 34(3)(b)(i) ... 2.116
- Section 34(3)(b)(ii) ... 2.118
- Benefits arising from the proposed arrangements ... 2.120
  - Optimizing the management and use of water resources
    - Water resource imbalances ... 2.124
    - Integrated supply network ... 2.135
    - Long-term resource planning ... 2.137
    - Leakage reduction and metering ... 2.138
    - Generation of additional water resources ... 2.139

Resource management and water conservation programme	2.140
Conjunctive use of water sources	2.141
Deferment of need for major new resource development	2.142
Other benefits	
Efficiency gains	2.143
Improved competition	2.144
Service standards	2.145
Finding under section 34(3)(b)(ii)	2.146
Other detriments arising from the proposed merger	2.149
Conclusion on the public interest	2.154
Recommendations	2.155
Related issues	2.166

The region

2.1. FDWS, SEW and MKW operate in most of Kent and East Sussex and part of West Sussex. Their supply areas (the areas for which they hold appointments) are interspersed with some of those of SWS (see Map 7). The areas within Kent, East Sussex and West Sussex in which FDWS, SEW, MKW and SWS supply water are termed 'the region' in this report. SWS is a much larger company than FDWS, SEW and MKW. It is both a water and sewerage undertaker. Its water supply areas are widely separated. They are Kent Thanet, Kent Medway, Hampshire, Sussex Coast, Sussex East and Sussex West and the Isle of Wight. By contrast, it supplies sewerage services across most of the south-east of England both to its own water customers as well as to the customers of FDWS, SEW and MKW. SWS owns and operates a large number of water resources throughout Kent, Sussex and Hampshire. A considerable number of its boreholes and reservoirs are situated in the territory of MKW, SEW and FDWS.

2.2. A large proportion of the water supplied in the region is extracted from boreholes in the chalk and greensand aquifers. These aquifers, on which FDWS is completely dependent, are delivering close to the maximum amount of water practicable. Opportunities for sinking further boreholes are very limited. The balance of supplies comes from surface water. Supplies are drawn from the river systems in the region to fill major reservoirs, most of which were developed in the 1970s. SWS has been much involved in the strategic development of resources in the region. The principal scheme which it operates is centred on the River Medway and its tributaries. Water is extracted from the Medway at Springfield and Yalding, and from the Teise at Smallbridge. Some of the water is treated and enters the public supply system. The remaining water is pumped upstream to a large surface reservoir, Bewl Water. Most of the pumping takes place in winter, when the river flows are at their greatest. Water is extracted from Bewl and treated on site when it is needed or released into the river to allow abstraction downstream at Springfield. MKW contributed 25 per cent of the costs of the Medway Scheme and is entitled to a similar proportion of the water. The scheme has recently been further developed to allow transfers of water from Bewl Water to the enlarged reservoir at Darwell, which supplies SWS's customers in Hastings.

2.3. Map 7 shows the major pipelines in the region. The Wigmore–Eastling, Selling–Fleete main runs along most of the northern boundary of Mid Kent's area. It is owned by SWS and forms the principal source of supply to its Kent Thanet region. Both MKW and SWS supply to and extract water from the main to meet the demands of the Medway area and the towns in north Kent. The main running south-east from Darwell reservoir is owned by SWS and is used to supply water from the Medway Scheme to Hastings.

The parties to the merger

2.4. GU is a wholly-owned UK subsidiary of Compagnie Générale des Eaux (CGE), a large French company controlling a group with world-wide activities principally in construction, water supply and waste water services and an annual turnover approaching £20 billion (1995 figure). GU has shareholdings in a number of UK water undertakers, as described in paragraphs 3.28 to 3.30, including FDWS in which it owns 74.1 per cent of the shares. Most of the remaining shares are held by SWS. FDWS had a turnover of £10.5 million for the financial year ended 31 March 1996.

2.5. SAUR is wholly owned by a French company, SAUR International SA (SAUR International), which is majority owned by SAUR SA. SAUR SA in turn is majority owned by a private investment company, SCDM SA. SAUR SA's turnover in 1995 amounted to approximately £1 billion. The minority shareholder in SAUR International is a holding company owned 35 per cent by Bouygues SA (Bouygues) and 65 per cent by Electricité de France International (EDF International). The minority shareholders in SAUR SA are Bouygues and a holding company representing certain employee shareholders (see paragraphs 3.41 to 3.43). SAUR SA, SAUR International and Bouygues, like CGE, operate in several industrial sectors both within and outside France and water supply is a significant activity for each of them. SAUR has two water subsidiaries in the UK: SEW, which is wholly owned, and Mid Southern Water plc, in which it owns 99.5 per cent of the shares. SEW had a turnover of £53.6 million for the financial year ended 31 March 1996.

2.6. MKW was formed in 1888 to supply water to the parishes of Halling and Snodland. One year later it became a statutory water company (SWC). In subsequent years its operations expanded gradually, eventually covering an area of 2,050 square kilometres in central and western Kent and East Sussex. MKW retained its status as an SWC until 1989. In March of that year MKH was formed as a public limited company and the stockholders of MKW were offered shares in MKH in exchange for their holdings of MKW stock. At the same time there was a rights issue and an offer of shares to customers and employees.

2.7. MKH became the holding company for MKW in 1989 at the time of water privatization and it currently owns 99.9 per cent of the ordinary share capital. The shareholdings in MKH are more complex. Currently, and as detailed in Appendix 3.7, GU holds 19.45 per cent of the voting share capital, SAUR 19.39 per cent and seven financial institutions, including GU's financial advisers Morgan Grenfell & Co, Limited (Morgan Grenfell), hold between them a further 40 per cent.[1] MKW had a turnover of £34.7 million for the financial year ended 31 March 1996.

2.8. MKH has a number of other subsidiaries, as shown in Figure 3.4. These subsidiaries accounted for 16 per cent of group turnover in the year ended 31 March 1996 but made virtually no contribution to profits.

Background to the reference

2.9. GU has, since 1988, held a proportion of MKW's 6 per cent ordinary stock. Early in March 1989 it acquired further stock in the form of redeemable preference shares (see paragraph 3.61). As a result, its share of the voting capital in MKW increased to 29.9 per cent, the maximum permitted under the Takeover Code without triggering an obligation to make a

---

[1]As a result of the obligation of MKH under its Articles of Association to redeem all its existing voting preference shares by 31 March 1997, the shareholdings will change as shown in Appendix 3.7.

full bid. In 1990 the acquisition of shares that had resulted in this increased holding (which was, by then, a holding in MKH) was referred to the MMC.

2.10. The MMC carried out an investigation[1] into whether a merger of two or more water enterprises had been created after 11 January 1989 between water enterprises under the control of GU and MKW. It was found that GU had acquired the ability materially to influence the policy of MKW and that such a merger had been created. Further, the MMC concluded that the merger situation might be expected to operate against the public interest in that it prejudiced the ability of the DGWS to make comparisons between different water enterprises.

2.11. Following the MMC's report, in March 1991 GU undertook to reduce its holding to not more than 19.5 per cent of the voting share capital and not to make arrangements that might result in holdings by associated persons to take its shareholding over that level. It also undertook not to seek (or if offered, accept) the opportunity to nominate any person to serve as a director of MKH or MKW. On 30 June 1992 GU reduced its holding in compliance with its undertaking (see paragraphs 3.62 to 3.64).

2.12. SAUR began to acquire voting stock in MKW in the spring of 1988. By March 1989 it had acquired 15.8 per cent of the voting stock. This was converted into a 15.8 per cent holding of the voting share capital of MKH in August 1989, following the establishment of MKH as a public limited company earlier that year (see paragraph 2.6). In November 1989 SAUR made further purchases of stock, bringing its share of the voting capital in MKH up to 19.5 per cent. The DGWS wrote to MKH in April 1991 saying that he would expect SAUR to operate in the spirit of the undertakings given by GU and to ensure that its shareholding did not exceed 19.5 per cent. He does not, however, appear to have written to SAUR in this vein until October 1996.

2.13. Morgan Grenfell purchased £5 million of preference stock in MKW in 1986. This gave it a 50.2 per cent share of the voting capital, and it subsequently agreed with MKW not to exercise voting rights over more than 29.9 per cent of the stock. Following a rights issue by MKW in 1988, Morgan Grenfell's share was reduced to 27 per cent. In March 1989 it sold just over half of its holding to GU and the remainder to SAUR. Subsequently, in June 1992 Morgan Grenfell bought back the stock that GU was obliged to dispose of by the undertaking given to the Secretary of State following the MMC report referred to in paragraphs 2.10 and 2.11. That transaction was accompanied by an agreement which provides that if Morgan Grenfell were to sell, GU would receive additional consideration equal to [*] per cent of any profit made by Morgan Grenfell. Any loss would be borne by Morgan Grenfell except in certain specified circumstances. These arrangements were notified at the time to the DGWS, the Office of Fair Trading (OFT) and the Department of Trade and Industry (DTI) who said that they were content with the arrangements. At present the shareholding of Morgan Grenfell amounts to 9.35 per cent of the total issued capital.

2.14. On 21 December 1995 GU and SAUR announced their intention to make a bid for the whole of the issued share capital of MKH, which now holds 99.9 per cent of the shares of MKW. GU and SAUR agreed under a JVA dated 20 December 1995 to form a company for this purpose. The agreement provides for the making of the announcement of their intentions and for making submissions to the MMC. It provides that the making of an offer is conditional on obtaining satisfactory regulatory approval and agreement of the offer price. The agreement states that neither party will acquire equity share capital in MKH or enter into any arrangement which would result in an infringement of GU's undertakings.

---

[1]*General Utilities PLC and The Mid Kent Water Company: a report on the merger situation*, HMSO, Cm 1125, July 1990.

*Figure omitted. See note on page iv.

2.15. Under the terms of the JVA dated 20 December 1995, GU and SAUR further agreed that once the share capital of MKH had been acquired, the principal operations of MKW would be divided into two geographically-distinct parts, as explained in Appendix 2.1. The supply business of the western half of MKW's operational area would be merged with SAUR's existing wholly-owned business, SEW, which currently adjoins the western boundary of MKW. The supply business of the eastern half of MKW's operational area would be merged with that of the adjoining FDWS, which has GU as its principal shareholder. Certain of MKW's water resource assets, as described more fully in paragraph 2.48, would remain under joint control.

2.16. GU and SAUR did not spell out in their public announcement the proposed time-scale for the division of MKW. Subsequently, in February 1996, they formally agreed that the arrangements would be completed within four years of the date of the take-over in order to ensure legal certainty. They told us that they would like to complete all stages as quickly as possible, and well within the four-year period.

Subsequent developments

2.17. MKH believes that the arrangements entered into by GU and SAUR, and referred to in paragraphs 2.14 and 2.15, infringe the terms of the undertakings given by GU in March 1991. In April 1996 it took proceedings before the High Court for a declaration that GU had breached its undertakings. The Court held that MKH had no *locus standi* to bring the proceedings. The Secretary of State declined to bring proceedings and stated that the undertakings of March 1991 remained in force.

2.18. Under section 32[1] of the 1991 Act it is mandatory for the Secretary of State to make a reference to the MMC where it appears to him that it is or may be the fact that arrangements are in progress which would result in the merger of two or more water enterprises, subject to conditions as to the value of the assets of the water enterprises concerned.

2.19. The Secretary of State referred the proposed arrangements between GU, SAUR and MKH to the MMC on 23 May 1996. The reference was varied on 13 September 1996, extending the scope of our inquiry to consider, in addition, whether there was an existing merger in place.

Terms of reference

2.20. Under our revised terms of reference (see Appendix 1.1) we are required to investigate and report on whether arrangements are in progress which, if carried into effect, will result in the creation of one or more such mergers of two or more water enterprises as are required by section 32 of the 1991 Act to be the subject of a merger reference. If we establish that such arrangements are in progress (or that the actual result of the arrangements is the creation of one or more such mergers), we are required to consider whether the creation of each such merger operates or may be expected to operate against the public interest.

2.21. We are also required to consider whether a merger of water enterprises belonging to MKH, GU and SAUR respectively, which is required to be the subject of a reference under section 32, has taken place otherwise than as a result of the carrying into effect of arrangements

---

[1] Read with section 33 and the Water Enterprises (Merger) (Modification) Regulations 1994 (the 1994 Regulations), SI 1994/73.

that have been the subject of a reference; and, if so, whether that merger operates or may be expected to operate against the public interest. We consider first the question of whether a merger has already taken place.

The existing situation

2.22. The effect of sections 34 and 35 of the 1991 Act is that, for the purpose of deciding whether or not a merger of water enterprises has taken place, the provisions of Part V of the FTA relating to enterprises ceasing to be distinct apply. Section 65 of the FTA provides that enterprises are to be regarded as ceasing to be distinct if they are brought under common control. The section further provides that if a person is able, directly or indirectly, to control or materially to influence the policy of a body corporate, but without having a controlling interest in it, that person may be treated as having control of it. Thus if a person who has control of one enterprise is able materially to influence the policy of a second enterprise, the enterprises may be regarded as having ceased to be distinct.

2.23. Section 77(1) of the FTA provides that associated persons, and any bodies corporate which they or any of them control, shall be treated as one person for the purpose of determining whether enterprises have been brought under common control. Section 77(4)(d) provides that any two or more persons shall be regarded as associated with one another if they are acting together to secure or exercise control of a body corporate or other association or to secure control of any enterprise or assets.

2.24. Thus a merger of water enterprises would have taken place if:

(a) (i) GU and SAUR had, either by virtue of the JVA they entered into on 20 December 1995 or otherwise, become 'associated persons' under section 77 of the FTA, with the result that they would be treated as one person for the purpose of determining whether enterprises have been brought under common control; and

(ii) together they have the ability to control or materially to influence the policy of MKH; or

(b) if either or both individually have the ability to control or materially to influence the policy of MKH,

and the MMC considered that GU and SAUR, together or individually as the case may be, should be treated as having control of MKH for the purposes of section 65(1) and (2) of the FTA. We look at each of these possibilities in turn.

Associated persons

Acting together to secure control

2.25. We consider first whether GU and SAUR have been acting together to secure control of MKH. GU and SAUR initially argued that in order for them to be 'acting together to secure control' it was necessary that they were taking action which could *itself* have the effect of securing control over MKH. Acting together with a view to securing control in the future was not sufficient. They were, through the JVA, simply making preparations for a possible future bid. Before any bid could be made, the necessary regulatory clearance had to be forthcoming. Entry into the JVA was, in their view, simply a way of formally triggering the regulatory process and establishing that arrangements were in progress. GU and SAUR would be in a position to contemplate acting together to secure control of MKH only if four conditions were met: the proposed offer was cleared by the Secretary of State; any conditions applied were acceptable; GU was released from its undertakings; and a suitable bid price was agreed. Subsequently they argued that section 77(4)(d) was ambiguous and its interpretation depended on the interpretation of section 65(3) (see paragraph 6.65).

2.26. The DGWS said that it was for the MMC to judge at what point steps taken in preparation for a bid actually became an action taken with a view to securing control. But in his view the clause in the JVA which prevented the merger from proceeding without the Secretary of State's consent was sufficient to ensure that GU and SAUR were not currently acting to secure control. If companies such as GU and SAUR came to the DGWS for a preliminary discussion of a bid which they were contemplating, he did not believe this should be regarded as an action taken with a view to securing control.

2.27. We are advised that section 77(4)(d) should not be given such a restrictive interpretation that it applies only to action which itself secures control. We do not consider that the action taken in this case is merely exploratory; GU and SAUR have entered into a formal legally binding agreement to seek the approval of the authorities to acquire MKH, and, if obtained in terms satisfactory to them, to make an offer at a price to be agreed. They have carried out Clause 4 of the agreement, which provides for the making of a preliminary announcement and the proceedings before the MMC. They have argued that arrangements are in progress which, if carried into effect, would result in a merger of two or more water enterprises. We do not consider that the fact that there are prior conditions to be satisfied before an offer is made means that GU and SAUR are not acting together to secure control of MKH. We therefore conclude that GU and SAUR are associated persons by virtue of the fact that they are acting together to secure control of MKH as a result of entering into the JVA.

2.28. It might be argued that since Morgan Grenfell is financial adviser to GU, it could be acting together with GU and SAUR to secure control of MKH and that GU, SAUR and Morgan Grenfell were associated persons. Morgan Grenfell told us that its roles as financial adviser to GU and as a shareholder in MKH were strictly segregated and carried out by separate divisions within the company. Its Structured Finance Division (SFD) was responsible for the holding of shares in MKH. In the light of legal advice it had received, the Investment Banking Division (IBD) of Morgan Grenfell, which was responsible for providing financial advice to GU, had concluded that the procedures in place for segregating the roles of the SFD and the IBD would mean that the SFD would not be acting with GU to secure control of MKH and that its holding of the shares would not be relevant for this purpose (see paragraphs 10.35 to 10.37). We note that the arrangements between Morgan Grenfell and GU relating to Morgan Grenfell's acquisition of the shareholding in 1991 provide for a continuing relationship between the companies and that those arrangements were accepted by the DTI and the OFT. We do not regard those arrangements or the additional fact that Morgan Grenfell is acting as financial adviser to GU of themselves to mean that Morgan Grenfell is acting together with GU to secure control of MKH. Notwithstanding some reservations about the efficacy of Chinese walls in general, we are not convinced that Morgan Grenfell is acting with GU (or SAUR) to secure control of MKH.

Acting together to exercise control

2.29. MKH argued that GU and SAUR had acted together to exercise control of MKH. MKH alleged that their voting behaviour at the MKH AGM and EGM in July had been co-ordinated beforehand. MKH said that GU and SAUR had been careful not to vote in the same way on every resolution; nevertheless they had succeeded in blocking three resolutions. On only one, an ordinary resolution, had it been necessary for them to vote in the same way.

With the exception of Morgan Grenfell's proxy vote against resolution 6, no other major shareholder had opposed any of the three resolutions, which were of a standard nature. In previous years GU and SAUR had always voted with the management or given the Chairman discretion.

2.30. We asked GU and SAUR whether they had consulted each other before the meeting and asked them to explain the reasons why they had exercised their voting rights in the way they had (see paragraphs 6.67 to 6.69, and Appendix 6.3). Each said that they had not consulted the other before the meeting. They had been through separate independent management processes to decide how to vote.

2.31. GU said that it had voted against resolutions 4 and 5 because it did not understand why MKH needed to raise further share capital and it was concerned about the lack of success of MKH's diversified activities. It had voted against the executive share plan at the EGM because the company's overall performance was not good compared with that of other water undertakers and the plan did not comply with the Greenbury recommendations.[1]

2.32. SAUR said that it had abstained on resolutions 4 and 5 because it had concerns about the dilution of its own shareholding and about the possibility of MKH diversifying further. It had voted against resolution 6, the proposed share buy-back, because this would have had significant cash implications and could have raised debt which would have to be repaid before any preference shares. It had also voted against the executive share plan because it was contrary to the recommendations of the Association of British Insurers[2] and the Greenbury recommendations.

2.33. We also asked Morgan Grenfell about why it had voted as it had. Morgan Grenfell voted by proxy against the proposed share buy-back and the executive share plan. Its SFD had decided that it was in the commercial interests of Morgan Grenfell to vote against these two resolutions. It did not vote on any of the other resolutions because these were immaterial to its interests (see paragraph 10.37).

2.34. This evidence does not in our view justify a conclusion that GU and SAUR (or that GU, SAUR and Morgan Grenfell) have been acting together to exercise control of MKH.

Material influence as associated persons

2.35. Having concluded that GU and SAUR are associated persons by virtue of acting together to secure control of MKH so that they (and any bodies corporate they control) should be treated as one person for the purpose of determining under section 65 of the FTA whether enterprises have been brought under common control, we turn to the question of whether their combined shareholding of 39 per cent confers the ability materially to influence the policy of MKH. GU, SAUR, MKH and the DGWS all considered that if GU and SAUR were associated persons then they would have the ability to exercise material influence over MKH. In past cases considered by the MMC a combined shareholding of this magnitude has been regarded as conferring material influence where the other shareholdings in a company are widely dispersed (which is the case for MKH). While GU has undertaken not to seek Board representation, it, together with SAUR, can block special resolutions and, in the ordinary course of events, they could be expected to be able to block ordinary resolutions proposed by the Board. We conclude that together GU and SAUR have the ability materially to influence the policy of MKH.

---

[1] Report of study group by Sir Richard Greenbury, 17 July 1995.

[2] Guidance note issued by the Association of British Insurers, 17 February 1995.

2.36. It might also be argued that the shareholding of 39 per cent confers the ability to control the policy of MKH. MKH said that there was a grey area between the exercise of material influence and the exercise of control. It depended upon the nature and size of the other shareholdings in a company. MKH said that it would certainly not deny that GU and SAUR's combined shareholding conferred the ability to control policy. GU too said that it was difficult to say where material influence stopped and *de facto* control started. SAUR said that a shareholding of 39 per cent would not, of itself, amount to an ability to control. We do not think it necessary to decide this question.

Section 65(3) of the Fair Trading Act 1973

2.37. Section 65(3) of the FTA provides that:

> A person or group of persons able, directly or indirectly, to control or materially to influence the policy of a body corporate, or the policy of any person in carrying on an enterprise, but without having a controlling interest in that body corporate or in that enterprise, may for the purposes of subsections (1) and (2) of this section be treated as having control of it.

2.38. GU and SAUR argued that if the MMC were to find that they were associated persons as a result of the JVA and that together they had the ability materially to influence MKH then, on the facts, they should not be treated as having control of MKH. The JVA itself made no provision for GU and SAUR to control MKH until the bid was successful. GU and SAUR only had a common interest in relation to the proposed bid. In order to set in train the process of obtaining regulatory approval, GU and SAUR were obliged under the 1991 Act to demonstrate that arrangements were in progress and not just in contemplation. If the prospective merger was prohibited, the JVA would cease to have effect and GU and SAUR would no longer have that common interest.

2.39. MKH argued that section 65(3) should not be regarded as permissive. Moreover GU and SAUR would still retain a common interest in influencing the management and policies of MKH even if the JVA ceased to have effect.

2.40. We are advised that section 65(3) confers on the MMC a discretion to treat, or not to treat, a person who has the ability materially to influence the policy of a body corporate (but without having a controlling interest) as having control of it for the purpose of section 65(1) and (2). The circumstances of this case are very unusual. The ability of GU and SAUR materially to influence the policy of MKH derives from the fact that they have entered into the JVA. That agreement makes no provision for the companies to seek to control MKH before any bid is successful. Furthermore, GU is under a continuing obligation by virtue of its undertakings not to seek Board representation. Any bid is conditional on regulatory approval being granted. If the bid is not made the agreement is terminated. Moreover, in order to set in train the process of obtaining regulatory approval, GU and SAUR were obliged by the 1991 Act to demonstrate that arrangements were in progress, not just in contemplation. It also seems to us relevant that we have not concluded that GU and SAUR have been acting together to exercise control. If they were in future to do so a merger would arise by virtue of section 77(4)(d) even if the JVA had ceased to have effect.

2.41. In these very special circumstances we conclude that GU and SAUR should not be treated as having control of MKH for the purpose of section 65(1) and (2).

Individual material influence

2.42. MKH also argued that GU and SAUR each had individually the ability materially to influence the policy of MKH. Each individually could, in practice, block a special resolution. Because of the JVA their interests coincided; each could, therefore, predict the voting behaviour of the other, and each could be sure that neither would oppose the other in casting its votes. MKH suggested that it was also possible that each could rely on Morgan Grenfell, GU's financial adviser, not to oppose it. GU and SAUR did not consider that there were any circumstances in which each was, individually, able to influence MKH.

2.43. As indicated above, we are not satisfied either that GU and SAUR or that GU, SAUR and Morgan Grenfell have been acting together to exercise control of MKH. We note that GU's present shareholding of 19.45 per cent has been permitted by the undertakings given following the MMC report, that Morgan Grenfell's present shareholding has been held since June 1992 and that SAUR's present level of shareholding has been held since November 1989. We note also that GU is prohibited by the undertakings from seeking Board representation. We do not believe that the mere fact that each of GU and SAUR has a similar interest in the proposed merger of itself confers on either GU or SAUR the ability materially to influence the policy of MKH. For either to have such an ability, it must receive the backing of the other (or other shareholders) or be sure that the other will abstain. It is clear to us that, whilst there is some commonality of interest between GU and SAUR in relation to the proposed merger, their commercial interests do not necessarily coincide. They are part of very different French groups. GU, in particular, has a diverse range of activities within the UK. MKH argued that Morgan Grenfell was unlikely to oppose GU and SAUR in view of its role as GU's financial adviser. We note that the DTI, the DGWS and the OFT were content with the terms of the arrangements under which some GU shares were transferred to Morgan Grenfell. Morgan Grenfell's interests in the policies of MKH do not appear to have been altered by the fact that it is GU's financial adviser in relation to the proposed bid, and we do not think there can be any certainty about Morgan Grenfell's voting behaviour. We are not satisfied that either GU or SAUR individually has the ability materially to influence the policy of MKH.

Conclusions on an existing merger

2.44. Accordingly we conclude that a merger of water enterprises belonging to MKH, GU and SAUR respectively has not taken place.

The proposed merger

2.45. Our terms of reference also require us to determine whether arrangements are in progress which, if carried into effect, will result in the creation of one or more such mergers of two or more water enterprises as are required by section 32 of the 1991 Act to be the subject of a merger reference.

2.46. GU and SAUR's proposals are complex. At Stage 1 of the proposed arrangements the joint venture company, in which GU and SAUR would have equal 50 per cent shareholdings, would acquire the entire share capital of MKH, and thereby acquire control of its subsidiary, MKW (see paragraph 2.14).

2.47. Stage 2 of the proposed arrangements involves the splitting of the assets of MKH into three parts. The bidders would create two separate water supply businesses, MKEast and MKWest, which would be approximately equal in value, and a non-operational water resource company, the JRC. MKWest would be acquired by SEW. MKEast would be acquired by FDWS.

2.48. The precise role and responsibilities of the JRC have been amended by the bidders in the course of this inquiry; it is now intended, as part of Stage 2, that the JRC would be under the joint control of the enlarged SEW and FDWS. It would not be a water undertaker, but it would have a number of assets of its own. These would comprise:

— all of MKW's existing water abstraction rights including necessary rights of access;

— all of MKW's existing rights to receive supplies of water from third parties;

— all new water abstraction rights in the MKW area; and

— the rights and licences associated with any major resource development, for example a reservoir at Broad Oak.

2.49. [*Details omitted. See note on page iv.*] They confirmed to us that they did not intend to operate these subsidiaries on a joint basis.

2.50. We looked at how the arrangements should be considered for the purposes of the FTA, as applied by the 1991 Act. There are a number of ways in which the proposed arrangements could be analysed for this purpose. For example, Stage 1 could be regarded as giving rise to two mergers (that is, each of GU and SAUR obtaining the ability materially to influence the policy of MKH) or alternately as one merger (that is, GU and SAUR as associated persons together obtaining a controlling interest in MKH). It could also be argued that Stage 2 gives rise to two further mergers under which GU and SAUR obtain a controlling interest in the enterprises MKEast and MKWest respectively.

2.51. GU and SAUR said that they regarded the total number of mergers as a technicality; there were a number of possible ways of analysing the proposals. Their goal was the creation of the two enlarged water companies which would retain a joint subsidiary, the JRC, for water resource sharing and planning purposes. They regarded the two stages of the proposed arrangements as inextricably linked. The companies would want to give effect to the spirit of Stage 2 as soon as the acquisition of MKH was completed. At that time FDWS would become involved with the management of the eastern part of MKW and SEW with the western part. The benefits from the overall transaction would start to accrue immediately because the two companies would undertake the planned new investment and demand management policies as soon as they could.

2.52. MKH said that the transaction should be regarded as giving rise to three mergers. Stage 1 would result in one merger, with GU and SAUR as associated persons acquiring a controlling interest in MKH. Stage 2 would give rise to two further merger situations under which each of GU and SAUR would acquire a controlling interest in a new enterprise, MKEast and MKWest respectively. They considered that control by GU and SAUR as associated persons was not the same as control by one or other individually and that the effect of section 77(2) of the FTA was not to prevent Stage 2 giving rise to two new merger situations in these circumstances. They also argued that arrangements were not in progress for Stage 2 and that the MMC had no jurisdiction to consider public interest issues arising out of Stage 2. In addition, they said that there were legal difficulties in carrying out Stage 2, for example GU and SAUR might not be able to exercise the right of compulsory acquisition of minority shareholders under the Companies Act 1985 and the arrangements for Stage 2 could give rise to breach of fiduciary duties by directors or an application to the High Court by minority shareholders under the Companies Act, for protection against unfair prejudice.

2.53. The arrangements are for GU and SAUR to make an offer for MKH through a joint venture company. We consider that it is appropriate to treat GU and SAUR as acting together to secure control of MKH and thus as associated persons together acquiring a controlling interest in MKH, rather than to regard them as each individually acquiring the ability materially to influence the policy of MKH.

2.54. We considered whether Stage 2 should be regarded as giving rise to further mergers of water enterprises. The JVA provides for GU, SAUR and the joint venture company to use all reasonable steps to procure that the reorganization is carried out as soon as reasonably practicable after the date of the take-over and in any event to procure such implementation within four years after the date of the take-over. We are not satisfied that the legal difficulties suggested by MKH are likely to prevent the carrying out of Stage 2. The agreement also provides that pending the implementation of the restructuring the day-to-day business of MKEast should be controlled by GU and that of MKWest should be controlled by SAUR. The division of MKH derives from GU and SAUR together acquiring a controlling interest in MKH. We consider that it would be artificial to exclude Stage 2 from consideration of the consequences of the acquisition of a controlling interest in MKH by GU and SAUR and to regard Stage 2 as giving rise to further mergers of water enterprises. Accordingly we have considered the arrangements for Stage 2 as part of the consequences of the merger of the water enterprise, MKW, with water enterprises controlled by GU and SAUR respectively.

Arrangements in progress

2.55. We are required by our terms of reference under the 1991 Act to decide whether arrangements are in progress. (By contrast, section 75 of the FTA under which pre-acquisition merger references are normally made refers to arrangements being in progress or *in contemplation*.) We have looked carefully at the JVA made between GU and SAUR on 20 December 1995 as amended by a subsequent agreement dated 12 February 1996. It provides for the making of a preliminary announcement, for proceedings before the MMC and for the establishment of a joint venture company to bid for the shares of MKH. It describes an understanding between the parties for the restructuring of MKW, with MKEast to be integrated with FDWS and MKWest to be integrated with SEW. It provides for GU and SAUR to use all reasonable endeavours to procure that the reorganization is carried out as soon as reasonably practicable after the take-over of MKH and that they shall in any event procure such implementation within four years after the take-over.

2.56. Thus a binding agreement has been entered into by the parties to make an offer for MKH (subject to their obtaining the necessary regulatory consents and agreeing the price to be offered); in the event of the offer being a success, the agreement provides for the division and reorganization of MKW within four years of the take-over of MKH. As mentioned in paragraph 2.27, we consider that the parties have been acting in pursuance of that agreement.

2.57. We also note that various agreements have been entered into between GU and SAUR and a number of financial institutions to provide finance and financial advice for the proposed take-over.

2.58. We conclude, therefore, that arrangements as described in our terms of reference are in progress which, if carried into effect, would result in the creation of a merger of two or more water enterprises. We now consider whether that merger is required by section 32 of the 1991 Act to be the subject of a merger reference.

Assets test

2.59. Under section 33[1] of the 1991 Act the Secretary of State is required not to make a reference under section 32 if the value of the assets taken over does not exceed £30 million or if the only water enterprises already belonging to the person making the take-over each have assets the value of which does not exceed £30 million, calculated in accordance with section 33. MKH currently controls the water enterprise MKW which had gross assets of £100 million at 31 March 1996. GU and SAUR each own a water enterprise (Three Valleys and SEW respectively) with gross asset values at 31 March 1996 well in excess of £30 million (see paragraph 3.87 and Appendix 3.9). We are satisfied, therefore, that the merger is required by section 32 of the 1991 Act to be the subject of a merger reference.

Conclusion on the first question of our terms of reference

2.60. Accordingly we conclude that arrangements as described in our terms of reference are in progress which, if carried into effect, will result in one merger of two or more water enterprises, being a merger which is required by section 32 of the 1991 Act to be the subject of a merger reference. The arrangements have not been carried into effect and accordingly the question in paragraph (1)(ii) of our terms of reference does not need to be answered.

The public interest

2.61. We therefore turn to consider whether the creation of the merger may be expected to operate against the public interest. In determining the question, the MMC are required by section 34(3) of the 1991 Act to:

(a) have regard to the desirability of giving effect to the principle that the Director's ability, in carrying out his functions by virtue of the 1991 Act, to make comparisons between different water enterprises should not be prejudiced;[2] and

(b) have regard to the desirability of achieving any other purpose so far only as they are satisfied—

(i) that that other purpose can be achieved in a manner that does not conflict with that principle; or

(ii) that the achievement of that other purpose is of substantially greater significance in relation to the public interest than that principle and cannot be brought about except in a manner that conflicts with that principle.

Structure and regulation of the water industry in England and Wales

2.62. We first look at the structure and regulation of the water industry in England and Wales and the role of the DGWS. Further details are set out in Chapters 3 and 4, and in Appendices 4.1, 4.2 and 8.1.

---

[1] As amended by the Water Enterprises (Merger) (Modification) Regulations 1994 (the 1994 Regulations), SI 1994/73.

[2] Amended by the Competition and Services (Utilities) Act 1992.

2.63. Economic regulation is used as a surrogate for market competition. Each water undertaker is subject to a cap on its annual price movements under its appointment. The cap is set by the DGWS for a period of ten years, reviewable at intervals of five years (the Periodic Review). The appointment also provides for interim determinations of price caps, to take account of particular changes in the undertaker's circumstances.

2.64. The price cap formula is RPI+K. The retail price index (RPI) indicates the rate of increase in prices of a wide range of goods and services. K is an adjustment factor (which may be positive, zero or negative) which is specific to each company and limits permitted annual changes in prices in real terms (that is, allowing for inflation as indicated by the RPI). It comprises $-X$ (to reflect improvements in efficiency) and $+Q$ (to allow for required quality improvements). K factors were last reviewed in July 1994.[1] They became effective on 1 April 1995 and will remain in force for the five-year period up to 31 March 2000.

2.65. During that Periodic Review the DGWS developed a structure for determining K factors based upon a matrix of purpose and cost categories. The purpose categories comprise base service provision (the maintenance of existing levels of service), enhanced service levels, the supply/demand balance and obligatory quality enhancements. Costs are divided between operational expenditure and capital maintenance (including capital expenditure).

2.66. Since the water industry was privatized in 1989 there have been a number of developments. First, there have been mergers between water and non-water companies: Norweb Plc (NORWEB) was acquired by North West Water Group plc in 1995; South Wales Electricity plc (SWALEC) was acquired by Welsh Water plc in January 1996; and Southern Water plc was acquired by ScottishPower plc in August 1996. In these cases, amendments to the appointments were agreed which were designed to preserve the financial and management independence of the water businesses within the merged group structures. It was also agreed that a Welsh Water plc preference share would be listed on the Stock Exchange by 1999.

2.67. Second, the Department of the Environment (DoE) published in April 1996 a consultation paper containing proposals to extend competition in the water industry.[2] There is currently some scope for competition within the industry through cross-border supplies of water for domestic purposes and for inset appointments (that is, appointments made to supply water or sewerage within another supplier's area). Recently, a number of applications for inset appointments have been made. The DGWS has given notice that he is preparing to vary the licence of Anglian Water to supply a commercial customer by an inset arrangement in the neighbouring area of Essex & Suffolk Water. The proposals in the consultation document would ease some of the current restrictions on inset appointments, for example by permitting time-limited appointments. Other proposals concern common carriage, which would enable a person who was not the existing undertaker for a particular area to supply customers (initially large users of water) in that undertaker's area on the basis of shared use of pipes; and cross-border supplies of water for non-domestic purposes.

The use of comparators

2.68. The system of comparative competition underlies the regulatory regime. It enables the DGWS to take account of objective differences in the operating environments of the companies and on the basis of comparisons between them, to make an informed assessment of how each

---

[1] *Future Charges for Water and Sewerage Services: the Outcome of the Periodic Review*, OFWAT, July 1994.

[2] *Water: Increasing Customer Choice*, DoE, April 1996.

company's performance compares with that of the most efficient companies. On this basis he sets price controls (see paragraphs 2.63 to 2.65) and performance targets specific to each company. Companies have the incentive, once these price limits have been set, to achieve cost savings by operating more efficiently. In this way a dynamic process is generated. The more independent companies operating in similar circumstances and conditions that are able to take part in this process, the greater the potential for efficiency gains and the more effective comparative competition will be. The benefits achieved are both local and national. The process of comparative competition maintains downward pressure on prices for all customers. A company performing well will act as a model for the others.

2.69. Comparators are used in a variety of ways. The DGWS told us that comparisons between companies were important not only in the price-setting process but also in the performance of his other functions that continued between price reviews. Thus, the DGWS compares companies' performance not only in the areas of operating and capital costs, resource management, quality enhancement and financial performance, but also in the areas of service to customers, tariff structures (the aim being to reflect better the costs of supplying different classes of customers) and transfer pricing (where the DGWS seeks to ensure that the appointed business is financially separate from the non-appointed activities of the group).

2.70. The use which the DGWS makes of comparators has continued to develop since he gave evidence to the MMC in the Lyonnaise/Northumbrian[1] inquiry. He told us, for example, that the water supply difficulties during the summer of 1995 had prompted him to carry out a detailed comparison of the companies' approach to leakage control; that work had resulted in substantial changes to some companies' estimated leakage levels and would allow better informed decisions in future on the management of water supplies. Another area where comparative competition had recently played a role had arisen from the sharing by some companies of efficiency savings with their customers, which had provided the stimulus for several other companies to announce similar packages. The DGWS told us that other uses of comparisons between water companies, which could not necessarily be predicted now, were likely to emerge in the future.

2.71. There are three main stages in the process by which data about the companies are collected, analysed and deployed for the purposes of setting performance targets and price controls. The first is the collection of the data from the companies and the analysis of those data in a way that enables comparisons between companies to be made. Whilst it may sometimes be possible to make comparisons between companies using the raw data, sophisticated statistical modelling methods may be needed to allow for the effects of different operating environments so that the appropriate comparisons of relative management efficiency can be made. The second stage is the use of the results of this analysis to set bench-marks. Here, the analysis may not give sufficiently reliable results to allow the company which performs the best to be chosen as the bench-mark; a company at the upper quartile of performance may instead be selected, or indeed sometimes only the average performance may be usable for the purpose. The third stage is the target-setting for each company based on the bench-marks. Here, the DGWS exercises an element of judgment in deciding how far towards the bench-mark each company can be expected to move.

2.72. We now turn to the main ways in which the data are deployed by the DGWS. Operating cost comparisons represent a major element in setting price controls. This is one of the areas where the DGWS has considerable difficulty in making comparisons between companies because their operating costs are strongly affected by differences in operating conditions. The Office of Water Services (OFWAT) uses econometric analysis and data envelopment analysis (DEA) to filter out differences in costs which are attributable to diverse

---

[1]*Lyonnaise des Eaux SA and Northumbrian Water Group PLC: a report on the merger situation*, HMSO, Cm 2936, July 1995.

operating conditions from those which are attributable to the actions of management. The results are then used to assist in the assessment of the relative efficiencies of companies and the setting of cost targets for each of them.

2.73. So far as the capital costs allowable to the companies for maintaining their existing asset bases are concerned, the DGWS has so far used a standard costing approach, a less sophisticated form of data analysis than econometrics or DEA. Broadly, on the basis of submissions made by the companies, the DGWS has derived bench-marks based on lowest standard costs, relating to typical examples of capital projects or the unit costs of typical capital works. The DGWS told us that in theory the difference between companies' standard costs showed different efficiencies in the specification, design and procurement of such capital projects. He said that OFWAT is currently developing, for the category of capital maintenance, a similar econometric approach to that already used in examining operating costs (see paragraph 2.72) and that it was his intention to adopt this approach at the next Periodic Review.

2.74. The DGWS also drew our attention to the value of comparators in ensuring that a company's appointed water business was kept financially separate from any other business which it might carry out, and that thereby water customers did not cross-subsidize activities not involved in the supply of water. Under the terms of their appointments, water enterprises were required to comply with the DGWS's Regulatory Accounting Guidelines on transfer pricing. The DGWS was carrying out further work on this subject to strengthen his controls. He told us that comparisons provided an invaluable means of determining the extent to which a company could be said to operate at arm's length from its parent.

2.75. On the question of financial performance, the DGWS explained to us that he found it useful if individual water companies had a Stock Exchange listing. This helped him to compare performance on dividends, gearing and the cost of raising equity and loan finance on the open market.

2.76. So far as customer service is concerned, each year OFWAT publishes a report on the companies' performance against a number of service level indicators covering matters such as interruptions to supply, water usage restrictions and responses to written and telephoned complaints (see paragraph 4.23). Other aspects of customer service are also reviewed, including, for example, debt and disconnections, optional meter schemes, services for customers with special needs and compensation payments. Reports on such matters are published periodically. With the encouragement of the DGWS, the Customer Service Committees (CSCs) also stimulate peer group competition between the companies, by highlighting aspects of customer service which are exemplary in their own and other regions. They also bring pressure to bear on the company or companies within their CSC region to emulate best practice elsewhere in the industry.

2.77. It was clear to us that the way in which the DGWS uses comparators is becoming increasingly sophisticated. We are in no doubt that comparators have an important role to play in the regulation of the water industry and have played a major part in encouraging healthy rivalry between companies and in bringing to public notice aspects of company performance which are either poor and need improvement or which should be emulated by others. But it was also clear to us that the variety and complexity of the comparative techniques now being developed and utilized by the DGWS mean that strictly quantitative comparisons between different water enterprises need to be interpreted with great care.

Prejudice to the DGWS's ability to make comparisons

Section 34(3)(a) of the 1991 Act

2.78. Under section 34(3)(a) of the 1991 Act we are required, in determining whether a merger operates or may be expected to operate against the public interest, to 'have regard to the desirability of giving effect to the principle that the Director's ability in carrying out his functions by virtue of this Act, to make comparisons between different water enterprises should not be prejudiced'. We refer to that principle as 'the comparator principle'.

2.79. Since 1990, when the MMC carried out their investigation of the merger situation between GU and MKW, the number of WoCs in England and Wales has fallen from 29 to 19. Five of these have asset values below the £30 million threshold for referral to the MMC set out in the 1991 Act.[1] Of the remaining 14, nine are associated with major corporate groups (GU, SAUR and Lyonnaise des Eaux (Lyonnaise)). The remaining five, including MKW, are regarded by the DGWS as independent (see Appendix 4.4).

2.80. Under GU's and SAUR's proposals, MKW would be acquired by GU and SAUR and the water supply business would be divided between FDWS and SEW, thus replacing three comparators by two. At Stage 1 data would continue to be provided by MKW but MKW would be under the control of GU and SAUR. Progressively, FDWS and SEW would begin to manage the two halves of MKW until at Stage 2 the data from SEW and MKWest would be amalgamated and similarly the data from FDWS and MKEast. In assessing possible prejudice to the comparator system there are two major areas on which we need to focus:

(a) the loss of the *independence* of MKW; and

(b) the *reduction in the number of comparators*.

Independence

2.81. It was clear to us that the DGWS places great weight on companies having different management styles. The DGWS told us that a diversity of ownership of water companies was likely to secure the greatest variety of management approaches and techniques. The industry was more diverse than it had been under public ownership and companies had continued to differentiate themselves one from another in the sector. Experience had shown that differences in performance were fundamentally affected by differences in management approach and priorities, which were themselves driven by differences in ownership. The more independent companies that were able to take part in this process, the more effective comparative competition would be. Separate appointments in the hands of a common owner were a poor substitute for separate ownership; for example, the DGWS told us that each of the French groups (GU, SAUR and to a lesser extent Lyonnaise) had its own management approach which permeated the whole group. This overall approach tended to lead to convergence in the performance of the individual companies in the group, thereby reducing their full value as comparators.

2.82. The DGWS told us that in making comparisons in the water sector the independence of the company concerned was of far greater importance than its size, save that very small companies, whether independent or not, were of limited value as comparators. MKW was one of only five remaining independent WoCs of a size that he found useful for comparative

---

[1] As amended by the Water Enterprises (Merger) (Modification) Regulation 1994, SI 1994/73.

purposes. If MKW were to lose its independence he would lose valuable independent data. The DGWS concluded, therefore, that the loss of MKW's independence would have a significant adverse effect on his ability to make comparisons. MKH made a number of similar points to us.

2.83. GU and SAUR argued that the loss of independence would be more than compensated by improved data from the enlarged SEW and FDWS which would be created at Stage 2. It was their intention to create two exemplary comparators in terms of demand management and water conservation. The merger would help secure adequate water resources for the two enlarged companies, without which GU and SAUR said they could not become exemplary comparators.

2.84. Although from Stage 1 of the proposals MKW would be under the control of the GU and SAUR joint venture company, FDWS and SEW would immediately become involved in the day-to-day management of their respective sections of MKW. As a result at Stage 1 the company must necessarily lose that capacity for independent and innovative management action which has been a feature of MKW's recent performance in some areas (see paragraphs 7.11 and 7.38) and which is the basis of at least part of its value as a comparator. Moreover, because of the involvement of FDWS and SEW the company will have a different style of management from its current style. We consider, therefore, that the data produced by MKW after Stage 1 and before Stage 2 will be of less value to the DGWS than that currently produced by MKW.

2.85. Accordingly, at Stage 1 of the proposals MKW would no longer be an independent comparator and we agree with the DGWS that this loss would materially affect the quality of comparative data available and thereby prejudice his ability to make comparisons between different water enterprises.

Reduction in the number of comparators

2.86. We noted that the number of comparator companies which the DGWS regards as desirable in order to make comparisons with confidence will depend upon the nature of the data and the type and degree of analysis required. Comparisons can be carried out with as few as two companies. However, where sophisticated analysis is needed, for example econometric analysis, before comparisons can be drawn between companies with diverse operating environments, it is important that the number of separate observations relative to the number of explanatory variables that should be included in any model is sufficient. As the number of observations reduces, the reliance which can be placed on the estimates is reduced.

2.87. GU and SAUR argued that the fact that the transaction would result in a reduction in the number of comparators available to the DGWS would not prejudice his ability to make comparisons. In their view they would be creating two enlarged exemplary comparators. These would be of the size preferred by the DGWS for making comparisons. The proposals should be viewed as involving the loss of FDWS, a small WoC with limited value as a comparator, and not the loss of MKW.

2.88. We do not accept GU and SAUR's argument. As a result of their proposals, an independent WoC (MKW) will become part of two larger corporate groups (GU and SAUR). We believe that size is not as important as independence. Companies which are part of large corporate groups do not have the full capacity for independent and innovative action which is the basis of at least part of the value of a comparator. We consider that the most significant change to the data available to the DGWS would be the loss of data from MKW, an independent water undertaker. In any event the DGWS told us that FDWS provided some useful statistical information; for example, its distinct operating conditions provided an indication of relative efficiency.

2.89. In the Lyonnaise/Northumbrian inquiry the DGWS gave evidence on how different types of merger would affect his ability to make comparisons. During this inquiry he told us that he had further developed that work to produce a matrix (see Figure 8.1) of detriments. The matrix showed six broad categories of harm ranked from A to F, depending on the size of the two companies and whether they are contiguous:

- A — Harm to water comparators
- B — Significant harm to water comparators
- C — Serious harm to water comparators
- D — Serious harm to both water and sewerage comparators
- E — Very serious harm to both water and sewerage comparators
- F — Critical harm to both water and sewerage comparators

Categories A to C covered cases where there was detriment only to comparisons in water supply. Categories D to F covered cases where there was detriment to comparisons in both water supply and the sewerage service and hence are not relevant here. Within each of these categories there would be a range of detriment, depending on the circumstances of a particular case. Mergers between contiguous companies, as was the case with the GU and SAUR proposals, were more detrimental than those involving comparable remote companies because of their additional impact on regional comparisons.

2.90. In the current case, given that the proposed arrangements involve companies which are members of large corporate groups, he would see the detriment from the proposed merger falling into category C, causing serious harm to the comparator regime for water supply. The DGWS said that, as a result of the ultimate loss of data from MKW, there would be material prejudice to his ability to make comparisons.

2.91. The DGWS said that he did not accept GU and SAUR's arguments about the benefits arising from the creation of two new 'exemplary' comparators in terms of the use of water resources. They had argued that more water resources were necessary before they could become exemplary comparators. But the DGWS considered that optimal water resource benefits could not be achieved without the involvement of SWS. The proposed merger was neither necessary nor sufficient to resolve the problems. Moreover, the DGWS provided us with evidence which showed that MKW had improved its efficiency in relation to operating costs more than FDWS or SEW. This made him doubt whether FDWS or SEW could turn MKW into an exemplary comparator in this important area.

2.92. In considering the possible prejudice to the comparator system arising from a reduction in the number of comparators we have had regard to the fact that a company may be valuable to the DGWS for modelling and other statistical purposes even if it is not currently performing at or near the frontier of operating efficiency. A company which is currently performing at or near that frontier is potentially useful as a bench-mark. These two aspects of the value of a comparator are useful to the DGWS for different aspects of the comparative process. We also take into account the various other ways in which the DGWS uses comparators in that process.

2.93. As regards the value of MKW as a comparator for modelling and other statistical purposes, we consider that the loss of MKW, one of only five independent WoCs of the size the DGWS finds useful for comparative purposes, would significantly reduce the amount of data available to the DGWS. The reduction in the quantity of the data would lead to the DGWS having less certainty about his findings which would lead to him reaching less precise conclusions on efficiency targets, leading to less stringent price caps and to prices being higher than they would otherwise have been. Accordingly, MKW has a role to play as a water comparator in the modelling process (using econometric and other sophisticated techniques) that is used to assess operating cost efficiencies and may be used to assess capital maintenance cost efficiencies in the future.

2.94. We now turn to the value of MKW as a bench-mark. Company performance changes over time and the system of comparative competition makes use of this dynamic process. As can be seen from the overall efficiency rankings for operating costs between 1992/93 and 1994/95 in Table 4.1, there is considerable 'leap-frogging' by companies in terms of relative efficiency rankings, implying that currently less efficient companies can attain higher rankings within quite short time-scales. Therefore while one company might now be more efficient than another, over a short period this situation could well change. MKW is valuable as a comparator because of its contribution to this dynamic process as well as because of its current level of efficiency.

2.95. The DGWS looks to the companies that are currently nearest to the frontier for providing the bench-marks at the next Periodic Review, while recognizing that companies that are currently further away from the frontier may be useful for setting the bench-mark at later Reviews. The loss of a frontier company would lead to lower targets for other companies and prices across the country being higher than they would otherwise have been. The DGWS told us that MKW was not yet in the upper quartile of efficiency but that it could possibly be a frontier company in 1997/98. MKH provided us with a range of analysis which showed MKW's performance improving over the last few years. It expects MKW to be close to the operating cost efficiency frontier in the very near future. GU and SAUR contended that MKW is currently a poor performer. It seems clear to us that although historically MKW may not have done well, it has improved its performance over recent years and does now seem to have the potential to reach the efficiency frontier in terms of operating costs. Its loss would therefore be prejudicial to the overall comparator regime.

2.96. As for GU's and SAUR's claim regarding the creation of exemplary comparators (by which is meant a company whose performance, in the foreseeable future, might be used to set the bench-mark for the industry in some areas of efficiency or service standards) particularly in the area of water resource management, we accept the possibility that at some time in the future the enlarged FDWS and/or the enlarged SEW might become such a frontier company. However, we have seen no evidence that this is more likely than MKW (or, indeed, the present SEW or FDWS) achieving this status in the absence of a merger. If anything, OFWAT's data suggested that MKW was making faster progress in terms of operating efficiency than SEW or FDWS. In the light of this, and the time it would take GU and SAUR to reorganize the enlarged companies and implement the demand management programmes, we thought it highly unlikely that such an exemplary comparator would emerge quickly.

2.97. Turning to the use of MKW as a bench-mark for customer service, both the DGWS and the OFWAT Southern CSC have provided evidence of MKW's recent improvements both in terms of a more customer-oriented approach and in respect of particular performance indicators (see Appendix 4.3). As for the latter, MKW is already performing well in respect of some (albeit relatively minor) areas, such as the effectiveness of complaints and queries procedures where improvements have been marked. We take the view that MKW is already a useful company for comparative purposes in respect of at least some aspects of customer service and that under GU and SAUR's proposals there was unlikely to be a significant improvement.

2.98. We conclude that the loss of MKW as a comparator would prejudice the ability of the DGWS to make comparisons between different water enterprises.

Valuing the loss of a comparator

2.99. The DGWS did not consider that it was possible to value all of the many and diverse ways in which comparators were used. However, he had developed a model to indicate the potential impact of the loss of the leading comparator on the price limits set for England and Wales. The effect of the loss of a company the size of MKW could be very substantial. If such a company would have become a leading comparator at the next review and is now lost as a comparator, the net present value (NPV)[1] of that loss for operating expenditure for water services would fall within a range of £20 million to £590 million with an average of £120 million. OFWAT's model did not attach any probabilities, which, if they were included, would reduce the average loss. On the other hand, the model was incomplete. It looked at only one of the ways in which comparators were used and we were told that it therefore significantly underestimated the true damage to comparative competition arising through loss of the leading comparator. If capital expenditure were included in the calculation, OFWAT said that the loss could be as much as twice as large.

2.100. MKH had also carried out work aimed at quantifying the loss of MKW as a comparator, based on the greater uncertainty, quantified in the form of wider confidence intervals, which resulted from its loss. In its view, this greater uncertainty would lead to the DGWS reaching less precise conclusions on efficiency targets which in turn would tend to lead to less stringent price caps and hence to prices to consumers being higher than they would otherwise have been. MKH's estimates for the loss in terms of operating costs produced a range of NPVs from £33 million to £72 million (average £48 million). Commenting on MKH's approach, the DGWS said that the loss of a comparator would clearly affect the confidence with which he could adduce results from his econometric analysis. He told us that the MKH work assumed that he always determined prices in the same mechanistic way. But that was not the case. However, the DGWS said that to the extent that the approach used by MKH was capable of generating valid estimates, these losses should be seen as additional to those identified in OFWAT's simulation analysis.

2.101. It was clear to us that the studies by MKH and the DGWS approached the valuation question in quite different ways. They were, in effect, valuing different aspects of the effects on the comparative system. Both models were partial in that they did not include effects on some cost categories, for example capital costs, customer services and water quality, and both the DGWS and MKH told us that the reliability of the quantified benefits was uncertain for a number of methodological reasons. Furthermore, the estimates did not include the potential development in the use of comparators.

2.102. GU and SAUR told us that they did not consider it sensible to try to estimate the value of losing MKW as a comparator. In their view, taking into account both MKW's poor performance and the gains from improvements in the use of water and resources across all three companies which the proposals would bring, there were sound arguments that the loss of MKW would not be a detriment and could be a benefit. GU and SAUR said that quantification was particularly difficult as it should include the difference between the benefits arising from the proposals and any detriment, or further benefit, attributable to the effects on the comparative process. They told us that any exercise of quantifying the value of losing MKW as a comparator must have some regard to the consequences of not losing MKW (that is, the adverse impact on the value of SEW and FDWS, which they intended to make exemplary comparators), if the proposals did not go ahead.

2.103. Having examined carefully the analyses presented to us by OFWAT and MKH for valuing the loss of a comparator and taking account of GU's and SAUR's views, there are

---

[1] The increased costs from the Periodic Review are discounted at 7 per cent to 2025.

clearly difficulties in any quantitative assessment of the loss of MKW as a comparator. OFWAT's model was based on the premise that every company had the potential to become a leading comparator at the frontier of efficiency for operating costs and to become an exemplary comparator in other respects. We see merit in OFWAT's approach but there are problems with its application. OFWAT had not sought to attach a probability of any particular company reaching the frontier. If such probabilities were attached they would result in a lower valuation of the loss. We noted that some of the somewhat arbitrary assumptions in OFWAT's simulations led to a very wide range of figures being generated and wondered what degree of certainty could be attached to an average figure of £120 million drawn from a range as wide as £20 million to £590 million. MKH's estimates were based on the greater uncertainty which resulted from the loss of an independent company. As with OFWAT's approach, we see merit in the approach adopted by MKH, but there are uncertainties attached to its estimates. The DGWS's approach to setting price limits is not as deterministic as assumed in MKH's analysis.

2.104. These two approaches attempt a valuation of the loss of MKW for an important aspect of the comparative system, that of operating costs, but just one aspect. The DGWS and MKH acknowledge this. The result, however, is that many dimensions in which comparators are used in the comparative process have not been valued. The overall loss in any one case will therefore be higher than the loss estimated on the basis of operating cost comparisons alone (though not necessarily as high as the top end of the range of such estimates). Nor can the approaches we have considered do justice to the particular contributions which are made by an individual company in specific comparative exercises. Moreover, the approaches adopted by the DGWS and MKH are not the only ones possible. We have necessarily been unable to explore all the possible options. We are unable, therefore, to quantify the loss which would be represented by the removal of MKW from the comparative process. For the reasons set out in paragraphs 2.93 to 2.95, 2.97, 2.103 and this paragraph, we think such loss would be substantial.

Minor issues affecting the comparator regime

2.105. We then went on to consider a number of more minor issues resulting from the proposals and which could affect the operation of the comparator regime, namely loss of a Stock Exchange listing, disruptions to trend data, and the creation of the JRC.

Loss of a Stock Exchange listing

2.106. The DGWS and MKH argued that a Stock Exchange listing was of help to the DGWS because it provided him with information about a WoC's price:earnings ratio, dividend yields and its cost of capital; data which would reflect the views of independent investors. GU and SAUR disagreed. They thought the information the DGWS required could be provided in other ways. Moreover, little could be gleaned from movements in the price of a stock such as MKH which was very little traded. We thought the DGWS and MKH had rather overstated the value of such a quoted stock to the DGWS. We also noted that the DGWS did have powers under the appointments to obtain financial information about the companies, though this fell short of providing a market assessment.

Disruptions in the collection and analysis of comparative data

2.107. We considered that there would be some disruptions to the continuity, and therefore the consistency, of comparative data provided to the DGWS as a result of the proposed reorganization of the companies. Trends could begin to be obscured immediately after the acquisition and would become increasingly blurred the more SEW became involved in the management of MKWest, and similarly the more FDWS became involved in the management of MKEast. However, this would not be a problem which would persist. Once the new companies were well established and data had been collected in the same manner for a few years, trends would begin to show again.

The creation of the Joint Resources Company

2.108. We then assessed whether the creation of the JRC would have any effect on the DGWS's ability to make comparisons between water enterprises. The JRC itself would not be a water undertaker and would, therefore, not fall directly under the regulation of the DGWS. It would have almost no tangible assets, would not be responsible for either the treatment or distribution of water and would have no involvement in any subsequent step in the water supply process.

2.109. The DGWS told us that he was concerned by the proposals for the JRC, which, he felt, was in any event unnecessary. The majority of the assets owned by the JRC would be abstraction licences and supply rights. The DGWS would prefer it if assets of such strategic value were not held jointly between otherwise potentially competing entities; this would tend to blur their individual distinctiveness for comparative purposes. The DGWS was also concerned that if the JRC were created outside his formal ambit, there would be no mechanism to prevent it from exerting increasing influence over the operations of SEW and FDWS, thereby reducing the distinctiveness of those businesses and causing further detriment to the comparator system.

2.110. MKH argued that one effect of the JRC would be to reduce the effectiveness of the enlarged FDWS and SEW as comparators. This was because neither of the enlarged companies would hold abstraction licences in the present MKW area, nor would they be responsible for the planning of major new developments. These were usual functions for water undertakers. The enlarged FDWS and SEW would thus not be vertically integrated and could not be compared with all the other WoCs.

2.111. We believe these proposals would lead to a loss of vertical integration and some blurring of the independence of action of SEW and FDWS, both of which would result in some damage to the ability of the DGWS to make comparisons, though not on the same scale as the damage caused by the loss of MKW.

2.112. We looked also at the issue of transfer pricing between the JRC and its two owners. Clearly the JRC would need to charge the enlarged FDWS and SEW for the services which it provided. These services would usually be provided by a regulated water undertaker, but the JRC would not be a water undertaker. It was possible, therefore, that the unusual nature and role of the JRC could lead to distortions in the data provided by the enlarged SEW and FDWS. However, we noted that GU and SAUR had said that the arrangements for the JRC would be transparent and in accordance with the regulatory guidance issued by the DGWS on transfer pricing. We think the DGWS would be able to deal with this within his existing powers.

Finding under section 34(3)(a)

2.113. We have considered carefully all of the arguments put to us in the course of our investigation, primarily by GU and SAUR, MKH and the DGWS. As indicated in paragraphs 2.85, 2.98 and 2.111, we conclude that the proposed merger would prejudice the ability of the

DGWS to make comparisons between different water enterprises. We have been unable to quantify this detriment although it is, in our view, substantial.

Other purposes

Section 34(3)(b)

2.114. Section 34(3)(b) of the 1991 Act requires us to have regard to the desirability of achieving any other purpose so far only as we are satisfied that (i) it can be achieved without conflict with the principle we have just considered, or (ii) that the achievement of that 'other purpose' is of 'substantially greater significance in relation to the public interest than that principle and cannot be brought about except in a manner that conflicts with that principle'.

2.115. The principal 'other purpose' which we have been invited by GU and SAUR to consider is the potential of the proposals to optimize the management and use of water resources in the existing FDWS, MKW and SEW areas. We have also looked at the potential for efficiency gains arising from the transaction, the potential for improvement in local competition and improvements in service standards.

Finding under section 34(3)(b)(i)

2.116. Section 34(3)(b)(i) provides for the MMC to have regard to the desirability of achieving any other purpose so far as they are satisfied that the purpose can be achieved in a manner which does not conflict with the principle referred to in section 34(3)(a), the comparator principle.

2.117. We concluded in paragraph 2.113 that the proposed merger would prejudice the ability of the DGWS to make comparisons between different water enterprises. Accordingly we are satisfied that any purpose of the merger can be achieved only in a manner which conflicts with the comparator principle. The DGWS argued that the term 'purpose' in section 34(3)(b)(i) should not be interpreted as being limited to purposes of the merger. However, neither the DGWS nor any other person drew our attention to any specific purpose to which we should have regard by virtue of section 34(3)(b)(i).

Section 34(3)(b)(ii)

2.118. As indicated in paragraph 2.114, we can only have regard under section 34(3)(b)(ii) to the desirability of achieving any other purpose if that other purpose is of substantially greater significance in relation to the public interest than the comparator principle. In principle, we do consider that in certain circumstances the purpose of optimizing the management and use of resources could be of substantially greater significance in relation to the public interest than the loss of a comparator. A water company that has inadequate resources to supply its customers is unable satisfactorily to fulfil its statutory duties under section 37 of the 1991 Act.[1]

---

[1] '(1) It shall be the duty of every water undertaker to develop and maintain an efficient and economical system of water supply within its area and to ensure that all such arrangements have been made—
    (a) for providing supplies of water to premises in that area and for making such supplies available to persons who demand them; and
    (b) for maintaining, improving and extending the water undertaker's water mains and other pipes,
as are necessary for securing that the undertaker is and continues to be able to meet its obligations under this Part.'

2.119. The DGWS argued that section 34(3)(b)(ii) of the Act meant that we could take into account only those benefits which are of substantially greater significance than the principle that the DGWS's ability to make comparisons should not be prejudiced and which could not be achieved without the merger. Both MKH and the EA took a similar view. GU and SAUR argued differently. They said that section 34(3)(b)(i) and (ii) were mutually exclusive. If an 'other purpose' of the merger could be achieved without conflicting with the comparator principle it fell within section 34(3)(b)(i). If it could be achieved only with conflict, then it fell within section 34(3)(b)(ii). The last phrase of section 34(3)(b)(ii) simply served to distinguish between the situations to which section 34(3)(b)(i) and section 34(3)(b)(ii) applied. In examining the suggested benefits we take account of these divergent views by considering in each case whether or not the suggested benefit could be achieved without the merger.

Benefits arising from the proposed arrangements

2.120. GU and SAUR told us that there would be a number of significant benefits from the proposed arrangements, including, in particular:

— the means of alleviating the present *water resource imbalance* in the combined area of the three companies;

— the provision by GU and SAUR of an *integrated supply network* which would optimize resource usage and improve security of supply for customers of all three existing water companies;

— the ability to carry out *long-term resource planning* on a regional basis. This would better enable companies in the Southern Region to have converging needs for a new major resource;

— the establishment of an *improved programme of leakage reduction and metering promotion* aiming at a reduction of 30 per cent of the water losses over the area of the water companies by 2004/05;

— *action to generate additional water resources*, for example from the Medway system (a report, commissioned for GU and SAUR, by consultants at the Institute of Hydrology gave them reason to believe that the water yield from the Medway system could be increased by 25 megalitres a day (Ml/d);

— *a resource management and water conservation programme* (involving action on customer education, tariff structures and other incentives, water conservation charters, etc);

— *provision for conjunctive use of surface and groundwater sources* to achieve both environmental benefits and security of supply benefits;

— *improvement of service standards* for MKW's customers; and

— *creation of better circumstances for genuine competition in the region* as a result of the proposed arrangements acting to remedy current regional water resource imbalances.

2.121. GU and SAUR claimed that:

— their proposals on infrastructure, leakage and metering would act to secure that *demand* over the area of the enlarged water companies *would be met until at least 2009/10* when MKW was thought to expect to reach deficit;

— the realization of the proposed additional Medway system resources could *defer the need for a major new resource* until around 2013 to 2016; and

— the proposed resource management and water conservation programme would also act to *defer this need*, possibly *for an additional three to five years*.

2.122. GU and SAUR told us initially that they proposed to finance the infrastructure and other programmes illustrated above from within the 1995–2005 charging limits determined by the DGWS. But subsequently the DGWS announced a Periodic Review of charging limits to take effect from 2000/01. GU and SAUR then told us that they would want their proposals to be recognized in this Review. Their proposals would mean the companies finding the equivalent of an estimated additional £19 million in capital investment over a period of eight years, and £6 million of operating costs, also spread over eight years (both estimates were at out-turn prices).

2.123. We have examined carefully each of the suggested benefits put forward by GU and SAUR.

Optimizing the management and use of water resources

Water resource imbalances

2.124. We recognize that there is a problem for FDWS and SEW over the availability of water resources in their areas. The proposed merger could go some way to redress the water resource imbalances between SEW, MKW and FDWS, but the imbalances between those companies are not large. In 1995 MKW had a slight resource surplus of about 8 Ml/d or 5 per cent based on average demand (taking into account their BSTs from SWS and with some potential for further groundwater development not conflicting with EA policy), FDWS and SEW slight deficits (4 Ml/d and 3 Ml/d respectively). In 1994, which was a more typical year (see paragraph 5.44), both MKW and SEW had small surpluses of 16 Ml/d and 8 Ml/d respectively. FDWS had a deficit of 2 Ml/d. It is SWS that holds most of the surpluses of water in the south-east of England (around 200 Ml/d) although these are generally concentrated in Hampshire. The proposed merger would have no effect on that state of affairs which is essentially the historic legacy of SWS (see Chapter 5). Moreover, SWS told us that if Bewl Water were raised MKW would have no rights to additional supplies under the terms of its existing agreement. SWS would be prepared to negotiate such rights if MKW contributed to the capital costs of the enlargement of the reservoir.

2.125. Arguments were put to us, most notably by the DGWS and the EA, but also by MKH and SWS, that there were already mechanisms available by which water imbalances between companies could be redressed so that the benefits claimed by GU and SAUR could be achieved without the merger. GU and SAUR, however, told us that over a number of years FDWS and SEW (alone and jointly and in conjunction with MKW and SWS) had explored all means of redressing the regional resource imbalances short of merger. These had failed because of the absence of a shared economic interest.

2.126. The DGWS and the EA said that BSTs already take place between a number of water undertakers in England and Wales, including those in the EA's Southern Region. If one company requests a BST from another and that request is unreasonably refused then the DGWS has powers under the terms of section 40 of the 1991 Act[1] to insist that a supply be provided and to determine its price (see Appendix 4.1). The DGWS said that given that MKW and, in

---

[1] As amended by section 44 of the Competition and Services (Utilities) Act 1992.

particular, SWS have surplus resources, he considered that it was unlikely that these companies would be unable to reach agreement with any company wishing to take a BST. He thought it was unlikely that he would be called upon to resolve any dispute over the terms because he felt that both SWS and MKW would be willing to negotiate a fair deal if each had water to meet its own requirements.

2.127. SWS said that it was always prepared to consider making BSTs available provided it was sure that it could first satisfy its own demands. Demands in the region were rising as a result of climatic change and economic growth. SWS said that by planning ahead, developing new sources and tackling leakage it had been able to derive maximum benefit from the resources available in its area. But its surpluses over demand were not as great as the EA's 1994 document *Sustaining Our Resources—The Way Forward* suggested (see Figure 5.7); and since they arose largely in Hampshire, were not in the areas adjacent to SEW, MKW and FDWS.

2.128. MKW told us that it was prepared to offer BSTs to SEW and FDWS and to provide the same protection for supply interruptions as it gave to its own domestic customers. It had approached both companies but only FDWS had been prepared to enter into serious discussions for a long-term agreement to supply 2 Ml/d from Barham.

2.129. In GU and SAUR's view, BSTs were not capable of resolving a long-term structural imbalance of the kind that prevailed in the region, or of prolonging the life of existing resources through an integrated solution. BSTs perpetuated the dominance of companies in surplus and thereby did nothing to increase the prospects of effective competition or to encourage those companies in surplus to save water. Moreover, BSTs represented handing over part of their business (the development and operation of water sources) to a competitor, with a consequent loss of revenue, profit, staff skills and career paths, leaving them unable to compete on an equal basis. Although the DGWS had powers to insist on supplies being made when they were requested, he did not have the power to create the kind of integrated regional resource solution which they were seeking from the proposed merger. BSTs only worked, they said, where there was a basis of reciprocity.

2.130. We considered these arguments carefully, but felt they were overstated. Clearly there is evidence of mutual suspicion and distrust between MKW and SWS on the one hand and SEW and FDWS on the other relating to the provision of BSTs. This had been made worse by the protracted hostile bid. But GU and SAUR's objection to bulk supplies seemed to be based on the assumption that it was not appropriate to be dependent on others for long-term supplies. We were informed that there were a number of opportunities for them to take BSTs but they had usually been unwilling to negotiate (see paragraph 9.32).

2.131. Whilst clearly BSTs would not meet all the wishes of the bidders, they would provide significant additional resources for FDWS and SEW. BSTs cannot entirely redress the supply imbalances between FDWS, SEW, MKW and SWS, but they do, in our view, offer the bidders additional flexibility.

2.132. Moreover, the DGWS appears to have sufficiently strong powers under section 40 of the 1991 Act to resolve disputes over BSTs. Neither SEW nor FDWS has applied to the DGWS stating its requirements and asking him to exercise his statutory powers in a case where negotiations have been unsuccessful. Had GU and SAUR done so and received an unsatisfactory response, we feel their case would have been stronger. We do not consider that they have fully tested the system and found it to be wanting.

2.133. GU and SAUR argued that the allocation of abstraction licences to FDWS and SEW following the acquisition of MKH would contribute to the redressing of the current imbalances. We considered the extent to which this could occur without the merger. We raised with the EA the extent of its powers to reallocate abstraction licences. The EA has a duty under section 19 of the Water Resources Act 1991 to take all such action as it considers necessary or expedient to conserve, redistribute or otherwise augment water resources; and to secure the proper use of such water resources. The EA told us that it had been advised that although apparently wide-ranging the duty did not itself confer powers to take specific action but applied only in relation to functions and duties conferred by other sections of the Act. Water abstraction licences became valuable assets; they were routinely transferred by agreement when property with abstraction rights changed hands. Although the EA had power to revoke licences these powers had hardly ever been used and never to revoke the licence of one water undertaker in order to transfer it to another. The EA did not consider that its powers to revoke licences extended to circumstances where the main purpose of such action was to reallocate water resources between two water undertakers in order to redress historic imbalances in available supplies and resources. Compensation might be payable by the EA where a licence is revoked. The amount of compensation payable in respect of the revocation of a major abstraction licence would present major problems for the EA. The EA would, however, have no difficulty in facilitating a redistribution of licences where that could be achieved.

2.134. We consider that there is little scope for the transfer of abstraction licences from MKW to either FDWS or SEW by agreement. Given the predicted climatic changes and the overall pressure on resources MKW would not be willing permanently to weaken its future position. This view is supported by the evidence of SWS (which has greater surpluses than MKW) which said that it found unattractive the prospect of selling some of its licences and placing its own customers at risk.

Integrated supply network

2.135. GU and SAUR told us that their proposals would establish key links from Canterbury to Ashford and from Canterbury to Barham which would enable water from Broad Oak, were it to be developed, to be moved effectively both to FDWS and to the Weald area of Kent. MKH commented that GU and SAUR's proposals were outdated and incomplete. Several of the proposed links duplicated mains which already existed. There were neither the supply difficulties nor sufficient surpluses of water within MKW's area to justify the expenditure.

2.136. We heard from MKW that it was already strengthening the supply infrastructure within its own operating area on a similar time-scale to that proposed by GU and SAUR. This, taken with the fact that most of the surplus water resources in the south-east of England are within SWS's operating areas in Hampshire, suggested to us that any additional benefits from the integrated supply network would not be of great significance. At the margin, there would be improvements in the flow of water across the existing boundaries between SEW and MKW and FDWS and MKW. But it would be well into the future, and only if Broad Oak or another major new reservoir were developed within the region, that the benefits would assume greater significance.

Long-term resource planning

2.137. We feel that GU and SAUR's argument that the merger would facilitate long-term resource planning in the region is unconvincing. SWS, with its major presence in the region and its ownership of significant water resources, would need to be involved in any major resource development. The proposed merger would not help to secure the participation of SWS.

Leakage reduction and metering

2.138. The EA was sceptical, in the absence of enforceable conditions, that the introduction of the bidders' improved programmes for leakage reduction and metering would lead to improved levels of leakage reduction across the two enlarged companies. We too are doubtful. We note that in the most recent information provided to OFWAT (see Table 5.4) the companies' proposed leakage targets for 1997/98 were 120 litres/property/day (l/prop/d) (MKW), 138 l/prop/d (SEW) and 144 l/prop/d (FDWS). OFWAT told us that the figures for SEW and FDWS were well above the target levels proposed by the companies as part of the 1994/95 Periodic Review. At that time both companies were aiming to achieve [*] l/prop/d, to be achieved by 1999 for FDWS, but not until 2020 for SEW. We also feel that there is a risk that incentives to improve demand management would be reduced because of the additional water resources gained from MKW.

Generation of additional water resources

2.139. We sought the views of the EA on GU and SAUR's proposal that additional water resources could be generated from the River Medway. The EA's agreement would be necessary before such proposals could be implemented. Following a meeting between GU, SAUR, the EA and the MMC in November 1996, the EA remained concerned about the possible effect on the quality of water in the estuary; unless the scheme involved winter storage of water for summer use it would conflict with its stated policy of no further abstraction without winter storage. Realistically, storage could only be achieved at Bewl Water and Darwell reservoir, owned by SWS, whose involvement would be essential. The EA was sceptical that a scheme that did not involve winter storage could maintain acceptable water quality in the river in a manner that was cost-effective.

Resource management and water conservation programme

2.140. We think that a resource management and water conservation programme directed at customers could, if effectively applied, have some small benefits, but it could be put in place in the absence of the merger. The merger, by redistributing MKW's small water surpluses amongst SEW and FDWS, would provide a greater breathing space for SEW and FDWS to secure the benefits of such an educational programme; but equally the companies could achieve the same result through bulk supplies.

Conjunctive use of water sources

2.141. We consider that the merger and, in particular, the infrastructure proposals would provide some scope for greater conjunctive use of surface and groundwater sources. GU and SAUR told us that there would be some reduction in the amount of water that had to be held in reserve to deal with supply outages (see paragraph 6.13). They would also be better able to rest sources which were under stress. But given the pressure on resources throughout the region and the major efforts all three companies have made to maximize the output of their sources, we doubt whether the effect would be substantial.

Deferment of need for major new resource development

2.142. A key element in the GU and SAUR case was that as a result of the combination of measures and changes which they had outlined there would be the possibility of substantial deferment of the need for a major new water resource development in the area. As indicated above, we believe the benefits to be obtained are not likely to be significant. We note, for example, that the abstraction of further water from the Medway is likely to be rejected by the EA in the absence of winter storage. We are not convinced that the merger could be expected to lead to a substantial deferment of the need for a major resource development.

---

*Figure omitted. See note on page iv.

Other benefits

Efficiency gains

2.143. GU and SAUR estimated that the proposed merger might lead to a saving of £1.25 million a year in head office administration costs. The reorganized companies would also absorb over an eight-year period the £19 million of capital costs and £6 million of operating costs associated with infrastructure development. The efficiency gains are not large.

Improved competition

2.144. GU and SAUR claimed that the proposed merger would create better circumstances for competition in the region. We are sceptical. The scale of water resource imbalances which would be remedied is small when compared with the remaining imbalances between SWS and the companies in the region. We are more concerned that the creation of a JRC, enshrining as it will a permanent degree of co-operation between the enlarged SEW and FDWS on water resource management, may actually make it less likely that the two new companies will compete for inset appointments across their shared border. The DGWS has similar reservations. We note that tariffs for SEW customers are currently among the highest in the country. If the current borders between SEW and MKW are removed as a result of the merger, there will be reduced scope for SEW's customers to benefit from competition now or in the light of the proposed legislative changes.

Service standards

2.145. Improvements in service standards for MKW's customers are already taking place (see Appendix 4.3). No convincing evidence was given to us which suggested that the further improvements proposed by GU and SAUR would be substantial or would not take place without the proposed merger.

Finding under section 34(3)(b)(ii)

2.146. For the reasons described above we consider that the benefits which would be derived from the merger are not as great as was claimed by GU and SAUR. There would be some advantage in redressing resource imbalances in the region, but only between MKW and SEW and FDWS where the imbalances are not significant and can be substantially redressed by BSTs. The additional benefits of the integrated supply network would be limited. The proposed resource management and water conservation programme directed towards customer education may have some small benefits but could be put in place without the merger. The proposals would provide greater scope for conjunctive use of surface and groundwater sources, but this benefit would not be substantial. Efficiency gains from the merger would be small.

2.147. As indicated in paragraph 2.119, the DGWS argued that we should not have regard to benefits which could be achieved without the merger. We have concluded that many of the benefits which would result from the merger could be achieved without it. Achieving the other benefits (that is, those which could not be achieved without the merger), whether relating to water resources or efficiency gains (and either individually or together), is not, in our view, of substantially greater significance in relation to the public interest than the comparator principle. GU and SAUR argued (see paragraph 2.119) that we should have regard to benefits obtained from the merger even if they could be achieved without the merger. We consider, however, that even the achievement of all the benefits which would derive from the merger (whether or not they could be achieved without the merger) is not of substantially greater significance than the comparator principle, particularly since many of those benefits could be achieved in other ways.

2.148. We conclude, therefore, that the conditions specified in section 34(3)(b)(ii) are not met.

Other detriments arising from the proposed merger

2.149. A number of detriments other than those arising from prejudice to the comparator principle have been suggested to us. For regulated water undertakers the DGWS ensures that when their K factors are determined, allowance is made to permit adequate funding for the maintenance of capital assets. This would not be possible for the unregulated JRC. However, we do not consider that this would be a problem because the bulk of the assets which would be held by the JRC would be intangible and of negligible book value, namely abstraction licences and land access rights.

2.150. MKH and the DGWS were concerned about the possible detrimental effect of the JRC on competition to supply water in the region. GU and SAUR had argued (see paragraph 2.144) that the effect of the JRC would be beneficial. We disagree. Indeed, for the reasons set out in that paragraph we believe the merger would adversely affect the development of competition in the region.

2.151. MKH expressed concerns that the proposed merger would result in a loss of competition in its non-regulated activities, for example water engineering and resource consultancy and underground pipe work both in the UK and overseas. MKH also said that its independent and innovative research and development function would probably be lost. [

Details omitted. See note on page iv.

] In any event we do not expect any significant loss of competition in non-regulated activities, because all the companies concerned are small.

2.152. MKH also drew our attention to a number of allegations relating to the behaviour of representatives of CGE and Bouygues in France which, if substantiated, they felt would cause detriment to the public interest if GU and SAUR were allowed to expand their UK operations. No such concerns were expressed by the DGWS. We do not consider that these allegations are a sufficient basis for concluding that it would be contrary to the public interest for GU and SAUR to take control of any further water or sewerage undertaker.

2.153. We concluded in paragraph 2.113 that the proposed merger would prejudice the ability of the DGWS, in carrying out his functions under the 1991 Act, to make comparisons between water enterprises, and that the prejudice would be substantial. We also expect that it would lead to reduced prospects for competition within the region. Even if we were permitted to take into account all benefits which we consider would be likely to derive from the merger as described in paragraphs 2.120 to 2.145, we do not consider that they would outweigh the detriments, and all the more so in the circumstances that many of them can be achieved in other ways.

Conclusion on the public interest

2.154. Accordingly, we conclude that the proposed merger of water enterprises resulting from the acquisition of MKH by GU and SAUR may be expected to operate against the public interest with the particular adverse effects specified in paragraph 2.153.

Recommendations

2.155. We are required under section 72(2) of the FTA (which applies to this reference by virtue of section 34(1) of the 1991 Act) to consider what action, if any, should be taken for the purpose of remedying or preventing the particular adverse effects which we have identified.

2.156. In the course of our inquiry, we discussed with the DGWS, the EA and the parties the possibility that we might put forward certain remedies to detriments that had been identified from the proposed merger.

2.157. The DGWS told us that in general the most effective remedy to the adverse effects of prejudice to his ability to make comparisons was likely to be through an improvement in the quality of comparators by the creation of an exemplary new comparator. The detriment caused by the proposed merger might be remedied through a package of measures designed to compel the newly-merged companies (FDWS and MKEast and SEW and MKWest) to become exemplary comparators. First, there should be a requirement to maintain or increase the quality of outputs and service to consumers whilst reducing costs. This could be achieved through immediate and significant price reductions towards the top end of the range of 10 to 15 per cent of the revenue of the merged enterprises. Secondly, each of the merged companies should undertake to retain those features of performance where any of the three original companies had been a leading comparator, and thirdly, the merged companies should be required to achieve an upper quartile assessment in all aspects of performance which he monitored.

2.158. As far as visibility was concerned, the DGWS thought there should be separate listings on the Stock Exchange of the entire UK water businesses of the GU and SAUR groups. The water enterprises should also accept amendments to their appointments requiring them to act separately from and independently of their parent companies. He would like to see trend data on costs, outputs and explanatory factors maintained until 1997/98, the base year for the next Periodic Review, for the existing MKW, SEW and FDWS operations.

2.159. The EA considered that the package of measures designed to remedy the loss of a comparator should also contain an Action Plan designed to make the merged companies exemplary comparators in terms of their management of water resources. The Plan would contain elements relating to leakage reduction, the installation of meters, tariffing, customer education, the use of BSTs and the alleviation of low flows in susceptible rivers.

2.160. MKH argued that the proposed merger should be prohibited outright. It said that the benefits claimed by the bidders were vague and inconsistent and could not conceivably outweigh the prejudice to the comparator principle. Moreover, there were few efficiency gains to be made. Efficiency gains were necessary to create an exemplary comparator and had thereby underpinned the price cuts recommended by the MMC in previous cases. MKW was not lagging in terms of efficiency.

2.161. GU and SAUR argued that the proposed merger would not create any major detriment to comparative competition. Price cuts were an inappropriate remedy. They were proposing to spend £19 million from within their existing K factor settlement to achieve the benefits of the proposed merger (though they would want that expenditure to be recognized in the forthcoming review of K factors) and they were prepared to move to the efficiency frontier in terms of demand management and customer services. GU and SAUR felt that the DGWS's proposed remedy of a Stock Exchange listing of all of their UK water interests was out of proportion to the detriment. Moreover, the information gleaned from the listing of subsidiaries whose parent companies were not listed would be of little value. They thought the information sought by the DGWS from a Stock Exchange listing could be provided separately in other ways.

2.162. We considered carefully all the arguments put to us. It is clear that the efficiency gains achievable through the proposed merger are small. In view of this, large price reductions from the merged companies would not be sustainable in terms of long-term cost reductions. This would be of no benefit to the comparator regime. The price cuts would need to be funded from the existing resources of the parent companies and the benefits would last only until the next Periodic Review. The damage to the comparator regime arising from the loss of an independent WoC would be permanent.

2.163. Nor are we convinced by the DGWS's proposed remedies for loss of visibility. We agree with GU and SAUR that there is little point in listing majority-owned subsidiaries. We think this would be artificial and it would provide information on which it would be unwise to rely.

2.164. Of the measures proposed by the EA, those relating to leakage and metering went only part of the way to remedying the loss of a comparator; the remainder, however desirable, do not seem to us to address the damage caused by the loss.

2.165. In summary, therefore, we see significant damage to the system of comparative competition arising from the proposed merger. MKW is one of only five remaining independent WoCs of a size the DGWS finds useful for making comparisons. If it were to lose its independence (Stage 1) and ultimately be lost altogether (Stage 2) this would adversely affect the usefulness of comparative data provided by the DGWS. The remedies proposed by the DGWS and the EA would in our view either be short-term in effect or partial or ineffective. Any gain to water consumers arising from these remedies would be temporary, but the comparator system would suffer permanent damage. They would have no effect on the loss of competition in the area. We consider, therefore, that in this case the proposed merger should be prohibited.

Related issues

2.166. We recognize the water resource difficulties FDWS and SEW face. But GU and SAUR's proposals as they currently stand do not seem to us likely to achieve their stated objective. GU and SAUR need to work much more closely with the other companies in the region and the regulatory agencies if they are to improve the situation.

2.167. We believe the DGWS and EA have between them the necessary powers and influence to help develop long-term strategic solutions for the region. Moreover, they should make every effort to do so and in doing so must bear in mind the commercial pressures on the water industry since privatization.

2.168. If all the water undertakers in the region were prepared to co-operate one with another and with the two regulators we have no doubt that satisfactory long-term solutions could be found which would be of benefit to all the consumers in the region.

Part II

Background and evidence

3 Background to the reference, the parties, their operations and financial performance

Contents

	Paragraph
Introduction	3.1
Merger proposals and basis for the reference	3.2
The water industry	3.5
Background to the region	
The Environment Agency's Southern Region	3.7
Water resources	3.8
Changes affecting the region	3.9
The current regulatory regime	
Financial reporting	3.12
K factors	3.18
Compagnie Générale des Eaux and its General Utilities subsidiary	
History and development	3.19
Current activities	3.20
Water	3.21
Construction	3.22
Energy	3.23
Waste management	3.24
Other activities	3.25
Financial summary	3.26
UK water businesses—GU	3.28
Three Valleys	3.32
North Surrey	3.33
Tendring Hundred	3.34
Folkestone & Dover Water Services	3.35
SAUR Group	
History and development	3.41
Current activities	3.44
Water	3.46
Energy and waste management	3.49
Design, engineering and other activities	3.50
Financial summary	3.51
UK water businesses—SAUR UK	3.53
Mid Southern	3.54
South East Water	3.55
The Mid Kent Group	
Mid Kent Holdings	
History and development	3.59
Significant shareholdings and the proposed bidders	3.61
Mid Kent Water	
History and development	3.68
Current activities	3.70
Commercial relationships with the potential bidders	3.74
Relationship with SWS	3.77
Financial summary	3.80
Non-appointed businesses of MKH	3.83
Assets test	3.87

Introduction

3.1. This chapter opens with a short description of the merger proposals and the basis for the reference, and goes on to present a review of the water industry, its organization in the Kent and Sussex area, the companies involved, their businesses and financial performance and the extent of existing relationships between them.

Merger proposals and basis for the reference

3.2. On 21 December 1995 GU and SAUR publicly announced their intention to make an offer for the whole of the issued share capital of MKH. GU and SAUR's announcement outlined the companies' intention to divide into two parts the principal operations of MKH, which are mainly the water-related businesses of MKH's main subsidiary, MKW; and to merge each part with GU's and SAUR's respective existing water-related businesses in the area, FDWS, a 74 per cent-owned subsidiary of GU, and SEW, a wholly-owned subsidiary of SAUR. Some of the water resource assets, in particular all the water abstraction licences in MKW's area and MKW's current bulk supply rights, rights of access and the rights and licences associated with possible major new developments, would be transferred to a third company, the JRC. Although, as originally proposed, the JRC would also own land associated with any future major water resources development, for example at Broad Oak, near Canterbury, the proposal was subsequently revised to exclude land ownership (see paragraphs 6.7 and 6.8). The JRC would be owned 50:50 by the enlarged SEW and FDWS.

3.3. The companies' announcement acknowledged that the proposed bid would be subject to a mandatory reference to the MMC. Their announcement stated that 'in the absence of a requirement for an MMC reference ... General Utilities and SAUR Water Services would have announced today a firm intention to make an offer for the ordinary shares of Mid Kent at a price of 440p per share'. This compares with closing prices of 353p on the day before the announcement, 430p on the day of the announcement and 640p on 4 December 1996 (source: *Financial Times*). Two stages were envisaged by the companies if the proposals went ahead:

— In Stage 1 GU and SAUR would acquire the entire issued share capital of MKH through a new company (Newco) specially formed for the purpose.

— In Stage 2, which was intended to be completed as soon as reasonably practicable after Stage 1 is set in motion and in any case within four years of completion of the take-over, MKW's assets would largely be divided into two parts, approximately equal by value. The eastern part would be amalgamated with GU's subsidiary, FDWS, and the western operations with SAUR's subsidiary, SEW. At the same time the JRC would be established.

The likely zone within which the division would occur is shown in Appendix 2.1.

3.4. The Secretary of State for Trade and Industry, under section 32 of the 1991 Act, referred the matter to the MMC on 23 May 1996 for investigation and report. On 13 September 1996 he amended the terms of reference to require the MMC to consider, in addition, whether any merger of water enterprises had taken place.

The water industry

3.5. The water industry in England and Wales now comprises ten water and sewerage companies (WaSCs) which provide sewerage services throughout England and Wales and water services over a large part of the country, and 19 companies, often with origins as SWCs, providing water services alone (WoCs). FDWS, SEW and MKW, which supply water services in the region, are all WoCs. Most of the customers of these WoCs receive sewerage services from SWS, which is one of the ten WaSCs. SWS also supplies water to, *inter alia,* other parts of Kent and Sussex (as shown on Map 7). The industry turnover in 1995/96 was £3.0 billion and £3.1 billion for water services and sewerage services respectively (making £6.1 billion in total), and the estimated daily quantity of water delivered was 13,286 Ml/d.[1] All ten WaSCs are listed within the top 600 UK companies by size of turnover.[2] This inquiry is not concerned with waste water sewerage services.

3.6. Since 1989 the number of companies providing water services has fallen from the original 39 to the current 29 as a result of mergers. The following companies have been formed through mergers of the companies shown:

— Bournemouth and West Hampshire (Bournemouth Water and West Hampshire Water);
— Essex and Suffolk (Essex Water and Suffolk Water);
— North East Water (Newcastle & Gateshead Water and Sunderland & South Shields Water);
— Severn Trent (Severn Trent Water and East Worcester Water);
— SEW (Eastbourne Water, West Kent Water and Mid Sussex Water);
— Sutton & East Surrey (Sutton & District Water and East Surrey Water);
— Three Valleys (Lee Valley Water, Colne Valley Water and Rickmansworth Water); and
— Northumbrian (Northumbrian Water and North East Water).

Background to the region

The Environment Agency's Southern Region

3.7. FDWS, SEW, MKW, SWS and Thames Water supply water to Kent and East Sussex. They fall within the Southern Region of the EA, as shown in Maps 2 and 3, which includes most of Kent and Hampshire, East and West Sussex, the Isle of Wight, part of south-east London and small parts of Wiltshire, Berkshire and Surrey. This Region is one of the more densely populated areas in England and Wales with a population of around 4.5 million.

Water resources

3.8. The role of water resources as a key factor behind the present merger proposals is discussed in Chapter 5. The region is one of the driest in England and Wales and bordered on three sides by the sea: there are no large rivers and some 77 per cent of water supplies comes from groundwater boreholes. The EA's assessment for 1995 of reliable yields and current annual average demand levels shows FDWS and SEW as having deficits of 4 and 2 Ml/d respectively, and MKW and SWS with surpluses of 5 and 58 Ml/d respectively. (Reliable yields are assessed on the basis of a drought of critical length appropriate to the source and taking account of the return period. Such yields may not be available during severe droughts such as those between 1988 and 1992 and in 1995/96.)

Changes affecting the region

3.9. Under the Water Act 1973 the four River Authorities for Kent, Sussex, Hampshire and the Isle of Wight and those water supply undertakings run by local authorities became the Southern Water Authority. The existing SWCs of the region were not affected and included:

— Portsmouth Water Company;
— Mid Sussex Water Company;
— Eastbourne Waterworks Company;
— West Kent Water Company;
— Mid Kent Water Company; and
— Folkestone & District Water Company.

---

[1] One megalitre = 1 million litres, or 1,000 cubic metres.

[2] See the *Times Top 1000 United Kingdom Companies 1996*.

In addition to these, the following water companies extended into the statutory area of the Southern Water Authority:

— West Hampshire Water Company (now part of Bournemouth & West Hampshire Water PLC);
— Mid Southern Water plc; and
— East Surrey Water plc (now part of Sutton & East Surrey Water).

3.10. The region has seen a number of changes since 1989. In particular, SEW has been formed out of the merger of Eastbourne, West Kent and Mid Sussex water companies following their purchase by the SAUR Group (see paragraph 3.6), and FDWS has become part of the GU group.

3.11. Table 3.1 shows the significant changes which have taken place since 1989. A fuller chronology of events involving GU, SAUR and MKW/MKH is given in Appendix 3.1.

TABLE 3.1 Main changes in the local water industry, 1989 to 1992

Company	Significant changes	Date
Folkestone & District Water Co	Take-over by GU	January 1989
MKH (MKW prior to share exchange)	(i) GU share of voting stock increased to 29.8% (ii) SAUR share of voting stock increased to 15.8%	March 1989 March 1989
Eastbourne Waterworks Company West Kent Water Mid Sussex Water	Take-over by SAUR	February 1989
Southern Water Authority	Privatized	October 1989
MKH	SAUR share of voting stock increased to 19.5%	November 1989
MKH	As a result of an MMC inquiry into the possible merger of the then Folkestone & District Water Company (a GU subsidiary) and MKH, GU was required to undertake to the Secretary of State for Trade and Industry to reduce its shareholding in MKH to not more than 19.5% by 30 June 1992	March 1991
SEW	Formed out of merger of Eastbourne, West Kent and Mid Sussex Water Companies	May 1991
Folkestone & District Water Company	Incorporated under Companies Act 1985 and changed name to Folkestone & Dover Water Services Ltd	June 1992

Sources: EA, OFWAT, GU, MKW and SAUR.

The current regulatory regime

Financial reporting

3.12. Under the 1991 Act, the supply of water by appointed water undertakers is subject to the economic regulation of the DGWS, whilst the undertakers' non-appointed businesses are free from such regulation. Consequently, OFWAT has developed its own requirements for the provision of financial information rather than relying on accounts filed under the Companies Act. These include a format for annual regulatory accounts relating to the appointed businesses of each company, and upon which the company's auditors are required to report.

3.13. The main differences between regulatory accounts and statutory accounts are, first, details of the appointed water businesses are shown separately; secondly, the formats of profit and loss account and balance sheet components, which are intended to be consistent and relevant to the water industry, are different; and thirdly, regulatory accounts are prepared under both historical cost (HCA) and current cost (CCA) accounting conventions.

3.14. For OFWAT accounting purposes, fixed assets are divided into infrastructure assets and non-infrastructure assets. Infrastructure assets are defined as underground mains and sewers, impounding and pumped raw water storage reservoirs, dams, sludge pipelines and sea outfalls. Non-infrastructure assets comprise all other fixed assets. Infrastructure assets are regarded as having an indefinite economically useful life provided they are adequately maintained: some are already more than 100 years old. Infrastructure assets are not depreciated, but an infrastructure renewals charge is made to the profit and loss account. This is the estimated average annual cost of maintaining the infrastructure base indefinitely and is derived from a formal Asset Management Plan (AMP) prepared by each company and periodically updated. The annual charge may be more or less than the cash expended in that year.

3.15. Fixed assets are valued for CCA balance sheet purposes at their depreciated replacement cost. This is derived from the concept of a Modern Equivalent Asset (MEA). The gross MEA value is the cost of replacing an old asset with a technically up-to-date new asset with the same service capability, allowing for any difference both in the quality of output and in operating costs. The net MEA is the depreciated value taking into account the remaining service potential of an old asset compared with a new one. Thus if a new MEA had an estimated life of 50 years and the existing asset was expected to last another 20 years, the net MEA value would be two-fifths of the gross MEA value.

3.16. Water abstraction rights (in the form of licences) have substantial values but, apart from, for example, the expenditure of consultants' fees to support licence applications, they have cost little or nothing to acquire. Accordingly, they do not appear in company balance sheets, unlike the capital costs of extracting water such as those of sinking boreholes and building pumping stations.

3.17. For the purpose of this inquiry we have focused on the CCA regulatory accounts as being the most suitable given the exceptionally long asset lives and low historical costs of fixed assets in the industry.

K factors

3.18. The DGWS uses a formula of 'RPI+K' in determining the limits by which the overall revenues of a water undertaker may be raised annually. RPI is the change in the RPI for each year expressed as a percentage and K is a number (which may be positive, zero or negative) which is specific to each company; the two combined limit the increase (or impose a reduction) in average prices which the company may charge in a particular year. The first period in respect of which K factors were set was for five years ending on 31 March 1995, known as period K1, and the second period is now for the five years following, ending on 31 March 2000, and known as K2. K factors may vary from year to year, or be constant for an entire K period.

Compagnie Générale des Eaux and its General Utilities subsidiary

History and development

3.19. CGE was established in 1853 to provide water to the city of Lyon, since when it has won contracts in a large number of towns and cities in France to provide water or waste water services. It now manages a number of that country's public services through concessions awarded by municipal authorities. The CGE group has diversified over the years and by 1994 water-related business accounted for 26 per cent of group turnover, the second largest division behind construction. It operates extensively outside France and believes that it is among the 30 largest companies in Europe.

Current activities

3.20. World-wide the CGE group had, in 1994, 215,000 employees and some 2,500 subsidiaries. Its biggest operations outside France are in the UK and account for 9 per cent of group turnover with some 20,000 employees. The main divisions of the group are outlined in the following paragraphs and financial information is given in paragraph 3.26.

Water

3.21. The CGE group states that it is now the largest water company in the world, supplying water, and often sewerage services, to some 40 million people of which 15 million are outside France. In France during 1994 CGE provided water and waste water services through about 50 subsidiaries; water supplied averaged 1,940 Ml/d to some 6.4 million customers representing 25 million people. In addition to its UK operations, described in paragraph 3.28 and following, CGE has expanded primarily into Spain, the USA and Italy with other operations elsewhere including Malaysia, Argentina, Mexico and Portugal, often exporting the French model of management contract. This typically involves the contracted manager assuming all forms of risk for a long term at fixed prices adjusted for inflation, a variation being that the manager may be required to replace fixed assets as necessary at its own expense. Other versions include 'build, own, transfer' contracts, and fee-based arrangements which exclude the financing of initial capital expenditure. Contract terms are typically for periods of up to 30 years.

Construction

3.22. CGE's construction activities are carried out mainly through subsidiaries, known as SGE and CBC, which participate in major civil engineering projects. SGE operates in more than 80 countries and, in Europe, has a 31 per cent interest in Cofiroute, a private European motorway company which both operates concessions and builds new motorways. Main construction markets are France, Germany, the UK (where it owns Norwest Holst) and Portugal.

Energy

3.23. Energy is handled by CGE's Sithe Energies subsidiary which, in France, has a portfolio of 40,000 contracts for the heating of buildings and heat management services, each for an average period of six to seven years. Outside France, Sithe Energies is primarily active as a power generation utility in North America, whilst in the UK it operates power stations fuelled by household waste in Birmingham, south-east London and Cardiff.

Waste management

3.24. CGE said that it is Europe's leading operator, and third world-wide, in this field which includes cleaning, collection, sorting, recycling, incinerating and landfilling. In the UK it has five contracts with local authorities for refuse collection from 6 million inhabitants, and one with Hampshire to treat 650,000 tonnes of waste annually for 25 years. Other clients include London Underground and Heathrow Airport. CGE said that it is Europe's leading paper and cardboard recycling operator.

Other activities

3.25. CGE's other activities include property development, communications, healthcare and community services such as transport and catering, both within and outside France. In the UK, General Healthcare provides healthcare through 30 hospitals and psychiatric services for some 900 people. The transport operation recently won a seven-year franchise to manage London's Network South Central commuter rail operation. CGE has a significant minority stake in General Cable, a publicly listed company, which is one of the largest providers of cable networks in the UK.

Financial summary

3.26. The divisional turnover of CGE is summarized in Table 3.2 and a financial summary is set out in Table 3.3. Further financial information is at Appendix 3.2.

TABLE 3.2 **CGE: HCA divisional turnover**

Years ended 31 December   £ million

	1991		1992		1993		1994		1995	
	Sales	Profit	Sales	Profit	Sales	Profit	Sales	Profit	Sales	Profit
Services sector										
Water distribution	2,525		2,797		3,114		3,365	} 609	3,502	} 626
Water-related construction, etc	1,515		1,609		1,472		1,599		1,647	
Thermal energy	2,168		2,319		2,556		2,515	} 416	2,893	} 501
Electrical engineering	1,317		1,360		1,163		1,230		1,323	
Independent power production					205		211		427	
Energy industries	191		191		179		189		195	
Waste management	974		1,070		1,166		1,359	228	1,510	230
Other activities										
Construction	5,159		5,149		5,119		5,332	0	4,835	112
Property	1,388		1,646		1,354		1,021	0	1,086	(191)
Communications	301		303		479		643	0	728	(36)
Healthcare	398		457		543		616	98	666	101
Community services	418		479		542		848	84	941	96
Other	0		0		0		0	201	0	26
Total	16,354		17,380		17,892		18,928	1,636	19,753	1,465

Source: GU.

Notes:
1. Sales comprise group turnover, whereas profits comprise operating income before depreciation. For 1994 depreciation charged against profits totalled £1,055 million.
2. Figures have been translated at FF8.25 = £1.
3. In the years 1991 to 1993 information on profits breakdown is not available.

TABLE 3.3 **CGE: HCA financial summary**

Years ended 31 December   £ million

	1991	1992	1993	1994	1995
Net tangible assets	612	1,037	1,562	1,826	998
Intangible assets	844	1,034	1,167	1,243	1,338
Goodwill	1,132	1,295	1,598	1,875	2,055
Net assets	2,588	3,366	4,327	4,944	4,391
Represented by:					
Shareholders' funds	2,226	2,906	3,832	4,176	3,658
Minorities	362	460	495	768	733
Equity	2,588	3,366	4,327	4,944	4,391
Profit before exceptional items	467	411	375	(26)	(529)
Exceptional items	12	15	29	429	102
Profit before tax	479	426	404	403	(427)
Cash assets less borrowings	(5,247)	(6,286)	(7,029)	(7,166)	(7,309)
Net debt:equity (%)	463	485	440	382	356
Interest cover (net)	3.2	2.7	3.2	2.5	(0.0)

Source: CGE/MMC analysis.

Notes:
1. Figures have been translated at FF8.25 = £1.
2. Debt:equity has been calculated after excluding goodwill and intangible assets.
3. Interest cover has been calculated on profits after inclusion of exceptional items.

3.27. The balance sheet contains substantial intangible assets, some of which represent water utility contracts where advance payments have been made to local authority and other contracting parties and which will be written off over the life of the relevant contract. Nevertheless, intangible assets and goodwill accounted for 63 per cent of net assets in 1994, making the debt:equity ratio high by UK standards. Interest cover has been calculated after inclusion of exceptional items, so the figure for 1994 is not realistic or comparable. Otherwise, the interest cover figures do not indicate difficulty in meeting debt service obligations.

UK water businesses—GU

3.28. CGE established GU in 1987 as a UK wholly-owned subsidiary to act as the holding company for its planned interests in the UK water industry. In 1988 GU announced bids which led to the acquisition of 100 per cent of Lee Valley Water Company (Lee Valley), North Surrey Water Ltd (North Surrey) and Tendring Hundred Water Services Ltd (Tendring Hundred) and 74 per cent of the voting capital of FDWS.[1] (Almost all of the remaining 26 per cent of FDWS is held by SWS.) GU then transferred Lee Valley to a wholly-owned subsidiary, Three Valleys Water PLC (Three Valleys), which made recommended share offers to acquire the Colne Valley and Rickmansworth water companies, and these three water companies were subsequently merged. Minority shareholdings in Three Valleys were later acquired to give CGE 100 per cent of Three Valleys. GU's UK group structure is shown in Figure 3.1.

FIGURE 3.1

GU's UK structure

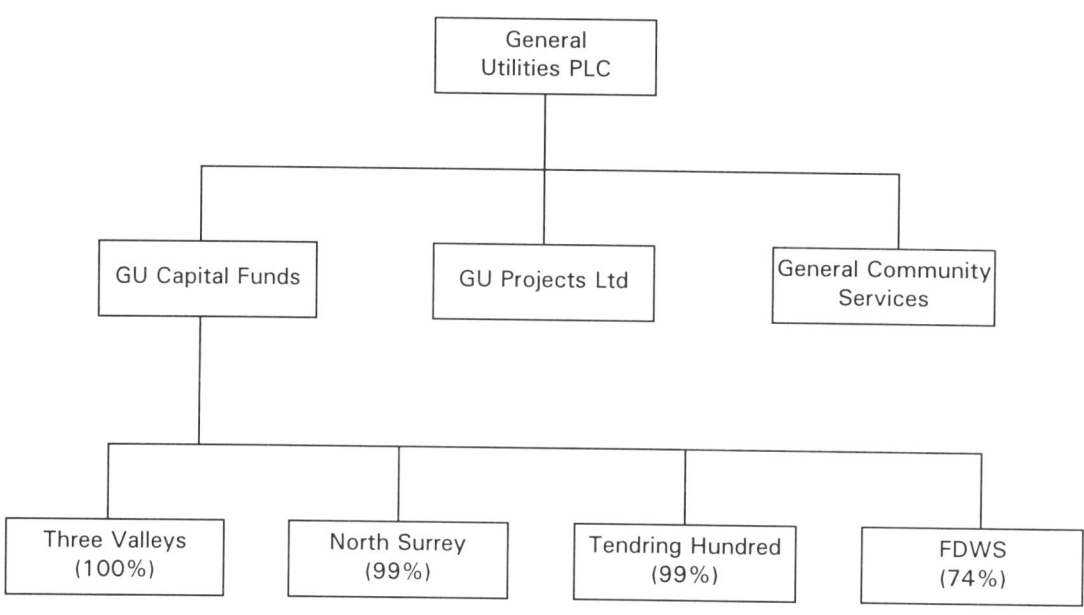

Source: GU.

3.29. GU Projects Ltd provides planning, engineering and laboratory services for the GU water subsidiaries; in the year ended 31 March 1996 it turned over £8.0 million and made a profit before tax of £321,000. General Community Services provides billing and administrative services to local authorities via two separate subsidiaries. In the year ended 31 March 1996 it turned over £6.4 million and lost £382,000 before tax.

3.30. In addition to the subsidiaries shown in Figure 3.1, at 31 March 1996 GU had the following minority interests, all of which are WoCs:

---

[1] Then known as Folkestone & District Water Company.

Company	Percentage held
South Staffordshire Water Plc	27.8
Bristol Water Plc	25.0
MKH	19.5

Note: Percentages held are of voting equity.

3.31. GU's stated policy is to encourage subsidiaries to act as independent local suppliers with operational autonomy; where it has a minority stake, it plays no part in management, neither does it have Board representation. The areas served by the respective companies are shown in Appendix 3.3.

Three Valleys

3.32. As referred to in paragraph 3.28, Three Valleys was formed by a merger of three companies. It now supplies 2.3 million people over an area of 3,213 sq km including a number of north and west London boroughs and parts of neighbouring home counties. The area is outlined on the map at Appendix 3.3. In 1995/96 Three Valleys supplied a daily average of 614 Ml/d or 4.6 per cent of the total regulated by OFWAT. Its average K factors for K1 and K2 were +3.8 and +2.5 respectively. Table 3.4 summarizes Three Valleys' financial performance since its formation.

TABLE 3.4 **Three Valleys CCA financial summary**

£ million

	Years ended 31 March					
	1991	1992	1993	1994	1995	1996
Turnover	*	*	*	109.1	113.8	122.3
Profit before tax				19.2	28.5	33.7
Profit after tax				18.9	22.6	25.2
Dividends paid and proposed				13.5	15.7	16.9
Current cost profit retained				5.4	6.9	8.3
Operating cash flow after interest, tax, and dividends				31.2	32.6	13.4
Capital expenditure				15.7	15.0	18.0

Source: Three Valleys.

*Results not consolidated.
Notes:
1. The figures shown include non-appointed activities, which for 1995 amounted to 1 per cent of turnover.
2. Capital expenditure represents cash expended on fixed assets and excludes infrastructure renewals expenditure but is after deducting capital contributions and proceeds from the disposal of fixed assets.

North Surrey

3.33. North Surrey was acquired by GU in 1988 and supplies water to approximately 478,000 people over an area of 500 sq km in parts of Surrey, Berkshire and the London boroughs of Ealing, Hillingdon and Hounslow, as shown in Appendix 3.3. Its average K factors for K1 and K2 were +8.1 and +2.0 respectively. In 1995/96 North Surrey supplied a daily average of 121 Ml/d or 0.9 per cent of the total regulated by OFWAT. Table 3.5 summarizes its recent financial performance.

TABLE 3.5 **North Surrey CCA financial summary**

£ million

Years ended 31 March

	1992	1993	1994	1995	1996
Turnover	19.6	21.5	23.6	25.5	26.4
Profit before tax	3.9	4.1	6.1	7.9	8.0
Profit after tax	3.7	4.2	5.8	5.7	6.4
Dividends paid and proposed	2.0	2.2	2.9	3.1	3.5
Current cost profit retained	1.7	2.0	2.9	2.6	2.9
Operating cash flow after interest, tax, and dividends	5.8	5.9	6.7	9.3	9.3
Capital expenditure	9.4	7.0	4.5	10.2	11.8

Source: North Surrey.

Note: Capital expenditure represents cash expended on fixed assets and excludes infrastructure renewals expenditure but is after deducting capital contributions and proceeds from the disposal of fixed assets.

Tendring Hundred

3.34. Tendring Hundred was acquired by GU in 1989 and supplies water to approximately 140,000 people over an area of 352 sq km in East Anglia between the Rivers Colne and Stour, taking in the towns of Harwich, Clacton-on-Sea, Brightlingsea and Manningtree. Appendix 3.3 shows the area served. In 1995/96 Tendring Hundred supplied a daily average of 30.3 Ml/d or 0.2 per cent of the volume regulated by OFWAT. Table 3.6 summarizes its financial performance and also shows its K factors for each year because they have varied considerably.

TABLE 3.6 **Tendring Hundred CCA financial summary**

£ million

Years ended 31 March

	1992	1993	1994	1995	1996
Turnover	8.2	9.3	10.8	11.1	11.6
Profit before tax	2.1	3.0	4.3	5.3	5.4
Profit after tax	2.0	2.9	4.1	3.9	4.0
Dividends paid and proposed	1.3	1.4	1.6	1.8	1.9
Current cost profit retained	0.7	1.5	2.5	2.2	2.1
Operating cash flow after interest, tax, and dividends	1.1	2.2	3.7	3.1	3.2
Capital expenditure	5.6	5.2	2.4	1.7	2.0
K factors	+22.5	+13.0	+11.0	+2.5	−0.5

Sources: Tendring Hundred, OFWAT.

Note: Capital expenditure represents cash expended on fixed assets and excludes infrastructure renewals expenditure but is after deducting capital contributions and proceeds from the disposal of fixed assets.

Folkestone & Dover Water Services

History and development

3.35. FDWS was established as an SWC in 1848 as Folkestone Water Works. Between 1950 and 1955 it acquired four adjacent water undertakings including those of Folkestone Corporation and Hythe Corporation. In 1970 it acquired Dover Corporation Waterworks and part of the business of East Kent Water Company. Its shares were listed on the Stock Exchange until 1992 when the company was registered as a private limited company and its ordinary and preference shares were delisted; its loan and debenture stocks, amounting to £2.6 million, continue to be listed. GU acquired 74 per cent of the voting ordinary shares in 1989 and almost all of the balance is held by SWS.

Current activities

3.36. FDWS serves a population of some 153,000 people through 70,000 connections over an area of some 420 sq km, covering a largely coastal area from just north of Dover to Dungeness, and inland nearly reaching Ashford and Canterbury. Almost all of its western boundary adjoins MKW's area, whilst its northern boundary and a small part of its western boundary adjoin separate areas served by SWS. The location is shown on Map 7. The annual daily average water volume supplied during 1995/96 was 44.1 Ml/d. This represents 0.3 per cent of the volume regulated by OFWAT.

3.37. As referred to in paragraph 3.8, FDWS has a shortfall between its annual average water requirement and the reliable yield of its resources. All of its water normally comes from its own groundwater sources of which it has 24, which it claims gives it the lowest average source output in the industry at 2.2 Ml/d. FDWS has 19 treatment plants, but the treatment required is mostly classified as 'simple, marginal chlorination'. A supply buffer is maintained via eight small untreated water reservoirs holding about 1.8 days' aggregate requirement, and 15 treated water reservoirs holding about 1.4 days' requirement.

3.38. FDWS had taken a BST from MKW's Barham source (also known as Kingston) which had operated for many years at a level of 2.2 Ml/d until 1992 when it was terminated. In 1996 FDWS expanded its resources by resuming a BST of 1.0 Ml/d from Barham; by bringing into use three disused surface reservoirs in Folkestone using a portable treatment plant to provide a further 2 Ml/d over two months; and in August by obtaining a licence to abstract 1.4 Ml/d from a disused Railtrack borehole at Dover Priory. Further information on water resources is given in Chapter 5.

3.39. The financial performance of FDWS over the past five years is summarized in Table 3.7. Its average K1 and K2 factors were +9.9 and −0.5 respectively. Further financial details are given at Appendix 3.4.

TABLE 3.7 **FDWS CCA financial summary**

£ million

	Years ended 31 March				
	1992	1993	1994	1995	1996
Turnover	7.6	8.6	9.6	10.2	10.5
Historical cost profit after tax	0.8	1.3	2.4	3.1	3.2
Current cost profit before tax	0.5	0.8	2.4	2.4	2.3
Current cost profit after tax	0.5	0.8	2.1	1.9	1.8
Dividends	(0.2)	(1.2)	(1.1)	(1.4)	(1.6)
Retained profits	0.3	(0.4)	1.0	0.5	0.2
CCA depreciation*	1.0	1.4	1.3	2.2	2.5
Operating cash flow after tax and dividends	1.4	2.0	2.7	3.4	3.7
Capital expenditure†	1.2	2.2	3.4	4.3	2.8

Sources: FDWS, MMC analysis.

*The figures shown for CCA depreciation exclude AMP expenditure on non-depreciated assets.
†Capital expenditure represents cash expended on fixed assets and excludes infrastructure renewals expenditure but is after deducting capital contributions and proceeds from the disposal of fixed assets.

3.40. Turnover levelled off in 1996 after substantial rises in the previous three years reflecting the change in K factor from +8.0 in each of the years ended 31 March 1993, 1994 and 1995 to −0.5 in 1996. Current cost profit before tax has declined marginally in 1996 reflecting increased operating costs against turnover up 3 per cent. Capital expenditure outflows in 1993, 1994 and 1995 were substantially above depreciation and reflected investment in additional assets as well as replacements: this mostly involved water mains many of which were to balance water flows between resources, but there was also a metering programme which is continuing. Aggregate capital expenditure for the five years shown exceeded operating cash flow after tax and dividends by £0.7 million, but in 1996 there was a cash flow surplus of £0.9 million because of both increased cash flow and reduced capital spending.

SAUR Group

History and development

3.41. The SAUR Group comprises the parent company, SAUR SA, together with its subsidiaries world-wide. SAUR SA was founded as a private company in 1933 for the purpose of carrying out water and sewerage utilities management and it remains privately controlled. By 1969 SAUR Group was operating in Africa particularly through its interest in SODECI (Société de Distribution d'Eau de Côte d'Ivoire) which had the water supply concession for the Ivory Coast. In 1984 the large French construction group headed by Bouygues acquired a 45 per cent interest in SAUR SA, with the original private shareholders retaining 51 per cent and employees 4 per cent through respective holding companies. Following this, SAUR Group extended its scope within Europe as well as into several other African countries, often in partnership with Electricité de France (EDF) as far as the energy business was concerned. In the early 1980s SAUR Group set up operations in Canada through its subsidiary Aquatech which later won water and sewerage contracts in the state of Quebec.

3.42. In July 1994 SAUR Group transferred its international interests into a new 65 per cent owned subsidiary, SAUR International, the other shareholder of which was a holding company owned 35 per cent by Bouygues and 65 per cent by EDF International. Figure 3.2 shows this structure.

FIGURE 3.2

Ownership of SAUR International

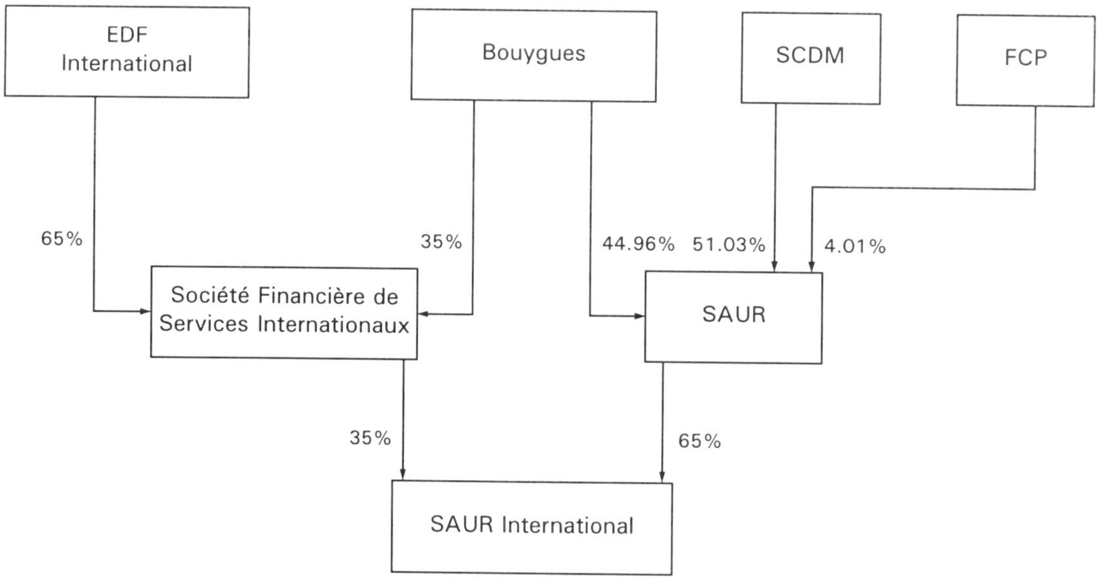

Source: SEW.

SCDM represents the original private shareholder interests, and FCP is an employee share holding company. Société Financière de Services Internationaux is an intermediate holding company.

3.43. In 1986 SAUR Group formed a UK holding company, SAUR (UK) Limited (SAUR UK), and also a joint venture with Trafalgar House PLC to provide access to the English and Welsh water supply market, which was to be privatized. Trafalgar House's interest was bought out in 1988 at which time shares in several SWCs were acquired. SAUR Group's UK water interests are all held through SAUR Water Services plc (SAUR), a wholly-owned subsidiary of SAUR UK. Figure 3.3 shows the UK corporate structure. The holdings shown for MKH amount to 19.39 per cent of the voting share capital (referred to in paragraph 3.65) because the preference shares carry voting rights.

Current activities

3.44. SAUR Group, including SAUR International, is based in Paris with day-to-day management delegated to its local companies. The group is a specialist in providing private management of public utilities, having many thousands of contracts with local authorities in France and other countries.

3.45. SAUR International is currently active in 18 countries outside France; three-quarters of its business is in water and energy services, with the remainder mainly in waste management, engineering and water process plant design, construction and operation. SAUR International's total turnover for the year ended 31 December 1995 was FF3,017 million (£366 million), of which FF1,118 million (£136 million) was attributable to water supply services. The main business activities of SAUR Group are summarized in the following paragraphs.

Water

3.46. The main activity is the provision of drinking water, whereby the contracting company is delegated responsibility by local communities for all operations from water collection through to distribution and management. In France SAUR Group has more than 6,000 long-term contracts which typically have the following features:

— SAUR Group has managerial and operating responsibility;

— ownership of assets remains with the local community;

— the local community finances new facilities;

— contract terms range from 10 to 30 years with price regulation; and

— revenues are shared between the local community for servicing asset finance, and the operator covers its costs and profit.

3.47. Elsewhere, SAUR Group adapts to the requirements of the local authority, ranging from managing a single plant to long-term concessions and 'build, own, transfer' contracts. World-wide, SAUR Group supplies water to more than 20 million people of whom more than 14 million are outside France; this activity accounted for some 48 per cent of SAUR Group turnover in 1995 and 37 per cent of SAUR International's. Further information on its UK activities is given in paragraph 3.53.

3.48. SAUR Group also designs, builds and operates sewerage systems, of which it manages more than 1,000 around the world; sewerage activities accounted for some 12 per cent of group turnover in 1995.

Energy and waste management

3.49. SAUR Group's energy activities comprise gas and electricity production and distribution, the whole of which is outside France and predominantly in French-speaking Africa, often in partnership with EDF. In 1995 energy-related industries accounted for some 14 per cent of SAUR Group's turnover and 38 per cent of SAUR International's. SAUR Group operates in all areas of public cleansing, industrial and urban refuse collection, waste processing and recycling, street and beach cleaning; it also operates landfill and waste disposal sites, which contributed 11 per cent of group turnover in 1995. In the UK this activity is carried out through the group's Ecovert group of companies which is 100 per cent owned, and which in 1994 generated a turnover in excess of £22 million through contracts with 16 local authorities.

FIGURE 3.3
SAUR International's UK structure

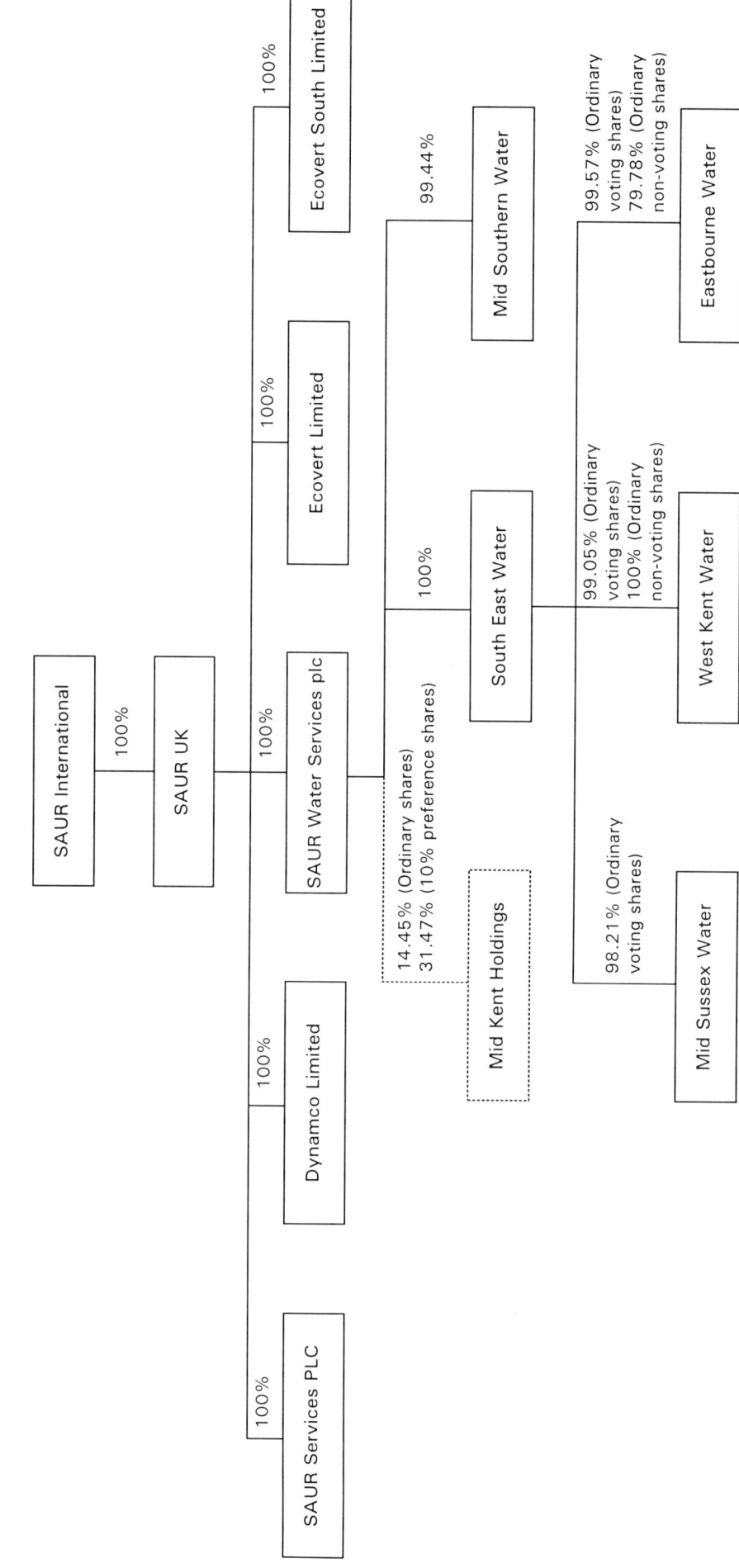

Source: SAUR.

Design, engineering and other activities

3.50. This sector mainly relates to the design, engineering and construction of water and sewerage treatment and recycling plants. Three-quarters of its turnover is in France and in 1995 it contributed 10 per cent of group sales.

Financial summary

3.51. SAUR SA and SAUR International are investment holding companies; Tables 3.8 and 3.9 show analyses of their turnover, and Tables 3.10 and 3.11 show consolidated financial summaries (including the results of their associated companies).

TABLE 3.8 **SAUR SA HCA consolidated divisional turnover**

£ million

Years ended 31 December

	1991	%	1992	%	1993	%	1994	%	1995	%
Sale of water	388	47.6	413	47.8	439	47.3	462	52.0	478	48.0
Sewerage	69	8.5	80	9.2	93	10.0	109	12.2	121	12.2
Cleaning	42	5.1	62	7.2	80	8.6	96	10.8	113	11.3
Energy	221	27.1	215	24.8	217	23.4	120	13.5	140	14.1
Works and other	96	11.7	95	11.0	100	10.7	102	11.5	144	14.4
Total	816	100.0	865	100.0	929	100.0	889	100.0	996	100.0

Source: SAUR UK.

Note: Figures have been translated at FF8.25 = £1.

TABLE 3.9 **SAUR International HCA consolidated divisional turnover**

£ million

	1993	1994	%	1995	%
Sale of water		116	39.3	136	37.1
Sewerage	Company	11	3.8	11	3.1
Cleaning	did not	19	6.5	33	9.0
Energy	exist	119	40.3	139	37.9
Works and other		30	10.1	47	12.9
Total		295	100.0	366	100.0

Source: SAUR UK.

Notes:
1. Figures have been translated at FF8.25 = £1.
2. The accounts do not show any profit analysis.

Table 3.8 shows SAUR SA's water sales moving up rather less than 20 per cent over four years; sewerage sales up by 75 per cent; cleaning sales nearly trebled; and energy sales down by nearly 40 per cent. Whilst the figures in Table 3.9 for SAUR International are for only two years, they show rising trends in all areas except sewerage which remained flat.

TABLE 3.10 **SAUR SA HCA consolidated financial summary**

£ million

	Years ended 31 December				
	1991	*1992*	*1993*	*1994*	*1995*
Net tangible assets	38	79	84	130	59
Goodwill and other intangible assets	93	192	195	183	164
Net assets	131	271	279	313	223
Profit/(loss) before tax and minority interests	9.7	19.1	21.0	80.6	(35.6)
Net debt:equity (%)	918	447	452	253	643
Interest cover (times)	1.3	1.4	1.7	3.3	2.5

Sources: SAUR UK, MMC analysis.

Note: Figures have been translated at FF8.25 = £1.

TABLE 3.11 **SAUR International HCA consolidated financial summary**

£ million

	Years ended 31 December				
	1991	*1992*	*1993*	*1994*	*1995*
Net tangible assets				75	80
Goodwill and other intangible assets				280	288
Net assets				355	368
Profit before tax	Company did not exist			17.6	22.1
Net debt:equity (%)				214	245
Interest cover (times)				2.8	2.5

Sources: SAUR UK, MMC analysis.

Notes:
1. Debt:equity is based on net debt and net tangible assets.
2. Interest cover is operating profit plus exceptional items divided by net financial expense.
3. Figures have been translated at FF8.25 = £1.

3.52. SAUR International increased profits in 1995 over the previous year, with net assets slightly increased although the debt:equity ratio and interest cover deteriorated somewhat. SAUR SA increased its trading profits in 1995 to the equivalent of £35.9 million from £7.9 million in the previous year, but losses of £63.1 million attributable to associated companies and additional goodwill amortization of £11 million resulted in a net loss for the year as shown in Table 3.10. By contrast, the 1994 profit was lifted by exceptional items, mostly profits on asset disposals, of £74 million. Further financial information on SAUR SA and SAUR International is given at Appendix 3.5.

UK water businesses—SAUR UK

3.53. These comprise Mid Southern Water plc (Mid Southern) and SEW and are held through a UK subsidiary, SAUR.

Mid Southern

3.54. Mid Southern was an SWC established in 1893 as the Frimley and Farnborough District Water Company and acquired by SAUR Group in 1989. It supplies water to an estimated resident population of 726,000 people at 275,000 premises over an area of 1,505 sq km in parts of Berkshire, Hampshire, Surrey and West Sussex as shown in Appendix 3.3. In 1995/96 Mid Southern supplied a daily average of 191 Ml/d or 1.4 per cent of the total regulated by OFWAT. Its average K factors for K1 and K2 were +8.1 and −1.0 respectively; Table 3.12 summarizes its financial performance.

TABLE 3.12 **Mid Southern CCA financial summary**

£ million

Years ended 31 March

	1992	1993	1994	1995	1996
Turnover	31.9	34.6	36.7	39.4	41.2
Profit before tax	8.6	8.9	13.2	12.3	12.8
Profit after tax	8.2	8.4	11.0	10.7	11.4
Dividends paid and proposed	3.1	4.8	5.4	5.2	5.4
Current cost profit retained	5.1	3.6	5.6	5.5	6.0
Operating cash flow after interest, tax, and dividends*	3.7	7.3	10.1	7.2	14.4
Capital expenditure†‡	0.9	6.2	8.2	9.1	14.8

Source: Mid Southern.

*Figures are for the appointed businesses. In 1993, however, the figure is for the whole business, of which non-appointed business is less than 5 per cent of total activities.
†Capital expenditure represents cash expended on fixed assets and excludes the infrastructure renewals charge.
‡Capital expenditure in 1995 is net of grants received of £3.2 million.

South East Water

History and development

3.55. In November and December 1988 SAUR Group made successful recommended offers to acquire the issued ordinary shares or stock and certain other securities of Mid Sussex Water Company, West Kent Water Company and Eastbourne Water Company. SEW was later formed as the holding company for these three companies and in 1994 the DGWS issued a single new appointment to SEW in exchange for the surrender of the individual appointments. SEW owns substantially all of the ordinary voting shares or stock in each company although there is a 20 per cent minority holding of non-voting shares in what is now Eastbourne Water plc. There are small holdings of debentures held by third parties remaining in all three companies.

Current activities

3.56. SEW supplies water to a resident population estimated at 617,000 at 252,600 premises over an area of 2,105 sq km in parts of Kent and East and West Sussex. Map 7 shows the area served, which includes Sevenoaks, Tonbridge and Tunbridge Wells in the north, Haywards Heath and Burgess Hill in the west, and Eastbourne and Bexhill in the south. In 1995/96 daily average volume of water supplied was 153 Ml/d or 1.2 per cent of the volume regulated by OFWAT. SEW has six river water sources supplying some 45 per cent of its output, and 32 groundwater sources accounting for 52 per cent. There are two treated BST import arrangements, with Sutton and East Surrey Water plc for just 0.05 Ml/d, and with SWS for 5.76 Ml/d, which account for the remaining 3 per cent. About half of its groundwater requires only simple chlorination by way of treatment, while the rest and the surface water requires varying degrees of more complex treatment. SEW has 89 service reservoirs holding in aggregate about two days' average supply. Further information on water resources is given in Chapter 5.

Financial summary

3.57. The financial performance of SEW since the businesses of its three subsidiaries were merged is summarized in Table 3.13.

TABLE 3.13 **SEW CCA financial summary**

Years ended 31 March — *£ million*

	1992	1993	1994	1995	1996
Turnover	44.3	48.0	50.4	50.9	53.6
Historical cost profit after tax*	2.5	5.8	9.6	10.5	13.5
Current cost profit before tax	2.9	3.3	8.3	11.4	14.6
Current cost profit after tax	1.9	3.2	7.5	10.0	12.5
Dividends	(0.6)	(0.7)	(1.0)	(1.1)	(1.2)
Retained profits	1.3	2.5	6.5	8.9	11.3
CCA depreciation†	8.5	9.3	8.6	7.2	8.1
Operating cash flow after tax and dividends	‡	8.8	13.8	15.4	20.7
Capital expenditure§	‡	12.9	13.3	12.2	17.8

Sources: SEW, MMC analysis.

*Historical cost figures are taken from statutory accounts, not from regulatory accounts.
†The figures shown for CCA depreciation exclude AMP expenditure on non-depreciated assets.
‡Information is not available.
§Capital expenditure is taken from net cash expended.

3.58. SEW's average K factors for periods K1 and K2 were +2.8 and −1.0 respectively: however, that for 1995 was nil against −1.0 for 1996. The table shows current cost profit after tax increasing more than sixfold over four years, an average annual increase of 60 per cent, while dividends have doubled. Capital expenditure has exceeded depreciation, indicating that additional assets have been acquired in addition to replacements. The cumulative cash flow during the last four years has exceeded capital expenditure by £2.5 million, and in each of the last two years there has been a net cash surplus of some £3 million. Further financial information is given at Appendix 3.6.

The Mid Kent Group

Mid Kent Holdings

History and development

3.59. MKH became the holding company for MKW in 1989 at the time of water privatization, when the SWCs were given the opportunity to relinquish their SWC status and become registered companies. In March 1989 MKH was formed as a public limited company and made a share offer to the stockholders of MKW whereby they could exchange their stock for shares in MKH. At the same time there was a rights issue and an offer of shares to customers and employees, both of which were completed in August of that year. MKH has since marginally increased its holding in MKW to 99.9 per cent of the ordinary share capital. Since privatization, MKH has reorganized and made a number of small acquisitions, detailed in paragraphs 3.83 to 3.86, which in the year ended 31 March 1996 accounted for 16 per cent of group turnover but made virtually no contribution to profits. The statutory provisions which previously applied to MKW as an SWC ceased to have effect on 30 November 1990.

3.60. A diagram showing the structure of MKH and its subsidiaries is at Figure 3.4.

Significant shareholdings and the proposed bidders

3.61. In 1988 GU acquired by tender offer 29.9 per cent of MKW's 6 per cent ordinary stock taking its share of the voting capital to just over 16 per cent. Discussion between the companies ensued during which MKW encouraged GU to make a full bid for the company, which GU did not do. MKW continued

FIGURE 3.4

The Mid Kent Group

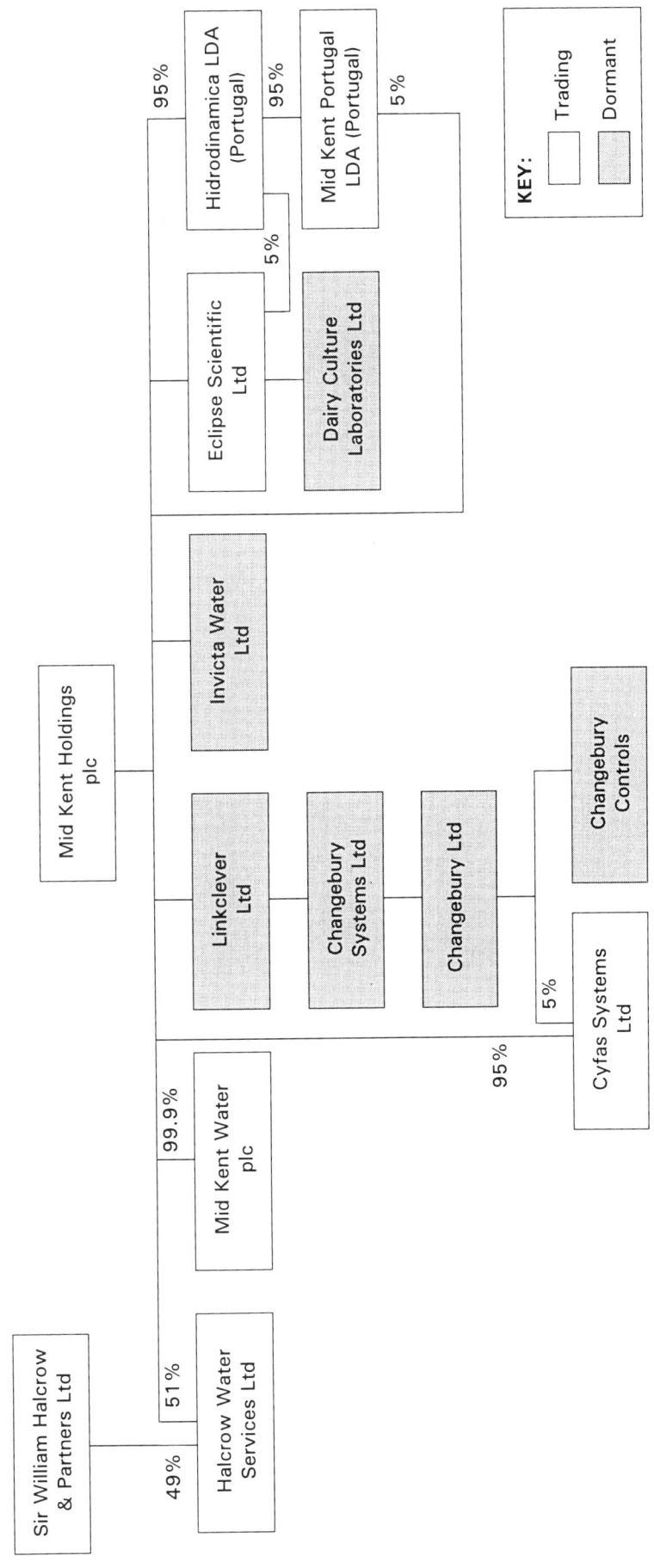

Source: MKH.

Note: Unless shown, shareholdings are 100 per cent.

the discussions with GU and also with SAUR during which the possibility of these companies raising their holdings in MKW was raised. MKW's stated objective was to gain a link with a large partner before regulation of the water industry began. However, GU acquired no further holdings until March of the following year, 1989, when it acquired £2.8 million nominal of MKW's 8.75 per cent redeemable preference stock 1997, taking its share of the voting capital to 29.8 per cent—virtually the maximum permitted under the Takeover Code without triggering an obligation to make a full bid. This holding (which had since become a holding in MKH—see also paragraph 3.11) was referred on 4 January 1990 to the MMC who published their report on 4 July.[1]

3.62. Undertakings by GU were given to the Secretary of State on 21 March 1991 under section 88 of the FTA to remedy the adverse effects identified in the MMC's report. They are set out in full in Appendix 6.2. These included the following obligations on GU:

(a) by no later than 30 June 1992, to reduce its holding in MKH to a level whereby it and the holdings of associated persons would be no more than 19.5 per cent;

(b) subsequently, not to increase its holding above the 19.5 per cent level; except in the event that the voting percentage increased through no action on GU's part, such as the redemption of preference shares; and

(c) not to seek nor to accept the opportunity to nominate a person to the Board of MKH or MKW.

3.63. There were changes to the senior management of MKH in 1991 and early 1992.

3.64. On 30 June 1992 GU duly reduced its holding to 19.5 per cent by way of a sale of shares to Morgan Grenfell. Morgan Grenfell continues to hold 9.35 per cent of the voting capital of MKH. The agreement under which Morgan Grenfell acquired the shares from GU provides that if Morgan Grenfell were to sell, GU would receive additional consideration equal to [*] per cent of any profit made by Morgan Grenfell. Any loss would be borne by Morgan Grenfell except in certain specified circumstances. These arrangements were notified to the DGWS, the OFT and the DTI who said that they were content with the arrangements. GU at present holds 19.45 per cent of MKH's voting capital.

3.65. The other potential bidder, SAUR, made various share acquisitions in 1988 and 1989 which have subsequently remained unchanged and now give it 19.39 per cent of the voting capital of MKH. MKH told us that on 30 April 1991 the DGWS wrote to the Chairman of MKH that 'he would expect SAUR to operate in the spirit of those guidelines [that is, GU's undertakings] and to ensure that their shareholding also does not exceed 19.5 per cent'. He wrote to SAUR in this vein in October 1996.

3.66. As at 30 September 1996 seven financial institutions, including Morgan Grenfell with its 9.35 per cent interest, held 40 per cent of the voting share capital of MKH. A table showing significant interests in the share capital of MKH at 30 September 1996 is at Appendix 3.7. MKH has two classes of voting share capital with equal voting rights: 17.123 million ordinary shares and 7.0 million 10 per cent preference shares which are due for redemption on 31 March 1997. Thus there are at present 24.123 million voting shares which will reduce to 17.123 million after the redemption date. At 30 September 1996 there were 1.862 million warrants to subscribe for ordinary shares at 600p each exercisable until 1999. There were also 0.39 million options exercisable at various prices and on various dates up to 2005. At 24 October 1996 30.04 per cent of the warrants were registered in the name of General Utilities PLC and 16.66 per cent in the name of SAUR Water Services plc.

3.67. In June 1993 SAUR raised with MKH the possibility of Board representation for itself which, after some consideration, was turned down. On 2 April 1996 MKH asked the High Court for a declaration that, among other things, GU's undertakings to the Secretary of State had been breached by the arrangements made with SAUR for the purposes of making the bid. The High Court (Mr Justice Knox), however, decided that MKH did not have the right to enforce undertakings obtained under the FTA.

---

[1]*General Utilities PLC and the Mid Kent Water Company: a report on the merger situation*, HMSO, Cm 1125, July 1990.

*Figure omitted. See note on page iv.

Mid Kent Water

History and development

3.68. MKW was formed as a limited company in 1888 to supply water to seven parishes in Kent including Halling and Snodland. That company was dissolved in 1898 and incorporated as an SWC under the terms of the Mid Kent Water Act of that year. The area served by the company has since been altered on 39 occasions. The predominance of groundwater as a source in the region enabled many small water undertakers to be established as viable enterprises, because the water required little, if any, treatment, and was readily available via wells and boreholes except on the Weald clay to the west of Ashford and Maidstone. During the 1960s there was a series of amalgamations with other water companies including those serving Faversham (1963), Ashford (1964), Canterbury (1968) and Maidstone (1970). The last significant change was in 1970 when part of the water supply area of the former East Kent Water Company was transferred from Mid Kent Water to FDWS.

3.69. Since 1971 there have been several internal reorganizations. In 1971 MKW was organized into three operating divisions based in Ashford, Canterbury and Maidstone, with central offices at the head office site in Snodland. Each operating division comprised a number of distribution districts, a supply department and administrative functions including cash collection and customer relations. In 1986 the number of divisions was reduced to two, based in Canterbury and Maidstone, and the number of distribution districts reduced from ten to six. In 1992 the company was restructured into a single operating unit based at Snodland, where all primary functions are located, and three distribution districts operating from offices at Ashford, Canterbury and Paddock Wood. The company's appointed area of supply now covers an area of 2,050 sq km with a resident population of 531,000 people within the boundaries of 12 local authorities in Kent and East Sussex. The main towns within the area are Ashford, Canterbury, Maidstone, Whitstable and Herne Bay. Sewerage services throughout the area are predominantly provided by SWS to which MKW provides billing and customer information.

Current activities

3.70. MKW supplies a daily annual average of nearly 170 Ml/d of water, rising to a daily weekly average of around 210 Ml/d in a dry summer such as that of 1995. Almost 90 per cent of its water comes from around 37 groundwater services, the output of some two-thirds of which requires only minimal chlorination treatment before being put into supply; the remaining one-third of the groundwater requires more complex treatment. The remainder of MKW's water comes from Bewl Water reservoir where it has its own treatment plant including pesticide removal, and from SWS's treatment plant at Burham on the River Medway. MKW's participation in the Medway Scheme is described in paragraph 3.78 and in more detail in paragraphs 5.20 to 5.22.

3.71. MKW's treated water is distributed to more than half a million people at 204,000 homes and 21,000 businesses located in its area of supply shown in Map 7. The widespread locations of most of its sources means that extensive large distribution mains have not generally been necessary; however, as resources have become more stressed in recent years, further investment in new mains has been necessary in order to relieve those areas where the stress has been most acute. Map 5 shows the layout of MKW's mains.

3.72. MKW's supply system incorporates service reservoirs containing treated water which provide a balance between supplies and demand, and a short-term back-up supply. MKW has 58 such reservoirs containing in aggregate 240 Ml or about 1.4 annual average days' supply. When weekend demand is predicted to be high, resource management techniques are used such as maximizing borehole output towards weekends so as to have service reservoirs full by Friday afternoons, followed by reduced pumping during the following Monday and Tuesday.

3.73. Almost all of MKW's business falls within its OFWAT appointment, the only exception being a small division which offers a repair service to customers' supply pipes. Details of MKW's performance under OFWAT's customer service measurements are given in Chapter 4. The water supplied by MKW accounts for 1.0 per cent of the total regulated by OFWAT in England and Wales.

Commercial relationships with the potential bidders

SAUR

3.74. MKW has no commercial relationship with SEW although it told us that it offered in principle a BST to SEW early in 1996, but this was declined as 'premature'. MKW listed seven water main connections between SEW and MKW which either exist and are closed, or could easily be reinstated, but these are all of 6" bore or less which limits the water volume which could be moved through them.

GU

3.75. MKW provided a BST to FDWS between 1970 and 1992 from its Barham (Kingston) source. This was restarted in May 1996 at 1 Ml/d albeit to a different delivery point to that previously supplied. This was subsequently increased to 2 Ml/d until late in October when FDWS requested that the supply be discontinued. Plans are now in hand to put the agreement on a medium-term basis. In the late 1980s FDWS joined with MKW and SWS in promoting the development of a new reservoir at Broad Oak by contributing 20 per cent of promotional costs, but the project was abandoned for the time being by common agreement between all the parties. Ad hoc arrangements are made from time to time between MKW and FDWS to facilitate engineering works, and there are four water main connections between MKW and FDWS which either exist or could easily be reinstated.

3.76. Apart from water transfers, MKW and FDWS belong to a billing software users' group in which GU has a 27 per cent interest. Until 1996 when it withdrew, MKW belonged to the EA Southern Region Water Control Area Project, a collaborative venture to provide best estimates of water demand at both company and regional levels. MKW supplied FDWS with laboratory testing services until 1993.

Relationship with SWS

3.77. MKW has a long history of contractual and commercial relations with SWS, details of which are contained in paragraphs 5.18 to 5.22.

3.78. In 1995/96 MKW was dependent on SWS for about 9 per cent of its water requirements by way of outright purchase, importing an average of 19.3 Ml/d and exporting 3.3 Ml/d (see paragraph 7.15). MKW is a minority (25 per cent) participant in the Medway Scheme where it has contributed 25 per cent to capital costs and continues to contribute to running costs thereby entitling it to 25 per cent of the output. The scheme is jointly managed and comprises a pumped storage reservoir at Bewl which provides both a direct supply to MKW for its own Bewl treatment works, and river regulation flows to augment abstractions downstream which supply the jointly funded Burham treatment works. In 1995/96 the Medway Scheme provided MKW with some 18 Ml/d or 10.9 per cent of its total resources.

3.79. Another important link concerns SWS's trunk main across north Kent from Wigmore, near Rochester to Eastling, and from selling to Fleete, near Margate (see Map 7). MKW both supplies to, and receives from, various points on this main. There are several other connection points between SWS and MKW, making 22 in all, although not all are currently in use.

Financial summary

3.80. The financial performance of MKW over the past five years is summarized in Table 3.14.

TABLE 3.14 **MKW CCA financial summary**

£ million

Years ended 31 March

	1992	1993	1994	1995	1996
Turnover	28.7	30.5	31.2	32.5	34.7
Historical cost profit after tax	5.0	4.2	5.5	6.9	9.9
Current cost profit after tax	4.0	2.4	3.5	7.4	9.8
Dividends	(2.6)	(2.3)	(2.5)	(2.7)	(4.7)
Retained profits	1.4	0.1	1.0	4.7	5.1
CCA depreciation*	3.3	3.6	4.0	3.7	4.0
Operating cash flow after tax and dividends	10.0	3.2	6.7	10.8	10.7
Capital expenditure†	11.4	11.2	11.8	7.3	7.1

Source: MKW, MMC analysis.

*The figures shown for CCA depreciation exclude AMP expenditure on non-depreciated assets.
†Capital expenditure is taken from net cash expended after deducting grants and contributions received.

3.81. The table shows a rising trend in profitability, noteworthy in that it continues into 1996 which is the first year of operation under the revised K factor. This was fixed at +1 for K2 compared with an average of +4.9 for K1. In 1996 MKW increased its dividend to its parent by 78 per cent, and its parent in turn increased its ordinary dividends to shareholders by 91 per cent (although its total dividend cost increased by only 69 per cent because of fixed preference dividends). In 1993 there were restructuring and redundancy costs of £2.1 million and cash flow was adversely affected by a small decrease in creditors compared with an increase of £3.8 million the previous year. Capital expenditure has reduced in the last two years from the relatively high levels of 1992 to 1994, reflecting completion of the more urgent items in the post-privatization era including MKW's share of the Yalding upgrade to the Medway Scheme at £4.5 million. Capital expenditure nevertheless still exceeded depreciation in 1996, which is indicative of spending on additional assets as well as replacements. In 1995 and 1996 capital expenditure was well covered by operating cash flow after tax and dividends which shows that overall the business is accumulating cash. Further details are given at Appendix 3.8.

3.82. In 1996 MKW's appointed business contributed 84 per cent of group turnover and virtually all of group profits.

Non-appointed businesses of MKH

3.83. At the time of privatization, MKW's laboratory services operation was transferred into a subsidiary of MKH to facilitate the building up of third party business in chemical and microbiological analysis. Since renamed Eclipse Scientific Limited (Eclipse), it was enlarged in 1991 by the addition of Northmore Laboratories Limited, based in Canterbury and specializing in pesticide residues. This was followed in 1995 by Dairy Culture Laboratories Limited, based in Somerset and specializing in food-related analysis. In the year ended 31 March 1996 Eclipse turned over £1.4 million, of which almost 60 per cent was intra-group, and earned £140,000 before tax.

3.84. In 1993 MKH acquired Cyfas-Restbury International Limited (CRI), which specialized in control room communications and radio equipment for emergency services and utilities, and in pipeline remote control and safety systems for the water and oil industries. CRI later acquired a small software systems producer and in April 1995 became responsible for MKW's information systems. In the year ended 31 March 1996 it turned over £6.6 million, of which 31 per cent was intra-group, and lost £59,000 before tax. Part of the business has since been sold, and the remainder restructured to concentrate on emergency radio services (with the company renamed Cyfas Systems Limited).

3.85. In 1995 MKH formed a joint venture, Halcrow Water Services Limited, with Sir William Halcrow & Partners Limited with the shares held 51:49 in MKH's favour. Its purpose was to enhance the efficiency of MKW's capital expenditure programme, and to provide MKW's former engineering function with access to the Halcrow network to assist in developing third party business. In its first nine months Halcrow Water Services Limited turned over £678,000, of which 81 per cent was intra-group, and earned £8,000 before tax.

3.86. MKH has also set up two wholly-owned Portuguese subsidiaries to develop services to local water supply companies; trading activities have not yet reached a material level.

Assets test

3.87. Appendix 3.9 contains summaries of the HCA balance sheets of GU's subsidiaries FDWS and Three Valleys, and of MKW and SEW which show total assets of a water enterprise exceeding £30 million within each of GU, MKH and SAUR on the basis set out in section 33 of the 1991 Act.

4 The regulatory framework and the role of comparators and competition

Contents

	Paragraph
Introduction	4.1
The current statutory regime	
The Water Act 1989 and the Water Resources and Water Industry Acts 1991	4.2
The system of comparative competition in the water industry	4.3
The use of comparators	4.6
The main stages in the comparative system	4.7
The areas where the DGWS uses comparative analysis	4.11
Operating cost comparisons in Base Service Provision	4.14
Capital maintenance comparisons for Base Service Provision	4.16
Resource management, and the balance between supply and demand	4.19
Quality enhancements	4.21
Financial performance	4.22
Customer service	4.23
Tariffs	4.25
Transfer pricing	4.26
The number of comparators	4.28
Valuing the loss of a comparator	4.37
Competition	4.50

Introduction

4.1. This chapter outlines the regulatory framework of the water industry and, in particular, discusses the role of comparators in the industry's regulation and the variety of uses made of comparators by the DGWS. It then examines the issue of the number of comparators and discusses attempts that have been made to value the loss of a comparator. Finally it looks at the extent of competition in the water industry. This chapter does not cover resource issues, which are dealt with in Chapter 5.

The current statutory regime

The Water Act 1989 and the Water Resources and Water Industry Acts 1991

4.2. Broadly, the Water Act 1989 had two principal regulatory purposes. It established a new quality regime for the water industry through the creation of the National Rivers Authority (NRA), now part of the EA, and the Drinking Water Inspectorate (DWI). At the same time, a new system of economic regulation was established under the DGWS. Consolidation in 1991 led to the 1991 Act, which governs the functions of the DGWS and the DWI, and to the Water Resources Act 1991 which deals with the constitution and functions of the NRA. A note by the DoE on the legal framework for the water industry and for water resource management is at Appendix 4.1. The operation of the current statutory regime is explained in more detail in the DGWS's note at Appendix 4.2.

The system of comparative competition in the water industry

4.3. The system of comparative competition[1] helps the DGWS to ensure that the regulated companies have incentives to improve efficiency and levels of service to consumers. On the basis of comparisons between companies, the DGWS makes an informed assessment of each company's performance and on this basis sets price controls specific to each company. Price controls are set by the DGWS for a period of ten years, reviewable at intervals of five years (the Periodic Review). The appointment also provides for interim determinations of price caps at the initiative of either the DGWS or the water company concerned. Other comparative exercises are carried out by the DGWS on a regular basis (for example, customer service levels). The DGWS told us that the results from these exercises inform the development of policy and enable the promotion of efficiency and effectiveness both nationally and at a regional level. The DGWS also carries out comparisons on an ad hoc basis (for example, an investigation into Yorkshire Water Services Ltd's performance). Ad hoc studies are typically carried out when problems occur. Usually these ad hoc exercises require a poorly-performing company to be compared with similar companies which are performing better. The DGWS told us that comparisons between companies were important not only at Periodic Reviews but also in the performance of his other functions that continued between Reviews (see paragraph 4.12). The DGWS's views are set out in detail in Chapter 8, whilst Appendix 8.1 contains his statement of the detailed use he makes of comparisons between companies.

4.4. The system of comparative competition seeks, so far as possible, to replicate the pressures of competitive markets, where firms face commercial pressures to improve service and quality at prices that the market is prepared to pay. The DGWS told us that the system encouraged active competition and initiative by management rather than reliance on continuous intervention by the DGWS. He said that comparison between companies made by the City, customers and companies themselves also drove the companies to improve their performance.

4.5. In general, making comparisons assists the regulatory process in three ways:

(a) it provides incentives for companies to operate efficiently as relative efficiency is taken into account at the time of the Periodic Review (between Review periods, companies have a financial incentive to improve their performance as reductions in costs against set price caps and performance targets lead to increased profitability and poorly-performing companies are penalized at the Review period);

(b) it applies continuing pressure to companies to improve their quality of service; and

(c) it provides a means of addressing the asymmetry of information which exists between the regulated companies and the DGWS. The regulator is largely reliant on the information collected from the companies to enable him to carry out his functions as a regulator. By collecting as wide a range of information as possible, the regulatory process aims to discourage companies from overestimating their costs by penalizing what could appear to be an inefficient performance. The more companies there are and the greater variety of information available to the DGWS, the greater the disincentive for companies to overestimate their costs as this can lead to them appearing to be inefficient resulting in a price cap which is tighter than it would otherwise be.

The use of comparators

4.6. In this section we look at the three main stages in the operation of the comparative system leading to the setting of targets and price controls. We then look at the areas where the DGWS uses comparative analysis.

---

[1] Also known as yardstick competition.

The main stages in the comparative system

4.7. There are three main stages in the operation of the comparative system leading to the setting of targets and price controls:

(a) collecting data from the companies and analysing it in a way that will enable a comparison between companies to be made;

(b) using the analysed data to set bench-marks;[1] and

(c) setting targets[2] for each company based on the bench-marks.

4.8. The first stage (data analysis) varies greatly in its sophistication depending on the data available and the extent to which data of a particular category need to be standardized. At one extreme it may be possible to make comparisons between companies without any transformation of the data at all. At the other extreme sophisticated statistical methods may be needed to reflect the effects of different operating conditions so that the appropriate comparisons of relative efficiency can be made. In between these two extremes it may be possible for the raw data to be transformed into standard forms, which can then be the basis for inter-company comparisons.

4.9. The second stage (setting bench-marks) is not always as simple as choosing the performance of the frontier company (the company that performs the best on the statistics available). In some cases the data analysis will not be sufficiently reliable, and in that case the performance of a company high up in the ranking, for example at the upper quartile, may be chosen as the bench-mark. When the data analysis is even less reliable, only the average may be usable for the purpose. The DGWS told us that when setting the price controls it might not be possible to rely on individual small companies as bench-marks.

4.10. The final stage of setting targets for each company (largely embodied in the form of the cost estimates that are the building blocks for the price control) is carried out by the DGWS deciding how far towards the bench-mark each company can be expected to move during the Review period. Failure to meet such targets will typically produce poor financial performance under the price cap regime and exceeding the targets will bring good financial performance. Thus, there is a financial incentive to exceed the targets and this encourages the dynamic process of improving efficiency in the industry.

The areas where the DGWS uses comparative analysis

4.11. Comparators are used in a variety of ways. Their use has changed over time and is likely to develop further in the future. As this inquiry is concerned with WoCs, we do not cover the use of comparators for sewerage services.

4.12. In respect of the 1994 Periodic Review and his other functions, the DGWS compares companies' performances in the following areas:

(a) operating costs for base service provision;

(b) capital maintenance[3] costs for base service provision;

(c) resource management and the balance between supply and demand;

(d) quality enhancements;

(e) financial performance;

---

[1] We use this term to mean the performance which other companies should in time be able to achieve.

[2] We use this term to mean the performance a company should achieve during the relevant Review period.

[3] Capital maintenance is the expenditure required to maintain service capability of assets for both current and future customers.

(f) customer services;

(g) tariff structures; and

(h) transfer pricing.

Whilst *(a)* to *(e)* refer to the DGWS's use of comparators for the Periodic Review and *(f)* to *(h)* refer to his use of comparators in connection with his other functions, there is considerable overlap in their use.

4.13. As indicated in paragraph 8.10, for the purpose of the 1994 Periodic Review the activities of each company were further divided into the following 'purpose' categories:

(a) base service provision—the maintenance of existing levels of service;

(b) enhanced service levels—the improvement in standards of service not driven by legal obligations;

(c) the balance between supply and demand—programmes for system expansion, control of leakage or demand management measures to meet any shortfall between forecast demand and existing capacity; and

(d) quality enhancements—obligatory improvements to water and waste water discharges to meet drinking water and environmental quality standards.

Operating cost comparisons in Base Service Provision

4.14. This category of costs is a major one in the context of setting the overall price control. It also involves considerable difficulty in terms of comparability between companies as it is strongly affected by differences in operating conditions. Sophisticated methods are thus needed (as mentioned in paragraph 4.8) to produce data that provide a firm basis for inter-company comparison. The DGWS has used mainly econometric analysis but also the DEA technique,[1] both of which utilized statistical comparisons between companies to differentiate between the differences in operating costs which were attributable to diverse operating conditions from those which were attributable to the actions of management. Those differences in operating costs which were not attributed to operating conditions were used to inform the resultant efficiency assessment.

4.15. The econometric analysis, undertaken on behalf of the DGWS by Professor Stewart of Warwick University, considered what quantifiable factors relating to the companies' operating environments might potentially explain differences in the companies' operating costs. With data provided by the companies, Professor Stewart used regression analysis to develop models which explained the variation of operating costs in terms of the identified factors. The relevant data for an individual company were then used to determine the expected costs of an averagely efficient company in that particular company's operating environment. A comparison of these expected costs with actual costs (reflected mathematically as the residual) was then used as a basis for ranking companies in terms of efficiency. The DEA results, the DGWS told us, tended to reinforce the conclusions derived from the econometric analyses. In addition the DGWS assessed a number of other unquantifiable factors before finally allocating companies into relative efficiency bands.

---

[1] DEA is a technique for comparing the overall productivity of companies. It uses linear programming to establish an efficiency frontier which is defined as the most efficient producers in the sample. Companies that form the efficiency frontier use the minimum quantity of inputs to produce the same quantity of outputs as other, similar firms. The relative efficiency of each firm is then determined by its position in relation to the efficiency frontier. A disadvantage of the technique is that companies which are dissimilar, that is use a different combination of inputs, may be located on the frontier as there are no other similar companies with which they can be compared.

Capital maintenance comparisons for Base Service Provision

4.16. In this area the DGWS has so far used a less sophisticated form of data analysis than econometrics or DEA and has resorted to a standard costing approach. In assessing capital maintenance costs, unit capital costs for specimen items collected from companies were compared to provide a basis for judgments of their relative efficiency. The standard costs selected reflected typical underground and surface asset works that were thought to characterize the companies' likely capital programmes. Some of the standard costs were unit costs of laying particular-sized pipes in typical conditions; in other cases they were of typical capital projects, for example building a standard-sized reservoir.

4.17. The DGWS told us that in theory the difference between companies' standard costs showed different efficiencies in the specification, design and procurement of capital works. The lower quartile standard costs provided a basis for the setting of bench-marks against which to compare the costs of other companies. The gaps between companies' estimates of their costs and the bench-marks indicated the scope for savings in setting price limits for a given level of output.

4.18. The DGWS told us that OFWAT was currently developing, for this category of capital maintenance, a similar statistical approach to that already used in examining operating costs (as described in paragraph 4.15). The DGWS said that in order that the statistical approach would be ready for use at the next Periodic Review, he had asked all companies and their reporters to identify potential influences on capital maintenance expenditure and had asked six companies to assist in the development of the statistical approach in detail.

Resource management, and the balance between supply and demand

4.19. The DGWS takes account of expenditure which he considers appropriate to meet growth in demand to maintain a balance between supply and demand. In reaching a view, the DGWS uses a relatively simple form of comparison, not involving statistical methods or cost transformations.

4.20. The DGWS has applied national unit cost bench-marks to companies' demand forecasts to determine expenditure levels. The bench-marks were derived from cost information provided by various companies. The DGWS told us that comparative data were also used in assessing the costs claimed for metering and the effects of metering upon demand levels, with a view to understanding and possibly challenging differences between companies in respect of forecasts of commercial demand, the ability of each company to manage leakage and the effects of leakage control on supply.

Quality enhancements

4.21. A fairly straightforward comparative approach was also used in assessing the costs of meeting the required quality enhancements; more sophisticated methods were not possible, but a problem of making comparisons for bench-mark-setting purposes remained. For the 1994 Periodic Review, the DGWS said that allowances for water quality enhancements fell into two groups: water treatment and water distribution. For treatment methods, the DGWS told us that it was possible to calculate unit costs for increased levels of treatment, but not to carry out bench-mark comparisons as the problems were too heterogeneous. Comparisons were used to identify expensive companies. For distribution, the DGWS said that comparisons of the costs of quality-related work to mains were also drawn from data provided by the companies. The DGWS told us that from the DWI's developing database on water quality, it would be possible to compare actual performance of companies by the quality of water supplied to customers.

Financial performance

4.22. The DGWS told us that if he was to be satisfied that companies were able to finance their functions, he needed to understand the implications of price limits both for the absolute level of profit (and hence financial indicators of concern to lenders and investors) and for rates of return. The DGWS said that he compared companies' financial performance in the following areas: dividends and dividend policy, financial indicators, profit headroom and other financial areas. For dividend policy, comparisons were made between the dividends paid by the parent companies and those paid by the appointee, on the assumption that the dividends actually paid by the parent represented the sustainable dividend. The DGWS said that in setting price limits he paid particular attention to the consideration of the overall return on capital. He told us that key financial indicators were interest cover, historical and current cost dividend covers and gearing. The DGWS said that he allowed sufficient headroom in profits to take account of company risks. He told us that financial comparisons between companies were also carried out as part of routine regulation, for example comparisons of profit margins, return on capital, capital maintenance charges, average interest cost.

Customer service

4.23. Each year OFWAT publishes its Levels of Service Report which shows the companies' performance against a number of service level indicators. There are currently nine service indicators, two of which (DG8 and DG9—see below) were added in 1995/96. Some indicators have more than one component. The nine service indicators and their DG reference numbers are:

  (a) the availability of raw water (DG1);

  (b) the pressure of mains water (DG2);

  (c) interruptions to supply (DG3);

  (d) water usage restrictions (DG4);

  (e) properties at risk of flooding from sewers (DG5);

  (f) response to written and telephone billing queries (DG6);

  (g) response to written complaints (DG7);

  (h) response to telephone contact from customers (DG8); and

  (i) proportion of metered accounts based on actual meter readings (DG9).

The performance of MKW, FDWS and SEW on certain service levels (DG2, DG3, DG6 and DG7) is discussed in Appendix 4.3.

4.24. The DGWS also reviews other aspects of customer service and periodically publishes reports on them. These include, for example, debt and disconnections, optional meter schemes, services for customers with special needs and compensation payments. The DGWS told us that these comparisons are valuable in promoting best practice.

Tariffs

4.25. The DGWS told us that the use of comparators in this area had been and would be to develop tariff structures to reflect better the costs of supplying different classes of customers, for example the difference between tariffs for measured and unmeasured supply, the level of standing charges for measured supply and tariffs for large users.

Transfer pricing

4.26. The DGWS drew our attention to the value of comparators in carrying out his duty to ensure that the appointed business was financially ring-fenced from the non-appointed business and that water customers did not cross-subsidize activities which were not connected with the supply of water.

4.27. The DGWS told us that transfer pricing was an area where individual performance had been very variable and that those companies whose implementation plans were well advanced and fully reflected the transfer pricing guideline[1] provided a powerful bench-mark against which companies with less-developed plans could be compared. The guideline, the DGWS said, was not prescriptive but provided a framework within which companies were responsible for ensuring compliance. It allowed the DGWS to compare and contrast the relative performance of individual companies. He expected that the extent of company compliance and the way in which the guideline had been interpreted would lead to areas of best practice within the industry. Best practice as evidenced by individual company performance was a valuable tool in encouraging, through peer pressure, other companies to make improvements to meet their duty to operate at arm's length. The DGWS told us that this area of work was at a relatively early stage in its development and comparative judgments provided an invaluable means of determining the extent to which an individual company could be said to operate fully at arm's length.

The number of comparators

4.28. One issue relating to the system of comparative competition that has often been raised is whether there is a minimum number of companies that might be said to be necessary or at least strongly desirable. The number of companies required to make effective use of comparisons will depend upon the nature of the data and the type of analysis envisaged. This varies a great deal, as discussed in paragraph 4.8.

4.29. At one extreme, certain comparisons can be carried out with as few as two companies. At the other extreme, where sophisticated statistical analysis is used as a means of drawing comparisons between companies with diverse operating conditions (as in the case of operating costs and possibly in the future capital maintenance costs), consideration needs to be given to the number of separate observations relative to the number of explanatory variables which might have to be included in any model. As the number of observations reduces, fewer explanatory variables can be included in the model and the reliance which can be placed on the estimates is reduced. If it is possible to develop a good and stable explanatory model with a small number of significant variables, then quite sophisticated analysis can be carried out with relatively few comparators. If there are many factors, a large number of special cases or not all the data are truly independent, it may not be possible to carry out sophisticated analysis even with many comparators.

4.30. Other reasons for maintaining a significant number of comparators have been put forward in the context of the rivalry between companies that encourages improvements in efficiency. While the most important comparators at any given point in time will be those companies which are the most efficient in each category, these 'frontier' companies are likely to change over time. The DGWS emphasized that comparative competition encouraged the less efficient to 'leap-frog' those more efficient than them; as a result, what was important was to maintain a range of different companies and not to limit the diversity of techniques and policies adopted within the industry. The DGWS provided data which showed the movements in operating cost efficiency rankings during the period 1992/93 to 1994/95 (see Table 4.1). The table shows that 15 companies have seen an improvement in their relative efficiency rankings, 13 companies have seen a fall and two companies have seen no change.

TABLE 4.1 **Movements in the relative efficiency rankings, 1992/93 to 1994/95**

Category	Number of companies
Up by more than 10 places	2
Up by between 5 and 10 places	8
Up by up to 5 places	5
No change in relative position	2
Down by up to 5 places	4
Down by between 5 and 10 places	6
Down by more than 10 places	3
Total	30

Source: OFWAT.

---

[1] Regulatory Accounting Guideline (RAG5)—Transfer Pricing in the Water Industry.

4.31. The DGWS also drew attention to the fundamental importance of diversity of ownership of water companies, which was likely to secure the widest diversity of management styles and techniques and was therefore also important for comparative purposes. As also shown in paragraph 8.20, he said that the key issue was the number of separately-owned companies rather than the number of separate appointments.

4.32. Table 4.2 shows the fall in the number of companies in the water industry since 1989.

TABLE 4.2 **Reduction in the number of companies in the water industry since 1989**

	WoCs	WaSCs	Total
1989	29	10	39
1990	26*	10	36
1991	23†	10	33
1992	22‡	10	32
1993	21§	10	31
1994	21	10	31
1995	20¶	10	30
1996 (September)	19¤	10	29

Source: OFWAT.

---

*Colne Valley, Lee Valley and Rickmansworth became Three Valleys; Newcastle & Gateshead and Sunderland & South Shields became North East Water.
†Eastbourne, Mid Sussex and West Kent became South East Water; Essex Water and Suffolk Water became Essex & Suffolk.
‡Bournemouth & District and West Hampshire Water became Bournemouth and West Hants.
§STW and East Worcester became STW.
¶East Surrey Water and Sutton & District became Sutton & East Surrey.
¤Northumbrian Water and North East Water became Northumbrian Water.

4.33. Between 1989 and 1996 the number of water undertakers fell from 39 (29 WoCs and 10 WaSCs) to 29 (19 WoCs and 10 WaSCs).

4.34. The DGWS told us that of the 29 companies (shown in Table 4.2), five had asset values below the threshold for referral to the MMC of £30 million set out in the 1991 Act whilst ten were owned, significantly influenced or controlled by either GU, SAUR or Lyonnaise. In his view this leaves a total of 17 major independent water groups comprising nine WaSCs, five WoCs and three corporate groups (GU with control of or influence over six WoCs, SAUR with control of two WoCs and Lyonnaise owning two companies including one WaSC—Northumbrian). The DGWS said that mergers between water and electricity companies did not involve the loss of an independent water comparator but that such mergers highlighted issues of the management and financial independence and visibility of a water utility business within a group structure (see paragraph 8.13). Appendix 4.4 shows the DGWS's view of the status of the water companies for comparative purposes.

4.35. GU told us that each of its operating companies (Three Valleys, North Surrey, Tendring Hundred and FDWS) operated independently of each other under its own Board. It said that in order to improve cost effectiveness, to promote best operational practices and to develop centres with a high level of expertise within the group, GU supported the four operational companies, at their request and as appropriate, in some specific and specialized areas such as laboratory services, project management, specialist technical expertise, treasury management, taxation, legal advice. It said that some information technology support was available from Three Valleys.

4.36. SAUR told us that regular meetings were held between operational staff of SEW and Mid Southern to discuss best practices on, for example, leakage and water quality issues. SAUR said that periodic meetings were held between the management teams to discuss strategic issues. It said that in addition to meetings, the two companies operated the same systems for billing, works management and financial control. SAUR told us that the two companies each had their own stockholdings, but, in emergencies, equipment such as specialist vehicles and emergency repair fittings could be shared.

Valuing the loss of a comparator

4.37. The effect of a merger between water enterprises is usually to remove two comparators and replace them by one, the one being the combination of the lost two. In order to facilitate an evaluation of the effects of such a merger on the comparative system, the effects are often considered in the simplified form of the loss of one comparator. It is not possible to generalize about the effects of a merger on the comparative system—it depends on precisely which companies are merging. The DGWS's views on the range of possible mergers and the relative scale of detriment arising from them is recorded in paragraphs 8.24 to 8.26.

4.38. There are four potential consequences of the loss of a comparator:

(a) The loss of a company which is at or near the frontier of efficiency and which is therefore potentially useful in setting a bench-mark may have an impact on the effectiveness of regulation. The comparative system is not, however, static: company performance does change over time.

(b) The loss of a comparator may affect the confidence with which the regulator carries out his duties by changing the quantity and quality of information available to him.

(c) The loss of a comparator may affect the promotion of efficiency and better service in the industry by changing cost-competition between companies.

(d) The loss of a comparator may change other aspects of the way in which the DGWS uses comparators, for example in his ad hoc exercises which he undertakes in response to changing circumstances.

4.39. To the extent that each loss of a comparator makes the task of the regulator more difficult, the detrimental impact upon his ability to make comparisons is likely to increase with each loss of comparator.[1]

4.40. We were provided with two estimates which sought to place a value on the loss of a comparator, one from the DGWS (see Appendix 4.5) and one from MKH (see Appendix 4.6). The two studies approached the question in quite different ways and were in effect valuing different aspects of the effects on the comparative system. Both were also partial in that they did not address some important factors, for example customer services, water quality and capital costs. Furthermore, the estimates did not include the potential development in the use of comparators. The DGWS told us that a few years ago he could not have anticipated the developments that had occurred in the use of comparators. The DGWS and MKH acknowledged that the reliability of their quantified benefits was uncertain for a number of methodological reasons. We look first at the DGWS's estimates and then at those provided by MKH.

4.41. The DGWS told us that while some of the detriments of the loss of a comparator could be quantified, at least in principle, not all of them could be given a monetary value and some could only be considered qualitatively. He said that the scale of the overall detriment could only be arrived at on the basis of a judgment involving a number of elements. The DGWS told us that the aim was to consider the position over the long run bearing in mind that individual companies would change their relative positions over time and the relative importance of various elements would change, often as a result of the emergence of a new factor.

4.42. The DGWS's analysis was based on the possible ranges of higher costs which the DGWS might be obliged to allow for in setting price limits because of the loss of a leading comparator (see paragraph 4.38(a)). The method simulated the effect, at the next Periodic Review, of a company becoming the leading comparator for operating expenditure (that is, the frontier company) and this being reflected in the price determination. The cost and price simulations were then rerun assuming the loss of this leading company. This resulted in a target level of efficiency which was lower than it would otherwise have been

---

[1]This point was raised by the then Minister for Corporate Affairs, John Redwood, in announcing the Secretary of State's decision on the Three Valleys merger in August 1990 when he said that any fall in the number of water enterprises available for comparison was likely to make it more difficult for subsequent mergers to be justified.

and which in turn resulted in prices in all other companies being higher than they would otherwise have been. A range of potential losses were derived by carrying out a large number of such simulations. The DGWS did not assign probabilities to the various outcomes. He did, however, illustrate how it might be possible to assist the qualitative judgment of the possibility of any of the companies being the leading comparator at future Periodic Reviews (see Appendix 4.5).

4.43. The DGWS said that the illustrative work he had carried out indicated that the impact of losing a company the size of MKW, assuming that it was a frontier company, could have a very substantial adverse effect on price limits set for England and Wales: aggregate target operating expenditure, expressed in terms of NPVs, for water services alone would be higher under different assumptions by between £20 million and £590 million with an average value of £120 million.[1] The DGWS said that as his work explored only one aspect of the many important ways in which comparators were used, it could not be used as an indication of the full value of a lost comparator and that his results significantly underestimated the potential damage to comparative competition. The DGWS told us that including capital expenditure in the calculation would make the value of the loss substantially larger, possibly by up to twice as large.

4.44. MKH's estimates of the effect of the loss of a comparator were based on the greater statistical uncertainty, quantified in the form of wider confidence intervals,[2] which result from the loss of an independent company in its representation of OFWAT's modelling work (see paragraph 4.38(b)). In its approach this greater uncertainty would lead to the DGWS reaching less precise conclusions on efficiency targets, which in turn would lead to less stringent price caps and to prices being higher than they would otherwise have been. MKH estimated that the loss of MKW, in NPV terms at 1994/95 prices, would be between £33 million and £72 million with an average value of £48 million.[3] Appendix 4.6 provides a fuller account of MKH's methodology.

4.45. We asked the DGWS for his views on the MKH study. He told us that although MKH used the unrealistic assumption that the DGWS would always act in the same way, conceptually the approach used was sound and capable of generating valid estimates. The DGWS told us that in his view MKH's estimates of loss were to be seen as additional to those identified in his simulation analysis.

4.46. As well as a difference in approach, the two studies used different assumptions. The main differences in assumptions between the estimates of the DGWS and MKH were that the DGWS used a 7 per cent real discount rate compared with a 5 per cent real rate used by MKH for its mid-point estimate (MKH also used a 2 per cent real discount rate for its upper bound estimate and 8 per cent for its lower bound estimate); and the DGWS's estimates were to 2025 whereas MKH used a time horizon of 20 years.

4.47. The DGWS also demonstrated the impact of a loss of a comparator on his ability to achieve service improvements by showing the reduced range of performances in the areas of disconnection figures and reliability of supply. The DGWS compared regional data with company data using a total of 30 companies. We asked him to carry out the same exercise but using a total of 17 comparators as he believed there were 17 major independent water undertakers (see paragraph 4.34). Table 4.3 shows the results of the DGWS's analysis.

---

[1]The DGWS's estimates relate to the loss of a comparator of the size of MKW, assuming that it was a frontier company. These estimates are based on operating costs of water services only using a 7 per cent discount rate to 2025.

[2]Confidence intervals provide a statistical measure of the range within which a variable has (say) a 95 per cent probability of being found.

[3]MKH's estimates relate to the loss of MKW as a comparator. Its estimates are based on operating costs of water services only. The lower bound uses a discount rate of 8 per cent, the mid-point uses a discount rate of 5 per cent and the upper bound a discount rate of 2 per cent. All estimates use a time horizon of 20 years.

TABLE 4.3 Potential impact of the reduction in number of company comparators on aspects of service levels

A: *Disconnection rates*

Rate of disconnections per 10,000 households 1995/96	Based on regions Number	%	Based on companies Number*	%	Based on companies Number†	%
0–2	7	70	11	37	9	53
2.1–5	2	20	10	33	5	29
5.1–10	1	10	6	20	1	6
10.1–15	-		2	7	1	6
15.1–20	-		1	3	1	6
	10	100	30	100	17	100

B: *Reliability of supply*

DG3 supply interruptions 1994/95 performance band (properties affected by interruption over 12 hours)						
Well above average (<0.05%)	1	10	13	43	5	29
Above average (0.05–0.10)	3	30	7	23	2	12
Average (0.01–0.20)	4	40	5	17	6	35
Below average (0.21–0.50)	1	10	3	10	2	12
Well below average (>0.50)	1	10	2	7	2	12
	10	100	30	100	17	100

Source: OFWAT.

*Based on total number of water undertakers as at 31 March 1996, excluding Cholderton and District Water Company.
†Based on the number of major water undertakers under separate control.

4.48. Table 4.3 shows the impact of reducing the number of comparators (an averaging effect) on the apparent range of performance. For example, the apparent performance of the industry in terms of disconnection rates is shown to improve and to be less variable as the number of comparators is reduced: based on 30 companies, 37 per cent achieved the lower rate of disconnections (0 to 2 per 10,000 households) and 10 per cent the higher rate (10.1 to 20 per 10,000 households) compared with 70 per cent and zero when a base of ten regions is used. A similar picture is shown for reliability of supply: the apparent performance is shown to improve and to be less variable as the number of comparators is reduced. When comparisons are made on the basis of 30 companies, 43 per cent have DG3 supply interruptions well above average and five companies (17 per cent) below and well below the average compared with 10 per cent and two regions (20 per cent) when a base of ten regions is used. The DGWS's views on other effects of the loss of MKW as a comparator are recorded in paragraph 8.31 onwards.

4.49. GU and SAUR told us that they did not consider it sensible to try to estimate the value of losing MKW as a comparator. In their view, as MKW was such a poor performer and taking into account the gains from improving water resources which the proposals would bring, there were sound arguments that the loss of MKW would not be a detriment and could be a benefit. GU and SAUR said that quantification was particularly difficult as it should include the difference between the benefits arising from the proposals and any detriment, or further benefit, attributable to the effects on the comparative process. They told us that any exercise of quantifying the value of losing MKW as a comparator must have some regard to the consequences of not losing MKW (that is, the adverse impact on the value of SEW and FDWS as comparators if the proposals did not go ahead).

Competition

4.50. Transportation costs are an important constraint on direct competition in the water industry and explain why no national water grid has been created. However, extending the present scope for competition through cross-border supplies for non-domestic purposes and inset appointments, and facilitating its development, is seen both by Ministers and by the DGWS as providing important underpinning for the system of comparative competition. Accordingly, the Government issued a consultation paper in April 1996 entitled *Water: Increasing Customer Choice*. This paper made proposals for:

(a) common carriage, that is the use of one company's pipes by another supplier, initially for large users of water;

(b) cross-border supplies of water for non-domestic purposes, for example agricultural or industrial uses; and

(c) easing some of the restrictions that currently apply to inset appointments, for example by permitting time-limited appointments.

In order to assist in the development of a suitable regulatory framework for common carriage, the DGWS issued a consultation paper to accompany the Government paper entitled *The Regulation of Common Carriage Agreements in England and Wales*.

4.51. The current legislation permits the DGWS to grant inset appointments (that is, a new supplier operating within the area of an existing undertaker) for either greenfield sites, that is a site not served by an existing undertaker, or customers using 250 M/l or more a year. The DGWS published a paper entitled *Competition in the water industry: inset appointments and their regulation* in July 1995. The paper outlined the criteria and the process for applying for insets, and to date he has received 18 formal applications. For one of these, the DGWS has given notice that he is proposing to vary the appointment of Anglian Water to supply a commercial customer within the area of Essex and Suffolk Water.

4.52. MKH told us that there were at present significant (although limited) opportunities for competition between water companies in south-east England (for example, through inset appointments) and that it was clear that there were very substantial prospects for competition in the future, cross-border along the boundaries between MKW and FDWS, and MKW and SEW, and possibly also through wholesale bulk markets in the Sevenoaks area (where five water companies could compete); such actual and potential competition would be adversely affected by the acquisition and the break-up of MKW and by the continuing long-term co-operation between GU and SAUR in running their proposed bulk resources joint venture. MKH said that in the longer term, if, as the Government hoped, genuine competition developed in the water industry through new rules on common carriage, through bulk supply contracts or through the emergence of wholesale markets, the facts that GU and SAUR would own and control, through their joint venture, a significant proportion of the bulk resources in Kent, and that they would jointly be responsible for operational matters at major new resources, would inhibit competition between the two groups, and create barriers to competition from third parties in and adjacent to the region.

4.53. GU and SAUR told us that the existing water resource and supply arrangements in the Southern Region effectively frustrated the scope for direct competition in Kent and Sussex. They said that if the proposals went ahead SEW and FDWS would be in a stronger position to compete. GU and SAUR told us that the JRC would not prevent SEW and FDWS competing with each other.

4.54. We asked the DGWS to provide information which shows the extent of actual competition in these areas. Table 4.4 shows the number of customers eligible for inset appointments and the number of applications for inset appointments.

TABLE 4.4 **Details of large user customers and inset appointment applications**

Company	Number of customers using more than 250ml a year	Number of inset applications
FDWS	3	0
MKW	4	0
SEW	0	0

Source: OFWAT.

4.55. The table shows that there are currently no applications for inset appointments in any of these companies' area. [*Details omitted. See note on page iv.*] Another indicator of the extent of competition may be the degree to which water companies have adjusted their prices. The DGWS told us that a number of companies in the water industry have introduced large user tariffs with the possible aim of preventing loss of customers. FDWS has a tariff for large users but no such tariff is offered by MKW, SEW and SWS.

5 Water resources in the region

Contents

	Paragraph
Introduction	5.1
Historical background to the management of water resources	5.2
The local setting	5.7
Water resources of the area	
Rainfall	5.12
Sources of supply	5.13
The Medway Scheme	5.20
The Belmont Scheme	5.21
Co-operation between MKW and SWS	5.22
The EA water resources strategy	
EA national strategy	5.23
EA regional strategy	5.25
Bulk supply transfers	5.27
Demand management	5.31
Metering	5.33
Loss reduction	5.38
Balance of demand and supply	5.44
Historic legacy	5.47
Demand forecasting	5.50
Water resource management: the bidders' proposals	5.57
Potential water sources	5.59

Introduction

5.1. This chapter sets out the water resources background to the proposed merger, based on submissions by the three parties, by the regulators and by SWS, the WaSC operating in the region. The issues covered include the water resources history of the region; the distribution, ownership of, and access to, the water resources; the balance and the management of supply and demand; and the options for future resource development.

Historical background to the management of water resources

5.2. The reorganization of the water industry for England and Wales under the Water Act 1973 was based on the principle of integrated catchment management. Ten multi-functional Regional Water Authorities (RWAs) were set up, each responsible for all aspects of the water environment within one or more river catchments, including water resource management, water supply—except in those areas supplied by SWCs—sewage collection and disposal, flood defence and environmental management.

5.3. From 1973 to 1989 the RWAs were charged with conserving, managing and developing water resources within their respective boundaries, which were drawn to encompass complete river catchments. The RWAs developed regional water resource strategies covering both the area which they supplied and those of any SWCs within their boundaries. Thus the development of all sources, including those developed by SWCs, was discussed and planned within the overall jurisdiction of the RWA.

5.4. At privatization in 1989, the RWAs' catchment-wide responsibility for water resource planning, conservation and management was transferred to the newly-created NRA, which became part of the EA in April 1996.

5.5. The water supply activities of the RWAs were transferred to the newly privatized WaSCs as was the provision of sewerage services to the whole of the old RWA area, including those areas for which water supply was the responsibility of the SWCs. Thus the WaSCs retained a catchment-wide responsibility for sewerage. The SWCs became WoCs with unchanged water supply responsibilities.

5.6. Southern RWA owned the majority of water sources located in its region (since it or its predecessors had developed most of them) in both its own and the WoC supply areas. At privatization, ownership of these sources passed to the WaSCs and no attempt was made to balance the ownership of resources with the demands within each company's supply area. This was because there was no provision in the Water Act 1989, the Water Resources Act 1991 or the 1991 Act for such balancing to be carried out.

The local setting

5.7. FDWS, SEW and MKW together supply water to most of Kent and East Sussex and part of West Sussex, as shown on Map 7. Their supply areas fall within the Southern Region of the EA (see paragraph 3.7 and Maps 2 and 3). They are interspersed with or border on five separate areas supplied by SWS. These are the Kent Medway, Kent Thanet, Sussex East, Sussex Coast and Sussex West zones. They also border on Thames Water and Sutton & East Surrey Water in the west. The EA's Southern Region also includes most of Hampshire and the Isle of Wight, part of south-east London and small parts of Wiltshire, Berkshire and Surrey.

5.8. In the past, industrial development was located mainly along the Thames and Medway Estuaries and around the south coast ports. The development of light industry and the extension of the London commuter belt has spread development more evenly but, as shown on Map 7, over 50 per cent of the population of Kent and East Sussex still live in urban areas located along the coastline and the two estuaries. This puts pressure on water resources since most treated effluent arises near the coast and thus the potential for effluent re-use is reduced. It also means that leakage is less likely to contribute to recharge of the aquifers (as happens in, for example, London and Birmingham). Agriculture and horticulture are important users of water, mainly for spray irrigation. The total population supplied by the four companies is about 3.4 million, compared with a total population served in the EA Southern Region of 4.5 million. The populations, quantities of water and areas supplied in 1995/96 by each of the water companies are shown in Table 5.1.

TABLE 5.1 **Population supplied by the companies, 1995**

	MKW	SEW	FDWS	SWS (water supply only)
Population supplied	528,000	614,000	151,000	2,100,000
Water supply (Ml/d)	163	175	51.5	629
Area served (sq km)	2,050	2,105	420	4,450

Source: EA.

Note: The total population supplied in the area of the EA Southern Region includes other water supply companies.

5.9. The topography of the area is characterized by the North and South Downs, formed of the chalk strata which dips in the north to the Thames and in the western parts, south to the English Channel. The Downs are typical chalk landscape with characteristic dry valleys on the higher ground and streams fed from chalk springs at the foot of the Downs. Between the North and South Downs lies the gently rolling landscape of the Weald of Kent, formed from clays and sands.

5.10. The main rivers in the area are:

— the Medway (also fed by the Eden, Teise and Beult), draining much of the Weald and flowing north through the Medway towns to meet the Thames at Sheerness;

— the Darent, draining the extreme west of Kent northwards into the Thames;

— the Stour system, draining much of East Kent and discharging to the sea south of Ramsgate; and

— the Sussex Rivers Ouse, Cuckmere, Brede and Rother, all draining south into the sea along the Sussex Coast.

The Ouse, Teise, Cuckmere, Brede, Medway, Rother and Stour are used for water supplies. Map 1 shows the river systems.

5.11. The River Darent, the Little Stour (part of the Stour system) and the River Dour (which flows into the sea at Dover) are designated by the EA as low-flow rivers (that is, suffering from over-abstraction either from the rivers or from the aquifers feeding them). The Little Stour and the Darent are on the EA list of 40 high-priority sites for low-flow alleviation in England and Wales.

Water resources of the area

Rainfall

5.12. The Southern Region (and particularly Kent) is one of the drier regions in England and Wales. Table 5.2 shows a comparison of the net effective rainfall (that is, the rainfall available to recharge aquifers and contribute to river flows after allowing for evaporation losses and water used by vegetation) across the EA regions. The net effective rainfall provides the resource from which all uses of fresh water must be met. These uses include both abstractive uses (for example, water for public supplies and agriculture) and instream uses (for example, fisheries and dilution of discharges).

TABLE 5.2 **Average net effective rainfall across England and Wales by EA region**

Region	Net effective rainfall (mm/yr)*
Anglian	210
Thames	280
Southern	350
Yorkshire and Northumbrian	400
Severn Trent	500
South West	720
North West	800
Welsh	870

Source: EA.

*Based on long-term average rainfall records over the period 1951 to 1980.

Within the Southern Region the annual average net effective rainfall ranges from 550 mm in the west to less than 200 mm in north-east Kent. This is shown on Map 3.

Sources of supply

5.13. The Southern Region obtains its water resources from a combination of groundwater (77 per cent) and surface water sources (23 per cent). The geology of the area (shown on Map 2) has strongly influenced the development of water resources and until the late 1960s the water supplies in the area (with the exception of surface water reservoirs in Sussex at Powdermill, Darwell and Weir Wood—see Map 1) were almost entirely from groundwater. The development of (more expensive) surface water sources only followed after the major groundwater sources became fully developed by the standards at that time. The key water resource schemes are shown in Appendix 5.1.

5.14. The major public water supply sources from groundwater are shown on Map 2. The chalk and underlying greensand of the North and South Downs are the main aquifers in the area. These aquifers are heavily exploited for public water supply and also provide base flow (that is, the long-term flow not caused by direct run-off from recent storms) to a number of rivers in the area from the high-quality water which filters through the chalk. The high level of groundwater exploitation has led the EA to establish the Kent groundwater management policy which sets out restrictions on resource development for each aquifer in each resource area. The EA told us that, with a few local exceptions, it was unable to license any further groundwater abstraction in Kent, although a number of recent schemes had been allowed, within existing abstraction limits, to increase flexibility of operations (by varying the location or timing of the abstraction of the licensed quantities). Examples of this were at Goudhurst (MKW) and Kemsing (SEW) where in each case a new borehole was licensed.

5.15. The balance of supplies comes from surface water. The existing major public water supplies (greater than 10 Ml/d) drawn from the river systems of the region are shown on Map 1. These sources are used to fill the major reservoirs and, in some cases, for direct supply after treatment. The development of the key surface water schemes (and in particular reservoir development) took place mainly in the 1970s when approximately 80 per cent of the present storage capacity was constructed. In Kent and East Sussex the most significant strategic developments are in the SEW and MKW areas and have been constructed by SWS to maximize use of its licences to abstract from existing sources and provide supplies to its geographically dispersed supply areas. Descriptions of these schemes are given in paragraphs 5.20 and 5.21.

5.16. FDWS obtains its supplies from 24 groundwater sources, all located within the area which it supplies. At present there is a facility for one significant inter-company transfer of up to 2 Ml/d into FDWS from the MKW Barham source (also known as Kingston). Discussions are still proceeding between the parties on the future of this transfer. In the EA's assessment, FDWS sources can only provide a reliable yield under drought conditions equivalent to 49 per cent of their combined licence total. For the other companies in the area the corresponding figure is over 70 per cent. There are a number of reasons for the difference between the volume of licensed abstraction and the output of the source under drought conditions. FDWS is entirely dependent on groundwater sources, for which the difference between licensed abstraction and reliable yield is greater than for surface water sources. Moreover, some of the FDWS sources are located in parts of the aquifer that are particularly sensitive to drought conditions.

5.17. SEW obtains 40 per cent of its supplies from 11 surface sources and the balance from 41 groundwater sources. SEW owns two key reservoirs in the region (Arlington and Ardingly). There is one significant bulk supply from SWS Sussex West zone (Weir Wood) of 6 Ml/d and a small transfer of 0.7 Ml/d from its Sussex East zone to SEW.

5.18. MKW obtains the majority of its supplies from 37 groundwater sources. Its main surface water supplies are from the River Medway Scheme, including Bewl Water reservoir (12 per cent). There is a net transfer of resources from SWS into MKW, the most important transfers being from the Medway Scheme and the Belmont Scheme which are described in paragraphs 5.20 and 5.21.

5.19. SWS (Kent Medway, Kent Thanet and Sussex East supply areas) obtains approximately 70 per cent of its supplies from groundwater sources. Of the remainder, 5 per cent comes directly from reservoirs and 25 per cent from rivers augmented by reservoirs.

The Medway Scheme

5.20. The Medway Scheme (see Map 7) was commissioned in 1976 by SWS's predecessor, the Southern RWA, with MKW as a participant and beneficiary. The scheme consists of abstraction from the River Medway system supported by a pumped storage reservoir (Bewl Water) formed by a dam on the River Bewl (a tributary of the River Teise which in turn is a tributary of the River Medway). The reservoir has little natural catchment but is filled by pumping surplus flows (mainly in winter) from the River Teise at Smallbridge. In 1995 the scheme's yield was increased by adding the abstraction of surplus water from the River Medway at Yalding. Water is released from storage in the summer to support abstraction at Springfield near Maidstone. The water is then treated at Burham and distributed to SWS and MKW consumers in north Kent. SWS is the owner and operator of the scheme but, in broad terms, MKW has contributed 25 per cent of the costs of the scheme and, through a series of agreements with SWS, is entitled to approximately 25 per cent of the yield of the scheme. Bewl Water reservoir is located on the border between the MKW and SEW areas of supply and is relatively remote from the customers of SWS whom it serves, although the point of abstraction, at Springfield near Maidstone, is much closer. The use of the Medway river system to carry water from the reservoir to the abstraction point provides a significant environmental benefit. The licensing of Bewl Water provides for a quantity of water which is only permitted to be used by a water undertaker other than SWS (in practice MKW). The formal agreements covering the original (1976) scheme were executed many years ago, but the draft agreement covering the Yalding extension is still in the process of being finalized as a formal contract. MKW told us that current arrangements are on the basis of commercial custom and practice, reflecting MKW's capital contribution. MKW receives bulk supplies of treated water from SWS's Burham treatment works and bulk supplies of raw water from Bewl Water which it treats and distributes. MKW has some degree of flexibility as to how its take is distributed between the two locations. The average yield of the scheme (including the Yalding extension) is 103.29 Ml/d, although SWS told us that the yield is currently limited by treatment plant capacity at Burham.

The Belmont Scheme

5.21. The Belmont Scheme was developed in the 1960s by Medway Water Board, which later became part of SWS. It exploits groundwater from the chalk aquifer south of Faversham by means of boreholes at Belmont, Selling and Throwley (see Map 7). Originally all the water was delivered to Eastling pumping station and then pumped west (through the Eastling–Wigmore main) to Wigmore service reservoir, south-east of Gillingham, to serve consumers in the Medway towns. From this scheme a bulk supply was provided from Matts Hill pumping station, south of Sittingbourne, to Maidstone & District Water Company (now incorporated in MKW). In the early 1980s, to meet peak deficits in its Thanet area, SWS developed further boreholes in the Belmont area (as part of the North Kent Groundwater Scheme promoted jointly with MKW) and laid the Selling–Fleete main connecting the Belmont Scheme sources to the SWS Fleete service reservoir which serves Thanet. The formal agreements between SWS and MKW (as modified in correspondence) provide for a bulk supply of 8 Ml/d average and 10.9 Ml/d peak, from SWS to MKW, via Matts Hill pumping station. During the 1980s, also as part of the joint SWS/MKW development of the north Kent chalk aquifer, MKW developed sources close to the Eastling main and reached informal agreements with SWS to share the use of the Eastling main to deliver this water to its consumers. Thus MKW now takes out (at several points) the quantity it has put in plus the agreed bulk supply of 8 Ml/d. In a form of common carriage, the inflows and outflows are accurately metered and operating costs are shared on an agreed basis. In addition MKW has access to the Selling–Fleete main as a transfer facility on an ad hoc basis provided that this does not jeopardize the security of supplies to SWS's consumers. MKW has made the necessary connections and used this facility in May 1995 to provide emergency supplies to consumers in the Whitstable area. Although the Eastling–Wigmore and Selling–Fleete mains are separate, the discontinuity in the main occurs at a major group of sources (Belmont/Selling/Throwley) and thus water can in effect be transferred across Kent by 'redirecting' some of the water from these sources.

Co-operation between MKW and SWS

5.22. There has been a history of co-operation between MKW and SWS since the mid-1960s and MKW has both promoted new source developments with SWS (for example, the River Medway Scheme) and has taken bulk supplies from SWS (for example, the Belmont Scheme). In some cases co-operation has gone beyond the formal agreements to a form of common carriage, as described in paragraph 5.21.

The EA water resources strategy

EA national strategy

5.23. The EA has a duty to take such actions as it considers necessary or expedient to conserve, redistribute or otherwise augment water resources in England and Wales and to secure their proper use.

The EA does not have specific powers to make the water companies manage resources in accordance with its policies and has to rely on its licensing powers to encourage the companies to do so. In using those powers the EA must have regard to the reasonable requirements of the applicants as well as the environmental and recreational aspects of any proposal. A fuller statement of the EA's powers, duties and functions is set out in paragraphs 9.3 to 9.12 and in Appendices 4.1 and 4.2.

5.24. The EA's preferred water resources strategy is based on the NRA's *National Water Resources Strategy,* published in 1994, and follows three principles:

(a) *Sustainable development:* There should be no long-term systematic deterioration in the water environment due to water resource development and water use.

(b) *The precautionary principle:* Where significant environmental damage may occur, but knowledge on the matter is incomplete, decisions made and measures implemented should err on the side of caution.

(c) *Demand management:* The management of the total quantity of water taken from sources of supply using measures to control waste and consumption.

EA regional strategy

5.25. In its Southern Region, the EA promotes a water resource strategy designed to address any potential inadequacy of existing sources by giving priority first to demand management and inter-company transfers, second to possible local development options and last to major new source development. The first three specific policies detailed in the Southern Region strategy are as follows:

(a) requiring water companies to achieve economic levels of leakage and metering (that is, the levels at which the cost of the measures needed is equalled by the savings in cost of the lost water, taking into account the EA's estimate of environmental costs) before new abstraction licences are granted for strategic developments;

(b) promoting water efficiency in industry, commerce, agriculture and use in the home; and

(c) where possible, redistributing water resources rather than developing new sources.

5.26. *Sustaining Our Resources—The Way Forward*, the NRA's November 1994 water resources strategy for the Southern Region, confirmed the view reached in earlier water resource planning initiatives that, assuming that the proposed future resource developments (see paragraphs 5.59 and 5.60) prove to be environmentally acceptable, the Southern Region as a whole is likely to be self-sufficient in water resources under a range of demand scenarios for future public water supply until at least 2021. This view was, nevertheless, dependent on the implementation of effective demand management measures and on the ability of the various parties within the region to develop mechanisms for addressing the uneven distribution of the supply/demand balance between the west and the east of the region and between the water supply companies. The NRA's forecasts are discussed further in paragraphs 5.50 to 5.55.

Bulk supply transfers

5.27. Where there are imbalances in access to water resources between neighbouring companies, the EA and the DGWS expect those companies with a water deficit to enter into BST agreements with those adjacent companies which have a water surplus, as a means of redressing these imbalances. Under a BST agreement, a supplier provides water (which may be either raw or treated) from a source (of which it retains the ownership) to a recipient company at a commercial rate, payable on a per-cubic-metre-of-water-supplied basis. By thus sharing any available surplus more evenly between the companies, the EA and the DGWS believe that the need for further resource development can be deferred. If a company seeks a BST from another, but is unable to negotiate acceptable terms and conditions, it can apply to the DGWS, who has powers under the 1991 Act as amended by the Competition and Services (Utilities) Act 1992 to order a supply to be given and to determine a fair price and conditions. Neither the EA nor the

DGWS has specific legal powers to require a company to take water under a BST although the DGWS told us that he may able to insist that a company take a BST using the powers of enforcement (under section 18 of the 1991 Act) to require the water undertakers to meet their statutory obligations to supply (section 37 of the 1991 Act). The DoE/Welsh Office paper *Water Resources and Supply: Agenda for Action*, published in October 1996, reports that the Government is considering whether the range of mechanisms (available to the regulators) could usefully be refined or extended.

5.28. If demand is rising, BSTs are likely to be provided by a supplier on one of two bases:

(a) a long-term 'guaranteed' supply where the supplier develops a source which it can only rely on to supply its own customers in the short term while the demand from the recipient builds up; or

(b) a short-term supply utilizing 'spare' water from a scheme which it has developed to meet the long-term needs of its own customers. In this case the recipient may need to develop another source to provide for the long-term needs of its customers as or when the BST ceases.

5.29. The EA told us that in determining licence applications it adopted a policy of not granting any new licences unless the applicant could demonstrate that it had taken all feasible measures to comply with the EA's policies on demand management and BSTs.

5.30. The EA has proposed the strategic transfers which it considers could solve the water resource problems in Kent and East Sussex (see Map 6). Essentially these consist of transfers from the west, which has a surplus of water, to the east of the region and from SWS to SEW and FDWS. They include transfers from:

— SWS Hampshire and the River Rother at Hardham to SWS Sussex West and Sussex Coast;

— SWS Weir Wood and SWS/MKW Bewl Water to SEW;

— SWS Kent Medway to SWS Thanet; and

— SWS Kent Thanet to FDWS.

The EA told us that, in accordance with its statutory duties, in proposing these transfers it took no account of the commercial implications for the companies involved.

Demand management

5.31. Central to the EA water resources strategy is the limitation or reversal of the growth in resources needed, through a policy of demand management. This policy has two elements: first, minimizing the per capita consumption of the consumer (consumption management), and second, minimizing the amount of water lost between the source and the consumer (loss reduction). Both are commonly referred to as demand management although the latter could be considered as supply, or distribution, management.

5.32. We deal first with consumption management. Although the growth of consumption can be reduced by public education campaigns, the policy which both the EA and OFWAT consider to be the most effective is the metering of domestic supplies. In the Southern Region, domestic supplies account for over 50 per cent of average consumption and for most of the additional consumption during peak demand periods. In 1994/95 the percentage of domestic supplies metered was 5.0 per cent in the FDWS area, 9.2 per cent in the SEW area, 6.1 per cent in the MKW area and 11.2 per cent in the SWS area (mainly on the Isle of Wight).

Metering

5.33. National metering trials were set up in 1989 based on approximately 60,000 properties (50,000 of which were on the Isle of Wight) to assess the cost and the effect on demand of metering domestic consumers. As part of these trials, some limited trials of a block tariff were carried out. Under a block tariff a higher charge is levied for discretionary use of water (for example, for car washing or garden water) than for water supplied for normal domestic purposes of cooking, washing and sanitation. This is intended to discourage non-essential use at peak periods or in periods of drought and to reduce peaking factors. In the metering trials a figure of 90 cubic metres a year was taken as the reasonable essential requirements of a family and a higher tariff was charged above this level. A wide range of block tariffs is in use around the world for demand management but the development of suitable tariffs is still at an early stage in England and Wales.

5.34. One of the key findings of the trials was the significant effect metering was found to have on demand. At the small-scale sites average demand fell, typically, by around 11 per cent over the three years of the trial; on the Isle of Wight distribution input fell by 22 per cent over the same period for the metered areas. The SWS report on the Isle of Wight trials attributed 44 per cent of the fall (about 10 per cent of distribution input) to metering, a similar proportion to a reduction in leakage (primarily the identification and rectification of leaks during meter installation) and 12 per cent (or 2 per cent of distribution input) to other factors. However, SWS also told us that average demand recovered to some extent after the trials ended and that the reductions in leakage on the Isle of Wight were matched by similar reductions in parts of the mainland where there had been a leakage reduction programme without any metering programme.

5.35. In the case of peak demand, the national water metering trials suggested that metering can have an even greater effect, with reductions of 30 per cent being recorded in peak month, week, day and hour demand in years with hot and dry summers.

5.36. The EA considered that metering could provide significant benefits in the Southern Region, by reducing both average and peak demand and, through producing a strong revenue stream from consumers with high water consumption (by means of block tariffs), providing a fairer way of paying for future investment in resource development. Figures provided by the EA to illustrate what might be achieved are shown in Table 5.3.

TABLE 5.3 **Potential effect of metering on average and peak demand, Southern Region**

Domestic properties metered by 2006 %	Reduction in average demand by 2021		Reduction in peak demand by 2021	
	Ml/d	%	Ml/d	%
30	35	(2.5)*	110	(6.2)*
90	78	(5.8)*	250	(14.0)*

Source: NRA, 1994.

*Reductions in demand expressed as a percentage of the NRA high scenario demand forecasts.

5.37. However, there is little long-term experience in the UK of the effect of domestic metering on demand. While all parties in the water industry in England and Wales agree that metering initially provides significant demand reductions, there is significant disagreement on the magnitude and sustainability of this reduction in the long term.

Loss reduction

5.38. We turn next to loss reduction. The EA estimated that some 25 per cent of the water input to the distribution system was lost between the source and the consumer in 1992. There is thus great potential to reduce the supply requirements by reducing this loss. In particular, in 1995 the NRA estimated that some 14.5 per cent of distribution input in England and Wales could be saved by controlling leakage. (Strictly speaking, losses are slightly more than leakage as they include overflows, swabbing, washing out and losses during repairs, but the two terms are often used interchangeably.)

5.39. There are two distinct elements of leakage, namely distribution leakage and supply pipe leakage. The former is the leakage between the supply (from the source or service reservoir) and the consumer's boundary or meter, and the latter is leakage within consumers' premises, from supply pipes, dripping taps etc. While distribution leakage can be fairly readily assessed, the leakage within consumers' premises is much more difficult to quantify.

5.40. Leakage is usually expressed in terms of litres per property per hour (l/prop/h) or per day (l/prop/d). By convention the hourly figure is not one twenty-fourth (as might be expected) of the daily figure but is taken as one twentieth (for reasons associated with the variation of leakage through the day). In rural or peri-urban areas with a low population density the measure of cubic metres per km of pipeline a day (m^3/km/d) is also used. This is often advocated as a fairer comparison between companies where considerably different lengths of pipelines (and thus correspondingly different potential for leakage) are needed to serve comparable numbers of consumers. Given the range of measures and the difference between total losses and distribution losses, great care needs to be taken in comparing the figures for different companies.

5.41. The EA and OFWAT have provided figures for total leakage by company, together with company targets and the industry average figures. These are shown in Table 5.4.

TABLE 5.4 **Total leakage levels (1994/95) and company targets**

Company	Total leakage, 1994/95		Rank, 1994/95		Targets, 1997/98	
	l/prop/day	m^3/km/d	l/prop/d	m^3/km/d	l/prop/d	m^3/km/d
FDWS	177	12.1	20	20	144	9.9
SEW	145	8.7	13	6	138	7.2
MKW	176	9.8	19	9	120	6.8
WoC average	152	11.4	-	-	141	10.6
SWS	139	10.2	12	11	103	7.6
WaSC average	255	17.6	-	-	195	13.4
Industry average	230	16.2	-	-	142	11

Source: OFWAT report 'Leakage of Water in England and Wales', May 1996.

Notes:
1. Total leakage includes losses from distribution and supply pipe.
2. Ranking is out of 29 water companies.

OFWAT told us that as part of the 1994/95 Periodic Review FDWS, SEW and MKW proposed target levels of leakage. These were [*] l/prop/d by 1999 for FDWS, [*] l/prop/d by 1998 for MKW and [*] l/prop/d by 2020 for SEW.

5.42. Techniques for reducing distribution losses are well established: pressure control (since increased pressure causes a disproportionate increase in leakage), district metering and mains renewal. District metering consists of dividing the distribution area into small districts into which the flow is accurately monitored. Thus by continuously monitoring and comparing the inflow with the expected or normal flow for the time of day, week and year, any leaks can be detected and fixed quickly; the smaller the district the higher the cost but the more effective the resulting leakage reduction.

5.43. Techniques for reducing supply pipe losses are linked to metering. Leaks in supply pipes are most likely to be identified in the process of installing meters and for this reason many companies offer free or low-cost repairs to, or replacement of, supply pipes as part of the meter installation package (and when replacing a communication pipe). Once a meter is installed, consumers will be more aware of the cost of water losses and therefore more willing to locate and repair leaks on their premises at their own cost.

*Figures omitted. See note on page iv.

Balance of demand and supply

5.44. Table 5.5, based on information provided by the EA and OFWAT, shows the resource balance in 1994 and 1995 by ownership of sources. 1995 was a particularly hot dry year whereas 1994 was more typical.

TABLE 5.5 Resource balance based on resource ownership

Company	Average demand (Ml/d)* 1994	1995	Reliable yield (Ml/d)†	Surplus/deficit (Ml/d) 1994	1995
FDWS	51	53	49	−2	−4
SEW	171	182	179	8	−3
MKW	162	170	178	16	8
SWS (E Sussex and Kent)					
Medway	125‡	130	180§	55	50
Thanet	54‡	55	66	12	11
Sussex East	27‡	28	25	−2	−3
Total	206	213	271§	65	58
Southern (total) including Hants and Sussex Coast	633‡	646	839§	206	193

Sources: *Data provided by companies to OFWAT. †NRA, 1994. ‡Provided by SWS. §Includes Yalding Scheme developed in 1995.

Notes:
1. Reliable yield refers to water availability in a drought and is roughly two-thirds of authorized licence totals except in FDWS area where it is approximately half.
2. It is argued that peak demand balance is equally important as the driver of new resource development but the relative positions of the companies are similar for peak and average demands.

5.45. Table 5.5 shows, in 1994 the FDWS and SWS Sussex East supply areas were in deficit on average demand while the SEW, MKW and SWS Kent Thanet and Kent Medway supply areas were in modest surplus. The areas in the west of the region (in particular the SWS Hampshire and Sussex Coast supply areas) had a significant surplus. This is consistent with the analysis of the resource balance in the Southern NRA Regional Strategy Document (NRA, 1994). Reliable yields have commonly been based on the '1 in 50 year drought' for surface water sources and on the worst historic levels for groundwater sources. In practice, since the severity of a drought is not known until it is over, restrictions are often introduced as a matter of prudence well before minimum reservoir or groundwater levels are reached. This accounts for the commonly quoted frequency of 1 in 10 years for demand restrictions. The DoE and Welsh Office paper *Water Resources and Supply: Agenda for Action* (1996) identified the need for water companies to reassess the yield of all their surface and groundwater sources in the light of climate change.

5.46. In 1995 recorded temperatures were significantly above normal with summer rainfall (April to September) for the region around 70 per cent of the long-term average. As a result, high, and in some instances record, demands were experienced. Hose-pipe bans were introduced at some stage by all the companies in at least part of their areas, although in the case of FDWS not until March 1996. Hose-pipe bans suppress demand and thus without them the surpluses may have been expected to be smaller and the deficits larger. Despite these bans, demand was some 4 per cent higher than in 1994, reducing the surpluses and moving SEW into deficit.

Historic legacy

5.47. SWS (and its predecessors) developed sources in the areas supplied by other companies because they were the water suppliers for areas in Kent and East Sussex with large populations but limited water resources. Both of these characteristics arise because SWS's areas of supply are on the coast or the Medway and Thames estuaries. In the 1960s the Medway Water Board could not find adequate sources to develop within the areas which it supplied and so it located and developed sources inland. In the 1960s, 1970s and 1980s, the Medway Water Board and subsequently the Southern RWA as the largest company in the area was the natural choice to promote or lead the development of major resources. In the case of the Southern RWA, its overall water resource management duty was a further reason for its leading role. Before privatization and commercial competition the smaller companies looked to it to take the lead and this is reflected in the Medway and Belmont Schemes. At privatization, to some extent, this role passed to SWS since the NRA did not have powers to develop water resources. This historic local legacy, together with the manner in which the water industry as a whole developed (see paragraphs 5.2 to 5.6), explains why SWS owns a number of significant sources located within the areas for which FDWS, SEW and MKW are the appointed water undertakers.

5.48. Table 5.6, based on information provided by the EA, OFWAT and SWS, shows the resource balances in each company's area in 1994 and 1995 after 'crediting' each company with those sources located in the area which it supplies regardless of ownership.

TABLE 5.6 **Resource balance based on resource location (regardless of ownership)**

Company	Average demand (Ml/d)*		Reliable yield (Ml/d)†	Surplus/deficit (Ml/d)	
	1994	1995		1994	1995
FDWS	51	53	63.5	12.5	10.5
SEW	171	182	205	34	23
MKW	162	170	239	77	69
SWS (E Sussex and Kent)					
Medway	125‡	130	84	−41	−46
Thanet	54‡	55	57	3	2
Sussex East	27‡	28	7	−20	−21
Total	206	213	148	−58	−65

Sources: *Data provided by companies to OFWAT. †NRA, 1994. ‡Provided by SWS.

Notes:
1. Reliable yield refers to water availability in a drought and is roughly two-thirds of authorized licence totals.
2. It is argued that peak demand balance is equally important as the driver of new resource development but the relative positions of the companies are similar for peak and average demands.

5.49. By comparing Tables 5.5 and 5.6 the differences in the degree of self-sufficiency in resource ownership in the areas which the various companies supply can be clearly seen. If each company controlled the sources within its own area of supply, FDWS, SEW and MKW would all move into significant surplus whereas SWS would move into significant deficit in its Kent Medway and East Sussex supply areas (while retaining a modest surplus within its overall area).

Demand forecasting

5.50. The forecasting of demand is a matter of some debate between the water supply companies and their regulators, the former often favouring higher forecasts than the latter. In 1994 the NRA Southern Region produced low and high demand forecasts for each water company in its area. These are summarized in Appendix 5.2. The low demand forecast assumed that all feasible measures to limit demand growth (for example, metering and loss reduction) would be implemented by the companies and that these would constrain the growth in per capita consumption. The high demand forecast assumed that such measures would be implemented slowly or poorly or would have limited effect. The NRA's 1994 low demand forecast assumed total leakage of 6 l/prop/h (roughly equivalent to 22 per cent of distribution input), and 30 per cent domestic metering with 10 per cent reduction in average per capita consumption. Under this scenario and assuming a number of BSTs between companies, the NRA concluded that no major new resources would be needed for 30 years. If this scenario could be achieved by following the NRA/EA policies on sustainable development, the EA believes that major reservoir schemes could be deferred for decades. Under the high demand scenario, assuming high growth rates in domestic and commercial demand, no leakage reduction and no increase in domestic metering, the NRA identified a number of potential resource developments in addition to the small local schemes, and these are listed in paragraphs 5.59 and 5.60. The EA is exhorting the companies to take all reasonable measures to ensure that actual growth is as close as possible to the low demand scenario.

5.51. The EA is now reviewing these forecasts, taking into account the higher than forecast demands in 1995/96. Underlying all the supply/demand projections is a degree of uncertainty in the extent to which demand management measures can limit effective demand growth and hence defer the need for major new sources. This uncertainty is reflected in the difference between the high and low forecasts by all companies.

5.52. Although the EA and OFWAT are strong advocates of demand management, some of the water supply companies consider that their expectations of what can be achieved by demand management in practice are optimistic. These water supply companies argue that uncertainties surround first the long-term efficacy of demand management, secondly the reliability of source yields in a period of climate change, and thirdly the future growth in per capita demand. Taking into consideration the lead time of up to 20 years for developing a major new source, they argue that these uncertainties make a strong case for having an adequate 'planning margin' of available resources to reduce the risk of water shortages over significant periods.

5.53. Revised forecasts from the water companies are shown together with the EA forecasts in Figures 5.1 to 5.8. It should be noted that the EA figures for 1996 were estimated in 1994 and the company figures are actual recorded figures.

5.54. Notwithstanding the lively debate on demand forecasting, the range of forecasts produced by the companies generally falls within the range of forecasts by the EA, that is, the companies' high forecasts are lower than those of the EA and their low forecasts are higher. The exception to this is SWS whose forecasts are higher than those of the EA for both low and high forecasts. The unanswered question is whether demand growth will be closer to the upper or lower forecast. The EA and OFWAT believe that demand growth can and should be forced to the lower forecast by demand management. Although the shallow gradient of the demand forecasts means that small changes in gradient will cause large changes in the timing of the requirement for new sources, the differences between the forecasts of the EA and the water companies are not so great as to make it unreasonable to use the EA's range of forecasts for the purposes of this reference.

5.55. On the basis of the EA's forecasts SEW and FDWS have, or are rapidly approaching, a deficit of supply compared with demand. MKW has a relatively small surplus of supply over demand. SWS has a larger surplus, although this is mainly located in the western part of its area. SWS argues that its surplus is overestimated by the EA and the bidders on the basis that the out-turn figures for 1995/96 demand were significantly higher than those in the 1994 NRA forecast.

5.56. The magnitude and timing of the need for future resource development is dependent upon:

(a) the effect of demand management measures (metering and loss reduction) to be implemented by the water supply companies; and

(b) the degree of implementation of BSTs between the various companies, as advocated by the EA and the DGWS.

Water resource management: the bidders' proposals

5.57. The bidders have told us that the primary objective and principal benefit of the proposed merger would be the improved distribution, management, planning and future development of water resources in the region (see paragraphs 6.17 to 6.19). In order to achieve this objective and realize the benefits, they propose enhanced leakage reduction programmes and enhanced demand management including public education campaigns and an extended metering programme. They also propose to construct a number of pipelines, reinforcing links within MKW's area and linking MKW sources and trunk mains to those of FDWS and SEW (see Map 4). By establishing these new links the bidders intend to set up what they describe as a 'mini-grid' in order to redistribute the water resources in the area, to enhance operational security and to optimize resources through conjunctive use, that is varying the output of sources so that one source can be used at maximum capacity while another is 'rested' to allow it to recharge more quickly or is taken out of service for alterations or remediation of pollution. Conjunctive use might also allow the resting of certain environmentally sensitive sources. The bidders have told us that to implement these proposals they would fund the equivalent of an additional £19 million in capital expenditure over eight years and £6 million in operating costs, also spread over eight years (both estimates at out-turn prices), all within existing price limits.

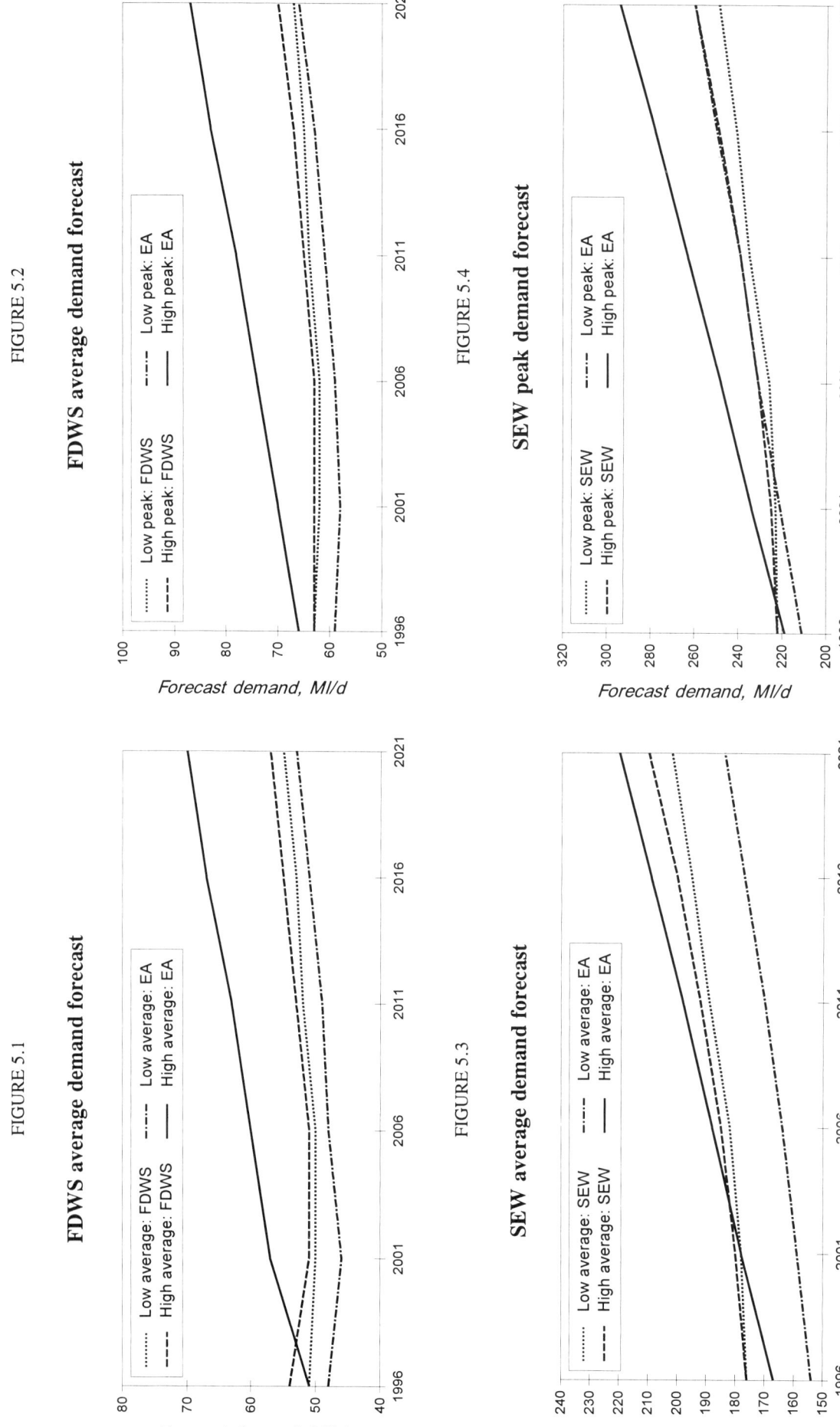

FIGURE 5.5

MKW average demand forecast

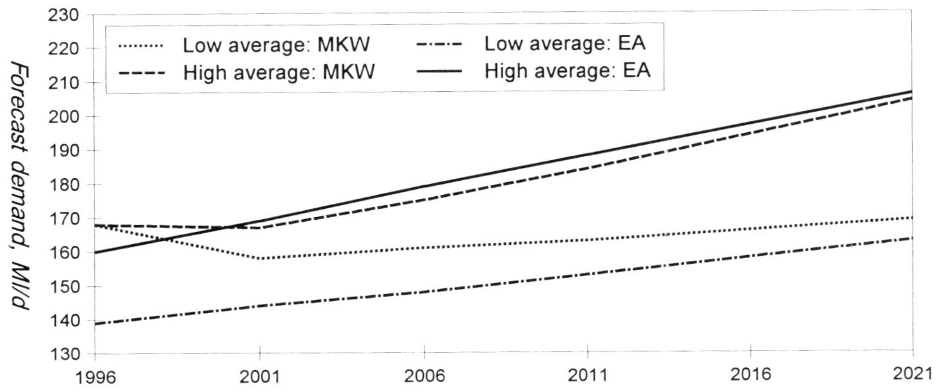

FIGURE 5.6

MKW peak demand forecast

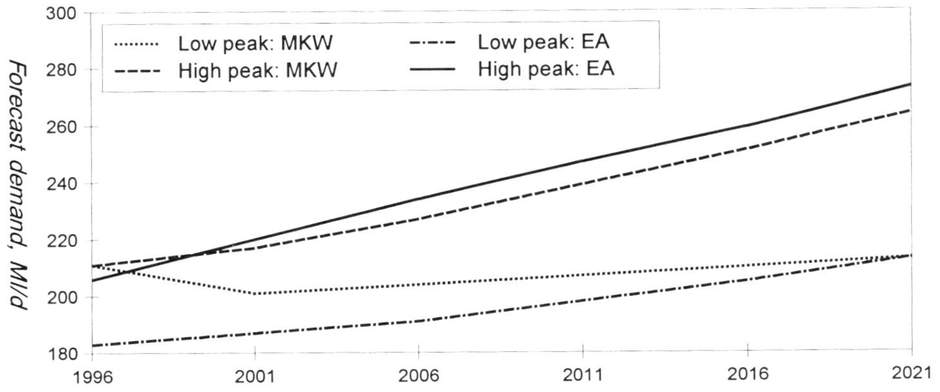

FIGURE 5.7

SWS average demand forecast

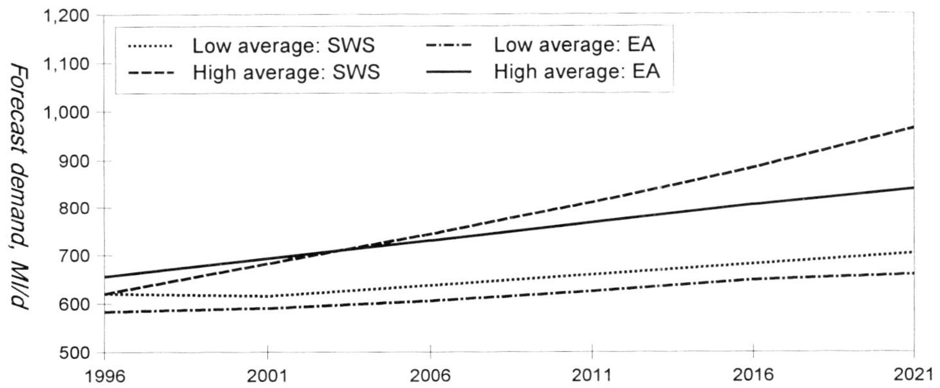

FIGURE 5.8

SWS peak demand forecast

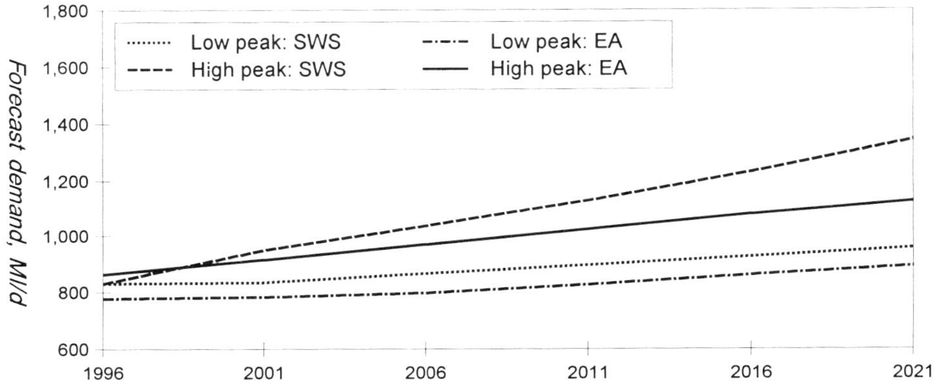

5.58. The bidders propose to develop an integrated supply network by connecting existing systems with the following pipelines (shown on Map 4):

(a) from Canterbury to Barham and from Howfield to Chilham, which together would enable the major Stour Valley groundwater sources of Chilham, Godmersham and Thanington to be linked to a new pipeline from Kingston (Barham) into the FDWS supply area. These pipelines would also help to facilitate future transfers of water from a major water resource development (such as Broad Oak) via Canterbury to FDWS and to other areas of the enlarged companies;

(b) from Kippings Cross to Cottage Hill, which would provide the ability to take water from the MKW treatment works at Bewl to supply Tunbridge Wells and Crowborough;

(c) to complete the link from Burham to Beech, west of Maidstone, which would provide the ability to feed treated Medway water into the West Kent area;

(d) to provide future reinforcement of east-west links across Maidstone linking into the Beech to Burham pipeline; and

(e) from Potters Corner, north-west of Ashford to Broomfield, east of Maidstone which, together with the above pipelines, would in effect link the MKW supply zones of Canterbury, Ashford, North Downs and Maidstone and thus link the Stour Valley groundwater sources with the areas supplied from the Medway Scheme. This link would provide the ability to operate the Stour Valley groundwater sources (and any future major source in East Kent—see paragraph 5.59) conjunctively with the Medway surface water source. The bidders have told us that, taken together with the existing and other pipelines listed above, this will facilitate transfer of up to 40 Ml/d from a new source in the Medway or Rother catchments or at Broad Oak.

Pumping stations are also proposed, at Canterbury, at Kippings Cross and near Barham.

Potential water sources

5.59. All the demand forecasts indicate that at some stage, when the EA's priority actions of demand management and BSTs have all been implemented, demand will ultimately exceed supply and further supplies will be required. A number of potential sources, either new or incremental developments of existing sources, have been identified within the region during the course of investigations to various levels of detail by the water companies in discussion with the EA. These include:

(a) the further development of the Medway system (in addition to the recent Yalding development), by raising Bewl Water with an additional yield of possibly up to 20 Ml/d;

(b) the development of a new reservoir at Broad Oak near Canterbury, storing winter flows from the River Stour with a possible yield of 40 Ml/d;

(c) the raising of the water level of Darwell Reservoir in Sussex, with a possible yield of 42 Ml/d; and

(d) a number of local resource developments identified by the EA (set out in Appendix 5.3).

5.60. Based on the present forecasts of the effects of climate change, the EA has declared a policy of refusing any further summer abstraction from rivers unless supported by winter storage, and has made it clear that this policy applies to the Medway system. At a meeting between the bidders and the EA, attended by staff from the MMC, the EA again made clear its view that the low flows in the Medway were less than needed to maintain acceptable water quality in the estuary and that any scheme for further abstraction would have to contribute to making good this deficit first. The EA also pointed out that the dischargers to the river had already undertaken the water quality improvement measures which were feasible at low to medium cost, leaving only the high marginal cost measures.

5.61. Additional schemes identified in the west of the EA Southern Region's area (some distance from the areas which FDWS, SEW and MKW supply) include further development of abstraction from the River Rother at Hardham (yield to be determined), Lower Hamble groundwater (10 Ml/d), further abstraction from the River Itchen (70 to 90 Ml/d), Havant Thicket Reservoir (30 Ml/d) and groundwater development in the Test Valley (20 to 30 Ml/d). These schemes would all have substantial transfer costs if used to supply Kent and East Sussex. These schemes could be used to replace SWS resources in Sussex which could then in turn be released for transfer further east, but the cost would be substantial.

6 The views of General Utilities and SAUR Water Services

Contents

	Paragraph
Introduction	6.1
General	6.3
Original reference: stages of the transactions and position of the Joint Resources Company	
General	6.4
Joint Resources Company	6.5
Planned infrastructure investment ('mini-grid')	6.12
Subsidiaries of Mid Kent Holdings	6.14
Timing of the expected benefits	6.15
Timing of changes to Mid Kent Water's status as a comparator	6.16
The expected benefits of the proposals	
Main benefits	6.17
Other aspects	6.22
Effect of proposals on the comparator system and competition	
Issues concerning numbers of comparators	6.24
Effect of the loss of Mid Kent Water as a comparator	6.25
Exemplary status for the enlarged water companies	6.28
Improvement of local competition	6.29
Effect of the proposed Joint Resources Company on the comparator system	6.30
Effect of the proposed Joint Resources Company on competition	6.33
Effect of the proposed Joint Resources Company on regulatory matters	6.34
Water resources	
Optimizing resource use	6.36
Involving Southern Water Services	6.37
Guarantees for Mid Kent Water's customers	6.38
Mutual co-operation as an alternative to the merger	6.39
Reasons to oppose bulk supply transfers as an alternative solution	6.40
Whether proposals are the only means of obtaining the expected benefits	6.44
Remedies	
General	6.45
Prices	6.46
Stock Exchange listing	6.47
Performance and proposed EA partial remedies	6.48
Miscellaneous legal issues	
Interpretation of section 34(3)(b) of the Water Industry Act 1991	6.52
Issues not directly deriving from mergers of water enterprises	6.54
Jurisdictional and legal issues concerning the original reference	
EC aspects	6.57
Arrangements in progress	6.58
Number of mergers	6.59
Assets test	6.60
Issues concerning the variation of the terms of reference (13 September) on a possible merger in being	6.61
Section 65(3) of the Fair Trading Act 1973	6.71
Public interest	6.74

Possible remedial action 6.78
Time limits affecting the MMC inquiry into any existing merger (section 34(4) of the
    Water Industry Act 1991) 6.79
Possible existing merger
    GU's views 6.84
    SAUR's views 6.85

Introduction

6.1. This chapter summarizes the views of GU and its subsidiary FDWS, and of SAUR and its subsidiary SEW. These views were provided in joint written submissions, in answers to questionnaires and at three formal hearings, major parts of which were joint hearings.

6.2. Evidence was sought from GU and SAUR on:

— the precise nature of the proposed transaction;

— the benefits they expected to flow from the proposals;

— the impact the proposals might have on the comparator system and competition;

— water resource issues in Kent and East Sussex, including the pros and cons of BSTs as a means of correcting resource imbalances;

— whether the benefits expected from the proposed merger might be achieved without the merger; and

— their understanding of jurisdictional and other legal issues associated with the original reference and the 13 September variation and, in connection with the latter, their views on whether a merger had taken place and, if so, its public interest consequences.

Finally, GU and SAUR were asked their views on the kinds of remedies that might be appropriate if:

(a) a merger with likely or actual adverse public interest consequences was already in being; and

(b) their proposed transaction was found to affect the public interest adversely.

General

6.3. GU and SAUR said that on 21 December 1995 they had announced their intention to make a bid for the whole of the issued share capital of MKH. This announcement recognized that the proposal would be subject to mandatory reference to the MMC. Under the terms of the JVA between them signed on 20 December 1995, GU and SAUR had agreed to form a joint venture company for the purpose of the bid and the proposed subsequent transactions. This company had not been formed pending the outcome of the regulatory process. Formally, the process was intended to be accomplished in two stages. Under Stage 1 the capital of MKH would be acquired. Under Stage 2 MKH's main subsidiary, MKW, would be restructured and divided approximately equally between SEW and FDWS. Certain MKW assets, however, principally abstraction licences, bulk supply rights and rights of access to land, would remain in a JRC. Appendix 2.1 gives a fuller synopsis.

Original reference: stages of the transactions and position of the Joint Resources Company

General

6.4. GU and SAUR considered that there would be little to distinguish each of the two stages of the proposed transaction. Stage 1 was simply a means to achieve Stage 2. The objective of GU and SAUR was to achieve Stage 2 as soon as possible following the acquisition of MKH. Stage 2 was dependent on a number of prior steps which would take time. For example, the values of assets for regulatory purposes and other regulatory aspects would need to be agreed with the DGWS. In operating terms, however, the companies would want to give immediate effect to the spirit of Stage 2 of the acquisition. FDWS would become involved in the management of the eastern part of MKH, and SEW in the western part, from the very beginning.

Joint Resources Company

6.5. The JRC would be held 50:50 by the two enlarged water companies, FDWS and SEW. This was because if, in the future, either SAUR or GU wanted to divest themselves of their water company, it would be important that the appropriate resource assets in the JRC went with the water company that was being divested. Within the JRC, therefore, the resource assets it held would be linked to the operating companies.

6.6. GU and SAUR said that the JRC was fundamental to their proposals. It would facilitate optimal management and distribution of the water resources held by MKW and would be used to develop and provide new strategic water resources for both enlarged companies.

6.7. At the outset of the inquiry GU and SAUR said that the following assets and rights would be transferred to the JRC:

(a) all existing abstraction licences located within MKW's current area that were now held by MKW;

(b) all MKW's current bulk supply rights;

(c) all necessary rights of access to land at the location of MKW's existing abstraction licences; and

(d) the land rights and licences associated with any major new development (for example, Broad Oak and Darwell).

The JRC would also own the physical assets associated with future strategic resources. GU and SAUR said that the structure, management and administration of the JRC would be kept as simple as possible, consistent with all statutory and regulatory requirements.

6.8. Subsequently, however, and in response to views expressed by the DGWS, GU and SAUR indicated that the JRC would not need to own the physical assets associated with the development of new infrastructure, whether major (for example, at Broad Oak or elsewhere) or minor. They envisaged instead that:

(a) the JRC would carry out the planning of all new major developments in the enlarged areas of FDWS and SEW and of all minor developments in the former MKW areas, on behalf of the two companies. It would hold the abstraction licences for these developments (as well as the existing licences in the MKW area, and the rights under BSTs in MKW's name);

(b) pursuant to a JVA or other similar arrangement, FDWS and SEW would jointly procure, construct, operate and maintain any major new resource and jointly negotiate any necessary agreements with third parties;

(c) the physical assets associated with any major new development would be directly controlled by FDWS and SEW jointly and not by the JRC; and

(d) smaller new developments would be invested in, developed and owned by the companies in whose areas they were situated, but with the abstraction licences held by the JRC.

6.9. GU and SAUR emphasized that they had no intention that other water undertakers should be excluded from participation in any future major new resource. They firmly believed that one of the many attractions of the proposal was the more equitable distribution of resources that would result between the water companies serving Kent and East Sussex. They considered that redistribution of water through their planned new infrastructure, the 'mini-grid' (see paragraphs 6.12 and 6.13 and Map 4) and the allocation of abstraction licences to those companies most in need of water would mean that the companies in the region would arrive together at a point when the next major resource development must be planned and implemented.

6.10. The reason why GU and SAUR considered joint ownership of abstraction licences and existing bulk supply rights in the MKW area essential was that each of the enlarged companies needed to have an equal right to the resources available over the entire MKW area, and from any major new resource. Only through both companies having equal rights to the water was it possible for the use of the resources to be optimized, and for rational decisions to be taken as to their development. Optimal use of those resources could not be achieved if their ownership were divided between the two companies on a geographical basis, because it would not be possible to predict in advance where the water would be needed in the future. Without joint ownership the parties would have to rely on purely contractual arrangements for the supply of water between them. GU and SAUR considered such arrangements unsatisfactory in the context of the resource issues facing this region (see paragraphs 6.40 to 6.43). Most important, only joint ownership would give each of the enlarged companies confidence to invest in the mini-grid in the knowledge that the resources of the area would remain available to it. Joint arrangements for similar purposes were not uncommon in other parts of the country.

6.11. Each of the enlarged companies would be committed to work together in the future on any major new resource for the area. A long-term commitment of this nature had never before been achieved between any of the companies of the region. It would allow for rational planning of the next major development. Without a jointly-owned company it would be necessary for the abstraction licences to be in the joint names of the water companies and for decisions to be taken by joint venture and management committees. Although such arrangements might achieve a similar result, GU and SAUR would be very reluctant to agree to this unless there were insuperable concerns about the existence of a separate legal entity. No such concern had been apparent to date.

Planned infrastructure investment ('mini-grid')

6.12. GU and SAUR's proposals for improving infrastructure in the MKW area for the benefit of the combined areas of the proposed enlarged FDWS and SEW are explained in Chapter 5 and illustrated in Map 4 (based on GU's and SAUR's understanding of the existing MKW primary network). The proposed strategic mains links (the 'mini-grid') were estimated to cost £16 million. GU and SAUR also planned a £9 million investment (of which £2.9 million would be capital expenditure) over eight years in enhanced demand management and conservation in order to secure a leakage rate of 5.5 l/prop/h by 2004. The total outlay of £25 million would be funded from within existing K limits, although GU and SAUR said they would expect that the extra capital and operating expenditure after 2000/01 would be recognized within the expenditure projections of the review of K factors in 1999 recently announced by the DGWS. With links from Canterbury/Barham into the present FDWS area, from Kippings Cross to Cottage Hill in the SEW zone and across Mid Kent through a new pipeline between Ashford and Maidstone, the developments were intended to benefit all existing customers of MKW, FDWS and SEW (see paragraph 5.58 for further details). GU and SAUR believed the region was unique in a number of respects:

(a) the scarcity of water resources (in this context they noted that a recent Government report had singled out Kent as the county most adversely affected by climate change);

(b) the very small size of the area's sources (on average about 3 Ml/d compared with a national average of 10 Ml/d); and

(c) the fragmentation of water distribution, with four companies active in a fairly small area through a number of separate networks.

6.13. They were convinced that the creation of the proposed mini-grid was the only approach to optimizing water resources in the region. Its creation hinged on the control of MKW because of its geographical location. Their proposal would reduce the three main networks that made up the distribution systems of SEW, MKW and FDWS to two linked networks with the further benefit of the JRC that would ensure transparency between the two. The flexibility which the mini-grid would bring about would enable the enlarged SEW and FDWS to achieve greater security of supply, opportunities for conjunctive use of sources (and consequent environmental benefits) and an overall improvement in the way in which they used their resources. GU and SAUR estimated that the amount of water which would ideally need to be kept in reserve to deal with outages would be reduced from a current total of 19 Ml/d to 8 Ml/d over the entire network.

Subsidiaries of Mid Kent Holdings

6.14. GU and SAUR could see no circumstances under which they would want to operate jointly any of the five MKH subsidiaries. MKW, which was MKH's main business, would be split evenly by value between FDWS and SEW. [*Details omitted.*
See note on page iv.   ] They did not, however, regard it likely that these subsidiaries would have any significant impact, either detrimental or beneficial, on the public interest consideration of the merger proposals.

Timing of the expected benefits

6.15. As far as GU and SAUR were concerned it did not make great practical sense to attempt to allocate the expected benefits of the merger proposals (see paragraph 6.17 onwards) to one or other of the formal stages. These stages were necessary steps on the way to completing all the arrangements. In practice the benefits would start to accrue immediately as it was the companies' intention to undertake the necessary investment and new demand management policies as soon as they could. They expected, for example, substantially to complete their proposed new strategic mains links within the MKW area by the year 2000.

Timing of changes to Mid Kent Water's status as a comparator

6.16. It was clear, in GU's and SAUR's view, that MKW would cease to be an independent comparator as soon as Stage 1 of the proposed arrangements was put into effect. Although the companies would intend at the same time to begin putting Stage 2 into effect, for example through having separate management of the new eastern and western areas, they accepted that until Stage 2 could formally be completed it would be necessary to continue to provide aggregated accounting and comparator information for MKW as an entity. The companies would be content to discuss and agree requirements with OFWAT.

The expected benefits of the proposals

Main benefits

6.17. GU and SAUR said that the proposed acquisition would have a number of significant benefits. Appendix 6.1, an extract from the affidavit submitted by Martin Smith (a solicitor acting for GU) in the course of the High Court proceedings in April 1996 brought by MKH against GU, provides a summary of the expected benefits. These would include:

— the means of alleviating the present water resource imbalance in the region;

— the provision by GU and SAUR of an integrated supply network which would optimize resource usage and improve security of supply for customers of all three existing water companies;

— a practical means of supporting the EA's resources strategy in the Southern Region;

— the ability to carry out long-term resource planning on a regional basis—this would better enable companies in the region to have converging views on when a new major resource would be required;

— the establishment of an improved programme of leakage reduction and metering promotion aiming at a reduction of 30 per cent of the water losses over the area of the water companies by 2004/05;

— action later on (2009) to generate additional water resources, for example from the Medway system through resource optimization on a catchment basis (a report, commissioned for GU and SAUR, by consultants at the Institute of Hydrology gave reason to believe that the water yield from the Medway system could be increased by 25 Ml/d);

— a resource management and water conservation programme (involving action on customer education, tariff structures and other incentives, water conservation charters etc as well as action on leakage and metering);

— provision for conjunctive use of surface and groundwater sources to achieve both environmental benefits and security of supply benefits;

— improvement of service standards for MKW's customers; and

— creation of better circumstances for genuine competition in the region as a result of the proposed acquisition acting to remedy current regional water resource imbalances.

6.18. The companies noted that:

— their proposals on infrastructure, leakage and metering would act to secure that demand over the area of the enlarged water companies would be met until at least 2009/10 when MKW was thought to expect to reach deficit;

— the realization of the proposed additional Medway system resources could defer the need for a major new resource until around 2013 to 2016; and

— the proposed resource management and water conservation programme would also act to defer this need, possibly for an additional three to five years.

6.19. The companies were also committed to ensuring that the expected benefits (at a cost of some £25 million) would be provided without extra cost to customers of any of the three companies. GU and SAUR would not seek to reopen the present K determination. In addition the postponement of a major new regional resource facility would mean deferral of major investment which they estimated at £80 million (at today's prices).

6.20. GU and SAUR questioned the EA's apparently sceptical attitude to their initial proposal to extract further water from the Medway. They found it surprising that the EA had indicated that it was unlikely that it would grant licences in relation to a proposal that was based on abstracting additional water in 2009, basing its view on studies completed as long ago as 1991. GU and SAUR wondered how the EA was able to express such a view so far in advance. GU and SAUR believed it was incumbent on the EA to give proper consideration to the potential for increased resources described in their consultants' report. By indicating that it would be unlikely to license a scheme such as that outlined by GU and SAUR, the EA appeared to be prejudging the viability of future schemes.

6.21. Following a very recent meeting, however, it seemed to GU and SAUR that the EA would in fact be prepared to look at any proposals which addressed the EA's concerns about the existing flow conditions in the Medway.

Other aspects

6.22. Besides the benefits described above, GU and SAUR also estimated that a saving of £1.25 million a year in head office administration might be achievable through changes to the top management structure and in the use of information technology.

6.23. GU and SAUR were asked why their claimed solution to the water imbalance in the region could be considered complete given that most of the available surplus resources lay with SWS. GU and SAUR were of the firm view that the proposed arrangements would work for a sufficiently long period ahead. They left open the possibility of co-operating with SWS, for example over a major new resource development when that proved to be necessary.

Effect of proposals on the comparator system and competition

Issues concerning numbers of comparators

6.24. In the view of GU and SAUR the fact that the proposed arrangements resulted in a reduction in the number of comparators did not of itself equate to any prejudice to the comparator system. It needed to be borne in mind that:

— the resource imbalances in the region operated to the detriment of comparative competition;

— MKW had been a consistently poor performer in the rankings of water companies by the DGWS and was, in their view, an inefficient company;

— the enlarged FDWS and SEW were intended to provide two exemplary comparators in terms of demand management and water conservation; in particular, they would provide better comparative bench-marks for SWS;

— the loss of independent data generated by MKW would be more than offset by the improved data from the enlarged FDWS and SEW;

— the net loss of comparators in regional terms would be the equivalent to the loss of the smallest company, FDWS, but would result in a new FDWS company that was closer to the DGWS's stated optimum population size band of 0.5 million to 1 million (the new FDWS would serve some 417,000 people); and

— even after the acquisition of MKW, there would still be four independent comparators in the EA's Southern Region (SWS, the enlarged FDWS and SEW, and Portsmouth Water Company). This was as high as in any other EA Region, and higher than in all but the Thames Region.

Effect of the loss of Mid Kent Water as a comparator

6.25. GU and SAUR considered the methodology proposed by OFWAT for calculating the cash equivalent in NPV terms of the loss of a medium-sized comparator such as MKW to be subjective and not scientifically-based. They refuted the suggestion that the value of loss of MKW from the range of comparators available to the DGWS at the next price review could be of the order of £100 million in NPV terms. They considered, for example, the value ranges in the methodology for assessing the loss to be so wide as to make it suspect. They also considered that it was not realistic to base the assessment on MKW becoming a frontier company in efficiency terms. They noted OFWAT's assumption that 3 per cent of the industry turnover was needed to set a robust industry bench-mark and observed that MKW's turnover (even if aggregated with that of SEW and FDWS) fell below this threshold. They believed that on OFWAT's own criteria the theoretical value of the loss of MKW would be no more than £9 million and that once the full implications of the proposals were taken into account there would be a net benefit to the system. In place of the disappearance of MKW, a poor comparator at present, not only would the average efficiency rating for the industry as a whole rise but also the East Sussex and Kent area would benefit from a solution to the present water resource imbalance. In addition GU and SAUR were proposing to create two new exemplary comparators.

6.26. To the argument that the dynamic nature of the comparator system implied that any company was capable of moving to the efficiency frontier and, therefore, of becoming an exemplary comparator, GU and SAUR considered that it was the quality, rather than the number, of comparators that mattered. While MKW might have the theoretical potential to move to the water industry efficiency frontier, they did not believe it would do so having regard to its performance to date.

6.27. GU and SAUR did not consider that the loss of MKH's status as a listed company would affect the performance of the DGWS's functions. They pointed out that the DGWS's evidence to the MMC in the Lyonnaise case emphasized that there were only ten major companies in the industry with a listing on the Stock Exchange and which had a significant turnover in shares (that is, the ten WaSCs). He had expressly recognized that the shareholdings in the listed WoCs were much more tightly held with very little share turnover.

Exemplary status for the enlarged water companies

6.28. GU and SAUR were asked whether FDWS and SEW could become exemplary comparators without the proposed merger. In their view exemplary demand and conservation management depended on the availability of resources. They could only obtain sufficient water by the proposed acquisition. Increased water resources would give GU and SAUR the breathing space to secure the development and the benefits of their exemplary programmes and the time necessary to enable them to evaluate the effect of the programmes.

Improvement of local competition

6.29. GU and SAUR considered that the proposed arrangements would improve competitiveness within the region. Although opportunities to compete were limited, they would be improved if companies locally had adequate water resources of their own and an adequate trunk main system providing the ability to transfer water to new customers. The proposed arrangements were expressly designed to secure this situation, which did not currently exist. At present competition could only work one way. Companies like SWS and MKW which had surpluses would be able to pick and choose FDWS's and SEW's best customers, especially if FDWS and SEW were at the same time reliant on BSTs provided by SWS and MKW.

Effect of the proposed Joint Resources Company on the comparator system

6.30. The JRC would have limited functions and would be transparent for cost purposes. The operating companies would continue to be wholly comparable with other water companies. The JRC would not be involved in the planning or day-to-day implementation of any of the proposed demand management or water conservation measures. Nor would it be involved with the fulfilment of any of the operating companies' levels of service to customers.

6.31. Nor did GU and SAUR consider that the existence of the JRC or any other form of joint ownership of resource rights would blur the distinctiveness of SEW or FDWS as comparators. The DoE and Welsh Office recent water resources report,[1] at paragraph 11.23, stated that 'Just as in times past major new resources were developed by water companies or water boards acting co-operatively, so might the present water industry consider the scope for joint ventures in promoting strategic water resource schemes'. GU and SAUR agreed with this and considered that much of the rest of this report, for example on leakage, education and planning, was very much in line with their own restructuring proposals.

---

[1] *Water Resources and Supply: Agenda for Action*, October 1996.

6.32. GU and SAUR said that they were aware of at least six schemes in England and Wales in which resources were owned or managed jointly by two or more companies. Similarly, GU and SAUR understood that there also existed other arrangements, for example that between Severn Trent and Anglian Water entered into in October 1995, between water companies for co-operation in other aspects of their businesses, for example joint billing arrangements. They were not aware that, in any of the existing joint arrangements between other companies, the DGWS had considered that co-operative arrangements would diminish the independence of the companies concerned for the purposes of comparative competition.

Effect of the proposed Joint Resources Company on competition

6.33. There was no reason, in GU and SAUR's view, why the JRC should limit competition between their water companies. If each had enough headroom, in terms of water resources, they could compete. The principle underlying the JRC was not different from joint ventures in the oil and gas industry. In the North Sea the companies in this industry were members of consortia. But in marketing the gas and oil, all were competitors.

Effect of the proposed Joint Resources Company on regulatory matters

6.34. GU and SAUR did not believe that the existence of the JRC or joint ownership would reduce the scope for cross-border competition between the operating companies. First, it should be pointed out that the potential for competition across the proposed boundary (whether by inset appointments or otherwise) was unlikely to be great given the predominantly rural nature of the area. Secondly, where there was potential for cross-border competition, the fact that the parties would have joint rights to the relevant resources would not make such competition any less likely. Indeed, the fact that joint ownership made a greater quantity of water available to each of the operating companies meant that there was greater scope for cross-border competition.

6.35. GU and SAUR did not believe that the existence of a separate, jointly-owned company would of itself create any regulatory problems, albeit that the JRC would not itself be a regulated company. They would be prepared to provide the DGWS with whatever information he required. They were prepared to enter into undertakings which would make the reporting requirements of the JRC equivalent to those of a regulated company and would work with the DGWS to address any regulatory concerns he might have. GU and SAUR did not consider that there would in practice be regulatory difficulties. For example, it was true that the JRC, which would not be a water undertaker, could not itself apply for drought orders under section 73(3) of the 1991 Act. However, SEW and FDWS could do so, and in such a way as to permit the JRC to take the necessary consequential action.

Water resources

Optimizing resource use

6.36. GU's and SAUR's main reason for their proposals was that they firmly believed a regional solution needed to be found to the question of resource availability and optimization of its use. The benefit of the proposals, in their view, was the implementation of a permanent optimization of water resources. When it came to the point of general resource shortage, the two enlarged companies would both arrive at the same point at the same time. Together they would be a positive and strong force for finding a new major resource; separately they would be less capable of managing the situation.

Involving Southern Water Services

6.37. Although SWS had substantial surplus resources in the Southern Region as a whole, the two companies did not believe SWS had significant surplus resources in this part of the Southern Region. Furthermore, they did not feel that either SWS or MKW was committed to resolving regional resource imbalances, or to reallocating licences on a fairer basis. SWS had withdrawn from the joint agreement with SEW to enlarge Darwell reservoir and from the promotion of Broad Oak reservoir with FDWS and MKW in 1993, once the EA had approved a new resource scheme at Yalding. MKW, which was a beneficiary of this scheme, had followed suit in 1994. SWS also later withdrew from the joint discussions with FDWS, MKW and SEW over resource optimization. Nevertheless, GU and SAUR were entirely content, in principle, for SWS to join in the development of future resource strategy for the region. In the meantime, they were satisfied that their proposals were sufficient for a long period into the future, possibly up to around 2020.

Guarantees for Mid Kent Water's customers

6.38. Because of their proposed improvements to infrastructure and their plans for demand management, GU and SAUR did not believe that existing MKW customers would suffer any loss of security of supply as a result of sharing the modest MKW surplus with those parts of the SEW and FDWS areas with shortages. Indeed GU and SAUR were committed to matching and improving on MKW's own predictions of resource availability. They noted that the supply problems which MKW had encountered during the summer of 1995 which had led to widespread hose-pipe and sprinkler bans were largely distribution-related, rather than the result of a shortage of water. The strategic mains links involved in the mini-grid would considerably improve distribution within the current MKW area.

Mutual co-operation as an alternative to the merger

6.39. GU and SAUR said that over a number of years FDWS and SEW had (alone, jointly and in conjunction with MKW and SWS) explored all means of redressing the regional resource imbalance short of merger. These discussions had failed because of the absence of a shared economic interest. Bulk supplies, whatever other objections the two companies had to them (see the next paragraph), only dealt with piecemeal aspects of the problem and were not necessarily available when needed. What was required was a permanent regional solution.

Reasons to oppose bulk supply transfers as an alternative solution

6.40. The two companies gave several reasons in support of their strongly held contention that BSTs would not be a satisfactory means of resolving the resource imbalances in this case, and also provided a supplementary joint submission on the issue. They said that:

— The benefits of the proposed arrangements would not be achievable through bulk supplies. The benefits arose from the construction of an integrated supply network, the management of resources on a catchment basis, the promotion of conservation and the conjunctive use of sources.

— BSTs were not capable of resolving a long-term structural imbalance of the kind that prevailed in the region, nor of prolonging the life of existing resources through an integrated solution.

— GU and SAUR had no 'philosophical' opposition to BSTs. They were, however, opposed to them where the two companies concerned were not in an equal position and could not make BSTs available to each other on a reciprocal basis.

— BSTs provided less incentive to the supplier to save water; they were inefficient in conservation terms, risky in terms of water quality, would perpetuate/aggravate imbalances, and would be costly to put in place. Furthermore, any infrastructure put in place to take BSTs would not be as useful as a system implementing a co-ordinated regional strategy. In addition, suppliers would tend to put the interests of their own customers first. When it came to a choice between cutting off a BST or reducing supplies to one's own customers, a supplying company would choose the former.

— BST agreements were difficult to enforce in practice. Where supplies were cut off the recipient's only possible remedy would be damages, which would not compensate for the damage to the recipient's customer relations and service levels. If any one of a series of bulk supply agreements was defaulted upon, it could upset the entire resource optimization strategy.

— Bulk supplies would perpetuate the dominance of companies in surplus. Companies providing such supplies were more likely to be granted additional abstraction licences than those receiving these supplies. Companies receiving bulk supplies had a more difficult task to demonstrate the need for new licences.

— BSTs weakened the competitive process. Not only would they distort comparative data provided to the DGWS, but they would also constrain the recipient when there was question of competing with the supplier. A company could only be a credible alternative supplier if it had sufficient water resources of its own.

— The supplier of a bulk supply would tend to be in a better position to compete at low prices for customers in the recipient's area, as a result of the fact that prices for bulk supplies were likely to be at comparatively high levels owing to the need to pay for additional infrastructure and, where the price was set by the DGWS, to allow the supplier a reasonable return on its capital.

— BSTs did not convey the same operational and commercial freedoms as ownership. The recipient, especially one who had little or no resource headroom, had no practical means of guaranteeing continuity of supply. This could cause severe problems even where such supplies represented a relatively small proportion of total demand.

— Although the DGWS had the power to set terms for BSTs, these powers were limited by the mandatory criteria in the legislation, for example not to put at risk the supplier's ability to discharge its existing obligations. Nor did the DGWS have the power to create the kind of integrated regional solution which GU and SAUR were proposing. Even if it were in fact possible to achieve a practical solution by using the DGWS's powers in this way, it seemed to GU and SAUR that it would almost be necessary for the DGWS to be in permanent session over a variation application under section 40A of the 1991 Act, acting as a hands-on micro-manager of the area's water resources. This line of reasoning would mean a reversal of the privatization process that gave rise to the new regime which the relevant legislation was aimed at implementing. GU and SAUR did not believe it was ever intended that the legislation should be used in this way, or that it would be practical to do so.

6.41. In GU's and SAUR's view, the situation in the region was one where their two companies were in or approaching deficit, while the other two companies, SWS and MKW, had a monopoly of the availability of surplus resources. These companies had no interest, therefore, in offering bulk supplies unless they were compelled to by the regulator. GU and SAUR did not feel that they could plan long term on the basis of possible new bulk supply offers which might or might not materialize. In any case they faced the objections set out above. These objections included the likelihood that SWS and MKW would reinforce their dominant position through the probability of obtaining additional licences based partly on having granted GU's and SAUR's companies some bulk supplies. FDWS referred in this context to the termination by MKW of their bulk supply at Barham in 1992 on three weeks' notice.

6.42. GU and SAUR were asked whether they would have a stronger case for their proposed course of action if they had first asked the DGWS for a satisfactory solution under a bulk supply arrangement. GU said that they had explored with the DoE, the NRA and OFWAT through a series of meetings in the first half of 1995 the question whether BSTs imposed by the DGWS could give the recipient effective control of the supply (equating to ownership). The purpose of the approach had been to establish whether long-term bulk supplies could work at a conceptual level before putting forward any particular proposal to the DGWS. The conclusion which GU and SAUR had themselves drawn from these discussions was that the level of control they desired was not achievable. GU and SAUR said that in their view:

— BSTs were unable to provide a satisfactory solution in the present situation;

— BSTs would weaken their competitive position; and

— overlaying BSTs on the present position where there was a fundamental imbalance in the resources held by the companies in the region threatened the survival of companies lacking resources like FDWS and SEW in the medium term and would do nothing to resolve the imbalance.

6.43. GU and SAUR said that in the present case any 'solution' involving BSTs, even if it offered a means of remedying resource imbalances in the region (which they believed it would not), would entail a substantial cost, for which there was no allowance in present Ks. Their proposals provided a real solution and one which they were willing to finance from within existing price limits. FDWS said that it had conducted a costing exercise to assess the likely costs of resolving its resources deficit. Using illustrative bulk supply tariffs based on [*] per cent of the standard tariffs of the relevant companies, FDWS estimated that it would be necessary to increase its price limits by just under 6 per cent.

Whether proposals are the only means of obtaining the expected benefits

6.44. GU and SAUR said that, even leaving aside their objections to the BST possibilities, they did not believe the expected benefits were obtainable other than through the proposed arrangements. Although MKW was in theory capable of making the demand management changes proposed by GU and SAUR, they doubted whether MKW would in fact do so. The customers of all three water companies would be faced with the likelihood of funding alternative resource solutions much earlier than would be the case under the proposals. In addition, the effectiveness of FDWS and of SEW as comparators would be eroded over time through increasing reliance on BSTs. Finally, the DGWS would be unlikely to obtain the two new exemplary comparators proposed under the arrangements.

Remedies

General

6.45. The two companies were asked to consider appropriate remedies, in the event of a finding by the MMC that the loss of a comparator was against the public interest, such remedies to act as the basis on which the acquisition might nonetheless proceed. GU and SAUR said that they believed there was no detriment. They were proposing a satisfactory permanent solution to an unsatisfactory major regional water resource imbalance, and the creation, in demand management respects, of two new exemplary comparators in place of an indifferent one. They were also proposing to invest £19 million and spend a further £6 million over eight years, all within existing Ks, to realize their proposals. The MMC might choose to regard this expenditure as a 'remedy', rather than as a positive ingredient of the solution which the two companies preferred. If the MMC considered this to be insufficient, however, it might even be inferred by GU and SAUR that they should reconsider the proposed acquisition, though this was not an all-or-nothing case, and their decision would depend on the overall economic package they faced.

Prices

6.46. If there were to be a recommendation that GU and SAUR should be required to introduce price cuts and possibly also meet performance criteria too, the companies would need to consider the cost and other conditions and whether this would affect the viability of their proposals. GU and SAUR would regard a price reduction (in addition to the investment inherent in their proposals) as a double penalty. They were already prepared to spend a great deal in order to solve the regional resource problems. A price reduction would be the equivalent of a further penalty for taking the initiative of solving the resource problems.

---

*Figure omitted. See note on page iv.

Stock Exchange listing

6.47. The suggestion that the regulated water businesses of both groups should be listed on the Stock Exchange as a price for the loss of one comparator would, in GU's and SAUR's view, be a quite disproportionate remedy. If, alternatively, for example, the listing of FDWS were contemplated, GU pointed out that even after the merger it would only be worth about £27 million in turnover. GU considered that the concept of listing an enlarged FDWS would be wholly irrelevant. Neither GU nor SAUR had the practice of listing their subsidiaries. If the purpose of listing was not so much the listing itself as to achieve some of the features associated with listing, such as information about trading with associated companies, it might be possible to come to a mutually satisfactory agreement with the DGWS. GU and SAUR understood that the DGWS had in any case been examining with ScottishPower alternatives to a full listing for SWS. GU and SAUR noted that SWS was a WaSC and therefore the listing issue was much more important than in this inquiry.

Performance and proposed EA partial remedies

6.48. The companies believed that the EA's proposals for demand and resource management suggested as partial remedies (see paragraph 9.40) were very much in line with their own proposals. They would be willing to comply with many of them, for example the concept of an enforceable action plan for balancing supply and demand, and exemplary approaches on leakage, metering, tariffs, etc. Not all the EA ideas were practicable, however, either in the form set or by the date suggested (for example, compulsory metering of garden sprinklers during hose-pipe bans).

6.49. Commenting further on EA's revised proposed 'partial' remedies, GU and SAUR said they did not accept that any measures beyond those they had already proposed were necessary to prevent or remedy an adverse effect on the public interest. However, they were pleased that the EA accepted in principle that a solution to the resource problems of the region was in the public interest, and that measures of the sort proposed by the parties would both deliver that solution and create exemplary comparators in demand management and water conservation. Indeed they noted that implicit in the EA's judgment was the acceptance that the purpose of the proposed merger was not only in the public interest but of substantially greater significance in relation to the public interest than any detriment that might result from the loss of MKW as an independent comparator.

6.50. On the hypothetical assumption that the MMC found an adverse effect on the public interest:

(a) GU and SAUR would accept the concept of enforceable Action Plans agreed with the EA and OFWAT though they believed that the proposed timetable of agreeing and implementing the Action Plans was over-ambitious given the proximity of the preliminary work for the next Periodic Review in 1999. They would accept that the Action Plan should demonstrate exemplary approaches to the matters set out by the EA, which were already included in GU and SAUR's proposals.

(b) GU and SAUR accepted the need for a full appraisal of the scope and value of all options for transfer of water resources and would be willing to participate fully in such an exercise. GU and SAUR envisaged that the exercise would cover all options for resource transfers including transfer of licences and joint ownership of resources as well as considering the wider implications of such options, including the extent of optimization of the resources, the relative impact on competition, environmental consequences of the options, levels of security of supply and fairness of resource allocation.

(c) GU and SAUR were willing to use their best endeavours to assist the EA in alleviating the low flows in the Darent, Little Stour and Dour catchments. They would be prepared to include in their Action Plans a commitment to an evaluation, within one year of the merger, of a programme for management of sources within the catchments of these rivers so as to maximize flows. Equally the EA would need to establish, on the basis of scientific evidence, that reductions in abstractions would have the desired effect on river flows. GU and SAUR could not agree to discard any licence entitlements without an equivalent compensation, and where additional expenditure was required they would need to secure funding at the next price review.

(d) GU and SAUR were also willing in principle to preserve the availability of information flows in respect of the old MKW area for a period of time so that data in respect of the enlarged SEW and FDWS could be disaggregated.

6.51. As far as the other EA proposals were concerned:

(a) GU and SAUR believed that following the restructuring they would be able to achieve a leakage level of 120 l/prop/d in their own existing areas and could commit to this within the period proposed. Achieving the MKW target of 120 l/prop/d by 1997/98 (a revised target that was only published after the announcement of the possible bid) would represent a dramatic improvement on the 1994/95 figure. GU and SAUR drew a clear distinction between targets and commitments. Before they had had an adequate opportunity to review the background to and justification for the MKW target, GU and SAUR would be reluctant to extend their commitment to 120 l/prop/d across the entire enlarged areas (that is, over an area including the whole of MKW's existing area).

(b) A free meter option in the new enlarged areas was acceptable, and was indeed one which GU and SAUR were in any case proposing.

(c) There were difficulties in imposing compulsory meters on garden sprinkler use while a hose-pipe ban was in force. But GU and SAUR were prepared to commit themselves to this measure as soon as the benefits of their restructuring proposals enabled them to do so.

Miscellaneous legal issues

Interpretation of section 34(3)(b) of the Water Industry Act 1991

6.52. GU and SAUR were asked for their views on the correct interpretation of section 34(3)(b). Their understanding of the effect of section 34(3) was that in assessing the public interest consequences of a merger of water enterprises the MMC must have regard to two things:

— the desirability of giving effect to the principle that the comparative competition process should not be prejudiced; and

— the desirability of achieving any other purpose.

However, it could only have regard to the desirability of achieving any 'other purpose' if the conditions of subparagraphs (i) or (ii) of section 34(3)(b) were satisfied. All possible 'other purposes' must of necessity fall within either subparagraph (i) or subparagraph (ii). They were mutually exclusive. Between them they covered all possible situations.

6.53. The factor that determined which of the two subparagraphs of section 34(3)(b) a given 'other purpose' fell into was whether or not, as a matter of fact, it could be achieved in a manner that conflicted with the comparator principle. If it did not, it fell within (i). If it did, it fell within (ii). These were the only two possibilities. The function of the phrase '... and cannot be brought about except in a manner that conflicts with that principle' at the end of subparagraph (ii) simply served to distinguish between the situations to which subparagraphs (i) and (ii) respectively applied.

Issues not directly deriving from mergers of water enterprises

6.54. GU and SAUR were asked to consider the issue whether the MMC should or should not take into account arguments relating to issues which did not directly derive from the creation of mergers between water enterprises. GU and SAUR did not consider that there were any material public interest issues in the present inquiry relating to the merger of non-water enterprises. Nor did they see any legal impediment preventing the MMC from taking account of any of the benefits they claimed for their proposals. In their view, the MMC clearly had the power to take account of any consequences flowing from the merger of water enterprises themselves, even where those consequences were felt in areas or markets other than those in which the water enterprises operated, and even if not related to issues of comparative competition. They included within this category any consequences of the coming under common control of assets which, while not owned by a water enterprise, were used for the benefit of or, in the words of section 33(2) of the 1991 Act, were 'appropriated to' a water enterprise. MKH's headquarters operation should be regarded as appropriated to MKW because the headquarters operation was largely devoted to the water enterprise.

6.55. Secondly, GU and SAUR would not make a distinction between the direct and indirect consequences of the merger of water enterprises. For any consequence to be taken into account there must be a sufficient degree of causal connection. This applied whether the consequences were direct or indirect. It would be a question of fact and degree in every case.

6.56. Whether the MMC should separately have regard to general competition concerns arising from a merger of non-water enterprises was not a relevant issue in the current inquiry. However, GU and SAUR doubted whether the MMC had the power under a reference under section 32 of the 1991 Act to consider the public interest consequences of the merger of enterprises other than water enterprises where those consequences did not affect the water enterprises or their merger, unless they were specifically empowered to do so under the terms of reference.

Jurisdictional and legal issues concerning the original reference

EC aspects

6.57. In the companies' view, there were no outstanding EC issues following the February 1996 amendment to the JVA. This was made to satisfy the European Commission that there was a binding legal commitment to complete Stage 2, that is to split MKW between FDWS and SEW. This was achieved by placing a specific long-stop date for completing Stage 2. The intention, however, was to move to Stage 2 early and to complete it as quickly as possible.

Arrangements in progress

6.58. GU and SAUR considered that they had established that arrangements were in progress within the meaning of section 32 of the 1991 Act. They had signed a JVA on 20 December 1995, the day before announcing their prospective bid, which set out the arrangements for establishing a jointly-owned company to make the joint offer for MKH. Among other things they had also held Board meetings to authorize the announcement, obtained approval from their respective parent companies and appointed legal and financial advisers. Further, the companies also believed that both stages of the merger proposals were covered by the arrangements in progress. Both were integral to the proposals and were expressly contemplated in the 20 December agreement. GU and SAUR believed, from the papers filed by MKH in the context of the litigation brought earlier in the year against GU in relation to the 1991 undertakings, that MKH too had accepted that arrangements were in progress. In his judgment Mr Justice Knox had noted that 'Both parties ... were agreed that there are indeed arrangements in progress which, if carried into effect, would result in a merger of two water enterprises within the meaning of section 32(1)(a) of the Water Industry Act 1991'.

Number of mergers

6.59. GU and SAUR were asked to comment on how the proposed arrangements should be analysed for the purposes of the FTA. They said that they regarded the total number of mergers as a technicality. They said that there were a number of possible ways of analysing the proposals. However, the ultimate objective was to achieve Stage 2. This was the merger of FDWS with MKEast, and that of SEW with MKWest, with the two enlarged water companies retaining a joint subsidiary, the JRC, for water resource sharing and planning purposes. GU and SAUR were asked to comment on the proposition that the MMC should treat the proposed transaction as one merger, commencing with GU and SAUR (acting as associated persons at the time of the possible bid) jointly acquiring a controlling interest in MKH and having as a direct consequence the achievement of Stage 2. In response GU and SAUR said that they would not dissent from such a proposition.

Assets test

6.60. Both GU and SAUR were companies whose existing water enterprises had assets exceeding £30 million in each case. Secondly, on the basis that Stage 2 should be considered as giving rise to two further mergers, it was their intention to split MKW, whose assets amounted to some £100 million, into two parts which they intended to make as near equal in value as possible, as well as providing for the JRC. The proposed JRC would be owned 50:50 by the enlarged FDWS and SEW. Its assets, at least in the early years, would consist mainly of abstraction licences without the underlying land or other tangible assets. It was clear, therefore, that the value of the assets taken over by FDWS and SEW would also exceed £30 million in each case. As far as the companies were concerned the assets test in the 1991 Act was satisfied.

Issues concerning the variation of the terms of reference (13 September) on a possible merger in being

6.61. GU and SAUR submitted joint written evidence in relation to the extended terms of reference; this covered whether GU and SAUR were currently acting together to secure or exercise control of MKH; possible remedial action; and the time limits affecting the MMC inquiry. Subsequently GU and SAUR were questioned separately, then together. After that GU and SAUR submitted a Counsel's opinion on some of the issues.

6.62. The only basis on which it appeared to GU and SAUR to be suggested that they had been or were acting together to secure or exercise control of MKH was by virtue of the 20 December JVA or their voting at the meetings of MKH shareholders held in July 1996. In order for two persons to become associated persons within the meaning of section 77(4)*(d)* of the FTA it was necessary for them to be taking action which itself could have the effect of securing or exercising control over the body. Acting together with a view in the future to securing control was insufficient. The effect of the JVA was, in GU and SAUR's judgment, that they were merely taking steps preparatory to launching a possible future bid for MKH (namely participating in the MMC process with a view to obtaining regulatory clearance). Whether they chose to launch a bid would depend, among other things, on the outcome of the regulatory process and whether they could agree between each other the price and other terms to be offered to MKH shareholders. Entry into and announcement of the JVA was the necessary prerequisite to establish that arrangements were in progress under section 32(1) of the 1991 Act and to ensure that MKH's shareholders were properly informed of what was proposed. Anything less than that would have created both regulatory and shareholder confusion. There was no other way the process of seeking regulatory approval for the proposed acquisition could have been put in train.

6.63. At least four further key steps would have to take place before GU and SAUR would be in a position to contemplate actually acting together to secure control of MKH:

(a) the Secretary of State would have to clear the proposed offer;

(b) any conditions which the Secretary of State might decide to stipulate would have to be acceptable to both parties (as contemplated by the JVA);

(c) the 1991 undertakings given by GU (see Appendix 6.2) would have to be released, or at least varied sufficiently to enable an offer to proceed; and

(d) in the light of whatever regulatory conditions might be imposed and taking account of all market (and other relevant) conditions prevailing at the time, GU and SAUR would have to agree a price to be offered to MKH's shareholders.

The point at which they announced a formal offer to shareholders was the earliest date on which it could be said that GU and SAUR would be acting together to secure control of MKH. In contrast, there was a lack of causal nexus between the current arrangements and the acquisition of shares in MKH. Too many significant intervening events were required, some of them outside the control of the parties and some of them within their control. At the present time, the parties were merely seeking to obtain the necessary clearances to enable matters to move forward.

6.64. A number of other aspects of the JVA should be noted. First, it ceased to be of any further force or effect if no offer was made or if an offer was made but did not succeed. Secondly, the agreement was totally silent about the way in which GU and SAUR should vote their respective shareholdings in MKH during the current regulatory process, because it was not GU and SAUR's intention, when entering into the JVA, to use their current shareholdings individually or together to influence the policy of MKH. Their plans were much more fundamental and could only be achieved by gaining full control of MKH, with a view to creating an enlarged FDWS and an enlarged SEW. In any event, GU would not have entered into such an arrangement, given the 1991 undertakings. Indeed, clause 3 of the JVA specifically provided, among other things, that they would not enter into any 'arrangement' which might result in an infringement of the undertakings. The JVA represented the totality of the arrangement between GU and SAUR.

6.65. Subsequently GU and SAUR submitted an Opinion from Counsel to the effect that there were two possible interpretations of section 77(4)*(d)* of the FTA. The first was that two persons are 'associated' where they act together with the joint purpose of in the future securing or exercising control over a body corporate. Under this interpretation the word 'to' means 'with a view to'. The second possible interpretation was that persons only become associated when they actually take a step which is a step towards securing or exercising control, for example buying shares with a view to obtaining control. The word 'to' in this construction means 'with the effect of'. On the first construction uncertainty arises as to when the merger occurs. That uncertainty would be unsatisfactory for two principal reasons. These are, first, because of the very serious consequences which can flow from holding that a merger situation exists; and, secondly, because of the uncertainty which it would create in terms of the application of the time limits under section 34(4) of the 1991 Act (see paragraph 6.79).

6.66. Counsel said that he would favour the second construction unless the FTA provided some mechanism whereby the fact that parties were associated did not inevitably lead to the conclusion that they therefore controlled the relevant company. He thought, however, that section 65(3) provided that mechanism (see paragraphs 6.72 and 6.73). If the section 65(3) mechanism worked in the way he advocated he thought that would tend to point in favour of the first construction. Once the effect of section 65(3) was recognized, the importance to be attached to the question whether GU and SAUR were associated to a large extent disappeared. The important question was therefore the proper interpretation of section 65(3).

6.67. The joint written evidence of GU and SAUR further submitted that they did not collude in any way, directly or indirectly, in relation to their voting at the AGM and the EGM of MKH in July 1996. A very conscious decision was taken independently by each company that they should not discuss these matters at all and their advisers were instructed accordingly. The two companies went through independent management processes (involving their respective external legal advisers) in order to decide how to vote. In the event, GU and SAUR had voted in a quite different manner on the various resolutions (see Appendix 6.3) which were put to the meetings. The two companies had voted as follows (see also Appendix 3.1):

Resolution	Type	GU	SAUR
1	Ordinary	Abstain	In favour
2	Ordinary	Abstain	In favour
3	Ordinary	In favour	In favour
4	Ordinary	Against	Abstain
5	Special	Against	Abstain
6	Special	Abstain	Against
Performance share plan	Ordinary	Against	Against
Class Resolution for preference shareholders corresponding to Resolution 6	Extraordinary	Abstain	Against

Source: GU and SAUR.

6.68. The only resolution against which both GU and SAUR voted concerned the performance share plan. They had each told their respective legal advisers that the reason they voted against this resolution was that they each, independently, considered that the performance plan was not in line with the

Greenbury Report or the ABI guidelines.[1] GU and SAUR felt it was significant that institutional shareholders who voted in favour of a number of other resolutions chose to abstain on this one. As far as resolution 6 was concerned (authority in respect of a share buy-back), GU had abstained and SAUR had voted against. SAUR told us that this resolution was conditional on the approval of preference shareholders at the separate general meeting. They said that before the vote was taken at the AGM the Chairman announced that sufficient proxy votes had already been received to defeat the resolution at the separate class meeting, and therefore the AGM vote was academic. At the separate meeting of preference shareholders, where the resolution would, if a poll were taken, have been defeated by proxy votes already received, SAUR was, it said, encouraged by the Chairman of the meeting to vote, in order to avoid the need for a poll. SAUR duly voted against the resolution, GU again abstained and the resolution was defeated. GU and SAUR told us that they subsequently discovered that the proxy votes were from a shareholder or shareholders other than GU or SAUR.

6.69. GU and SAUR considered that it was almost inevitable during a regulatory process as long as this particular one that the target of a possible offer would have cause to put resolutions of one sort or another to its shareholders. That being the case, it was inevitably the case that GU and SAUR might, independently, decide to vote the same way on one or more resolutions. Of itself, this did not cause them to be associated persons. Any other proposition would effectively mean that, in order to avoid the possibility of it being suggested that they were associated persons, they would have had to disenfranchise themselves, by agreeing not to vote. That would have been a surprising and unprecedented proposition. Moreover, agreement not to vote would itself have been an act of collusion amounting to a form of negative control. An alternative which might be suggested was that GU and SAUR should, by agreement, have voted with the Board on everything. That would, they considered, have amounted to action designed to secure control of the company. The only proper course, and the one which GU and SAUR followed, was for each of them to vote independently.

6.70. Finally, GU and SAUR rejected the argument that the events at the AGM-EGM in any way undermined the ability of MKH to manage the company and its finances independently.

Section 65(3) of the Fair Trading Act 1973

6.71. If, for these reasons, GU and SAUR were not to be treated as associated persons within the definition of section 77 of the FTA, there was no basis on which they could be said currently to 'control' MKH within the definition of section 65. There was therefore no existing merger situation. However, even if the MMC were of the view that GU and SAUR were associated persons, it would be perfectly open to the MMC to conclude that in the particular circumstances of this case that association did not give them 'control' within the meaning of section 65(3) of the FTA. The effect of that subsection was that a person able directly or indirectly to control or materially to influence the policy of a body corporate, but which did not have a controlling interest in that body corporate, might be treated as having control of it, but was not automatically deemed to have control. In this context GU and SAUR considered it important that they had only come together for the purpose of making a possible bid; that apart from that possible bid there was nothing that linked them; that if it failed their 'association' would end; and that there was no collusion between them in relation to the voting of their respective shareholdings. In those circumstances the correct conclusion was that there was no completed present merger because their link was not such as meant they exercised control. In brief, GU and SAUR did not accept the proposition that there was or might be a completed merger by reason of their coming together in order to effect a prospective merger and for no other purpose.

6.72. After the hearing GU and SAUR submitted an opinion of Counsel which indicated that it was plain from section 65(3) that even where the MMC were dealing with one person who was able materially to influence policy, it did not necessarily follow that that one person should be treated as controlling the relevant body corporate. The fact that that one person was in fact two persons treated as one by the FTA did not obviate the need to examine the circumstances in which that shareholding was held and how it was likely to be voted. That, in turn, would involve consideration of the relationship between the two

---

[1] (1) 'Directors' remuneration': report of study group by Sir Richard Greenbury (17 July 1995). (2) 'Share option schemes': guidance note issued by the Association of British Insurers (17 February 1995).

relevant blocks of shares. It was difficult to see how the matter could properly be described as a matter of discretion.

6.73. GU's and SAUR's Counsel said that the argument that the JVA of itself led to the conclusion that GU and SAUR had control was fallacious. That agreement involved no element of control until the bid, if it was made, was successful. It might be contended that the JVA created such an identity of interest between GU and SAUR as to how to vote, at least in relation to those resolutions which might affect their bid, that the JVA inevitably led, even without collusion, to joint voting on critical resolutions. The argument then went that they should therefore be treated as exercising control by voting together. It was plain that GU and SAUR were not voting together on all issues. In relation to the suggestion that they were voting on issues which might 'affect their bid' there was no suggestion that the resolutions on which they did vote together fell within that category. That category was, in any event, almost incapable of definition. In any event the fact that two shareholders had identity of interest, as they very often would have, could not of itself mean that they should be regarded as together controlling a company. For example, the fact that two or more institutions, publicly, adopted similar policies about how they would vote their shareholdings on such issues as share options or directors' remuneration did not thereby render them in control of those companies where they, together, constituted a sufficient minority to influence policy on those issues.

Public interest

6.74. Even if the act of coming together with a view to bringing about a future merger was to be found to have led to the creation of an existing merger, GU and SAUR did not believe any public interest issues would arise separately from those raised by the proposed future merger. If the future merger was cleared those public interest issues were by definition addressed. If it were not, the alleged existing merger would fall away along with the prospective merger. Leaving aside any consequences of the proposed merger, GU and SAUR considered that there was no separate possible detriment to the comparator system which might result from any merger in being. If there were found to be any elements of material influence, these would be wholly transient in nature, because GU and SAUR would either make a bid at the end of the regulatory process, or would not. Either way there would be no long-term effect on the comparator process arising from any merger in being.

6.75. GU's and SAUR's Counsel had also said that if the MMC concluded that there was no collusion, but the commonality of GU's and SAUR's interest as a result of the JVA was such that they invariably voted together on any resolution which might affect the outcome of the possible bid, and they thereby should be treated as having control, it was very doubtful that that would be against the public interest. Where two existing shareholders decided to make a joint bid, it was unrealistic to suggest that it was 'against the public interest' that they did nothing, individually, with the shares whilst they progressed the bid that might damage the bid.

6.76. Counsel said that it was in the public interest that proposed bids be considered by the MMC. It was not in the public interest that the proposal should not even be considered because, if GU and SAUR were correct, it had significant benefits for customers. If that result involved there being in existence a merger which had no other effect save to permit the consideration of the proposed bid, it could have no adverse effect on the present independence of MKH, and was not therefore contrary to the public interest. If the proposed bid did not proceed the relationship between GU and SAUR would cease and there would be no prospective damage to the public interest.

6.77. In any event, even if it could be said that the merger, which on this hypothesis had already occurred, was against the public interest, no remedial action would be required because the relationship would cease upon the failure of or non-proceeding with the possible bid.

Possible remedial action

6.78. Even were the MMC to conclude that a merger situation currently existed and that it operated, or might be expected to operate, against the public interest, no remedial action would be necessary or appropriate in respect of that merger situation. The only basis on which such a merger situation might be found to exist, in their view, was the existence of the JVA itself. If the proposed merger did not proceed, the JVA fell away and with it the basis on which GU and SAUR would have been found to have acted together to secure or exercise control of MKH:

(a) If no offer was made to MKH shareholders, the JVA on its face would fall away. On that basis, GU's and SAUR's status as associated persons (which they denied) would fall away with the demise of the JVA itself.

(b) If the parties were cleared to make an offer and made a successful offer the issue would become moot. The function of the JVA would be superseded and the public interest would be protected by such undertakings (if any) as might be given by GU and SAUR to the Secretary of State before the offer proceeded.

(c) If the offer proceeded but failed, for whatever reason, the JVA on its face again would fall away.

Time limits affecting the MMC inquiry into any existing merger (section 34(4) of the Water Industry Act 1991)

6.79. For the purpose of section 34(4), GU and SAUR considered that the relevant transaction was the JVA. It was made in December 1995 and the DTI was notified of it in advance of its being concluded. At the time of the original reference to the MMC (23 May 1996), the President of the Board of Trade did not refer any suggested completed merger to the MMC. Between December and May there were extensive and detailed discussions between GU, SAUR, the OFT and the DTI. More than six months after making known to the DTI the facts which allegedly led to a completed merger GU and SAUR were entitled to assume that, in the absence of further material not known to the DTI at the date of the original reference, it could not be varied so as to add an alleged completed merger. A variation in this way, without new material facts having come to their notice, would effectively deprive GU and SAUR of the protection of section 34(4).

6.80. In addition, section 71 of the FTA would only permit variation to a merger reference where the variation related to the prospective uncompleted merger already covered by the existing reference. To seek to add retrospectively by way of variation a separate, supposedly already completed merger would effectively circumvent the protection given to GU and SAUR by section 34(4) of the 1991 Act. As a matter of law, the decision taken by the President of the Board of Trade on 13 September amounted, in GU's and SAUR's submission, not to a variation of a merger reference but to the making of a new reference. As such, it was made outside the six-month period referred to in section 34(4). Accordingly, if the MMC concluded that a completed merger had already taken place they should, pursuant to section 34(4), state that fact and nothing else.

6.81. That would be an unfortunate consequence from a public interest point of view because it would mean that the MMC's consideration of the proposed merger would have to assume an aggregated shareholding of approximately 39 per cent held by GU and SAUR. This strengthened GU's and SAUR's views that there was no existing merger situation.

6.82. In a joint hearing, GU and SAUR noted points put about doubts whether or not the time limits in section 34(4) of the 1991 Act applied. Subsequently GU and SAUR made further submissions on this matter. They said that Counsel had advised them that section 34(4) was intended to give parties protection, not only from remedies which might be imposed on a merger, but also from the negative effects of the publication of a report on the matter. Given that there was doubt whether or not they applied, the MMC suggested that it might be safer to investigate and report on a possible merger situation to which the section 34(4) time limit was ultimately shown to have applied, than not to do so and risk the judgment that they should have done. GU and SAUR replied in a letter that it was not open to the MMC to decline to determine whether or not section 34(4) applies, and thereby to deprive GU and SAUR of the intended protection, simply on the ground that the proper legal construction of section 34(4) was uncertain. To do so would deprive section 34(4) of its effect. Appreciating the difficulties that would ensue if a court found, contrary to the MMC's view, that section 34(4) did not apply to a particular merger, Counsel's advice was nevertheless that the correct course was for the MMC to form a view as to the application of section 34(4) and report accordingly.

6.83. GU and SAUR were also asked for their views on the application of section 66A of the FTA to this case. GU's and SAUR's response was that in the present case the JVA was on one analysis one transaction, of a type referred to in section 66A(2), in a series of transactions giving rise to a prospective merger. It could be taken into account under the terms of the original reference as such, and if the prospective merger did not take place within two years from the JVA the position was not affected because section 75(4)*(aa)* (combined with section 66A) deemed the future transactions to take place on the day before the reference. Under the terms of reference announced on 13 September, the JVA had now also been referred to the MMC as a completed merger. If it was a completed merger it took place on 21 December 1995 and so the reference was out of time. The fact that it might also be a step towards a prospective merger did not affect this. Section 75(4)*(aa)* did not apply because it had been referred for investigation as a completed merger. Section 66A could not have the effect of bringing within the scope of the reference of the completed merger the transactions that had not yet occurred because section 66A dealt only with mergers that had already taken place.

Possible existing merger

GU's views

6.84. In a separate hearing with GU representatives the MMC raised with them a number of issues arising from the variation in the terms of reference. The main points put by GU during this hearing were:

   (a) *Ability of GU individually to influence MKH*. GU did not consider that its 19.45 per cent shareholding in MKH gave it any influence on the company or any rights beyond those of normal shareholders. While GU might be able materially to influence or control if it got together with another major shareholder to do so, it had not done so. Simply alleging that GU had similar interests to those of another company, for example on the Greenbury recommendations, and had voted in the same way as that other company, did not mean that GU was able materially to influence the policy of MKH. It had no interests arising through nominees and there were no other shareholders who might be regarded as acting with it to secure or exercise control. The price paid by Morgan Grenfell, which was GU's financial adviser for the proposed merger, for the 9 per cent of shares bought from GU in 1992 was not underwritten by GU, except in very narrowly defined specific circumstances (such as insolvency or default and compulsory acquisition of shares). The agreement provided that if Morgan Grenfell were to sell, GU would receive additional consideration equal to [*] per cent of any profit made by Morgan Grenfell. These arrangements were notified to OFWAT, the OFT and the DTI who had said they were content with the arrangements. The present shareholding of Morgan Grenfell amounted to 9.35 per cent of the total MKH issued capital. As far as the forthcoming redemption of preference shares was concerned on 31 March 1997, as a result of which GU's percentage holding of the ordinary shares would rise from 19.45 to 24.5 per cent, GU could not see any particular consequences for it of that redemption. It would in any case continue to comply with the undertakings given to the Secretary of State for Trade and Industry. Those undertakings had already specifically catered for the redemption situation.

   (b) *Associated persons (and acting together)*. GU said that it and SAUR were not 'associated persons'. There was no sense in which they were acting together to secure or exercise control. The 'acting together' which was occurring was essentially the preparatory steps that needed to be taken for GU and SAUR to be in a position which might, in due course, lead to their seeking to 'secure or exercise control'. GU and SAUR certainly had the intent to get to a position of securing or exercising control but were not engaged in doing so. They had not even decided whether they were going to proceed. There was no contradiction between the GU and SAUR argument that 'arrangements were in progress' and their view that their present 'acting together' was not to secure control, but to complete the prior regulatory process. To the argument that the JVA embodied the concept of acting together to secure control, the GU answer was that the only commitment in the JVA was to GU and SAUR jointly going through the regulatory process. In

---

*Figure omitted. See note on page iv.

GU's view, if the very act of agreeing to put a proposal for merger to the authorities for adjudication created an existing merger situation, then that would be a massive deterrent to making such proposals; at one and the same time both a past and a future merger would be created. Generally, GU felt strongly that if shareholders had a commonality of interest, for example over the Greenbury recommendations, this was an inadequate basis for treating such companies as acting together. GU was simply trying to get through the regulatory processes prior to furthering a proposal it believed to be in the public interest. It would be amazing if, having gone through these prior processes with this aim in view, it were to find itself at risk of being punished for bringing a matter of public interest to the MMC.

(c) *The MKH AGM and EGM*. In relation to these meetings, GU confirmed that it had had no direct or indirect contact with SAUR with regard to other matters to be debated or voted on either at the AGM or the EGM. GU also confirmed that it had had no discussions or relations with any other shareholders, including Morgan Grenfell, about the direction or policy of MKH, nor about how changes to MKH policy could be brought about, nor how voting should take place on any particular resolutions. GU had independently considered each resolution one by one, and came to a decision how or whether to vote on each (see Appendix 3.1). On *resolution 1* (the dividend) GU abstained; the high dividend appeared possibly to prejudice the company in the longer term by raising the regulatory risk for the company (the DGWS was on notice as saying that he was focusing on dividend declarations). On *resolution 2* (re-election of Mr Perkins) GU had no view and abstained. GU voted in favour of the reappointment of the auditors, *resolution 3*, as it appeared a statutory matter. Taking *resolutions 4 and 5* (authority to allot shares) together, GU voted against. It did not understand why MKH should need to raise further share capital, given its low gearing. In addition, GU was concerned, given that MKH's diversification activity had not been a success, that it might be considering further acquisitions. As far as *resolution 6* was concerned (share buy-back), GU abstained. It was worried that the resolution might have been motivated by short-term considerations, coming on top of a large and unforecast profit and dividend increase, and that the company would not be able to support the same performance longer term. The *executive share plan* resolution at the EGM was opposed by GU for two main reasons. First, MKH's performance had not been particularly good by comparison with other water undertakings. Secondly, there were features in the plan which did not comply with the Greenbury recommendations.

(d) *Material influence and control and section 65(3)*. GU accepted that if it and SAUR were associated persons their combined shareholding of nearly 39 per cent would enable them materially to influence the policy of MKH. When asked whether that combined shareholding would confer the ability to control policy, GU said that it was difficult to say where material influence stops and *de facto* control starts.

(e) GU accepted, in connection with section 65(3) of the FTA, that someone who had less than legal or *de facto* control might be treated as having control because that someone had the ability to influence policy. But this was a *permissive* enlargement of the MMC jurisdiction—the word to focus on in the section was '*may*'. In any event, however, GU did not accept that it had material influence (either individually or as an associated person). GU did not accept that the concept of influence or control was present. There had to be something to bridge the gap between such common interests and acting together. If, purely hypothetically, the MMC were to regard GU and SAUR as associated persons it would be necessary to define what their material influence or control amounted to. It could only amount to what was in the JVA, as there was no evidence of collusion. The JVA was a purely transient concept which would disappear if the merger proposal did not proceed.

SAUR's views

6.85. In a separate hearing with SAUR representatives the MMC raised with them a number of issues arising on the variation to the terms of reference. The main points put by SAUR during this hearing were:

(a) SAUR's ability individually to influence MKH. SAUR confirmed that its interest in MKH was confined to its 19.39 per cent shareholding, and that there were no interests held through nominees and no other shareholders who might be regarded as acting with SAUR to secure or exercise control over MKH. SAUR's attempt in 1993 to secure Board-level representation in MKH had been motivated by the normal desire of a major shareholder to secure such representation. As to its own position, a 19.39 per cent shareholding might in certain circumstances give rise to ability to have material influence. But ability materially to influence was not the end result of having a 19.39 per cent holding. SAUR did not consider that there were any circumstances in which it was indirectly currently able to influence MKH. After 31 March 1997, when its preference shares were redeemed, bringing its total shareholding down to 14.45 per cent (and assuming MKH remained independent), SAUR would regard itself as free to decide what to do about any further share acquisition, assuming the limitations imposed by the JVA had by then fallen away.

(b) Associated persons (and acting together). SAUR's objective, since the JVA was signed on 20 December 1995, was to move through the regulatory processes and then to decide, depending on the outcome, whether or not to launch a bid. The objective of the JVA was to take GU and SAUR through the regulatory process to the point at which, in the light of the Secretary of State's decision, they could take that decision. It would be perverse if SAUR, whose proposals were, it believed, in the public interest, were to be found to have acted against the public interest by becoming an associated person as a result of its part in the JVA. In answer to the question whether the JVA, made with the ultimate objective of obtaining control of MKH, was not on all fours with a reading of section 77 of the FTA that could be taken as acting together *for the purpose* of securing control, SAUR said that the JVA was simply a preparatory act which had no 'control' effect present or prospective. If SAUR or GU started to acquire shares pursuant to an agreement, then they would have started acting so as to secure control. But that point had not been reached. Other than as part of the regulatory and MMC process, SAUR had had no formal contact with GU.

(c) The MKH AGM and EGM. There had been no discussion with GU on how SAUR would vote on the resolutions at the AGM-EGM. SAUR had supported the first three resolutions. It had abstained on *resolutions 4 and 5* (authority to allot shares) although SAUR had some concerns about the possibility of MKH diversifying further as this had not been a success. *Resolution 6* (share buy-back) would have had significant cash implications and could have raised debt above those for the preference shares. As a significant preference shareholder, therefore, SAUR voted against, although the class resolution would in any event have been defeated by proxy votes of one or more preference shareholders other than GU or SAUR (see paragraph 6.68). While its voting pattern on resolutions 4 and 5 might have differed from that at previous AGMs on similar resolutions, at the earlier events SAUR had been concerned to give MKH management its support for various ventures, such as diversification. At the 1996 AGM SAUR did not feel MKH had shown a sufficiently successful track record. It had also voted against the performance share plan resolution.

(d) Material influence and control and section 65(3). Although, if it were assumed that GU and SAUR were associated and their shareholding could be aggregated to 39 per cent, such a level might confer ability materially to influence the policy of MKH, SAUR did not agree that this of itself would amount to ability to control. SAUR did not accept that it and GU were associated persons. As to whether, if they were associated persons, GU and SAUR should be treated as having control under section 65(3) of the FTA, SAUR considered that on the facts it should not be so treated. The provision was a permissive one, and allowed the MMC to conclude that because of the limited and temporary nature of the association between GU and SAUR they did not in fact 'control' MKH. SAUR did not consider that there were any circumstances under which it was, individually or with GU, currently able materially to influence MKH or that it should be treated as in control of MKH.

7 The views of Mid Kent Holdings

Contents

Paragraph

Introduction 7.1
The effect of the proposals, and of any merger (or mergers) in being, on the comparator system
    General 7.3
    The loss of MKW and its worth 7.4
    The prejudice to competition 7.11
    The effect of any merger(s) in being 7.13
Resource issues and benefits
    Co-operation 7.14
    Optimizing water resources and other proposed benefits 7.16
    Objections to bulk supply transfers 7.22
    Joint Resources Company 7.26
    Infrastructure proposals 7.31
Other proposed benefits of the merger proposals or of the merger(s) in being 7.34
Other public interest detriments 7.36
Remedies 7.42
Jurisdictional and legal issues on the original reference
    EC Merger Regulation 7.47
    The undertakings to the Secretary of State for Trade and Industry 7.48
    Water Industry Act 1991, section 34(3)(a) and (b) and the Fair Trading Act 1973, section 84 .... 7.49
    Section 84 of the Fair Trading Act 1973 .... 7.52
    Arrangements in progress 7.53
    Statutory assets test 7.56
    Analysis of the proposed transaction 7.57
    Non-water elements of merger proposals 7.58
    Further legal issues 7.59
Issues, including legal issues, arising from the variation of the reference
    Merger in being 7.61
    Section 65(3) of the Fair Trading Act 1973 .... 7.64
    Timing and time limits 7.65

Introduction

7.1. This chapter summarizes the views of MKH. These were provided in a number of written submissions and at three hearings.

7.2. The MMC sought evidence and assessments from MKH on:

— the effect of the proposed arrangements, and of any merger in being, on the ability of the DGWS to make comparisons between different water enterprises;

— the impact of the proposed arrangements on resource issues and the supply of water in the MKW, SEW and FDWS areas including consideration of BST agreements as a means of correcting local imbalances, and the benefits that might flow from the proposed transaction or from any merger(s) in being;

— whether other public interest effects might result from the proposed arrangements and/or any merger(s) in being; and

— a number of legal issues associated with the original reference; and, in connection with the variation of the reference, in particular on whether GU and SAUR had been acting together to secure or exercise control of MKH.

MKH was also asked for its opinion on possible remedies, if it should be found that there was a merger (or mergers) in being which might be expected to operate against the public interest; and/or that the proposed transaction might be expected so to operate.

The effect of the proposals, and of any merger (or mergers) in being, on the comparator system

General

7.3. MKH provided its view of the comparative competition system and an analysis of its development and method of operation. Particular points made on the issue of a possible reduction in the number of comparators included:

(a) The loss of any comparator would be prejudicial because the comparative competition system was dynamic, with relative performance changing over time.

(b) The improving sophistication of efficiency measurement in the system increased the number of relevant variables being identified. This required a greater number of observations and more, not fewer, degrees of freedom (and hence comparators).

(c) The fewer the comparators the less rigorous the standards and bench-marks set, the less pressure on companies to perform well and the more likely the DGWS was to find irremediable deficiencies in the process of, for example, allocating costs.

(d) The danger to the comparative system represented by a decline in competitors was the more acute and increasing, because it was irreversible.

(e) A decline could be expected to reduce aggregate efficiency targets measurably and in perpetuity.

(f) Alternative solutions for the loss of a comparator were in most cases inadequate to remedy the detriment.

The loss of MKW and its worth

7.4. The effect of losing MKW as a comparator would be particularly detrimental to the comparative competition system because:

(a) MKW was one of a reducing number of WoC comparators. The 29 at privatization in 1989 had declined to 19 now. Nine of these were members of three large groups, and five were below the £30 million assets threshold and therefore could disappear without MMC scrutiny (see paragraph 2.59). That left just five which, together with the three large groups, made eight fully effective WoC comparators. One of these was MKW.

(b) 'Stand-alone' quality of MKW's water business data, by comparison with the necessarily more subjective cost allocations between the different businesses of a WaSC, made it particularly valuable to the DGWS and was enhanced by its wide use of competitive tendering and arm's length dealing with group companies.

(c) MKW was one of only nine WoCs fully listed on the Stock Exchange, and its shares were the most actively traded of these. Neither of the merged entities resulting from the current proposals would be listed. Yet listing enabled the DGWS to obtain important financial information for estimating the cost of capital, and for establishing realistic financial constraints for all regulated stand-alone water enterprises. Omitting the infrequently-traded small WoCs, there were now only 11 listed water companies (six WaSCs and five WoCs) which would be reduced to ten by the merger.

(d) Loss of MKW as an independent management unit and its absorption into two large water groups at Stage 1, together with the setting up of a JRC and joint control arrangements at Stage 2, would involve considerable information sharing by the two groups; so much so that these two groups might cease to be comparators which were truly independent of each other.

(e) By 1994/95 (the most recent comparative data available), MKW was the second most improved water company in efficiency in England and Wales since the DGWS's bench-mark year of 1992/93. Using DEA models, MKW was only 4 to 12 per cent behind the estimated efficiency frontiers for 1994/95. In 1994/95 MKW had further reduced real operating costs by 13 per cent, while raising output by 5 per cent to record levels; this further, and sustainable, cost-cutting was likely to make MKW frontier-defining in 1995/96 and beyond. In this event MKW's direct comparator value to the DGWS at the 1999 Periodic Review would be very substantial, as it would be the referent company for many companies including SEW.

7.5. MKW was also a particularly valuable comparator in terms of the key financial and cost dimensions employed by the DGWS in making comparisons. The greater the number of companies, the less uncertainty involved and the better the resulting estimates. The loss of any comparative information would lead to a rise in uncertainty, more lenient price caps and hence higher costs to users across the country. Given this, it was essential to quantify the cost of losing a comparator such as MKW. MKH had therefore sought to quantify the effect of losing MKW as an operating expenditure comparator.

7.6. The methodology inevitably made use of assumptions to which some degree of uncertainty attached. It centred first on quantifying the additional degree of certainty that MKW provided as one of the (then) 30 observations on operating expenditure in 1994, and the degree of uncertainty of operating expenditure predicted for the remaining companies. This would have been 0.032 per cent a year had MKW not been present. The second stage was to apply the annual reduction of 0.032 per cent a year to industry total operating expenditure. This process showed that the potential efficiency savings that the DGWS could identify with the required degree of certainty, if MKW was not available as a comparator, would have been reduced by a sum rising to £4 to £5 million a year by 2015. Thirdly, the NPV of these savings was calculated. This was in the range £33 to £72 million (assuming a 2 per cent or 8 per cent real discount rate) over the 20-year period following the Periodic Review, with a central estimate of £48 million (assuming a 5 per cent real discount rate).

7.7. MKH calculated that the value of MKW as an operating expenditure comparator in the future was at least of this order. The real value was undoubtedly much greater, partly because there were already only 28 comparators, rather than the 30 available in 1994, but mainly because it was a lower bound estimate that did not take account of MKW as an operating expenditure 'chaser' or potential frontier definer. And it did not assign any value to MKW's other comparator roles.

7.8. MKW's high value as a comparator also arose from the quality and scope of its computerized information on its infrastructure assets and its notably efficient capital maintenance costs which were markedly lower than those of FDWS or SEW. It held its own in price of water against FDWS at 68p/m^3, and was much cheaper than SEW's 93pm^3. MKW was at the frontier of capital investment in remedying polycyclic aromatic hydrocarbons problems in the region and iron failures. And, generally, its management was characterized by its independence of approach. MKW was a particularly valuable comparator for SEW, having a similar operating environment and size but, in MKH's contention, being more efficient. GU and SAUR might say that the enlarged FDWS and SEW companies would be better comparators for the DGWS to use in assessing SWS. But this reasoning would be incorrect. SWS was a WaSC; the DGWS had no shortage of other WaSC comparators. It was hard to see how a large WoC would form a useful comparator for it. Moreover the merged companies would still be much smaller than SWS.

7.9. MKH submitted that the most fundamental characteristic of a comparator was its independence. MKH was truly independent, on this analysis, whereas FDWS and SEW belonged to conglomerates. The proposals would destroy an independent comparator and replace it with inferior alternatives linking two of the biggest groups of water companies. Because of the proposed JRC and joint control arrangements, FDWS and SEW would no longer have, separately, many of the functions of a water company, and would therefore be of questionable relevance for comparisons; this would represent a loss of three existing comparators.

7.10. Contrary to the public statements made by GU and SAUR during the inquiry, MKH provided high levels of customer service and compared very favourably with FDWS and SEW over the measures of service levels published by OFWAT.

The prejudice to competition

7.11. MKH considered that, in line with the Government's policy of developing effective market competition, its own approach and practices put it among the most competitive companies. MKH believed that, though it was limited in the short term, there was considerable potential for competition in the region, given that a number of independent companies operated there. Possibilities existed for competition in, for example, inset appointments (although this was limited), bulk supplies, common carriage, and cross-border supplies. In the area of unregulated activity it was the only water undertaker to open supply pipe connection work to competition. It had competed with SWS for contracts, and was continuing to look for opportunities to compete with its neighbours. MKH was also competing in other activities, such as water resource consultancy (in which MKH's subsidiary Halcrow Water Services Limited competed in the regional market against GU's and SAUR's subsidiaries) and plumbing via Waterlink Services.

7.12. The GU and SAUR proposals would, in MKH's analysis, eliminate 55 per cent of the total 345 km boundary between MKW and its competitors. There would be a significant detriment to actual and potential competition. It was inconceivable that the new boundary between the GU and SAUR companies that would be created would stimulate competition, and in any event MKH considered that such competition was unlikely to emerge given that they would be partners in a JRC.

The effect of any merger(s) in being

7.13. MKH submitted that the merger(s) in being it considered to exist would entail equivalent and greater prejudices to the comparative competition system than the MMC had identified in paragraph 8.51 of the 1990 report on the GU/MKW merger situation,[1] that is progressive influence over policy, increasing exchanges of information and, consequently, a reduction in the independence of data provided by MKW to the DGWS. The greater prejudice lay in GU's and SAUR's greater voting power, especially if supported by GU's advisers, Morgan Grenfell, with a 9 per cent stake in MKH, and their ability to place representatives on MKH's Board (though GU was currently prevented from doing so by its undertakings). It also lay in exchanges of information being likely to occur between all water companies in the GU and SAUR groups, nine including MKH.

Resource issues and benefits

Co-operation

7.14. MKH submitted that balancing resource supply with demand, which GU and SAUR were apparently pursuing through their proposals, required, among other things, constructive relationships with neighbouring companies. There were currently no links with SEW on resources; MKW's proposed discussions on possible bulk supplies, following SEW's claims about shortages earlier in 1996, were turned down. FDWS had, however, responded positively to MKW's recent BST offers, and a BST of

---

[1] *General Utilities PLC and the Mid Kent Water Company: a report on the merger situation*, HMSO, Cm 1125, July 1990.

1 Ml/d, rising to 2 Ml/d, had been agreed and implemented with the work in progress to develop it into a long-term arrangement.

7.15. MKW's links with SWS were more extensive. There were several joint schemes, the location of which can be seen on Map 7. MKW had contributed 25 per cent of the cost of all joint components of the River Medway Scheme. This was 75 per cent owned and operated by SWS, and MKW met its proportionate share of the running costs. MKW was entitled to 25 per cent of the scheme's yield under the terms of the abstraction licences. Secondly, MKW also received a BST of marginally below a quarter of the yield of the Belmont Scheme, another SWS development. Thirdly, co-operative development and use of the Belmont Scheme together with the adjacent Wigmore–Eastling Selling–Fleete main, with which it was integrated, allowed both companies to make joint use of assets and achieve maximum operational flexibility (see paragraph 5.21). The operation was a demonstration of what constructive management and co-operation between independent water companies could achieve. In 1995/96 MKW received a total average import of water from SWS of 19.33 Ml/d and exported 3.31 Ml/d in return. Finally, MKW held the title to the land, jointly acquired with SWS, which would be required for any new raw water reservoir at Broad Oak, should this facility be needed in the future. Although FDWS had originally been involved, alongside MKW and SWS, in the promotion of the scheme, it had declined to contribute to the land acquisition.

Optimizing water resources and other proposed benefits

7.16. MKH rejected the main claim by GU and SAUR that the merger proposals could be justified in terms of optimizing water supply in this part of south-east England. The benefits claimed were either not realistic benefits, for example the proposal to take a further 25 Ml/d from the Lower Medway which would almost certainly be impracticable and refused by the EA, or were unnecessary because they were already available, such as key elements of GU's and SAUR's proposal for new infrastructure (the so-called 'mini-grid'); or were misconceived. First, the EA had not identified an overall shortage of resources in the Southern Region. Secondly, the most recent published evidence (relating to 1992/93) showed no significant resource imbalance, in terms of average yield per head, as between MKW, FDWS and SEW (whereas SWS had a significantly larger average yield). There was currently no overall shortage of resources in the area of the three companies, contrary to the impressions given by GU and SAUR. Thirdly, the ability to carry out long-term resource planning in the region as a whole, and secure convergence of dates by which a major new regional resource was needed, existed already. A merger was not necessary to achieve it. Finally, the GU and SAUR claims to justify the merger on the basis of improving water conservation, demand management and service standards to MKW customers needed to be set against the position that MKW had set itself, and was achieving, more testing demand management goals than FDWS or SEW and that the level of its customer satisfaction was high.

7.17. The issue of water resource optimization, the chief claimed benefit of the proposed arrangements, brought the provisions of section 34(3)(b) of the 1991 Act into focus. Under these it had to be shown that:

(a) the arrangements could achieve the required purpose; and

(b) that purpose was of substantially greater importance than the prejudice to comparative competition; and

(c) the merger was the only way of achieving that purpose.

7.18. In MKH's contention:

(a) as SWS held the significant balance of surplus resources in the region, and as MKW had a record of better demand and resource management than either FDWS or SEW, the proposed arrangements could not achieve the purpose of improving resources;

(b) given that (i) the effects of losing a comparator were national (as opposed to the local nature of the resource issue) and (ii) the NRA's Southern Region November 1994 report *Sustaining Our Resources—The Way Forward* showed that the region had enough resources not to require a major

new resource until, probably, after 2010, it was not possible to substantiate a case for saying that the resource issue was of 'substantially greater significance' than the loss of a comparator; and

(c) the merger, involving the loss of a comparator, was not the only way of solving resource imbalances. FDWS and SEW could achieve the same ends by (i) taking BSTs from SWS, from MKW, and from Thames Water; (ii) better demand and resource management; (iii) if necessary, developing their own new resources; and (iv) possibly, if imbalances were significant, transferring licences.

7.19. MKH rejected the notion that, if a merger proposal satisfied the test that it was the only way of achieving a purpose, it automatically satisfied the test that the purpose was of substantially greater significance than the prejudice it entailed to comparative competition; such a notion was tantamount to a failure to apply the balancing test in section 34(3)(b) of the 1991 Act. In addition, if it was possible both to achieve the stated resource benefits *and* to retain the comparator, that is to achieve the benefits without a merger, then, by definition, eliminating the comparator *could not* yield benefits of substantially greater significance than the effects of retaining the comparator.

7.20. Moreover, as there was no significant disparity in the resources available to each of MKW, FDWS and SEW (in terms of average daily yield per head), FDWS and SEW could attain the same resource situation as was enjoyed by MKW, which had imposed no hose-pipe restrictions this year. They could do so by adopting the kind of demand and resource management measures which MKW had been pursuing in the past few years, taking BSTs (the DGWS had appropriate powers to arrange and enforce a BST agreement); remediating boreholes; taking innovative steps such as aquifer storage recovery or re-use of marginal/brackish water; requiring sprinkler users to meter their usage; setting more stringent leakage targets etc. On the facts of the present case, it was clearly possible to achieve the resource benefits while retaining MKW as a comparator (that is without a merger) so that eliminating MKW as a comparator could not yield resource benefits of substantially greater significance. Also, as a matter of principle, it seemed to MKH virtually impossible that a water company could ever be in the position that it needed to acquire another in order to optimize resources. If, having exhausted the options outlined above, it still faced a resource shortage, or undeveloped resources in the region, there were routes to a solution which did not involve prejudice to the comparator principle. This could include obtaining abstraction licences, including from within other companies' areas.

7.21. In support of its claim that MKW had a better record in resource management than the GU and SAUR companies, MKH cited the following:

(a) MKW had lower standing charges for meter use and, unlike FDWS and SEW, no pricing disadvantage for the use of metered water.

(b) Its compulsory metering of sprinkler users was more effective in demand management than the optional 'free metering' policy of FDWS and SEW, and was a policy recommended by the DGWS.

(c) Its leakage reduction target of 6 l/prop/h by 1998/99 was more stringent than those of FDWS and SEW.

(d) While MKW had had no hose-pipe ban in 1996, both FDWS and SEW had imposed bans on all their customers.

(e) MKW had given higher priority to investment in optimizing water resources than FDWS or SEW. Between 1990 and 1995 MKW had invested £18.1 million, FDWS £2.1 million and SEW £9.6 million. Per capita MKW's record was twice as high as the others.[1]

(f) In the same period MKW had allocated 25 per cent of total investment to water resources; FDWS 12 per cent; SEW 9 per cent.[1]

---

[1] *1994–95 Report on Financial Investment and Performance*, OFWAT.

(g) It had a more proactive policy on the exploitation, use and remediation of existing resources, for example on boreholes. MKW also had more innovative strategies for future resource management. It was one of only six companies that joined with the EA and the British Geological Survey to investigate the US technique of aquifer storage recovery in Great Britain.

(h) MKW also had considerable expertise in other innovative types of resource developments, such as in the use of 'marginal' (brackish) water.

Objections to bulk supply transfers

7.22. The objections of GU and SAUR to taking BSTs to optimize resource balances were ill-founded. To begin with, MKH submitted, the MKW area could not be operated without bulk supplies. GU and SAUR would have to rely on them. BSTs accounted for almost 10 per cent of MKW's distribution input. If GU and SAUR were claiming that a merger was necessary to create convergence of the dates by which water companies in the area would need a major new resource, the system of BSTs would itself have this effect. BSTs were one of the standard tools available to water companies. They were common practice throughout the industry; they were specifically envisaged under section 40 of the 1991 Act as the way to solve resource imbalances, and they were recommended as such by OFWAT and the EA.

7.23. It would not be true to argue that BSTs gave less incentive to suppliers to save water; were risky in water quality terms; would perpetuate regional imbalances; or would be costly to install in terms of infrastructure. The idea that BSTs involved a lack of security because suppliers would tend to put the interests of their own customers first was not a real fear. In MKW's extensive experience, BSTs had proved to be a reliable arrangement, through all kinds of conditions; MKW had provided an uninterrupted BST for over 20 years to FDWS; it was only when FDWS refused to accept proper commercial terms that it had been withdrawn. In any case the GU and SAUR companies' needs for BSTs (assuming the proposed arrangements did not proceed) would not begin to approach high levels by industry standards until after 2010.

7.24. Further, in MKH's view, the argument that BSTs perpetuated the dominance of companies with surpluses because they would be more likely to be granted new abstraction licences was not relevant or accurate. It was not relevant because the company with the surpluses was SWS; and it was not accurate because, for example, while MKW was a net recipient of BSTs it had been successful in being granted new abstraction rights. In any event, the recipient company would still be able to demonstrate the need for its own new licences when the BST had been fully utilized.

7.25. It had been argued that BSTs weakened the competitive process; that they distorted the recipient's data to OFWAT; and that they deterred recipients from competing with suppliers. MKH pointed out, however, that this was hard to reconcile with the DGWS's advocacy of BSTs, and with the legislation which established the comparator regime itself, in particular section 40 of the 1991 Act empowering the DGWS to order BSTs 'for the purposes of securing the efficient use of water resources'. As far as competition was concerned, there was no automatic competitive advantage in being a BST supplier rather than the recipient; MKW competed with SWS, though a net recipient of BSTs from that company. Nor did ownership of resources necessarily offer greater operational flexibility and commercial freedom. The flexibility required could be negotiated as part of a BST contract. And there were no significant limitations on the DGWS's powers to enforce a suitable BST contract; in practice, those powers operated as an effective sanction.

Joint Resources Company

7.26. In MKH's view the proposed JRC, with rights of access to, rather than ownership of, the land relating to its groundwater abstraction licences, could not be granted abstraction licences under the Water Resources Act 1991. As a result, the proposal would be prejudicial to the public interest generally. In MKH's view, section 35(3) of the Act required an applicant to be the occupier, or potential occupier, of the land rather than merely having a right of access, because 90 per cent of MKW's licences were groundwater licences. In addition the EA, in considering an application for a licence, was required by section 38(3)(b) of the Act to have regard to the 'requirements of the applicant' (that is the JRC). However, the JRC would not be a water undertaker (a water undertaker *would* have such requirements in that it had duties to supply). So the EA would be likely to decide that the JRC did not have a requirement for the purposes of section 38(3)(b) and, hence, to refuse the application.

7.27. The JRC would also be beyond OFWAT's regulatory control (as would the associated joint entity, mentioned by GU and SAUR in their modifications to the proposed arrangements for Stage 2, which would procure, construct and operate any major new resource, and negotiate any necessary agreements with third parties). The JRC would not be subject to requirements to provide information to the DGWS on standard regulatory features such as on capital expenditure, on costs and pricing, on leakage control and metering and on planning costs for any major new developments. In addition, on top of the elimination of MKW as a comparator, the effect of the proposed JRC and joint control arrangements would be to remove two other companies from being effective comparators as they would no longer separately have many of the functions of a normal water company, such as holding abstraction licences in the present MKW area, or planning major new developments, and being responsible for operational matters at major new developments.

7.28. The degree of co-operation between FDWS and SEW (and hence between GU and SAUR) necessary for the JRC proposal to work was significant; so much so that it would imply the creation of just one effective comparator out of nine existing WoCs (on the basis that GU would own or have a material influence in six WoCs, SAUR in two, and both would have a 50 per cent share in MKW). MKH believed that GU's and SAUR's proposals to create a framework of joint resource ventures between them for their enlarged areas unquestionably increased the severity of the loss of comparators. In undertaking any of FDWS's operational functions as a vertically integrated water company, for example, the joint venture arrangements and the JRC would result in the creation of a WoC which was not vertically integrated and therefore could not be compared with all the other WoCs. This reduced or eliminated the remaining comparator value of the enlarged FDWS. Moreover the co-operative arrangements established between the GU and SAUR groups would:

  (a) create a nexus for the exchange of comparator information submitted by them to the DGWS; and

  (b) render improbable the prospect of comparative (or market) competition between FDWS and SEW.

These losses to the national comparator and competitive systems would be in addition to the potential costs the joint ventures could indirectly impose on the water consumers of the enlarged areas. 1.3 million people in this region would be supplied by a chain of water companies that successive regulators were finding progressively harder to regulate. Because they would be progressively less well vertically integrated companies, by the next century neither the final retailers (SEW and FDWS) nor their upstream suppliers would be effectively regulated. The water industry's regulators would then be dealing with what MKH viewed as a single, incomparable, octopus.

7.29. In addition if, as proposed by GU and SAUR, the JRC were to be responsible for holding abstraction licences but not for distributing or supplying water, MKH considered that the EA would be less able to carry out its duties of conserving water resources. Its duties under section 19 and section 20 of the Water Resources Act 1991, in this respect, related to arrangements with water undertakers, and the JRC would not be such an undertaker.

7.30. Consequently the alleged resource benefits, which were supposed to derive from Stage 2 of the bid and the establishment of the JRC, might never be achievable.

Infrastructure proposals

7.31. MKH had considered the information, provided from GU and SAUR source material, on the proposed infrastructure developments or 'mini-grid' (see Map 4). It considered that the proposals were based on outdated and incomplete data, were unnecessary, and were unworthy of the name 'mini-grid'. The proposals were outdated principally because they appeared to be based on a plan of the MKW primary network that was up to 20 years old. In effect the proposal was just a series of unconnected pipes. In particular, the plan submitted by GU and SAUR did not acknowledge the cross-county Wigmore–Eastling Selling–Fleete trunk main (see Map 7). GU and SAUR appeared to want to duplicate this further south between Potters Corner and Broomfield. MKW's overall system was in any case more modern and extensive than implied by the plan, and there were other technical weaknesses with the plan, for example not all sources currently available to MKW were shown connected to the infrastructure. MKW's existing primary network and its proposed new mains under the company's strategic business plan are shown in Map 5. The proposed Beech–Burham link main had already in effect been built. The proposed Chilham–Howfield link already existed; and the proposed Canterbury–Barham link was not needed to facilitate transfers to FDWS. The only link likely to be necessary was the Kippings Cross–Cottage Hill pipeline to transfer water to SEW. This, however, did not require a merger. It could simply be built to provide long-term bulk supplies.

7.32. As far as the aims of the mini-grid proposals for the short term were concerned, within MKW's area there were simply not the supply difficulties nor water surpluses which would justify significant expenditure of the type proposed. In any case, as noted, most of the proposals were unnecessary.

7.33. For the longer term the proposals would only make sense if there were substantial surpluses in the MKW area. There were not, however. The bulk of the surpluses remained with SWS. The proposal by GU and SAUR to extract a further 25 Ml/d from the Lower Medway could hardly be invoked in support. The River Medway was already 'fully regulated' (that is, there was no 'spare' water). MKH considered that the EA would be unlikely to license any such scheme but that, in any case, there was nothing to prevent GU and SAUR from pursuing this option independently of any merger. Any surpluses MKW had were already allocated to be used by MKW customers by 2006, so could not be made available without depriving these customers of security of supply.

Other proposed benefits of the merger proposals or of the merger(s) in being

7.34. MKH considered that there was no possibility of benefits other than the alleged resources benefits discussed above. Prospective efficiency gains, if these were available, would need at least (as it was a lower bound estimate) to match the MKH estimate of the £33 million to £72 million cost of losing MKW as a comparator (see paragraph 7.6). But GU and SAUR were explicitly not offering any offsetting efficiency gains. Furthermore, such gains as might be available could be, and were being, brought about without the loss of MKW as a comparator. Far from achieving efficiency gains, the merger proposals would appear to entail a loss of efficiency.

7.35. Overall, the alleged benefits were, in MKH's view, largely illusory and certainly not 'of substantially greater significance' than the prejudice to comparative competition. It remained the case that the purposes which the merger proposals were designed to achieve could be achieved without the prejudice to comparative competition entailed in the proposed or actual merger. And even if this were not the case the benefits alleged by GU and SAUR were, in MKH's view, wholly irrelevant to the public interest detriments arising from the material influence over MKH resulting from the actual merger (see paragraph 7.13). All the alleged benefits would depend on proceeding with both Stage 1 and Stage 2. They would not be achieved by the merger(s) in being.

Other public interest detriments

7.36. MKH believed there were a number of public interest detriments which would result if the proposed arrangements were allowed to proceed and which the MMC should take into account. These resulted from GU's and SAUR's strategy, together with Lyonnaise, to acquire dominance in the UK water industry. The main consequences were likely to be a concentrated industry and higher prices (MKH cited trade press reports that the French Environment Minister had quoted average water prices in 1995 for the private tender sector in France, where the three companies originated, at more than three times higher than the levels in England).

7.37. Unless checked, such concentration would include permanent co-operation between GU and SAUR through their proposed JRC and other joint control arrangements, and would have a number of public interest detriments. For example:

— there would be standardization of approach between companies, weakening innovation;

— water supply would cease to be the main concern of companies with group priorities;

— decisions were more likely to be taken centrally, remote from local needs;

— equity and debt capital would not be obtained on an arm's length commercial basis;

— support services might be procured intra-group and, therefore, at sub-optimal prices, to the disadvantage of the consumers; and

— the water industry would as a result be harder to regulate.

7.38. Further, the proposed arrangements would be detrimental to market competition in non-regulated activities such as MKH's current activity, via its Halcrow Water Services Limited offshoot, in water engineering. MKH's disappearance would also weaken its competitive activity overseas (it had set up two entities to develop capacity to exploit the market for water supply and waste management support services in Portugal). The loss of MKH would also be a setback to efficiency improvement, to resource management, to research and development, and to innovative and decentralized management, in all of which MKH had a better record than others including the GU and SAUR companies.

7.39. There would also be significant regulatory and enforcement difficulties for both the DGWS and the EA as a result of the proposed JRC (for the reasons discussed in paragraph 7.25 and following). These were a public interest detriment additional to the prejudice to comparative competition.

7.40. Finally, MKH considered that there were serious questions about the fitness of the parent companies of GU and SAUR to extend their influence over regulated entities in this country. In this connection MKH drew the MMC's attention to various judicial investigations in France. These concerned alleged offences, involving either CGE or Bouygues, relating to water quality and pricing.

7.41. The merger(s) in being, which MKH believed to exist, also entailed other public interest detriments, including: the threat to MKH's efficiency and staff motivation, by the GU and SAUR action in voting down the proposed performance share plan; the threat to MKH's directors' ability to optimize the company's financial structure (by, on 18 July, preventing the company from using an entirely uncontroversial method of raising its gearing); and the threat to MKH's independence of approach in areas such as resource management.

Remedies

7.42. In MKH's view the proposed mergers would operate against the public interest, and were not necessary for achieving any of the benefits alleged by GU and SAUR. They could not outweigh the detriment to comparative competition, nor the other detriments identified under section 84 of the FTA. There was, therefore, no remedy short of outright prohibition.

7.43. As far as possible price cuts were concerned, this case was very different from the Lyonnaise/Northumbrian case; in this case no efficiency savings were put forward by GU and SAUR. The proposed arrangements would not, therefore, produce exemplary comparators; indeed, no true comparator would survive the dismembering of MKW. In any case, the scale of the detriment was higher, implying, as the arrangements did, both elimination of MKW (in itself a particularly valuable comparator, moving fast towards the efficiency frontier) and continued co-operation between the GU and SAUR companies. If price cuts were recommended, however, they should apply to all the GU and SAUR companies.

7.44. MKH also regarded output performance targets as inappropriate and difficult to enforce, and a separate Stock Exchange listing as an inadequate remedy.

7.45. Nor did MKH consider the EA proposals on partial remedies (see paragraph 9.40 and following) an adequate response to the proposed arrangements. In MKH's view the EA proposals were either already being adopted by MKW or were not as beneficial as might at first sight appear. For example, MKW already had in place the kind of effective policy to make use of BSTs and to encourage the wider use of metering which the EA was advocating; indeed, if GU and SAUR were willing to endorse the EA's proposals on continued use of existing BSTs, and future use of additional BSTs, that undermined their arguments against BSTs. On the other hand the EA's wish to see reductions in abstraction in the Stour catchment area could entail major costs to consumers, which required further consideration, as they could accelerate the need for a major new resource. Both the DGWS and Ministers were very sensitive to such implications.

7.46. As far as the merger(s) which MKH considered to be in being were concerned, it seemed clear to MKH that the current situation could not be allowed to persist. This entailed material influence being exercised over MKH which was even more prejudicial than that which the 1990 MMC report,[1] on the then GU/MKW merger situation, was designed to prevent. Any remedies to the new situation would, therefore, need to be binding on SAUR as well as on GU and their financial advisers and would need to require a sufficient reduction in the maximum shareholdings permitted to GU and SAUR to remedy the situation in which they could, both together and individually, defeat special resolutions. In MKH's view the combined shareholding of the two companies should be required to be below 10 per cent. This would take time to effect; so in the interim each company would need to give an undertaking not to vote more than 5 per cent of the total shares issued by MKH.

Jurisdictional and legal issues on the original reference

EC Merger Regulation

7.47. MKH told the MMC that it had submitted, in a paper of last January to the Merger Task Force of the European Commission's DGIV, that the proposals did not constitute a concentration with an EC dimension under the EC Merger Regulation (ECMR), and noted that the Task Force had, apparently, agreed. Thus, in its view, the ambit of the MMC inquiry was not limited by the ECMR.

The undertakings to the Secretary of State for Trade and Industry

7.48. In MKH's view, the arrangements entered into between GU and SAUR were unlawful, in that they infringed the terms of the statutory undertakings given by GU following the 1990 MMC report on the merger situation between GU and MKW. It did not consider it appropriate for the MMC to be asked to investigate unlawful behaviour, though it left it to the MMC to reach their own conclusions on the issue and agreed to co-operate fully in the inquiry. On 2 April 1996 MKH had asked the High Court for a declaration that, among other things, GU's undertakings to the Secretary of State had been breached by the arrangements made with SAUR for the purposes of making the bid. The High Court (Mr Justice Knox), however, decided that MKH did not have the right to enforce undertakings obtained under the FTA.

Water Industry Act 1991, section 34(3)(a) and (b) and the Fair Trading Act 1973, section 84

7.49. MKH considered that the MMC's public interest appraisal of the GU and SAUR proposals was governed by section 34(3) of the 1991 Act and, to the extent that there was no conflict with the 1991 Act provision, by section 84 of the FTA. In particular, under section 34(3)(a), the MMC must primarily have regard to the desirability of giving effect to the principle that the DGWS's ability to make comparisons between water enterprises should not be impaired. The MMC might have regard to achieving any other purpose 'so far only as they are satisfied' that the criteria in section 34(3)(b)(i) or (ii) were satisfied.

---

[1] Op cit.

7.50. Under section 34(3)(b)(i) it must be demonstrated that the 'other purpose' could be achieved in a manner that did not conflict with the principle of making comparisons. In MKH's view GU's and SAUR's proposals would impair the comparator principle.

7.51. Under the alternative, section 34(3)(b)(ii), it was MKH's view that the MMC might only have regard to claimed benefits under this provision if they were satisfied that the achievement of such purpose met two criteria: first, that the purpose (or alleged benefit) was 'of substantially greater significance' in relation to the public interest than the principle of comparative competition; and secondly, that it 'cannot be brought about except in a manner that conflicts with that principle'. In MKH's view the proposals by GU and SAUR failed both parts of this test. MKH considered that their interpretation corresponded with the natural meaning of the words of section 34(3)(b)(ii) and with the underlying philosophy of the water legislation. This was to ensure the protection of comparative competition through a 'public interest' test which differed from that for ordinary mergers by requiring a more stringent justification from those seeking to eliminate a water comparator. Its view, in essence, was that the words 'cannot be brought about except' in the section mean that the MMC must be satisfied that there was *no other way* of achieving the alleged benefit than by prejudicing comparative competition through the merger; that the benefits could *only* be achieved by the merger; and that the merger was *necessary* for the achievement of the alleged benefit.

Section 84 of the Fair Trading Act 1973

7.52. In its submission, MKH considered that previous MMC reports had established that the MMC were entitled to have regard to public interest issues under the wider test in section 84 of the FTA, in addition to taking into account the 'comparative competition' test under section 34(3) of the 1991 Act. Though considering its ability to comment fully on public interest issues to be hampered by the lack of detailed, or by continually changing, information on GU's and SAUR's plans, and by the inconsistencies in statements put out by GU and SAUR (for example, on the date for building a major new resource), MKH nonetheless considered that there were a number of section 84 detriments to be taken into account. (These are set out in paragraphs 7.34 to 7.39.)

Arrangements in progress

7.53. Noting that the MMC had been asked to investigate, in respect of each of the two stages of GU's and SAUR's proposals, whether arrangements were in progress which, if carried into effect, would result in the creation of one or more mergers, MKH considered that it was doubtful whether the arrangements contemplated by GU and SAUR for Stage 2 were sufficiently far advanced to be said to be in progress rather than just in contemplation. MKH compared the state of the GU and SAUR proposals with those recorded for Severn Trent,[1] and stated in the MMC report (especially in paragraphs 2.26 and 2.27) to be the basis for concluding that arrangements were 'in progress': 'An implementation plan has been finalized, drawing on detailed research conducted in preparation for the acquisition. It sets out in some detail the proposed integration of important functions of the merged enterprise.' MKH contended that the preparations of GU and SAUR for Stage 2 fell well short of this. While the provisions of the redacted version of the JVA shown to MKH during the April High Court proceedings indicated that an implementation plan had been finalized for Stage 1, the position regarding Stage 2 was very different. There were no similarly detailed provisions at all; recital E stated that GU and SAUR 'intend' (rather than 'have agreed') to identify those parts of MKW which would be merged with each of FDWS and SEW; clause 8.1 showed that the assets to be held jointly had not been agreed; and while clauses 15 and 16 had provisions for the management of MKH up to the 'split date', there were no provisions for what happened after the split date, that is for Stage 2.

7.54. MKH also detected a lack of clarity in the detail of key proposals by GU and SAUR. There were differences and discrepancies between recent GU and SAUR statements and earlier ones on the details of their proposals. These especially affected the timing of any major new resource, the proposed JRC, and the new infrastructure proposals. On GU's and SAUR's own admission the JRC proposal was

---

[1] *Severn Trent Plc and South West Water Plc: a report on the proposed merger*, HMSO, Cm 3429, October 1996.

incomplete in that it was dependent on more detailed appraisal work. It made it inconceivable, in MKH's view, that arrangements were 'in progress' for Stage 2 (rather than merely in contemplation).

7.55. Generally, therefore, in view of the absence of a Stage 2 implementation plan, and of the lack of clarity and the discrepancies, MKH considered that as a matter of law the MMC should consider whether there were arrangements in progress in respect of Stage 2. While the broad aim of Stage 2 might be argued to be settled in the most general of terms, there were no arrangements in progress to achieve that aim as the details kept changing; and new developments were occurring. Further, the statement by GU's solicitor in the High Court proceedings in April that the JVA 'is not an agreement which could possibly result in the acquisition of shares in Mid Kent ... A further agreement is necessary to achieve this' (paragraph 40 of the Affidavit of Martin Smith, a solicitor acting for GU) was inconsistent, in MKH's view, with any contention that arrangements were in progress. MKH had concluded that while arrangements for Stage 1 were in progress, it seemed clear to it that, as at 23 May, arrangements for the merger situations at Stage 2 had not been in progress, and therefore that the MMC had no jurisdiction to consider public interest matters arising out of Stage 2. (This was without prejudice to its view that arrangements for Stage 2 were not in progress even at this later stage.) If the MMC were to concur, none of the benefits alleged by GU and SAUR to arise from Stage 2 could be taken into consideration in the MMC's conclusions on the public interest.

Statutory assets test

7.56. As at 31 March 1966, the book value of the gross assets of MKH was £108.3 million, and that of MKW was £99.8 million. In MKH's view it was clear that the GU and SAUR proposals gave rise to a merger situation qualifying for investigation, under section 33(1)(a) of the 1991 Act, though there was an issue whether Stage 2 constituted a separate merger situation (or situations) which might not qualify for investigation. MKH also did not dissent from the hypothesis that, as explained by GU and SAUR, the JRC would broadly control up to about £15 million of MKH's assets, the remainder being divided, if the proposals went ahead as planned, more or less evenly between GU and SAUR.

Analysis of the proposed transaction

7.57. MKH was asked for its comments on how the proposed arrangements should be treated for the purposes of the FTA and in particular on a provisional MMC intention to treat the proposed transaction as one merger, arising from GU and SAUR as associated persons jointly acquiring a controlling interest in MKH. In reply MKH said that while it agreed that Stage 1 of the proposed transaction would only involve one merger situation, it seemed to MKH that Stage 2 would give rise to two further merger situations: one, under which GU alone would acquire a full controlling interest over those enterprises which currently comprise the water supply business in the eastern part of Mid Kent; and the other by which SAUR alone would acquire a full controlling interest over those enterprises currently comprising the water supply business in the western part of Mid Kent. In this connection, MKH emphasized in particular the following points:

(a) Although section 77(1) of the FTA provided that 'associated persons ... shall ... be treated as one person' for the purposes of section 65, this did not mean that the 'one person' was the same person as each of the associated persons which were deemed to constitute it. In short, control by GU and SAUR as associated persons was not the same as control by GU or control by SAUR individually.

(b) Section 77(2) made clear that section 77(1) could not have the effect of excluding from section 65 'any case which would otherwise fall in that section'. In short, the fact of GU and SAUR assuming control over MKH at Stage 1 could not exclude the separate acquisitions of control individually by GU and SAUR at Stage 2 from being counted as merger situations.

(c) A move from a situation where each had material influence to one where each had a controlling interest was to be treated as a merger situation, by reason of section 65(4). Notwithstanding the use of the word 'may' in section 65(4), this had never been understood to be merely permissive.

(d) 'Enterprise' was defined in section 63(2) as 'the activities, or part of the activities, of a business'. There could be no doubt, in MKH's opinion, that the eastern part of MKW's water supply business, and the western part, might both be regarded as 'enterprises' for the purposes of section 65.

Non-water elements of merger proposals

7.58. The MMC had asked MKH's view on whether or not merger inquiries under the 1991 Act should take account of consequences other than those which derived from the merger of water enterprises. MKH said that in its view there was no reason to exclude any matters from the MMC's investigation provided that they were consequences which the merger in question had or might be expected to have. In its view nothing in the 1991 Act limited the MMC's consideration of the consequences or effects of the merger referred. Indeed section 34(2)(b) excluded the normal power of the Secretary of State under the FTA himself to impose a limit on the ambit of the MMC's investigation to certain elements or consequences only of the merger. Equally, therefore, it considered that the MMC were obliged to have regard to all the effects of a merger of water enterprises whether or not they related directly to the water businesses themselves, subject only to the proviso that alleged public interest benefits ('purposes') must be subject to the tests set out in section 34(3)(b) of the 1991 Act. In short, the merger which the MMC were required to investigate was the merger of water enterprises; but such merger, if it also involved other enterprises, had consequences which were wider than just those which specifically related to the water businesses. MKH believed the MMC's duty related to all public interest consequences arising from the merger. There was no limitation, either in the legislation or in the terms of the present MMC reference, relating to whether those consequences impacted on the water enterprises.

Further legal issues

7.59. MKH considered that the provisions of the Companies Act 1985, together with the requirements of the City Code on Takeovers and Mergers and the London Stock Exchange Listing Rules, might make it difficult or impossible for GU and SAUR to move successfully to Stage 2 (the restructuring of the MKH business) after completing Stage 1 (acquiring control of MKH); and that it could not, therefore, be assumed that if GU and SAUR were permitted to acquire MKH they could automatically proceed to Stage 2. At Stage 1, GU and SAUR could well succeed in acquiring control (that is 50.01 per cent) of MKH. However, in order to implement Stage 2 without restriction from minority shareholders GU and SAUR would need to acquire 100 per cent of MKH. MKH said that to do this, they would need to be able to exercise the compulsory acquisition rights provided by the Companies Act. For these to operate GU and SAUR would have to acquire, or contract to acquire, not less than 90 per cent of the shares to which their offer related. Under Companies Act rules these shares would exclude those already held by GU and SAUR. The effective threshold, therefore, was almost 94 per cent, as opposed to 90 per cent. If, because of apathy or resistance, GU and SAUR were not able to reach the threshold, they would not be able to exercise compulsory acquisition rights, and the continued existence of a minority shareholding interest could cast serious doubt on the ability of the bidders to implement their Stage 2 proposals. Nor, therefore, would the alleged benefits of the merger be achievable.

7.60. In addition, if MKH remained listed on the Stock Exchange, under the Exchange's Listing Rules, the restrictions dealing with 'transactions with related parties' would apply. These had to be approved by the company in general meetings but the related parties could not vote. 'Related parties' included, among others, shareholders with 10 per cent or more of the votes of a company at its general meetings, or associates of such shareholders. This would mean that GU and SAUR would not be able to vote on the transfer of MKWest and MKEast to SEW and FDWS respectively. In MKH's view, therefore, in such circumstances, it was doubtful that the minority shareholders would agree to the restructuring of MKH. Even if MKH were delisted, and the restrictions of the Listing Rules removed, implementation of Stage 2 against the wishes of the minority shareholders could be a breach of the fiduciary duties of the directors; and the minority shareholders could apply to the court for an order under section 459 of the Companies Act (protection of company's members against unfair prejudice).

Issues, including legal issues, arising from the variation of the reference

Merger in being

7.61. MKH submitted that, in addition to the arrangements referred to the MMC on 23 May for investigation under section 32(1)(a) of the 1991 Act, a merger of water enterprises had taken place within the meaning of section 32(1)(b). It resulted from MKW coming under the 'control' (in the sense of the ability to exercise material influence over its policy) of a 'person' which was GU and SAUR. GU and SAUR were associated persons within the meaning of section 77(4)*(d)* of the FTA (which applied by virtue of section 34 of the 1991 Act). And associated persons were deemed to be one person for the purposes of determining whether enterprises were under common control.

7.62. GU's and SAUR's ability to block resolutions coupled with what MKH saw as their co-ordinated behaviour at the AGM and EGM on 18 July demonstrated, in MKH's view, the existence of a merger, or mergers, in being. MKH said that while GU and SAUR were careful not to vote in the same way on every resolution at the AGM-EGM, it was clear that their voting conduct was co-ordinated pursuant to understandings between them (see Appendix 3.1 and paragraph 6.67 for a record of voting behaviour, and Appendix 6.3 for the texts of the resolutions). There were a number of factors behind this conclusion:

— GU and SAUR were the only significant shareholders to oppose resolutions, other than Morgan Grenfell's proxy vote against resolution 6.

— GU's and SAUR's voting conduct was in contrast to that at the previous four Mid Kent AGMs at which they had either voted with the management or given the Chairman discretion.

— GU had asked for a poll vote on resolutions 4 to 6, yet it had not voted on 6 (it was SAUR which voted against on 6). This implied that its request was made on SAUR's behalf as well as its own.

— The reason for their *both* voting to defeat the performance share plan resolution at the EGM was that it was an ordinary resolution and they could not afford for one of them to abstain.

Moreover, GU and SAUR representatives were seen by MKH staff to be conferring following the meeting. The voting behaviour could not be explained by fears that the contested resolutions could make a GU and SAUR bid more expensive. MKH considered that there was nothing in the resolutions, which were standard resolutions, to disadvantage a putative bidder. MKH understood that the MMC had learned from GU and SAUR that, when resolution 6 was being discussed at the AGM, MKH's Chairman had announced that it could not pass because proxies sufficient to defeat it had already been received at preference share level. MKH said that neither Jeremy Leigh Pemberton, Chairman, nor Simon MacLachlan, the non-executive director who chaired the meeting of preference shareholders, had any recollection of having said anything to this effect.

7.63. It also appeared to MKH that two other mergers in being had taken place, as a result of:

— MKW coming under the 'control' (material influence) of GU; and
— MKW coming under the 'control' (material influence) of SAUR,

because each could be sure at least that neither would oppose the other in casting their votes. This was borne out by their voting behaviour at the MKH AGM and EGM on 18 July. GU and SAUR had shareholdings of 19.45 per cent and 19.39 per cent respectively. Given the total number of votes cast at most AGMs, this meant that individually they were able to block special resolutions (requiring 75 per cent of votes cast). In MKH's view, another major shareholder, Morgan Grenfell, was likely to support GU and SAUR in view of its role as GU's financial adviser; Morgan Grenfell had a shareholding of 9.35 per cent. There was, in MKH's view, a strong possibility of a veto over ordinary resolutions if either GU or SAUR *and* Morgan Grenfell abstained and the other voted against. MKH considered that GU and SAUR were individually able to exercise material influence over MKH, as well as able to do so acting together, because in its view the voting pattern at the recent AGM-EGM depended on expectations of the way in which each of the parties, including Morgan Grenfell, would vote.

Section 65(3) of the Fair Trading Act 1973

7.64. MKH was asked by the MMC for its views on whether, under the provisions of section 65(3) of the FTA, GU and SAUR should be treated as having control of MKH because they were directly or indirectly able to control or materially to influence the policy of MKH. This would be as a result of having become associated persons through the JVA. MKH was further asked whether it agreed that, if the proposed merger were prohibited, the JVA as a transitory agreement would cease to have effect; and that it would not be reasonable to treat the parties as having control for the purposes of section 65. MKH said that section 65(3) was not permissive. The MMC had always previously treated a person who had the ability materially to influence the policy of a company as having control of it. Moreover, it would not be correct to assume that, if the proposed merger were to be prohibited, all relationships between GU and SAUR would cease:

— They were still companies neighbouring MKH and still with the resource difficulties they claimed to have.

— It would be difficult to conclude that their common interest to influence MKH would simply fall away.

— Their combined level of shareholding would have an adverse effect on MKH's independence.

— In any event it was not MKH's case that such GU and SAUR control as existed derived from the JVA alone. So even if that fell MKH would say that the control did not fall.

— Having failed in their first approach, GU and SAUR might wish to rely all the more on the influence they could exert by co-operating through their shareholdings in MKH.

Timing and time limits

7.65. As to when the merger(s) in being took place, MKH had no view on the date when GU and SAUR became associated persons. Instead it considered that the relevant question was when the merger(s) became a matter of public knowledge, in accordance with the provisions of section 34(4) of the 1991 Act. In its view this did not happen in December: GU had specifically denied to the High Court in April 1996 that there was any arrangement or agreement with SAUR to vote shares together or act in conjunction to secure or exercise control over Mid Kent (GU's outline submissions to the Court, paragraphs 5.12 and 5.14). Further, the Secretary of State for Trade and Industry would have been bound to refer a merger (or mergers) to the MMC with the original May reference if it had appeared to him that it (or they) might be in existence. As GU's High Court statement had also said that GU and SAUR would be associated persons if they had agreed or arranged with each other that they would vote their shares together, and as they had done so at the AGM-EGM events on 18 July, the fact of their acting in conjunction to exercise control (that is, material influence) over MKH only came into public view then, including in subsequent press coverage of the event.

7.66. On time limits, according to MKH's interpretation, the 1991 Act provided in section 34(4) that unless the reference to the MMC was made within six months after the later of (a) the day on which the merger(s) took place and (b) the day on which material facts about the resulting transactions first came to the notice of the Secretary of State or the Director General of Fair Trading (DGFT) or were made public, any MMC report must be confined to stating that the reference was not made within the time period. As it was clear to MKH that the merger(s) occurred or were made public at and following the AGM-EGM, it seemed to MKH that the time limits for the purpose of section 34(4) of the 1991 Act were six months as from the end of July. However, MKH agreed that it could be argued that the section 34(4) time limit had not been reached on any merger that was found to have arisen in December 1995. This was because the reference on the issue could be held to be a variation of the May 1996 reference. Hence the most appropriate course might be for the MMC to answer the question as to the public interest of such an existing (December) merger.

8 The views of the Director General of Water Services

Contents

	Paragraph
Introduction	8.1
Possible merger in being	8.3
The public interest effects of an existing merger	8.7
Remedies	8.8
The use of comparators	
The importance of comparators	8.9
Changes in the structure of the industry	8.13
Developments in the use of comparators	
Efficiency and competitiveness	8.14
Financial ring-fencing	8.16
Capital expenditure	8.17
Leakage	8.18
Developments in the scope for direct competition	8.19
Relative value of comparators	
General	8.20
Cost comparators: inter-company variations	8.21
Spectrum of loss to the comparator system	8.24
Quantifying the value of a comparator	8.27
The loss of Mid Kent Water as a comparator	8.30
The detriments of the proposed acquisition	8.31
Mid Kent Water's dynamic potential	8.32
Mid Kent Water's performance	8.33
Reduction of the number of separate water undertakers	8.34
Reduction in quality of data	8.35
Loss of a separately listed company	8.36
Loss of potential cross-border competition	8.37
Availability of alternatives to the proposed arrangements	8.44
Section 34(3)(b) of the Water Industry Act 1991	8.52
Absence of countervailing benefits	8.54
Possible remedies	8.56
Costs and prices	8.58
Outputs	8.60
Visibility	
Market information	8.61
Management independence	8.65
Other comparative information	8.66
Joint Resources Company	8.67

Introduction

8.1. This chapter summarizes the views of Mr Ian Byatt, the DGWS, which were provided to the MMC in written submissions and at three hearings. One of the written submissions was a background paper on water resources in East Sussex and Kent, jointly prepared by the EA and OFWAT.

8.2. The MMC sought evidence from the DGWS on the key aspects of the reference, including the variation to the reference (whether a merger had taken place and, if so, whether it might be expected to operate against the public interest); and on the original reference (the expected consequences of the proposed merger for the public interest). In particular the MMC sought comments on:

— the effect on his ability, in carrying out his functions, to make comparisons between different water enterprises; his views on the interpretation of section 34(3)(b) of the 1991 Act; whether he expected any benefits to flow from any actual merger on the proposed acquisition and, if so, whether they could be achieved in the absence of the merger;

— any safeguards which he thought might be appropriate if the MMC concluded that the actual or potential merger might be expected to operate against the public interest; and

— any other issues which he considered relevant.

The DGWS provided detailed evidence on the use currently made of comparators in regulating the industry, the relative value of comparators and the impact of the proposed merger. Some of this evidence is discussed at greater length in Chapter 4. The DGWS also gave the MMC his views on appropriate remedies for the adverse effects.

Possible merger in being

8.3. On the information available to him, the DGWS considered that there were two bases on which it might be suggested that GU and SAUR had been 'acting together' in relevant respects: either as a result of the steps taken pursuant to their agreement of 20 December 1995; or in connection with their voting conduct at MKW's AGM and EGM on 18 July 1996.

8.4. As for the steps taken pursuant to the agreement of 20 December 1995, GU and SAUR had been 'acting together' in a sense, in that they had entered into the agreement, made joint representations and so on. However, it did not appear to the DGWS that such actions should in themselves be regarded as 'acting together to secure or exercise control' within the meaning of section 77(4)(d) of the FTA, particularly given that the agreement between GU and SAUR specifically restricted either party from acquiring further shares in MKH without consent of the Secretary of State. Actions with a view to obtaining consent were not the same as actions 'to secure' control.

8.5. If any kind of joint preliminary steps were to be taken as acting together to secure or exercise control, where would the line be drawn? Both GU and SAUR had visited OFWAT in the autumn of 1995 to have discussions before their decision to act in relation to the proposed acquisition. If such discussions, because they might ultimately lead to an acquisition, were interpreted as actions to secure control, the position of the DGWS and the DGFT would be untenable. Mergers requiring a mandatory reference to the MMC could be deemed to have arisen at the outset. Hence, in his view, no mergers existed at this stage.

8.6. On the events surrounding MKH's AGM and EGM on 18 July, the DGWS had noted the way in which GU and SAUR cast their votes on the relevant resolutions. The DGWS found this evidence inconclusive, but considered that it warranted further investigation by the MMC.

The public interest effects of an existing merger

8.7. The DGWS considered that a merger resulting from GU and SAUR acting together to secure or exercise control of MKH would indeed prejudice his ability to make comparisons. Such co-operation between GU and SAUR and the resulting control over MKH would in his view lead to a loss of distinctiveness between GU and MKH, between SAUR and MKH and indeed between GU and SAUR *inter se*. The consequence would be that the appointed businesses which the three companies controlled could not be treated as truly independent comparators. The DGWS could see no benefits in such mergers. Any benefits claimed could be achieved without mergers.

Remedies

8.8. If a merger was found already to exist and the arrangements originally proposed proceeded subject to remedies of the kind suggested by the DGWS (see paragraph 8.56 and following), then the adverse effects of the existing merger would be addressed by the remedies attaching to the proposed arrangements. If, however, an existing merger were found to have arisen but the proposed arrangements did not proceed, then the DGWS considered that alternative remedies would be required to bring the existing merger to an end. That could be achieved by enforcing the 1991 undertakings against GU and requiring similar undertakings from SAUR to ensure that the two companies ceased to act, and did not again act, as 'associated persons'. An alternative and more definitive remedy, which the DGWS preferred, would be to require both GU and SAUR to divest shares in MKH to a level at which they could not in aggregate exercise material influence over the policy of MKH. Finally, if a merger was not found already to exist and the arrangements originally proposed were allowed to proceed subject to remedies, but did not, the DGWS considered that the remedies would need to ensure that both GU and SAUR did not in future act as 'associated persons'. He considered that the Secretary of State for Trade and Industry had powers to ensure this in the context of remedies for the proposed arrangements.

The use of comparators

The importance of comparators

8.9. The main evidence from the DGWS on the use of comparators and the effects of losing them is set out in Appendix 8.1. He stated that the value of comparisons between companies in the industry and the vital role played by the DGWS's use of them had been noted by the MMC in their report on the Lyonnaise/Northumbrian merger. The MMC had concluded that:

— the DGWS's use of comparisons permeated the regulatory system;

— it was of critical importance, informing quantitative and qualitative assessment of a wide range of activities;

— it had increased efficiency in the industry and enhanced the information available to the regulator; and

— it was fundamental to the operation of comparative competition in the future and to the continued dynamism of the process and companies' responses to it.

In the DGWS's view, events since the Lyonnaise/Northumbrian reference had served only to reinforce the MMC's conclusions, as his use of comparisons had developed further.

8.10. The DGWS stated that he used comparators not only in determining price controls but across the range of his functions. He provided a detailed description, updated since the Lyonnaise/Northumbrian report, of the use of comparators. This is in Appendix 8.1. At the last (1994) Periodic Review, the DGWS used comparators within each of four purpose categories (base service provision, enhanced service levels, supply/demand balance and quality enhancement). There were three cost categories (operating costs, capital maintenance and the return on capital) by reference to which he analysed companies' activities. In addition, comparisons were used in other areas including:

— customer service, including comparisons of performance in delivering service, in speed of response, in providing compensation for service failures, and in implementing optional meter scheme;

— tariff structures, including comparisons of companies' approaches to structuring their tariffs the better to reflect the costs of supplying different classes of customer;

— financial performance, including comparisons of companies' policies on dividends and comparisons of their respective financial indicators (such as interest cover, dividend cover and gearing); and

— transfer pricing, including comparisons of the ways in which and extent to which companies implemented the DGWS's Regulatory Accounting Guidelines, which dealt with the relationships between appointed and non-appointed activities of water companies.

8.11. Further, the MMC in the Lyonnaise case had recognized the usefulness of comparisons at a regional level. The MMC had also stated that stock market information, such as price:earnings ratios and dividend yields, enabled useful comparisons to be made.

8.12. In the DGWS's view, an important consideration was the pressure exerted on independent companies by competition for corporate control: the threat of take-over could force less efficient companies to improve their performance, including reducing their costs. It was preferable that pressure came from outside the industry, since mergers between water companies were subject to greater regulatory scrutiny and control.

Changes in the structure of the industry

8.13. Whereas in 1989 there had been 39 appointed water undertakers, 29 of which were WoCs and ten WaSCs, this number had already reduced to 29. Mergers had brought the number of WoCs down to 19. Five of those 19 were small and therefore could not provide an effective basis for comparison in judging the larger companies. Of the 24 larger companies (WoCs and WaSCs taken together), ten were owned or controlled by one or other of three corporate groups, GU, SAUR and Lyonnaise. This gave an effective total of only 17 major separately-owned water comparators (nine WaSCs, five WoCs and three corporate groups). In addition, mergers between water and electricity companies had taken place since the Lyonnaise/Northumbrian report (Welsh Water and SWALEC, North West Water and NORWEB along with the take-over of SWS). Whilst not involving the loss of an independent water comparator, this activity had highlighted issues of the management and financial independence and visibility of a water utility business within a group structure.

Developments in the use of comparators

Efficiency and competitiveness

8.14. In the view of the DGWS, the dynamic nature of the comparative approach worked to provide companies with incentives continuously to improve their performance. Evidence was now beginning to appear of the changes in efficiency ranking which the DGWS had forecast in his evidence to the MMC in the Lyonnaise/Northumbrian case. All three companies directly involved in this inquiry, for example, had improved their efficiency rankings between 1993 and 1995.

8.15. The value of independent comparators in the regulatory regime had also been further demonstrated by levels and quality of service. For example, on compensation payments for poor service, the ability to use comparators to demonstrate good practice had been vital in achieving recent improvements. In particular, comparisons of companies' customer charter schemes had highlighted what efforts companies were making beyond their minimum legal requirements. Another example was comparison of customer complaint handling procedures and policies. Comparative competition had also played a role in the sharing by companies of efficiency savings with their customers which had commenced in the last year.

Financial ring-fencing

8.16. Further, as the utility businesses were operating in an increasingly diversified and changing environment, so financial ring-fencing was becoming an increasingly important aspect of the DGWS's duty to ensure that water and sewerage undertakers were able to finance their functions. Again, comparative analysis had proved valuable. For example, the DGWS had initiated investigations into ring-fencing arrangements within the largest companies and groups of companies. Teams of independent consultants had visited companies to review the extent to which OFWAT's transfer pricing guidelines were followed in practice. Companies had taken a variety of approaches to implementing the guidelines (see Appendix 8.1, paragraph 144 and following).

Capital expenditure

8.17. The DGWS's approach to assessing efficiency in capital expenditure, which had been endorsed by the MMC during the review of price limits for South West Water and Portsmouth Water in 1994/95,[1] was now being refined and complemented by the development of further econometric models to explore the different influences on capital maintenance expenditure by different companies. These would allow better informed and more robust judgments to be made in future price reviews and could thus result in greater efficiency savings being built into price limits. The number of independent datasets was important in the development of this work. As with the models previously used for operating costs, this work would depend upon having a large enough number of independent and diverse comparators available.

Leakage

8.18. A further use of comparators had been highlighted as a result of the water supply difficulties during the summer drought of 1995. The DGWS had carried out a detailed analysis of companies' methods of balancing the various components of their water supply and demand and estimating the economic level of leakage. This work had involved comparing companies' estimates of the water balance components such as unmeasured domestic consumption and challenging those who appeared not to be employing best practice. The work had resulted in substantial changes to some companies' estimated leakage levels and would allow better informed decisions on the investment and management of water supplies.

Developments in the scope for direct competition

8.19. There was limited scope for direct competition within the water industry. Some competition could be achieved through cross-border supplies of water for domestic purposes and by inset appointments (that is, appointments made to supply water or sewerage within an existing supplier's area). The Government's recent proposals would increase the scope for competition across borders. Any further mergers between water companies would reduce the number of potential competitors in the industry; mergers between contiguous companies, as was proposed in this case, would also reduce the scope for cross-border competition.

Relative value of comparators

General

8.20. The effects of the loss of a comparator in the water industry would vary with circumstances. Any merger would lead to some loss of comparative data, and this would not be remedied by maintenance of separate appointments. Although separate appointments might help to identify some of the variation in costs between operating in different natural environments, differences of management style and management priorities had revealed themselves as key factors in performance in the last five years. They were likely to become more important in the future as the water industry became increasingly more diverse than it had been under public ownership. Companies had continued to differentiate themselves. And the differences in management style seen so far derived largely from differences in ownership. In the DGWS's view, therefore, even if separate appointments could be maintained these would be a poor substitute for comparisons between separately-owned companies.

---

[1] *South West Water Services Ltd: a report on the determination of adjustment factors and infrastructure charges for South West Water Services Ltd*, HMSO, July 1995. *Portsmouth Water plc: a report on the determination of adjustment factors and infrastructure charges for Portsmouth Water plc*, HMSO, July 1995.

Cost comparators: inter-company variations

8.21. So far as his operation of the regulatory regime was concerned, the DGWS considered that the effects of losing a listed comparator included:

(a) reduced ability to estimate the minimum operating and capital expenditure which should be allowed for in setting price limits;

(b) inferior stock market and other financial information on which to base assumptions about the economic cost of capital and other financial parameters to be assumed in setting price limits; and

(c) reduced ability to press companies for:

(i) better outputs such as higher water pressure, faster responses to queries;

(ii) better information and systems for collecting information;

(iii) better arrangements for charging and better tariffs;

(iv) better transfer pricing and ring-fencing policies;

(v) better compensation for poor service and better resolution of complaints;

(vi) better policies for disadvantaged customers; and

(vii) better policies for sharing benefits with customers either in the form of rebates, by making less than full use of the price headroom in K, or by discretionary investment.

8.22. Given the DGWS's duty to act in the manner he considered best calculated to secure that companies could finance their functions, his ability directly to apply cost estimates drawn from one company to the operations of another was limited. It was therefore important that he had a range of different companies from which to select a comparator. For example, costs allowed for in setting the price limits for larger companies had to be consistent with the experience of comparable companies. The operating environment of all companies was influenced by local conditions. For large companies the effect was averaged across their region. For smaller companies, there was more variation as specific local conditions could dominate.

8.23. Although there were limitations to applying information from small companies to bigger ones, the range of costs incurred by smaller companies revealed the importance of local factors. As water was expensive to transport, local differences would remain important: hence the importance of comparisons within a region and the detriment resulting from the loss of a regional comparator. The DGWS believed that local circumstances would be increasingly relevant in identifying costs to be allowed in setting price limits.

Spectrum of loss to the comparator system

8.24. The MMC had found useful, in the Lyonnaise/Northumbrian inquiry, to be aware of the spectrum of mergers identified by the DGWS from consideration of the range of uses of comparison, from the most harmful to the least harmful. As there described, this had been as follows:

Most harmful — merger of two contiguous WaSCs;
— merger of two non-contiguous WaSCs;
— merger of two independently-controlled large companies in the same region;
— merger of two large companies in different regions;
— merger of a large company with a small company.

Least harmful — merger of two neighbouring small companies. This could be more likely to produce a better comparator, but would not necessarily do so.

8.25. The DGWS had considered the matter further in relation to MKW. He had developed a matrix, reproduced as Figure 8.1, which set out in greater detail the range of possible mergers and the relative scale of detriment arising from them. The matrix showed six broad categories of harm ranked, in ascending order, from A to F. Within each of these categories there was, however, a range of detriment. In each category mergers between contiguous companies were more detrimental than those involving comparable remote companies because of their additional impact on regional comparisons and cross-border competition.

8.26. Within *category A* the DGWS regarded the take-over by neighbouring large companies of companies too small to be protected under the 1991 Act as more detrimental than mergers between two such small companies. Within *category B* the DGWS would regard any merger as causing significant harm but mergers involving large WoCs and WaSCs would be more serious than those between WoCs. *Category C*, which broadly encompassed the present merger proposals (two WoCs owned by large groups, one of which was a large WoC, and a contiguous large WoC), involved the loss of one of the larger water comparators. Again increasing size and contiguity gave rise to greater detriments. *Category D* would result in the loss of both a water and a sewerage comparator. *Category E* involved mergers with large water and sewerage operations. These were extremely detrimental. They created a new entity at the extreme end of the industry size range while losing a company more directly comparable with others in the industry. Finally, *category F* involved mergers with the largest water and sewerage operations, and were even more detrimental than those of category E.

Quantifying the value of a comparator

8.27. In the DGWS's view it was not possible to devise a means of quantifying the value of a comparator capable of reflecting the many and diverse ways in which he and OFWAT's CSCs used comparisons. While some detriments might be quantified, at least in principle, not all of them could be given monetary values. Some could only be considered qualitatively. Neither was it possible to state definitively which of the detriments was most important, in part because the importance of individual issues changed. For example, while disconnections had become less of a problem as their occurrence had reduced, leakage had become more significant in the light of recent weather conditions and changes in demand for water supplies. However, in some areas it might be possible to devise models that illustrated possible effects of losing a comparator, although these would be dependent on the precise assumptions on which they were based. Such quantification could only be illustrative, since the very essence of the comparative approach to regulation was its dynamic nature.

8.28. Nevertheless, in his evidence in the Lyonnaise/Northumbrian inquiry, the DGWS had included an analysis of the possible effect which losing the leading comparator would have had on one aspect of the 1994 price-setting review. This work had indicated that the loss of a comparator, shown to be near the efficiency frontier, could have resulted in setting price limits which were significantly higher, perhaps by £50 million a year, than those actually set in 1994. This analysis had assumed movement of the average company halfway to the position of the frontier company.

8.29. Since then, the DGWS had looked again at possible means of illustrating the value of a leading comparator (or frontier company) at a quinquennial review. Using a typical set of assumptions about the derivation of efficiency assumptions at a Periodic Review, he had developed a model to indicate the potential impact of the loss of the leading comparator. The loss of even one of the smallest companies could have a very substantial effect. The model and the recent work done are discussed and explained further in paragraph 4.37 onwards and in Appendix 4.5.

The loss of Mid Kent Water as a comparator

8.30. In the DGWS's view, the proposed acquisition of MKH and its division and annexation into the GU and SAUR groups respectively would materially prejudice his ability to make comparisons in the regulation of the water industry and prejudice the benefits to the consumer that result from comparative competition. The proposed merger would reduce from 17 to 16 the number of major separately-owned water comparators (see paragraph 8.13). Maintenance of a sufficient number of separate undertakers was important to secure a satisfactory base for reliable econometric modelling. Such

FIGURE 8.1

Matrix showing detriment to economic regulatory regime resulting from the loss of a comparator

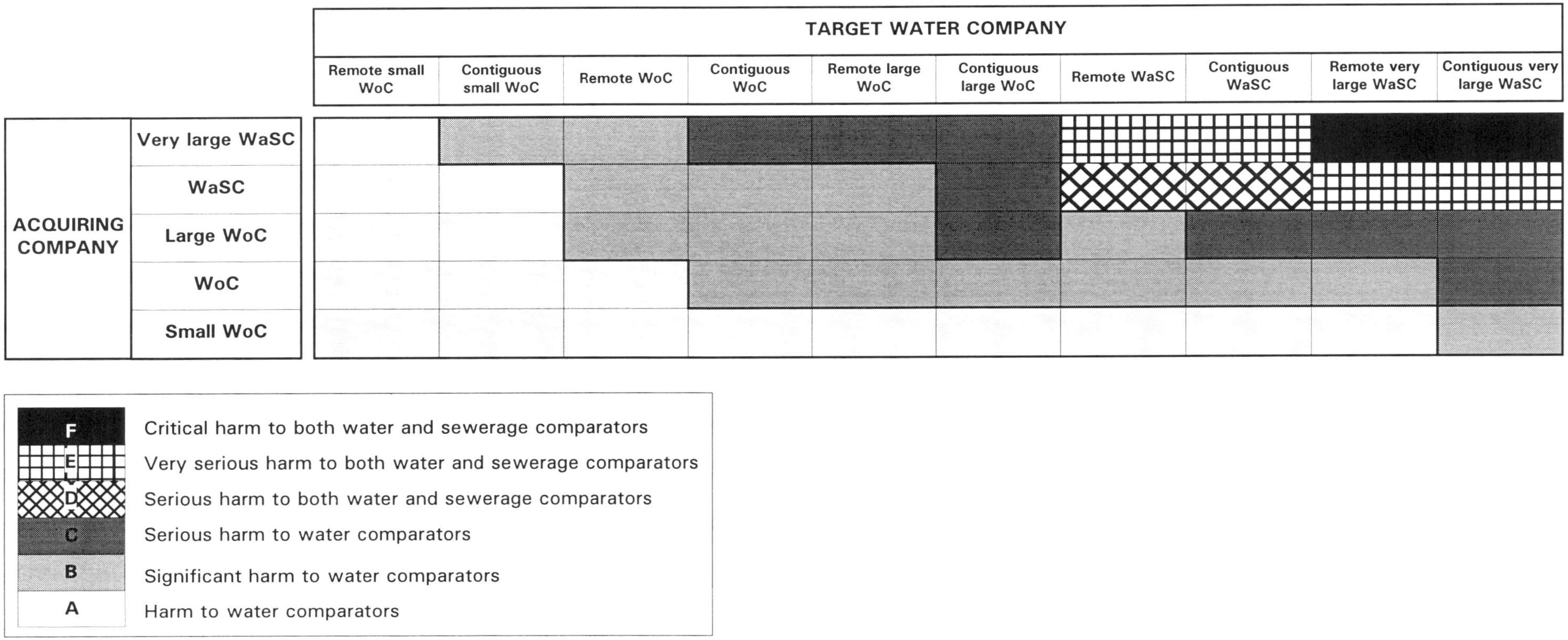

		TARGET WATER COMPANY									
		Remote small WoC	Contiguous small WoC	Remote WoC	Contiguous WoC	Remote large WoC	Contiguous large WoC	Remote WaSC	Contiguous WaSC	Remote very large WaSC	Contiguous very large WaSC
ACQUIRING COMPANY	Very large WaSC	B	B	C	D	D	D	E	E	F	F
	WaSC	A	B	B	C	C	D	E	E	E	E
	Large WoC	A	A	B	B	C	C	C	C	C	C
	WoC	A	A	A	B	B	B	B	B	B	B
	Small WoC	A	A	A	A	A	A	A	A	A	A

Legend:
- F: Critical harm to both water and sewerage comparators
- E: Very serious harm to both water and sewerage comparators
- D: Serious harm to both water and sewerage comparators
- C: Serious harm to water comparators
- B: Significant harm to water comparators
- A: Harm to water comparators

Source: OFWAT.

Notes:
1. The differences between the categories are important, but it should not be forgotten that there are also differences within categories which are also significant.
2. The detriments described are based upon the number of comparators in existence at 1 April 1996.

benefits as might be claimed for the proposed acquisition, in particular in relation to water resources, could be realized without the merger and did not outweigh the detriments to comparative competition (see paragraph 8.54). Illustrative work carried out by OFWAT had indicated that losing a company the size of MKW could have a very substantial adverse effect on price limits set for England and Wales, with an NPV ranging from £20 million to £590 million with an average of £120 million. This work had explored only one aspect, namely operating costs, of the many important ways in which comparators were used and could not therefore be used as a full indication of the value of a lost comparator.

The detriments of the proposed acquisition

8.31. As MKW was currently a significant independent water company in a part of England dominated by the subsidiaries of the two major groups, GU and SAUR, it was particularly valuable, both actually and potentially, as a comparator against which to judge the conduct of other WoCs in south-east England operating in comparable conditions. The detriment to the DGWS's ability to make comparisons arose from the loss of an independently-owned comparator. This independence would be lost as soon as GU and SAUR together acquired the entire share capital of MKH.

Mid Kent Water's dynamic potential

8.32. The DGWS said that MKW's actual performance relative to others at any particular time was of less importance than the fact that as an independently-owned and -managed undertaking it retained the potential to leap-frog other companies. This was an intrinsic part of the process of comparative competition.

Mid Kent Water's performance

8.33. Moreover, according to the DGWS, MKW had been improving its performance, for example:

— in levels of service, having previously been poor in its handling of customers' complaints and queries;

— in respect of interruptions to water supplies MKW's performance was well above average (and well above SEW);

— although MKW's performance in terms of water pressure was average, its information systems were believed by OFWAT to produce good-quality data; the ability of a company like MKW to produce data of reasonable quality in this area was a valuable example when encouraging companies to improve their information systems; and

— in addition, MKW was one of the companies which largely complied with the DGWS's charging policies as set out in *Paying for Water*;[1] for example, it had removed the differential between the tariffs for measured and unmeasured supplies and had reduced its measured standing charge to below the DGWS's target level. Again, the existence of such companies with appropriate charging policies was extremely useful in negotiations with other companies.

Reduction of the number of separate water undertakers

8.34. For the DGWS, absorption of companies into large groupings reduced the diversity and thus the dynamics of comparative competition. In the case of SAUR, for example, the DGWS had already raised concerns over the extent to which Mid Southern Water and SEW could be considered individually. Although the water supply companies had separate operational teams, they were headed by the same Managing Director. The working capital of the water companies was financed by a loan facility

---

[1] *Paying for Water: The Way Ahead* (OFWAT), a statement of the DGWS's conclusions, December 1991.

established at the level of SAUR. It was not clear to what extent the companies had control over their dividend policies. A full report was still being prepared.

Reduction in quality of data

8.35. The DGWS said that the proposed arrangements would result in the loss of separate data for MKW's activities. And for each of the two enlarged concerns the data post-merger would cease to be comparable with the data pre-merger, breaking the continuity of comparisons.

Loss of a separately listed company

8.36. As in the case of Northumbrian Water, MKH would not be separately listed and would become part of larger groups for which there was no UK stock market listing. Listing provided, in the DGWS's view, valuable benefits for the regulatory regime:

— it provided comparative data on market performance indicators such as price:earnings ratios, dividend yields and market valuations;

— it put external pressure on management to run the company effectively;

— it also exposed the company to the risk of take-over and the incentives which that produced for efficient management; and

— generally, it provided an independent market view on the performance of a company which was not available in any alternative arrangement.

Loss of potential cross-border competition

8.37. Within the current legislative framework the DGWS considered that there was potential for cross-border supplies (for water for domestic purposes) between MKW and SEW and between MKW and FDWS. There was also potential through inset appointments for competition between SEW, FDWS and MKW. The GU and SAUR companies might argue that they needed sufficient water resources available in order to compete. If so, the DGWS would reply that if FDWS and SEW did not feel able to compete it would be because, so to speak, they had tied their hands behind their backs by not fully investigating what might be done by way of BST arrangements and transfers of abstraction licences to obtain sufficient water.

8.38. If the proposed acquisition proceeded, the removal of an independent company would reduce the scope for such competition. Although there would still be a border dividing MKW, because of the formation of the proposed JRC it was unlikely, in the DGWS's view, that either GU or SAUR would try to attract the other's customers. Moreover, GU and SAUR would have less incentive to compete with each other not least because an integral part of their proposals was to operate resources jointly. He understood that GU and SAUR contended that the proposed arrangements would put the new companies in a better position to compete for new inset appointments. He felt, however, that there was little force in this view.

8.39. Current tariffs showed very wide variations between the areas. SEW had the highest tariffs in the country and the differential across the border with MKW currently ranged from 16p per cubic metre to 38p per cubic metre. If this border were removed it would limit the scope for customers currently in SEW to gain full benefits of competition now or when the legislation changed.

8.40. The DGWS said that his staff had met GU and SAUR representatives to discuss the JRC. As a result GU and SAUR had made some changes to their proposals. The proposal was something of a muddle, and it kept changing shape. It would confuse things, and would especially do so if the respective water groups were to be listed (as a precondition of any agreement to the proposed arrangements). The

DGWS continued to regard the proposed JRC as a detriment to the comparator system. In his view the JRC:

— was not needed to own assets, physical or intangible. The assets could be jointly owned by the parties without an intervening corporate entity or better still divided between them, particularly in the case of the existing abstraction licences;

— did not provide a solution to any potential long-term supply imbalance between the enlarged SEW and FDWS. GU and SAUR argued that any substantial difference between their need for, or use of, the jointly-owned resources was unlikely. The DGWS, however, had not seen sufficient evidence to substantiate this assertion. He believed that the issue was one of careful forecasting and management of supply and demand in the enlarged region of each of the surviving water companies. The JRC was not necessary for this and could even reduce the incentives for careful resource management in each area. In the absence of a JRC, any divergence in demand could be addressed by a separate bilateral BST agreement between the parties or other parties; and

— was not necessary to solve problems arising from the requirement for the parent companies to fund any investment on an equal basis and at the same time. It was proposed that a JVA would be entered into between SEW and FDWS for the provision of finance to develop new resources. Each party could, however, make an independent decision on investment based upon its interests at the appropriate time.

8.41. The DGWS noted that the parties had now decided that it would not be necessary for the JRC to own physical assets associated with major new developments. Under the revised proposal, such assets would be owned directly by SEW and FDWS. This change to the proposal (and the fact that the JRC would be owned by the appointed businesses themselves and not by their parents) provided the DGWS with a degree of comfort that each of the appointed businesses would be able to control its physical assets, as was required under Condition K of its licence.

8.42. However, the DGWS was concerned that the JRC would still own intangible assets such as the existing and new abstraction licences. These had considerable financial and strategic value (especially in the south-east of England). The DGWS would prefer that assets of such importance were not held jointly between otherwise potentially competing entities since this tended to blur distinctiveness for competition purposes. If a JRC were created outside the formal ambit of the regulators, there would be no mechanism to prevent it from growing in influence over the operations of SEW and FDWS. For example, it was envisaged that the JRC would plan and develop major resources. Should this happen, the result could be a significant reduction in the distinctiveness of the two appointed businesses, causing further harm to the comparative regime. In addition, the existence of a joint agreement for the development of new resources would tend to reduce the potential for cross-border competition between SEW and FDWS.

8.43. The DGWS was also concerned that the JRC could prove to be an unstable arrangement. He had seen no evidence that there was a convergence of need for resources. A potential supply imbalance and differing priorities for investment could set up tensions between the two shareholders that could make the JRC inoperable. Indeed, there were no provisions in the JRC proposals which addressed this possibility. This suggested that the two parties might have no intention of jeopardizing their relationship, for example by competing with each other. Should the JRC become inoperable, a sharing out of the abstraction licences would probably be inevitable.

Availability of alternatives to the proposed arrangements

8.44. GU and SAUR claimed that the proposed arrangements would enable them more effectively to manage water resources in the areas covered by the three companies. However, the DGWS believed that the proposed arrangements were not necessary to achieve a satisfactory resolution of supply/demand issues in this region. Indeed, in so far as the arrangements did not involve SWS, which held most of the available additional water resource, they could in any event be of only limited benefit. Apart from seeking a better supply/demand balance through agreeing the transfer of abstraction licences voluntarily as a normal commercial transaction, which could well not be straightforward, there were two more practical approaches which might be adopted:

— by reducing demand for water through effective programmes of metering and leakage control. The companies involved in the proposed arrangements did not have a history of effective demand management; and

— by obtaining water from other companies through BSTs. If they had concerns that unreasonable terms or conditions were being demanded by the supplier they were able to ask the DGWS to set the terms under which water should be provided. He had powers to ensure that the terms were fair.

8.45. As amended by the Competition and Services (Utilities) Act 1992, sections 40 and 40A of the 1991 Act gave the DGWS the power to set the terms and conditions of any bulk supply agreement. Section 40 provided that where:

(a) it appears to the Director that it is necessary or expedient for the purposes of securing the efficient use of water resources, or the efficient supply of water, that the water undertaker specified in the application ("the supplier") should give a supply of water in bulk to the applicant, and

(b) the Director is satisfied that the giving and taking of such a supply cannot be secured by agreement,

the Director may by order require the supplier to give and the applicant to take such a supply for such period and on such terms and conditions as may be provided in the order.

8.46. The DGWS considered that both these approaches should be adopted and that both offered an alternative, and perhaps more satisfactory, solution to local problems than was likely through the proposed arrangements. He understood that the possibility of arranging additional BSTs had been on offer to SEW and FDWS from SWS and MKW but, for whatever reason, these offers had not been pursued except in part. In his view, bulk supplies could provide an efficient way of addressing resource imbalances in the region. Bulk supplies worked successfully in many areas, including parts of Kent and East Sussex.

8.47. The Act stipulated that the DGWS should have regard, *inter alia*, to the desirability of:

— the supplier recovering the expenses of complying with its obligations and securing a reasonable return on its capital;

— the supplier being able to meet its existing obligations, and likely future obligations, to supply water without having to incur unreasonable expenditure in carrying out works; and

— not putting at risk the ability of the supplier to meet its existing obligations, or likely future obligations, to supply water.

His powers, which are set out in Appendix 4.1, had some limitations. He could not, for example, initiate the process of requesting a BST (see Appendix 4.1, paragraph 15). However, the DGWS was satisfied that he had adequate powers to arrange a solution once a request to him had been made, even where the potential supplier might be unwilling.

8.48. Indeed he could go further. If the DGWS were satisfied that a company was in breach of its general supply duty in section 37 of the 1991 Act, he would be able (even required) to demand remedial action. Assuming that the real cause of the company's failure was a deficiency of available water, he could require the company to correct it. Depending upon the circumstances, that might happen in several ways, for example by further measures to control leakage, or the creation of further links between the company's existing resources, if the deficiency were localized. If the failure could not be so corrected, the DGWS would have to decide whether the company's proposals were suitable, in terms of cost and performance. Any suggestions for the development of new resources (whether by abstraction or impounding) would have to be judged against the availability of BSTs, which would take advantage of resources already available to another company.

8.49. The DGWS could require the company to seek bulk supplies. Failing its agreement so to do, his powers of enforcement could be used to that end. The company need not feel that enforcement action would put it at risk of being held to ransom. There was already provision for disputes about the terms of agreements for bulk supplies to be resolved by the DGWS. Given the breadth of his enforcement powers, it would be open to him to impose a timetable for the achievement of these ends and to require the company, in default of agreement, to request that he settle the terms of the BST.

8.50. The DGWS had never been called upon to determine a disputed bulk supply agreement where, for example, the supply was considered by the supplier to jeopardize the supplier's ability to meet existing or likely future obligations to supply water. Should a supplier claim a bulk supply would so jeopardize its ability to supply, the DGWS would seek evidence to this effect from the supplier, ask advice on resource availability from the EA, ask an independent reporter to verify the supplier's position and review information already received by OFWAT on the supply and demand balance. The DGWS could then determine a bulk supply agreement against the wishes of the supplier if it appeared to him that it was necessary or expedient for the purpose of securing the efficient use of water resources or the efficient supply of water.

8.51. Further, given that both MKW and, in particular, SWS had surplus resources, the likelihood of the above happening was considered by the DGWS to be slight. He was not inclined to accept the proposition that, if FDWS and SEW sought adequate BSTs, they would fail.

Section 34(3)(b) of the Water Industry Act 1991

8.52. The DGWS was asked for his interpretation of the provisions of section 34(3)(b). In his response he said that, as to section 34(3)(b)(i), he agreed that the MMC could have regard to other purposes whose achievement did not conflict with the principle of comparative competition. This might (at least in theory) arise where the number and quality of companies after the merger would be such that the merger would not prejudice his ability to compare. Other purposes might also be taken into account under section 34(3)(b)(i) where achieving them would involve stopping the merger, since that *ex hypothesi* would avoid conflict with the principle. The DGWS had also obtained Counsel's opinion which argued that the term 'purpose' in section 34(3)(b)(i) should not be interpreted as being limited to purposes of the merger. But neither the DGWS nor any other party argued that the MMC should have regard to any purpose under section 34(3)(b)(i).

8.53. The DGWS also argued that there was a contrast between subparagraph (i) and subparagraph (ii) in that the former dealt with purposes achievable *without* conflict with the comparator principle whilst the latter dealt with purposes whose achievement did conflict with the principle. However, he could not agree that for subparagraph (ii) to apply the only condition that needed to be satisfied was that the benefits were of substantially greater significance than the principle. Such a construction simply flew in the face of the plain wording of the statute. Section 34(3)(b)(ii) expressly provided that the MMC 'shall have regard to the desirability of achieving any other purpose so far *only* as they are satisfied ... that the achievement of that purpose is of substantially greater significance in relation to the public interest than that principle *and* cannot be brought about except in a manner that conflicts with that principle' (DGWS's emphasis added). Thus the MMC might have regard to 'other purposes' under subparagraph (ii) only if *two* conditions were satisfied: first, if the benefits were of substantially greater significance than the damage to the comparative regime represented by the proposed merger; and second, if their achievement could not be brought about except in conflict with that principle (that is, their achievement was dependent upon the merger).

Absence of countervailing benefits

8.54. The proposed arrangements would result in damage to the DGWS's ability to make comparisons. Therefore, any possible benefits arising from them could only be taken into account if they satisfied section 34(3)(b)(ii) of the 1991 Act. The DGWS considered that the possible benefits outlined by GU and SAUR were either not benefits at all or failed both tests of section 34(3)(b)(ii). Where a benefit could be identified it was of minor significance in comparison to the detriment the proposal would cause, and furthermore could be achieved without the merger and the concomitant harm to the regulatory regime.

8.55. Most importantly, the proposed arrangements could not resolve the resources imbalance within the region in the long term, which would require the participation of SWS. Specific DGWS comments on the possible benefits were:

(a) Alleviation of water resource imbalances in the area of the three companies. The arrangements could not resolve the resource imbalance in the long term, which would need to involve transfers of resources from SWS. So any benefit would be limited to the short term. The DGWS believed that GU and SAUR had not adequately investigated alternative means of alleviating the resource imbalance involving SWS.

(b) An integrated supply network. This could only provide a short-term means of alleviating the resource imbalance, following MKW's integration into SEW and FDWS. The price limits set in 1994 for MKW already specifically allowed for the expenditure needed to develop strategic links and therefore increased the scope for transfers within that company's area. In the longer term, there were alternative ways of resolving the resources imbalance and the contribution made by the proposed arrangements would only be short term and therefore of minor significance, when compared with the long-term loss of a comparator.

(c) Enabling long-term resource planning on a regional basis (and convergence on when a new major resource is needed). This could be achieved without a merger through closer co-operation between the parties, and was therefore not a benefit of the merger in the DGWS's eyes.

(d) Improved leakage reductions and metering performances. There was no reason to suppose that improved demand management would result from the proposed arrangements. It was highly desirable that the companies should take action on this front, but all could do so independently. All three companies were taking some action. In so far as the proposals might result in an increase in supply, it might, of course, take away the pressure on them to pursue this action sufficiently vigorously.

(e) Generation of additional resources from the River Medway system. This could help to resolve the resources imbalance, but a merger was not required to achieve it. Development of new resources might not necessarily be the most economic solution; bulk supplies might be a cheaper alternative.

(f) Resource management and conservation programmes. The DGWS had not seen details of these possible benefits. He did not understand how it could be argued that a merger was a precondition to such measures.

(g) Enabling conjunctive use of surface and groundwater sources. This in itself was another way to assist alleviation of the resources imbalance. A merger was not required to achieve this benefit and it might not be the most economic solution.

(h) Improving service standards for MKW customers. It had already been shown that the comparative regime was an effective route to bring about improvements. Because such benefits would emerge from the operation of comparators they could not be claimed as benefits solely of a merger.

(i) Creation of better circumstances for genuine competition. The proposed arrangements could be expected to inhibit competition between GU and SAUR. It would reduce cross-border competition by significantly reducing the length of the boundaries in this area. The present structure of several companies encouraged the development of cross-border competition. If the parties combined to work together, for example through a JRC, this was also likely to reduce competition. The DGWS would, therefore, expect the arrangements overall to be detrimental for competition.

Possible remedies

8.56. For the DGWS, the detriments were aspects of the consequences of the loss of a comparator. Section 34(3)(a) of the 1991 Act set up a presumption that such a loss might be expected to operate against the public interest, because of its effect upon the ability to make comparisons. Since the ability to do that permeated the regime, the prejudice also permeated it. In the view of the DGWS, the most effective remedy for the reduction in the number of comparators was likely to be through the improvement in quality of comparators, by the creation of exemplary new comparators. This might be achieved by a package of measures, an important part of which would involve a reduction in the costs which the company was able to support, brought about through a reduction in the revenue which it was permitted to collect. In order to be a remedy for the damage caused by the merger, the exemplary merged company would need to be required to perform at a level better than that which would have resulted without the merger through the normal operation of the price review mechanism.

8.57. The remedies proposed by the DGWS were all designed to improve the quality of the new comparator, in order to alleviate the reduction in quantity. To that extent, all the proposed remedies went to the same adverse effect, the damage caused to the comparative regime by the loss of a comparator. If a new comparator was to be effective for the regulator its performance must be visible to him as well as exemplary. Any remedy must, therefore, in his view, consist of a package of measures to:

— reduce costs and prices;
— maintain or improve outputs for customers; and
— improve visibility of the regulated business.

Costs and prices

8.58. The DGWS considered that the enlarged companies should undertake to make significant reductions in prices as evidence of their acceptance of the need to become exceptionally efficient and to operate with significantly lower costs than would otherwise have been assumed at the next price revue.

8.59. Account had to be taken of the scale of the merger relative to previous cases and of the fact that successive mergers had become increasingly difficult to justify because of their cumulative impact on the regime. The DGWS therefore believed that price reductions towards the top of the range 10 to 15 per cent of the combined revenue of the three merged entities, that is MKW, SEW and FDWS, would be appropriate. This would be equivalent to £10 million to £15 million a year, £143 million to £214 million NPV.[1] Such price reductions should have a significant immediate effect on increasing efficiency and in pushing the companies beyond the efficiency frontier. The DGWS considered that an effective remedy could be implemented only through amendments to appointments. In the Lyonnaise/Northumbrian merger the MMC accepted that an appropriate remedy for the loss of a comparator was the creation of an exemplary comparator through the imposition of price cuts giving an incentive to efficiency.

Outputs

8.60. The merged companies should undertake to retain those features of performance where any of the merging companies is a leading comparator within the industry in order to prevent the averaging down which might otherwise result from the merger. More generally the merged companies should be required to achieve an upper quartile assessment in all aspects of performance monitored by OFWAT.

Visibility

Market information

8.61. Under the current proposal, the independent listing for MKH would be lost. The GU and SAUR groups were not listed in the UK at all. Furthermore the comparative value of information

---

[1] 7 per cent discount rate to 2025.

obtained from regulatory accounts for companies under common ownership was reduced by their lack of independence, for example in respect of financing arrangements. The DGWS therefore believed that GU and SAUR should each be required to list on the Stock Exchange their UK water businesses as enlarged by the merger to improve the visibility of the UK water interests of the French groups to the regulator and the public. Such listings would be analogous to that agreed by Lyonnaise as a condition of its take-over of Northumbrian Water.

8.62. The DGWS would prefer the quoted companies of the two groups to be purely concerned with the provision of water services. However, he would be prepared to regard the listed companies' stock market performance as a proxy for that of such a company provided that unregulated activities constituted less than 15 per cent of the listed group totals, measured by reference to each group's gross assets employed and operating profit (that is, profit before interest and taxation).

8.63. Although such listings could not directly remedy the loss of MKH as a separately listed company it would mitigate the loss to some extent by providing new stock market information, for two groups of companies. They would also contribute to the creation of exemplary comparators by increasing the transparency of the enlarged water businesses of GU and SAUR, requiring them to report on a stand-alone basis to shareholders under the Listing Rules, and by exposing them to external pressures to improve their performance.

8.64. The increase in efficiency (through price reductions) was of greatest importance. However, the DGWS also attached considerable significance to the issue of visibility, particularly listing. He would regard it as a significant contribution to the creation of exemplary comparators if the companies were to commit to the early listing of their UK regulated water interests and to amendments to appointments designed to increase the independence of the utilities within their groups. The additional transparency, financial information and thus scope for active competition would act as an additional spur to improved efficiency and performance and could have some influence on his view as to the precise level of the remedial price reduction.

Management independence

8.65. A number of companies in the industry had already agreed to amendments to appointments which would secure management separation. These included provisions to ensure that the utility acted independently from the parent company (via appointment of independent non-executive directors to the utility Board; annual certification that adequate management resources were available, additional control over contracted-out facilities and purchases by utility business from associated companies). In the DGWS's view these should be included in any remedy.

Other comparative information

8.66. Given the particular stage of the regulatory cycle, with a potential price review in 1998/99 there would be some value in maintaining access to trend data on costs, outputs and explanatory factors for the existing MKW, SEW and FDWS operations through to 1997/98, which would be the base year for the 1999 review.

Joint Resources Company

8.67. The DGWS believed there was no need for the JRC, and that it could even add to the harm caused to the comparative regime. The creation of a JRC could also delay discussions as to how MKW's assets should be split. He had therefore concluded that if the arrangements were allowed to proceed, they should do so only subject to remedies in addition to those remedies outlined above. The JRC structure could be replaced by a sharing out of the assets; alternatively, the JRC's activities could be constrained by undertakings from the parties that there should be no transfer of assets or capital from the parties into the JRC without the DGWS's consent.

9 The views of the Environment Agency

Contents

Paragraph

Introduction 9.1
The role of the EA
    General 9.3
    Protecting and enhancing the environment 9.4
    Demand forecasts and joint working with OFWAT 9.5
The EA's licensing function
    Licensing criteria 9.7
    Situation in the EA Southern Region 9.13
Water resources in Kent and East Sussex
    Resource availability 9.15
Resource management
    Joint Resources Company 9.19
    GU's and SAUR's infrastructure proposals (the 'mini-grid') 9.22
    Medway proposal 9.25
    Leakage 9.29
    Metering 9.30
    Bulk supply transfers 9.31
Detriments, benefits and remedies
    Detriments 9.35
    Benefits 9.38
    Remedies 9.39
Possible merger in being 9.47
Interpretation of section 34(3)(b) of the Water Industry Act 1991 .... 9.49

Introduction

9.1. This chapter summarizes the views of the EA which were provided, mainly by the EA's Southern Region, in written submissions to the MMC and at two hearings. The EA and OFWAT also provided a joint background submission on water resources in East Sussex and Kent.

9.2. The MMC sought evidence from the EA on any existing merger and on the proposed arrangements. The MMC were concerned to establish whether GU's and SAUR's proposals or the possible existing merger might have any effect on the EA's ability to administer the abstraction licensing system; whether the EA considered that the proposals were desirable to secure better water resource use in the region; and whether the aims of the proposals were capable of achievement other than through the proposed mergers. The EA's views were also sought on any remedies the EA thought appropriate if the MMC concluded that any of the mergers might be expected to operate against the public interest and on any other issues which the EA considered relevant. Some of the EA's views, especially on resource issues, are shown in greater detail in Chapter 5.

The role of the EA

General

9.3. The EA's regulatory functions are set out in Appendices 4.1 and 4.2. In its evidence the EA explained that when the industry was privatized in 1989, responsibilities for water resources planning were passed to the NRA. The NRA had developed national and regional policies between 1989 and 1996, which reflected international and national policies on sustainable development. The NRA advocated demand management and transfers between companies before major new resource developments. All those policies had been adopted by the EA, as the successor organization to the NRA from 1 April 1996. The EA had a general duty to manage water resources with powers to conserve, redistribute, augment and secure their proper use. This duty was mainly achieved through determining abstraction licence applications and through national and regional water resource development strategies, for example as set out in *Sustaining Our Resources—The Way Forward* published by the NRA's Southern Region in November 1994, now in the process of being updated. The EA's general duties on managing resources had attracted criticism from the water industry on the grounds that the EA's activity did not adequately reflect the commercial realities of the water industry post-privatization. In the EA's view this was largely because the relevant legislation (the Water Resources Act 1991) was in essence a continuation of pre-privatization legislation, notably the Water Resources Act 1963. The legislation was therefore specifically related to the proper management of water resources and was not designed to cope with commercial competition.

Protecting and enhancing the environment

9.4. The EA also had a duty to protect and enhance the environment. Where river flows had been reduced by over-abstraction the EA sought to remedy matters with the companies concerned. The Darent in north Kent was a local example. EA environment policy emphasized the principles of:

— sustainable development;

— the precautionary principle (for example, to refuse applications, where there was a risk of adverse impact on the environment); and

— demand management.

These principles had important implications for the merger proposals.

Demand forecasts and joint working with OFWAT

9.5. In addition, the EA had a duty to publish demand forecasts, and on this worked closely with OFWAT which used forecasts from the water companies as a basis for the economic regulatory regime. One of the key components of demand forecasting was leakage. Both OFWAT and the EA took a keen interest in company leakage levels. OFWAT published annual comparisons of performance, while the EA Southern Region water resources strategy provided indicative leakage level targets of 6 l/prop/h or 120 l/prop/d. These were taken as starting points in considering 'reasonable need' (see paragraph 9.11) in determining abstraction licence applications.

9.6. A further area of joint working with OFWAT was on BSTs between companies. There were good water resource reasons for using such transfers. In using its powers to order BST agreements, OFWAT was statutorily required to consult the EA.

The EA's licensing function

Licensing criteria

9.7. In determining abstraction licence applications, the EA said that it must balance the reasonable need of the abstractor against the impact on other abstractors and the environment. In assessing a water company application the following issues were paramount:

— was total leakage (from water company distribution and customer supply pipes) down to an acceptable and economic level, taking into account both operating costs and capital costs of new sources;

— had the company promoted to its customers water conservation and demand management, particularly through meter installations and appropriate tariffs; and

— were there surplus water resources available from neighbouring companies which could be transferred for up to 10 or 15 years?

9.8. The EA was asked about the full extent of its powers. It said that it had a duty under section 19 of the Water Resources Act 1991 to take action in accordance with the directions of the Secretary of State for the Environment, where necessary to conserve, redistribute or otherwise augment water resources in England and Wales; and to secure the proper use of such water resources. Although apparently wide-ranging, it was advised that the duty did not itself confer powers to take any action but applied only in relation to functions conferred by other sections of the Act.

9.9. It was implicit in the issue of licences in perpetuity and of right that a water abstraction licence should become a valuable property right or asset. Licences were routinely transferred by agreement and negotiation when property with abstraction rights changed hands. However, the EA did have powers, dating back to the Water Resources Act 1963, to revoke licences, for which compensation might be payable following a valuation by the Lands Tribunal. The powers had hardly ever been used and certainly not 'aggressively' to revoke a water company licence for transfer to another company. The EA did not consider that its powers to revoke licences extended to circumstances where the main purpose of such an action would be to reallocate water resources between two water companies in order to redress historic imbalances in available supplies and commercial competitiveness.

9.10. If major public water supply licences were to be revoked, the compensation claimed might be the cost of replacement resources, perhaps £1 million to £2 million per Ml/d of source yield. Compensation payment of, say, £50 million for the loss of a 25 Ml/d source would obviously present major problems to the EA which had a regional annual water resources income of about £7 million. (The national annual income for the EA was about £85 million.) The EA believed its powers were available to redress the balance between abstraction and the aquatic environment. In 1992 the NRA Board had resolved to use these powers unilaterally to reduce abstraction licences held by Thames Water which were drying up flows in the River Darent, in north Kent. In the event, Thames Water had agreed to a voluntary reduction of 30 per cent of licensed abstractions, but it had suggested it might claim about £50 million compensation for loss of 23 Ml/d abstraction yield.

9.11. The EA said that in 1994 SAUR and GU had proposed to the NRA and OFWAT that SWS's Darwell licences should be revoked and transferred to SEW. This the NRA considered inappropriate and impractical. Although the Secretary of State for the Environment had powers under section 52 of the Water Resources Act 1991 to direct the EA to formulate proposals for revoking licences, he did not do so. This proposal had not featured in SEW's 1994 strategic business plan. The EA would, however, have no difficulty in facilitating a redistribution of licences where this could be mutually agreed between the parties concerned.

9.12. It had been argued that the EA had a statutory duty to make water available for a water undertaker who had not got sufficient water, and where a BST arrangement could not be imposed because it would put at risk the potential supplier's ability to meet its statutory obligations. The EA said, however, that this argument was based on a misunderstanding. Section 19(1) of the Water Resources Act 1991 was a wide-ranging duty on the EA but section 19(2) of the same Act put the responsibility for resource development squarely with the undertaker. 'Nothing in this section shall be construed as relieving any water undertaker of the obligation to develop water resources for the purpose of performing any duty imposed on it by virtue of section 37 of the Water Industry Act 1991.' Certainly the EA would expect to assist an undertaker, in accordance with section 19(1), but the concept of the EA being obliged to make water available was erroneous. Furthermore, EA policy nationally was not to become involved in resource development schemes, and only in exceptional circumstances would it promote a scheme. This could occur if, for example, there were a number of beneficiaries, or if the scheme had a large environmental benefit.

Situation in the EA Southern Region

9.13. At present the EA saw plenty of scope in its Southern Region for:

— leakage reduction;
— demand management; and
— BSTs.

If water resources were managed making use of these techniques, in line with the low demand assumptions (which the EA considered the more likely) made in the NRA's national strategy paper 'Water: Nature's Precious Resource' (NRA, 1994), there should be sufficient resources for the Southern Region as a whole up to around 2021.

9.14. This judgment took account of information supplied by the companies themselves and by the EA's own consultants. The view was also robust when set against long-term predictions, for example those in the recent DoE *Review of the Potential Effects of Climate Change in the United Kingdom* (HMSO, 1996). The long-term reductions in rainfall in the south-east of England which were forecast made it important to manage demand properly and to deter unessential use through a policy of metering coupled with differential tariffs.

Water resources in Kent and East Sussex

Resource availability

9.15. A detailed analysis of resource issues, including information from the EA, is incorporated in Chapter 5. In essence, however, the EA believed that, although there were areas of deficit within East Sussex and Kent, there was an overall surplus in the region. On the basis of the EA's low demand scenario (which was considered by the EA to be the more likely scenario) no major new resources should be needed for 30 years or more.

9.16. In contending that the imbalance of water resources within the East Sussex–Kent area could be resolved through the integration of the distribution systems and water resources of the three companies, GU and SAUR had, in the EA's assessment, also assumed that there was groundwater available for development in the MKW area. However, there was no guarantee of this.

9.17. However, the EA considered that transfers of water from the west of its Southern Region (see paragraph 3.7) coupled with effective demand management would delay the need for a major new resource development. If this did not happen there was likely to be increased stress on the local groundwater in Kent, whether or not the merger proposals proceeded.

9.18. Another possible option to increase resource availability for the two companies FDWS and SEW was the transfer of resources between companies through abstraction licence revocation and re-issue. The EA said that, in principle, transfer of resources through licence transfer could be either:

(a) by mutual agreement between donor and recipient; or

(b) by 'aggressive' revocation by the EA and subsequent re-issue.

The EA referred to the recent DoE and Welsh Office report *Water Resources and Supply: Agenda for Action* which pointed out that the existing legislative and administrative procedure enabled water companies to reach agreement among themselves for the redistribution of abstraction licences. As indicated in paragraph 9.11, the EA considered that it would have no difficulty in facilitating such a redistribution; and there had been a recent case in the Southern Region of a water company 'purchasing' a licence from another organization, albeit not another water company. However, the indications so far from SWS were that it would not be willing to transfer licences by agreement, although it had offered BSTs on a number of occasions. The DoE report did not deal with case *(b)* but the EA's current view was that the legislation did not in practice envisage such a course of action by the EA (see paragraph 9.9) in circumstances such as these.

Resource management

Joint Resources Company

9.19. In the EA's view, the short-term implications for water resource use of the proposed JRC were as yet unclear. Should effective demand management be achieved, however, the need for major scheme development, which would be the JRC's most significant planning function, would be delayed for the foreseeable future. Consequently the role of the JRC might be less important than issues such as demand management.

9.20. In assessing the proposed functions of the JRC, the EA commented on its principal features as follows:

(a) *Planning* new major developments in the two enlarged areas and minor developments in the former MKW area. In the EA's view a separate corporate identity was not needed for planning purposes.

(b) *Promoting* new major resources (for example, Broad Oak) including negotiation with third parties (for example, SWS). The EA saw some small practical advantages arising from a JRC. The main benefit might be to have two more equally matched entities (JRC and SWS) entering into joint promotion.

(c) The *ownership* and control of major new assets would remain with FDWS and SEW, not with the JRC. In the EA's view this seemed seriously to undermine the case for a JRC. If the JRC did not own the assets it would merely be a planning device, which did not need a corporate status to be effective.

(d) *Minor sources* would be owned and developed by the separate companies, yet the licences would be held by the JRC. The EA could only receive licence applications from *occupiers* of land on which abstraction takes place and it appeared that the JRC might not be the legal occupier. Enforcement of licence conditions should be against the operator of the source, not a third party. The EA doubted that the JRC could be classified as a water undertaker and so might not be eligible to apply for drought orders for licences it held.

9.21. The EA maintained that co-operation between companies and the use of BSTs would ensure that companies arrived together at the point when a major new resource was to be planned without the need for a JRC. Whilst the proposals to pool SEW/MKW/FDWS resources in the short term could introduce a partial convergence of need, it would be at the expense of extra pressure on groundwater and did not address the more important imbalance between the GU and SAUR companies and SWS. The EA would be bound to view any new proposals to build Broad Oak reservoir in the light of the overall availability of resources in the Kent catchment.

GU's and SAUR's infrastructure proposals (the 'mini-grid')

9.22. The EA had also been shown an outline of the proposals by GU and SAUR for new infrastructure development in the MKW area to facilitate and optimize resource use across the area of the three present WoCs. In general, the EA considered that the connection of demand centres to strategic sources and the infilling of gaps in existing trunk mains improved the resilience of any resource system and was in line with EA policy. The proposals provided benefit to FDWS by effectively reallocating the Barham source, and improved supplies to Ashford in Mid Kent through the intended connection from Maidstone. The connections from Bewl Water, via Kippings Cross towards Tunbridge Wells, would improve the most vulnerable part of SEW's area. There was therefore a potential benefit to all three company areas (see Map 4).

9.23. In more detail (on which see also paragraphs 5.58, 6.12 and 6.13), the proposed pipelines from Canterbury to Barham and from Godmersham to Canterbury would enable the Barham source to be reallocated to FDWS, provided that the shortfall in Ashford could in turn adequately be made up from the west. Reallocation of Barham in this way had long been a feature of NRA/EA strategy and the proposal was therefore entirely consistent with this. However, the EA was seeking to reduce abstractions at Barham because of its impact on the Little Stour. This source would therefore be of limited value to Folkestone. This would have implications for the capacity of the pipeline required into Ashford from the west.

9.24. The proposed connection from the Medway Scheme at Bewl Water into Tunbridge Wells was also consistent with the NRA resources strategy. The supply would come from Mid Kent's existing entitlement at the reservoir. However, the extent to which further groundwater developments in the MKW area could contribute to supplies for Canterbury and for Folkestone and Dover would be dependent on the results of further investigation work to quantify likely outputs, and on the extent to which the EA would license them. As far as the EA was aware, most of this investigation work remained to be done.

Medway proposal

9.25. A key feature of the merger proposals was to be the generation of additional resources from the existing Medway system of some 25 Ml/d. On the face of it, however, the field trials carried out by the EA were unlikely to give any support to the GU and SAUR proposal submitted to the EA in the summer of 1996. This proposal could reduce notional fresh water residual flows below levels considered safe.

9.26. The NRA had carried out detailed investigations over two or three years to identify the most appropriate abstraction regime for the tidal Medway Estuary. In addition to hydrological modelling of the type carried out by the Institute of Hydrology for GU and SAUR, the EA had undertaken extensive water quality modelling of, and detailed monitoring of conditions in, the estuary (including trials of a 'bubbler barge'). This had allowed the EA to identify possible reductions in fresh water residual flows as a result of improved water quality following tighter discharge consents and multi-million pound investment in treatment by dischargers (mainly paper mills and SWS sewage works). The public water supply licences for the Medway Scheme were varied accordingly and over 100 other abstraction licences were varied to reduce the minimum residual flow conditions. However, the existing flow to the estuary still fell significantly short of that required to meet the estuary water quality objective. As a result the EA would be extremely unlikely to support proposals which reduced the notional fresh water residual flows any further.

9.27. The EA had at a late stage in the MMC inquiry met GU and SAUR, at their request, to explain these conclusions and findings to them. The EA was always willing to work with water companies to develop sensible proposals. It had made it clear to GU and SAUR that the water quality objectives for the Medway Estuary took into account recent effluent improvements. The EA was always prepared to consider proposals that would further treat effluent discharges so that the water quality objective could be met by lower fresh water flows, or by a scheme which provided additional fresh water low flow to the estuary. The EA could say with certainty, however, that the GU and SAUR proposals, as originally submitted (and allowing for the minimal supporting technical detail), were unlikely to be licensable. Any new proposals which the companies might put forward would, in the EA's view, face challenging, difficult and uncertain circumstances. It was doubtful that they could be cost-effective. They might be achievable, though at a high cost, but would in any case need very thorough investigation.

9.28. However, if additional storage were created at Bewl Water, the output from the Medway might be increased. The proposed strengthening of the mains around Maidstone envisaged as part of GU's and SAUR's 'mini-grid' would then be appropriate. Any scheme to enlarge the reservoir at Bewl would, however, have to be with the agreement of the owner, SWS.

Leakage

9.29. According to the EA, in England and Wales the smaller WoCs had a consistently better leakage record than the larger WaSCs. In Kent and East Sussex, however, the WaSC, SWS, had consistently outperformed the WoCs. And for 1997/98, while SWS was setting a target of 103 l/prop/d (a reduction of 33 l/prop/d), MKW's target was 120 l/prop/d and those of SEW and FDWS were some 20 l/prop/d higher (see Table 5.4). In its submission the EA said that exemplary performance in demand management (leakage and metering) was unlikely to be achieved by the merging companies without the stimulus of an enforceable recommendation from the MMC.

Metering

9.30. Metering targets for the three companies were also dissimilar. Although the EA considered that MKW had a better track record in achievement of targets, its aim by 2005 was a less challenging 23 per cent of households on meters, compared with 51 per cent and 53 per cent for SEW and FDWS respectively.

Bulk supply transfers

9.31. The EA said that it was well aware that SEW and FDWS argued that there were commercial and operational reasons why BSTs between themselves and SWS or MKW were unacceptable. The NRA previously, and now the EA, had, however, consistently taken the view that there were good water resource reasons for using transfers as the key option for securing proper use of water resources. Together with the DGWS, the EA had encouraged SEW and FDWS to take advantage of the opportunities available for BSTs on a number of recent occasions. This policy was also reflected in the EA's licensing policy and determinations. Neither company had yet had the opportunity to appeal against NRA/EA decisions and put their case to a public inquiry, although two small SEW abstraction applications were to be the subject of an inquiry in June 1997.

9.32. At the publication of the NRA Southern Region strategy document *Sustaining Our Resources—The Way Forward* in November 1994, companies had issued statements giving their position on transfers. SWS had said that it was willing to make supplies available; SEW and FDWS had said that it was not their company policy to take new bulk supplies. MKW had recently offered BSTs to both SEW and FDWS. The EA continued to promote such transfers as a means of meeting deficits and OFWAT had the necessary power to determine a fair price and conditions where there were disagreements.

9.33. In the EA's view, as SWS in particular had spare resources, they should be taken up as bulk supplies by SEW and FDWS. However, on the basis of information put to the EA by the two companies, there appeared to be a possibility that SEW and FDWS might seek to rescind the existing MKW/SWS agreements for BSTs if the mergers proceeded. If this were to happen it would have a very serious effect. It would put the companies in the position of needing to develop new resources much sooner than was necessary or anticipated.

9.34. In essence, the EA's view was that additional water resources and optimizing resource use could be achieved by the two companies without a merger, if they accepted BSTs. This was the preferred route from a water resource management point of view. It reduced the need to exploit groundwater in MKW's area, and postponed the need for further resource developments longer than would otherwise be the case.

Detriments, benefits and remedies

Detriments

9.35. The EA considered that the proposed arrangements could or would affect the duties of the EA in the following functional areas:

— managing and distributing water resources;
— securing proper use of water resources;
— protecting and enhancing the environment; and
— balancing the needs of the water customer, shareholder, other legitimate uses and the environment.

9.36. The EA considered that the loss of a comparator and information about water resources, resulting from the loss of MKW through the proposals, would affect the EA's ability to undertake the above functions. While, in its view, the use of comparators was not a precise science, it provided a critical frame of reference for identifying strategic and operational management issues. For example, where one company introduced a free meter option for sprinkler users, other companies in the area were likely to develop similar initiatives. The loss of a comparator was viewed by the EA as the loss of a source of ideas, solutions and incentives to improve the effectiveness and efficiency of water resource management.

9.37. For the EA, the proposals also clearly entailed the development of further groundwater in Kent. It would seem likely that potential development might be needed sooner than proposed by MKW if the companies, as the EA feared, did not accept further BSTs.

Benefits

9.38. The EA considered that most of the prospective benefits claimed by GU and SAUR for the proposals, such as improved infrastructure, resource optimization and better demand management, were achievable without the proposed acquisition. However, the proposed acquisition probably offered the only means of achieving better conjunctive use of sources (resulting from infrastructure improvements). There would be benefits to the environment, such as reductions in licensed abstractions from low-flow rivers such as the Darent. The EA doubted whether the proposed improvements could be relied on to take place without the proposed acquisition and a commitment by the companies to achieve quantifiable targets, enforceable as a result of MMC recommendations.

Remedies

9.39. The EA considered that, on balance, the proposed arrangements were likely to operate against the public interest. Most of the claimed water resource benefits could be achieved without a merger. However, the achievement of 'exemplary' comparator status by the bidding companies, as a result of an enforceable set of remedies covering demand management and other matters, could be regarded as a purpose of substantially greater significance in relation to the public interest. This purpose was probably not achievable without the proposed mergers.

9.40. The EA believed that carefully expressed and enforceable remedies could provide new industry-best water resources comparators for this most stressed part of south-east England; and that these would in time serve as industry bench-marks in England and Wales and thus assist as a partial remedy to the detriment of the comparative regime. The EA proposed that each of the companies controlled by FDWS and SEW, as a condition of the merger, be required to:

(a) prepare an Action Plan for balancing supply and demand over the next 25 years; this plan to be to industry-best standard;

(b) agree to specific short-term interim actions; and

(c) give commitment to implementing and maintaining the Action Plan.

9.41. The Action Plans should be prepared to a content, format and methodology agreed by the EA and OFWAT. All stages of the development of the Action Plans should be subject to independent certification by the company reporters. A full draft of the Action Plans including reports from the reporters should be submitted to both regulators within 12 months of the merger. Following discussion with the regulators the Action Plan, including reports from the reporters, would be finalized to address all the regulators' concerns within 15 months of the merger. If necessary the contents of the plans, once approved, could be incorporated into the companies' terms of appointment and thereby enforced by OFWAT. The Action Plans would be kept under review and regularly updated in the light of changing circumstances. They would be key documents in any EA abstraction licence determinations. They would also form part of the companies' submissions of OFWAT in the event of a Periodic Review of price limits occurring in 1999.

9.42. The EA submitted that the Action Plan should demonstrate exemplary approaches to:

— customer and company leakage reduction;

— installation of domestic and non-domestic meters;

— promoting efficient use of water to customers;

— customer tariffs;

— continued use of existing BSTs;

— economic appraisal of costs and terms for additional medium-term BSTs (with reference to OFWAT, if necessary);

— alleviation of low flows by voluntary reduction of abstraction licences in the Darent, Little Stour and Dour catchments; and

— providing current and historic data at sub-company level on leakage, per capita consumption, metered domestic/non-domestic consumption, transfer volumes and operational costs.

9.43. As specific interim actions, the EA would like to see both companies achieve:

— total leakage levels better than 120 l/prop/d by 31 March 1998, for reporting in the 1998 July returns;

— a free meter option in the two enlarged company supply areas, within 12 months of the merger; and

— compulsory metering of garden sprinkler users in the two enlarged company supply areas, within 12 months of the merger.

9.44. Clearly it would be necessary for each company to be committed to implementing and maintaining the agreed Action Plans. Details of their performance standards for customer service, targets for leakage, planned activity levels and investment proposals should be published. The companies should be required to provide to the Secretary of State enforceable undertakings with respect to the Action Plans and interim measures as a partial remedy to the harm to the regulatory regime that would arise from the merger, failing which orders under the FTA or amendments to appointments should be made.

9.45. The EA also put forward a number of specific longer-term demand management and other proposals. These are set out at Appendix 9.1. The EA said that these proposals should be subject to detailed cost-benefit analysis and compared with alternative supply management and development options, such as transfers, enhanced supply grids and new source development. The EA would expect each company to carry out this work for its own enlarged supply area, and to provide an additional joint report covering matters pertaining to the proposed JRC.

9.46. The EA considered that, in the event of a finding by the MMC that a merger was already in being, the disbenefits perceived under the proposed arrangements would still result once Stages 1 and 2 of the proposals had been implemented. The EA would therefore continue to recommend the above remedies.

Possible merger in being

9.47. The EA said that, based on its dealings with the companies on water resources issues, it had no evidence or perception that a merger was in being. The GU and SAUR submission to the EA in February 1996 set out a number of proposals for the management of water resources after the proposed merger, and it was the EA's understanding that none of these had yet been implemented. Whilst it might be argued that the recent BST agreed between MKW and FDWS at Barham constituted a step towards the wider scheme of resource management envisaged in the submission, the EA understood that this BST was subject to full commercial negotiations and not therefore the type of transfer expected in a unified supply area.

9.48. Both SEW and MKW were progressing individual abstraction licence applications which did not seem to the EA to be part of a larger strategy. All three companies had shown the EA different water efficiency plans. The EA did not therefore consider that a merger was in being.

Interpretation of section 34(3)(b) of the Water Industry Act 1991

9.49. The EA considered that the primary public interest consideration for the MMC was the desirability of giving effect to the principle that the DGWS's ability to make comparisons between different water companies should not be prejudiced. The desirability of achieving any other purpose was subject to that primary consideration. Section 34(3)(b)(i) enabled the MMC to have regard to any other purpose that could be achieved in a manner that did not conflict with the principle but in so far only as the MMC were satisfied that such other purpose could be so achieved. This proviso could not sensibly be read so as to include all situations where the other purpose could, in theory, be achieved in a manner that did not conflict with the principle.

9.50. It had been suggested that any other purpose not falling within section 34(3)(b)(i) necessarily fell within section 34(3)(b)(ii), subject only to the requirement that achievement of that other purpose was of substantially greater significance. However, the EA considered that section 34(3)(b)(ii) applied to situations where the other purpose could only be brought about in a manner which conflicted with the principle and not merely to situations where purposes could be achieved in a manner which conflicted with the principle but not exclusively so. The MMC were not entitled to have regard to a purpose of substantially greater significance unless the second condition (that the achievement of that purpose could be brought about only in a manner conflicting with the comparator principle) is found. So, where the purpose was capable of being achieved in a manner which did not conflict with the principle (for example, by co-operation), the MMC may not have regard to that purpose under section 34(3)(b)(ii), even if it was of substantially greater significance. Whether the MMC were entitled to have regard to that purpose under section 34(3)(b)(i) will depend upon the extent to which it can be achieved under the merger proposals, without any such conflict.

10 The views of other parties

Contents

Paragraph

Introduction	10.1
Government departments	
Department of the Environment	10.2
OFWAT's Southern Customer Service Committee	10.3
The water industry	
Southern Water Services Ltd	10.16
Cambridge Water PLC	10.21
Mid Southern Water plc	10.23
North Surrey Water Ltd	10.26
South Staffordshire Water Plc	10.28
Tendring Hundred Water Services Ltd	10.29
Three Valleys Water PLC	10.32
Major shareholders in MKH	
Morgan Grenfell	10.35
The Equitable Life Assurance Society	10.38
The Prudential Assurance Company Limited	10.41
The Royal London Mutual Insurance Society Limited	10.44
Local authorities	
Kent County Council (County Planning Department)	10.45
Ashford Borough Council	10.48
Maidstone Borough Council	10.50
Shepway District Council	10.51
Swale Borough Council	10.52
Tonbridge & Malling Borough Council	10.54
Tunbridge Wells Borough Council	10.57
Addington Parish Council	10.58
Bethersden Parish Council	10.59
Birling Parish Council	10.60
Borough Green Parish Council	10.61
Boughton Monchelsea Parish Council	10.62
Brenchley Parish Council	10.63
Broomfield & Kingswood Parish Council	10.64
Doddington Parish Council	10.65
Ditton Parish Council	10.66
Egerton Parish Council	10.67
Parish Council of Farningham	10.68
Great Chart with Singleton Parish Council	10.69
Lenham Parish Council	10.70
Plaxtol Parish Council	10.71
River Parish Council	10.72
Rolvenden Parish Council	10.73
Sholden Parish Council	10.74
Smeeth Parish Council	10.75
Westbere Parish Council	10.76

Other public bodies
    English Nature 10.77
    East Kent Health Authority 10.78
    Brighton Health Care NHS Trust 10.80
    Eastbourne & County Healthcare 10.81
    South Kent Hospitals NHS Trust 10.82
Business and consumer organizations
    The Water Group, Canterbury Friends of the Earth 10.83
    The Chartered Institution of Water and Environmental Management 10.90
    Kent Chamber of Commerce & Industry 10.91
    Maidstone and Mid-Kent Chamber of Commerce and Industry 10.94
    Shepway Chamber of Commerce & Industry 10.95
    Business Link (Kent) Limited 10.96
    The Kent Dimension 10.102
    Kent County Agricultural Society 10.103
    Stour Fishery Association 10.105
Trade unions
    UNISON 10.108
Businesses (including major water users)
    Ashworth Frazer (Home Counties) Ltd 10.113
    Aylesford Newsprint Ltd 10.114
    Babtie Group Ltd 10.117
    Belmont International Limited 10.118
    Brettell Bros 10.119
    P J Burke (Kent) Ltd 10.120
    Eternit UK Ltd (Pipes Division) 10.121
    Eurotunnel 10.123
    Fleet Cost Management 10.125
    Ford Motor Company Limited 10.126
    Hays Chemical Distribution Ltd 10.128
    Invicta Trucks Ltd 10.129
    JKN Polymers Ltd 10.130
    Kentec Tool Hire (Medway Handling Engineers Ltd) 10.132
    Kent Technical & Draughting Services 10.134
    MCS Cleaning Contractors Ltd 10.136
    Medway Travel Limited 10.137
    Sabre Security 10.138
    Safeway Stores plc (Directorate of Engineering) 10.140
    SCA Packaging Limited 10.142
    Sensus Metering Limited 10.144
    Shepherd Neame 10.145
    G Stow PLC 10.146
    Swale Business Supplies 10.148
    T M Products Ltd 10.149
    T N Printers Ltd 10.150
    Truck Crane Services Ltd 10.151
    Uponor Ltd 10.152
Members of Parliament and Members of the European Parliament 10.153
Private individuals 10.157

Introduction

10.1. Views were invited from Government departments, OFWAT's Southern CSC, the water industry, major shareholders in MKH, local authorities and other public bodies, business and consumer organizations, trade unions, businesses including major water users and other interested parties.

Government departments

Department of the Environment

10.2. The DoE submitted evidence on the regulatory framework for the water industry with particular reference to the mechanisms for securing water resources. The full text of this evidence is reproduced at Appendix 4.1.

OFWAT's Southern Customer Service Committee

10.3. The Chairman of the Southern CSC, Professor Judith Rees, submitted evidence and attended a hearing.

10.4. The SCSC's principal statutory duties (contained in section 29 of the 1991 Act) included:

(a) keeping under review all matters appearing to affect the interests of customers of the four WoCs and one WaSC in the region;

(b) consulting these companies about those matters;

(c) making appropriate representations to the companies; and

(d) investigating complaints made or referred to the SCSC which relate to the carrying out by those companies of their functions.

10.5. On the issues raised by the variation of the reference (that is, whether there was a merger in being) the SCSC said that it had no evidence that GU and SAUR had made any attempts to influence MKW's decision-making in relation to customer services. Nor was it possible for the SCSC to say whether GU and SAUR had colluded and acted together at the MKH AGM. It was certainly conceivable that they had individually decided to vote in the way they had.

10.6. On the original reference, the SCSC said that it had consistently argued that in a relatively water-short area such as south-east England it was necessary to ensure the strategic development of resources to benefit customers in the region as a whole. The SCSC believed the EA had the power to use the licensing system to encourage strategic co-operation between companies, as on the 75:25 split arranged between SWS and MKW for the Medway Scheme. The SCSC's concern had been to avoid inefficient capacity development, with each company seeking independently to secure supplies rather than working together to promote the least-cost solution for the region. At the time of the Periodic Review, for example, the SCSC was dismayed to find that extremely high cost options including desalination plants were included in the proposed investment programmes of SEW and FDWS, rather than arranging BSTs with SWS. SEW's reluctance to enter such agreements was subsequently restated to the SCSC at its public meeting on 20 January 1995, when the Managing Director of the company clearly set out the SAUR Group's policy in this area. Great emphasis was placed on the ownership of resources and SAUR's unwillingness to be dependent on another company for supplies. On the GU side, only very recently, in response to the 1995/96 drought, was there evidence that discussions were taking place. One relatively small bulk supply had been arranged from MKW to FDWS.

10.7. It was the SCSC's belief that there could be no solution to the resource situation without the involvement of SWS; this company held most of the 'available' reserves of water in the region. All the companies involved in the proposed arrangements were short of water resources at peak periods. Recent evidence of increased demand and higher ratios for peak to average use suggested that only very limited supply surpluses would actually be available. Further, potential urban and industrial development along the Thames corridor to the Channel Tunnel, the possible effects of climate change, and the fact that historically MKW had frequently needed to resort to hose-pipe restrictions in peak demand periods also led the SCSC to conclude that any surplus was likely to be small and short-lived. The SCSC had some concern that the proposed arrangements might actually exacerbate the problem because:

(a) SEW had consistently refused to enter into BST arrangements with SWS, though co-operation between them would be essential; and

(b) there might be a danger that GU and SAUR would in the short term merely strip MKW of its water resources which would not be to the advantage of MKW customers.

10.8. The proposal to split MKW appeared to be arbitrary. The SCSC had concerns about how the proposed JRC would actually operate. The existence of the JRC also raised questions concerning its position in the regulatory structure, reporting requirements and its relationship with the SCSC. The SCSC's view was that it was essential that any such company remained part of the core company, and that channels of communication and accountability between the JRC and customers (including the SCSC) were maintained.

10.9. Finally, the SCSC shared the view of the DGWS that any resource benefits which might conceivably follow the proposals could be achieved without the proposals, and were not linked in any way to such a structural change. The current imbalance in the present allocation of resources in the region could be overcome through the use of BSTs. Such arrangements would need to be complemented by a continued commitment to leakage reduction and demand management.

10.10. The SCSC would also regret the loss of an independent water company from the region. It had benefited from being able to use comparative information from the companies within the region and also outside it. This information had been particularly helpful in assessing the performance of the companies in a number of service areas, and these assessments had been vital in encouraging the companies to adopt best practice. For example, initially all the companies in the region were reluctant to allow the SCSC free access to their internal complaint files. However, MKW was the first company to invite the SCSC to its offices to undertake an audit of its complaint files. MKW's decision had prompted the other companies to follow suit.

10.11. MKW was the first company openly to offer its customers weekly instalment payment arrangements. It was also the first in its region to produce, in consultation with the SCSC, a leaflet that encouraged customers experiencing payment difficulties to contact the company and agree a mutually acceptable payment method. The company had also been very responsive to the SCSC's suggestions for improving its customer information literature. It had moved away from lengthy technical detail to plain English, with a focus on the customers' information needs. The company's billing literature had received a 'crystal mark' from the Plain English Campaign. FDWS, on the other hand, had been slow to improve its material, and all the documentation for SEW was in the SAUR Group style. The SCSC was rarely involved in the development of such literature, except where consultation was a regulatory requirement.

10.12. The SCSC was convinced it was important that MKW was independent. Since MKW was not part of a group structure, it was not subject to outside influence. Group influence could have a significant impact on the SCSC's relationship with a water company, if group policy reduced the local company's freedom to negotiate with and respond to SCSC initiatives.

10.13. GU and SAUR claimed that the creation of two enlarged companies would provide two stronger companies for the purposes of comparison. However, the SCSC doubted this. The new companies would be part of diversified groups, with other subsidiaries undertaking construction, mains-laying and a host of other services for them. There would be a loss of transparency, greater potential for transfer pricing abuses and possible difficulties concerning accountability to customers.

10.14. Although GU and SAUR had stated that the proposals would improve the level of service to customers, no specific details were made available to the SCSC. It was worth noting that in terms of performance, all three companies had a somewhat patchy record. None of them could claim to be among the best performers in the country in levels of service (for example, pressure of mains water, response to billing queries), numbers of complaints, cost of water delivered and efficiency, and debt and disconnection. The SCSC remained sceptical of the ability of the proposals to produce improvements in service standards. It stressed that the improvements made by MKW in responding to billing enquiries and customer complaints were as a direct result of comparative competition. Moreover, the SCSC pointed out that the performances of SEW and FDWS had not (to date at least) markedly improved as a result of their ownership by larger groups.

10.15. If the proposed acquisition were to go ahead, the SCSC's belief was that safeguards would be particularly important in the following areas:

(a) The JRC should be seen as an integral part of the core businesses, and therefore subject to the same regulatory conditions and scrutiny as other parts of the two water companies. The SCSC would wish to have current access arrangements safeguarded.

(b) MKW customers allocated to the new western company should be safeguarded from price averaging, which would in effect result in them cross-subsidizing customers in the higher-priced SEW area.

(c) MKW customers should also be protected from bulk supplies being taken out of their area without the approval of the DGWS. There was no doubt that customers would react with hostility if resource transfers out of the Mid Kent area increased their vulnerability to supply restrictions in peak periods.

(d) GU and SAUR should be asked to make more concrete their claims about improved service standards, with explicit targets that would allow their progress to be monitored and taken into account in price reviews.

(e) The enlarged companies should be required to work co-operatively with SWS for the strategic development of resources in the region.

The water industry

Southern Water Services Ltd

10.16. SWS submitted information to the MMC and attended a hearing.

10.17. SWS said that, as a WaSC, it provided water services to 2.1 million customers in the south-east of England and sewerage services to these and, amongst others, the customers of MKW, FDWS and SEW (see Appendix 3.3). Its own projections of supply and demand showed that under average conditions demand would not exceed supply in its areas until after 2012, though it would be earlier under peak conditions. Currently SWS was thought to have surplus capacity of around 130 to 135 Ml/d, or 65 Ml/d under peak conditions. The bulk of this was in Hampshire and the Isle of Wight. Most of the shortages were in the east. The situation in Hastings had begun to improve as a result of the new Bewl–Darwell link.

10.18. The effects of any merger on the public interest were likely to be adverse. SWS thought it was difficult to envisage the division of MKW between FDWS and SEW as providing any additional resources for customers of MKW. Whilst the proposals would, if implemented, lead to some reallocation of MKW's 25 per cent of the yield of Bewl Water reservoir to SEW's customers, this objective could be pursued in the absence of the acquisition proposals, through BST agreements; though SWS noted a reluctance on SEW's part to discuss BSTs. Any redistribution of MKW's current resources to the customers of other companies would inevitably hasten the day when a major new regional resource was needed. Water from such a resource might be expected to cost more than existing supplies, thus facing MKW customers with higher bills earlier than would otherwise have been the case. Commenting on the number and nature of BST and other supply agreements between SWS and MKW, SWS said that there was no expectation that a change of ownership of MKW, if that was agreed, would of itself disturb the operation of these agreements.

10.19. In the longer term SWS remained ready to take the interests of neighbouring water companies into account in developing strategy. The company had not ruled out Broad Oak or Darwell as sites for eventual major resource development, but currently it was looking to a possible increase in the capacity of the Bewl Water reservoir. In contrast to the present arrangement under which MKW had a 25 per cent share in Bewl, SWS did not have any obligation to provide 25 per cent of any increased capacity to MKW (or to any other company). However, SWS would be willing to discuss BSTs with adjoining companies and would expect the EA to have an input in this regard in view of the licensing implications.

There was no fixed time-scale yet, but developing Bewl would allow resources to flow, via Weir Wood, to the Horsham and Crawley areas; take some of the pressure off SWS's Hardham works; and increase the supplies to the Hastings area via the new link to Darwell. SWS's plans also included looking at options for bringing water from the west into the Hardham or Sussex Coast parts of its area.

10.20. Wherever resources permitted SWS saw BSTs as a sensible approach which could have the effect of avoiding the redistribution of MKW's current resources thereby deferring for their customers the cost of funding expensive new reservoir schemes. BSTs were also preferable to transfers of abstraction licences. Water undertakings necessarily worked to relatively short time horizons on water availability, and licence transfers of any short-term surpluses could well exacerbate longer-term capacity problems. For its part SWS would consider the prospect of selling some of its abstraction licences, and possibly placing its customers at risk, as an unattractive one. BSTs could, however, provide both short- and long-term solutions. It was not right to argue that there was an inherent lack of security in BSTs; the 60-year arrangement at Weir Wood with SEW could almost be classed as an in-perpetuity BST, and such long-term agreements were particularly feasible at the planning stage for new resources. Nor would SWS see its critical planning dates as limiting factors if, as the company was doing its planning, it was able to make due allowance for the BST needs of other companies. Despite any conditions attached to bulk supply agreements allowing a supplier to suspend delivery of water in specific circumstances, it was, in practice, most unlikely that supplies would be interrupted except in the event of some *force majeure*, for example a burst pipeline. SWS considered that it might well be cheaper for SEW and FDWS to use BSTs to solve resource problems in their areas rather than develop their own resources. SWS was currently completing internal consideration of a potable water link from its Turner's Hill service reservoir to Buchan Hill service reservoir to enable water from Weir Wood to be moved towards Crawley. This main would enable the company's longer-term objective of transferring additional resources from Weir Wood to the Crawley area to be achieved, ultimately using water transferred from an enlarged Bewl Water. When implemented there would seem to be an opportunity to make additional resources available from Weir Wood reservoir to SEW on a BST basis.

Cambridge Water PLC

10.21. Cambridge Water PLC, which is an independent WoC, had concluded that a merger had not taken place. On the occasion of MKW's AGM in July, GU and SAUR had both raised important questions and voted against resolutions. In considering whether it might be taken to imply that GU and SAUR were acting together because both voted against resolutions, it was necessary to ask how a prudent shareholder who had expert knowledge of the water industry and its regulatory framework might have voted. Cambridge Water would have considered that MKH's increase of 90 per cent in dividend was exceptional, both in terms of the ability of a company to sustain such a dividend in future years and from the point of view of the DGWS, who was looking to see a fair balance between the benefits paid to shareholders and to a company's customers. For such reasons, the fact that GU and SAUR both voted against resolutions was inconclusive evidence that they were acting together to secure or exercise control over MKW.

10.22. In Cambridge Water's view, a small company, even if it was well run, might reach the limit of efficiency gains more rapidly than a large company. In these circumstances a small company could only achieve further gains, without the risk of losing shareholder support, if it was able to expand its business, for example through reorganizations in the industry which had the effect of spreading a company's overheads over a larger customer base. If such reorganizations could take place without loss of comparators, the DGWS's objectives might be advanced. In a regulated public service, the structure of the operating units rather than the issue of ownership should be the primary consideration. The MMC's decision in the MKH case should not be one which might prevent other reorganizations of operating units from being proposed.

Mid Southern Water plc

10.23. Mid Southern is a subsidiary of SAUR. It said that a large amount of effort had been put in by both FDWS and SEW over recent years to try and break the deadlock over the misallocation of water resources between water companies. It could not be right that SWS, MKW and Portsmouth Water had surplus licences and water, whilst SEW and FDWS had a deficit. It considered it ludicrous that major resources such as Weir Wood, Bewl Water and Darwell were located within the boundary of SEW but were not available to SEW. Without adequate water resources under their own control SEW and FDWS would be unable to guarantee supplies, and it was difficult to see how they could compete with their neighbours.

10.24. In the company's view the imbalance of resources in the south-east of England could not be resolved by taking BSTs from the companies in surplus. BSTs had no place in the current competitive, privatized water industry. At times of peak demand of water shortages, the bulk supplier would always protect its own customers at the expense of the company receiving the BST.

10.25. Mid Southern was aware of various reports showing MKW's levels of service and other performance measures to be at the bottom of the league. The loss of MKW as a comparator would not, in its view, make any difference to the DGWS's ability to carry out comparisons between companies. An enlarged SEW and FDWS would be better and more significant comparators than they were now.

North Surrey Water Ltd

10.26. North Surrey said that GU currently held 99 per cent of the company's voting share capital. It supported the proposed merger. GU had consistently emphasized the importance of local management and local circumstances and issues. So the development of North Surrey within the GU group had reflected its own particular circumstances. At the same time, benefit had accrued from being able to compare and contrast all the companies within the group. In addition, membership of the GU group had provided advantages through ready access to group expertise (for example, technical and scientific support) both in the UK and in France.

10.27. The company also submitted that ownership by GU had brought the following benefits:

(a) to management—by providing access to experts and the means to identify best practice through inter-group discussions;

(b) to customers—by improved service and better water quality, through responsive local management;

(c) to staff—through wider opportunities for career development; and

(d) to regulators—through ready, open access to good-quality information and an efficient comparator against which to measure others.

South Staffordshire Water Plc

10.28. South Staffordshire Water Plc said that it had insufficient knowledge to determine whether there was a merger in being. As to the public interest of the proposed acquisition, the result of the MMC process should be one in which a sound, viable and transparent system of competition was able to operate.

Tendring Hundred Water Services Ltd

10.29. Tendring Hundred said that it was acquired by GU following an agreed bid. It supported the proposed acquisition of MKW and emphasized the GU group's commitment to high standards. Since becoming part of the GU group, Tendring Hundred had continued to operate with a very high level of local autonomy. Group companies met regularly to report progress and discuss and exchange ideas and initiatives to improve performance in all areas of activity. This provided a stimulating and competitive environment and comparators were used extensively to help develop and improve performances by the group companies. For instance, customer service standards had been improved throughout the company.

GU had made this a major issue and work was progressing throughout group companies to develop a comprehensive 'customer charter'.

10.30. Tendring Hundred had a good record of achievements in leakage control and in persuading customers to use water wisely. On leakage it had consistently achieved about the best overall performance of all water companies in all the main leakage indicators in use, whilst further published data from OFWAT showed Tendring Hundred to have one of the lowest household per capita consumption figures. Together with the other GU group companies, it was in favour of water metering. As well as offering customers a heavily subsidized meter option, Tendring Hundred had recently decided to require all sprinkler users to be metered.

10.31. On the strength of this kind of local achievement, the company suggested that present customers of MKW would be assured of a well-focused and reliable water supply service were the proposed acquisition to proceed, and that the proposal would not be against the public interest.

Three Valleys Water PLC

10.32. Three Valleys said that it was a wholly-owned subsidiary of GU and that it had been formed in 1990 by the merger of three former companies, Colne Valley Water, Lee Valley Water and Rickmansworth Water. The merger of these three companies had been extremely successful. Tangible benefits had been passed on to customers in the form of lower charges, improved customer service and improved water supply and distribution systems. At the time of the merger it had been anticipated that there would be greater self-sufficiency and flexibility in the use of water resources, including more efficient and effective use and the future development of an integrated distribution network. This had certainly been achieved with the bringing together of major sources of supply under common ownership and management. The following benefits had arisen:

(a) conjunctive use of major water resources;

(b) reduced reliance on BSTs;

(c) construction of major pipelines to transfer water to those parts of the new company area which had previously suffered from resource problems;

(d) ensuring that operations were as close as possible to the communities served; and

(e) creation of a water resources centre to manage and control the strategic movement of water around the enlarged area to ensure greater security of supply.

10.33. In its view none of these benefits would have been achieved successfully if the companies had remained separate. Three Valleys, although part of GU, did retain considerable local autonomy and was, therefore, an important comparator for the DGWS. The Three Valleys merger, together with the benefits of the support from GU, had also resulted in improved efficiency with unit operating costs falling from 44 p/m^3 in 1991/92 to just 38 p/m^3 in 1994/95. This was against an increase in the industry unit operating cost from 42 p/m^3 in 1991/92 to 44 p/m^3 in 1994/95. (Source: OFWAT's 1994/95 Report on The Cost of Water Delivered and Sewage Collected.)

10.34. Another major benefit of the merger and of being part of an international group was the ability to access the considerable research facilities of CGE world-wide. During the last five years since the merger, the company had reduced the leakage rate on its own mains by about one-third and it was still working to reduce it even further. Three Valleys did not believe this would have been possible to the same extent had the three former companies remained separate.

Major shareholders in MKH

Morgan Grenfell

10.35. Morgan Grenfell, whose Investment Banking Division was a financial adviser to GU, gave the following information to the MMC about its own role in MKH matters:

(a) *Structured Finance and Investment Banking Divisions.* Structured Finance Division (SFD) was the banking division of Morgan Grenfell. It carried on all the activities of general commercial banking including export credit, leveraged buy-outs, leasing and tax-based lending. The MMC would appreciate the distinction between these activities and the corporate finance activities of the Investment Banking Division (IBD) of Morgan Grenfell. Strict Chinese walls were in operation between SFD and IBD; in particular, IBD operated from its own segregated and secure area and the divisions had separate reporting lines. Officers and staff of the two divisions operated independently of each other and did not share information unless permitted under proper compliance procedures. The procedures for maintaining the Chinese walls were set out in the compliance manual and relevant officers and staff were required to undertake to comply with the manual.

(b) *9.4 per cent holding.* In 1991 GU undertook to the Secretary of State for Trade and Industry to reduce its shareholding in MKH to a level of not more than 19.5 per cent (the 'undertaking'). Following the undertaking, on 30 June 1992, SFD purchased 2,256,000 10 per cent redeemable cumulative preference shares of £1 each in MKH (the shares) from GU (see Appendix 3.7). This holding represented almost 9.4 per cent of the voting rights in the share capital of MKH. Under the purchase agreement for the shares (the Agreement) there were provisions for payment of deferred compensation by GU to Morgan Grenfell in certain circumstances to maintain an agreed return to Morgan Grenfell as a result of the purchase. There were no constraints imposed on Morgan Grenfell's voting rights or rights of disposal (although the compensation payments might be affected under certain circumstances). Morgan Grenfell received legal advice that it was not 'associated' with GU or CGE or any of its subsidiaries under section 77(4) of the FTA by virtue of the Agreement and confirmed this to OFWAT before completion of the Agreement. Morgan Grenfell understood that GU was similarly advised that it and Morgan Grenfell would not be associated under the Agreement and that the Agreement did not confer upon GU any interest in the shares. Morgan Grenfell further understood that there were discussions over the terms of the Agreement involving GU or its advisers, the DTI, the OFT and OFWAT before the Agreement was entered into. On 30 June 1992 Morgan Grenfell notified MKH of the acquisition in accordance with section 198 of the Companies Act.

(c) *Financial adviser.* After the acquisition of the shares, SFD had been solely responsible for managing the holding. It had not consulted IBD on the holding as regards voting rights attached to the shares or otherwise. Similarly, SFD had not been involved in IBD's role as financial adviser to GU. IBD accepted its appointment as financial adviser to GU in connection with MKH on 15 December 1995 and following independent legal advice. In the light of legal advice received, IBD concluded that Morgan Grenfell's procedures for segregation of roles described above would mean that SFD would not be acting with GU to secure control of MKH and that its holding of the shares would not be relevant for this purpose. Further, IBD was aware that any change in control would be subject to investigation by the MMC and a bid by GU would require it to be released from the undertaking. As such, IBD could not in any meaningful sense act with GU to acquire control until such time (if ever) as following the MMC report the undertaking was relaxed.

10.36. Morgan Grenfell voted by proxy against resolution 6 (authority to purchase own shares) proposed at the AGM of MKH held on 18 July 1996 and against the extraordinary resolution proposed at the separate general meeting of the holders of 10 per cent redeemable cumulative preference shares 1997 on the same date (see Appendix 6.3). It did not vote in relation to any other resolutions proposed at those meetings.

10.37. The decision on how to vote/abstain at the meetings was taken by SFD without reference to IBD. The SFD personnel concerned concluded that it was in the commercial interests of SFD to vote against the two resolutions referred to above and that the other proposed resolutions were immaterial to its interests. In particular:

(a) SFD concluded that the passing of the proposed resolutions could not be to its advantage as preference shareholder (irrespective of the Agreement).

(b) SFD had received legal advice that voting in favour of or abstaining from voting on any resolution which could affect the value of the preference shares might affect compensation rights under the Agreement and that, therefore, the cautious approach, to avoid any doubt, would be to vote against any such resolution. SFD had followed this advice.

(c) SFD considered that the passing of the resolutions might be part of a defensive strategy by MKH to discourage bids (by any person, not just GU/SAUR) for the company which might prevent SFD from maximizing its value in the shares should a successful bid at an appropriate price otherwise be made (and cleared by the MMC).

The Equitable Life Assurance Society

10.38. The Equitable Life Assurance Society (Equitable Life) said that it was not aware of the existence of a formal agreement between GU and SAUR to act together although that did not mean that one did not informally exist.

10.39. It did seem possible that, in the event that a bid did not take place, GU and SAUR could exercise creeping control of MKH, perhaps by installing friendly directors on the Board. It was difficult to gauge whether this would operate in the public interest or not. Whichever parties were in control, they would be regulated by OFWAT. The consumer would therefore be protected against higher than necessary price rises, deterioration in the quality of service and reductions in capital expenditure. Hence, Equitable Life did not believe that the universe of water enterprises would be so significantly affected by such a merger as to prejudice the DGWS's ability to set bench-marks and make comparisons.

10.40. However, it had been suggested that the main motivation behind GU's and SAUR's intention to bid was to secure access to MKW's supply of water. If this was the case, then it might be said that a take-over of MKW could be operating against the public good—at least as far as MKW's customers were concerned. Ultimately, it was in the interest of Equitable Life's policyholders (as indirect shareholders in MKH) that there should be more clarity in the situation. Either both companies should be disallowed from bidding (and either or both companies should have to reduce their holdings in MKH), or they should be allowed to put a formal offer on the table. What was unacceptable was for GU and SAUR to exercise control without paying a premium to other shareholders for that control.

The Prudential Assurance Company Limited

10.41. The Prudential Assurance Company Limited (the Prudential), which owns 1,681,900 ordinary shares and 1,375,900 preference shares in MKH, said that it was unable to provide the MMC with any evidence which might indicate that GU and SAUR had been acting together to secure or exercise control of MKH. The Prudential had not communicated with either GU or SAUR or with their advisers. However, the statement made by these companies on 21 December 1995 which indicated that any discussion with the Board of MKH about the proposed offer would be subject to mandatory reference to the MMC might be taken as an indication that GU and SAUR would not act to secure or exercise control of MKH until MMC clearance had been obtained.

10.42. With the prospect of a bid being made for MKH in the foreseeable future it was not surprising that some shareholders in MKH might come to the conclusion that it would not be in their interests for either the share repurchase proposal or the management incentive scheme to be approved. Shareholders in listed companies generally had a very wide range of views on matters which might affect their economic interests. In the particular situation of MKH the fact that GU and SAUR voted as they did at the meetings on 18 July 1996 could not be taken as evidence that they were acting together to secure or exercise control of MKH.

10.43. Although the Prudential did not support the contention that the public interest would be adversely affected if there were an existing merger, it did not at this time believe there was or might be an existing merger. However, if it were to be found that there was a merger in being, the Prudential did not believe it would prejudice the ability of the DGWS to make comparisons between different water enterprises.

The Royal London Mutual Insurance Society Limited

10.44. The Royal London Mutual Insurance Society Limited (Royal London) said that it did not have any reason to believe there had been collusive behaviour by GU and SAUR via their large shareholdings in MKH. Indeed, Royal London had traditionally viewed the two companies as rivals for influence over the company. The fact that both companies voted against the controversial performance share plan was unsurprising given the nature of the plan. Royal London's final decision was to abstain, although it could understand why other shareholders should have taken a more adverse view.

Local authorities

Kent County Council (County Planning Department)

10.45. As the strategic authority for Kent, Kent County Council (KCC) was not directly concerned with issues of monopoly and competitiveness. But it was concerned with their consequences upon present and future residents, the economy and the environment. KCC said that it had received very diverse evidence about the efficiency and effectiveness of SEW, FDWS and MKW. KCC sought an organization for, and pattern of, water supply and re-use in the county which provided secure, high-quality and equitable provision for the future. It was aware that in parts of the county, notably east Kent, the level of future supply was such as to place at risk the needs of residents and the local economy. East and north Kent were priority areas for economic development under KCC's structure plan and in terms of Government regional policy.

10.46. KCC considered that major initiatives on water conservation and water transfer within Kent were needed before expensive water storage schemes were considered. It understood that the DGWS and the EA could require co-operation or co-ordination between suppliers, with or without company reorganization and merger. It believed that the need for co-operation and co-ordination was clear; the means to achieve the necessary high level of integration of supply was a matter for the DGWS and the EA.

10.47. The improvement of supplies remained the prime requirement. And in the event that the primary objective of securing sustainable and long-term water supplies could be achieved without company merger, then this would provide an *a priori* case for ensuring a basis of competitive water supply in the county.

Ashford Borough Council

10.48. Ashford Borough Council (ABC) said that it was concerned by the attempted hostile take-over of MKW by two multinationals, GU and SAUR. This appeared to breach the MMC recommendation of 1990 and the undertakings given by GU to the Secretary of State at that time. ABC therefore opposed the proposed acquisition and urged protection for the interests of the water consumers of the borough.

10.49. ABC, whose concerns were also conveyed by Sir Keith Speed MP (Ashford), believed that the DGWS's use of comparators between water companies as a basis for price controls would be eroded if MKW disappeared.

Maidstone Borough Council

10.50. Maidstone Borough Council said that its Policy and Resources Committee considered that there was no objection to the proposed acquisition, subject to the water market in the south-east of England still having sufficient diversity of ownership for comparisons to be drawn between the performance of water companies, and the DGWS being satisfied that the protection of customers' interests was not prejudiced.

Shepway District Council

10.51. Shepway District Council (SDC) said that FDWS served the majority of the Shepway area. Only a small part of the SDC area was served by MKW. SDC's main concern was to ensure that, whatever the outcome of company ownership, residents within the existing MKW area continued to receive supplies of high-quality water and associated services at an acceptable price. Given the restrictions of water supplies over the last two years as a result of drought conditions, it might be that a larger company covering a wider catchment area had the ability to ensure a continuing supply of water throughout the whole of the area.

Swale Borough Council

10.52. Swale Borough Council (SBC) had noted the developments concerning MKW with some alarm. What was a well-managed water provider appeared to be threatened with the aim of supplying its water to other areas, where management did not appear to be as good, to the detriment of the community in the MKW area. SBC was, therefore, concerned that the proposed merger was not in the interests of the public presently served by MKW. Both the potential purchasers' subsidiaries were experiencing difficulties in meeting demand. The intention, as SBC understood it, was to optimize water resources over a larger area. SBC did not find this argument convincing. Spreading scarce resources over a wider area might well lead to a deterioration of service, and a levelling down rather than a levelling up.

10.53. The management and operational performance of MKW had been good and SBC would not wish to see any deterioration of service to customers. There was a significant risk that the loss of MKW's independence would not be in the public interest. SBC would oppose the proposed take-over.

Tonbridge & Malling Borough Council

10.54. Tonbridge & Malling Borough Council (TMBC) did not feel it was in a position to comment on whether GU and SAUR had been acting together to secure or exercise control of MKW. If the MMC found that there was an existing merger then TMBC believed this might give rise to concerns that it would not operate in the public interest. The essence of these concerns was the same as TMBC had for the proposed merger. This was that a reduction in the number of independent water enterprises would lessen the ability of the public to effect comparisons of performance. This could result in a reduction of pressure to secure infrastructure improvements which were needed to preserve and safeguard the quality and adequacy of water supplies.

10.55. It followed, therefore, that TMBC considered that the ability of the DGWS to make comparisons between different water enterprises would be prejudiced. It was difficult to see what remedy might be available to prevent that prejudice other than disallowing the proposed merger, whether through enforcement of GU's 1991 legally binding undertakings or through the exercise of such statutory powers as were available under relevant enactments. TMBC asked the MMC to consider very carefully the interests of water consumers during the course of their investigations.

10.56. Other particular concerns were:

(a) The existence of independent suppliers in various areas, whilst not directly providing choice and competition for consumers, did provide the opportunity for bench-marking of performance and price. This could facilitate informed debate and lead to improvements in performance.

(b) If the take-over were permitted, a virtual monopoly would be created in the area. Customers would not easily be able to judge performance and the new body would have less incentive to manage its resources effectively.

(c) MKW had managed its supplies effectively in the difficult climatic conditions that had prevailed; for example, it currently did not have a hose-pipe ban in place. It was understood that such bans were in force in nearby areas served by GU and SAUR. If the take-over were allowed, then

water resources from the Mid Kent area could be piped to other areas to alleviate supply difficulties. TMBC's concern was not that it was wrong that water resources should be pooled for the benefit of the overall population. Rather, it was that the possibility of imposing a hose-pipe ban in Mid Kent and transferring the resources saved to other areas might be a more attractive proposition than addressing fundamental issues such as leakage levels and capital expenditure on infrastructure improvements.

Tunbridge Wells Borough Council

10.57. Tunbridge Wells Borough Council expressed concern that a merger of this kind could result in the formation of very large companies and a consequential reduction in competition.

Addington Parish Council

10.58. Addington Parish Council said that it did not wish the proposed take-over of MKH to take place. The general feeling among residents was satisfaction with the service given by MKW, which had achieved this success by taking BSTs and by having invested more than twice as much per head in water resources in the period 1990 to 1995 as had FDWS or SEW.

Bethersden Parish Council

10.59. Bethersden Parish Council expressed its concern at the proposed acquisition of MKH, and said that there was no real justification for losing this valuable independent water company which had served Mid Kent successfully.

Birling Parish Council

10.60. Birling Parish Council said that the proposed take-over was not necessary and was not needed to achieve improved water supplies or service standards; and it would eliminate an independent comparator, making it harder for the DGWS to set stringent price controls and service standards. MKW had had no hose-pipe bans in 1996, unlike FDWS and SEW, because it took BSTs and had effective resource management policies, investing more than twice as much per head on water resources between 1990 and 1995 as FDWS or SEW.

Borough Green Parish Council

10.61. Borough Green Parish Council said that it was most disturbed to hear about the proposed take-over of MKH and wished to register support for the continuance of an independent MKW. There was particular concern about the reduction in competition that would result from a take-over, and about the ability of a different water supplier to make the necessary investment in, and commit the required levels of maintenance to, the infrastructure.

Boughton Monchelsea Parish Council

10.62. The Boughton Monchelsea Parish Council (BMPC) strongly objected to the proposed take-over of MKW by GU and SAUR. Local residents had always enjoyed a very reliable service from MKW. MKW, unlike other water companies, had not had a hose-pipe ban in 1996. By exercising effective resource management it had managed to maintain an uninterrupted water supply. BMPC very much doubted whether GU and SAUR had the same concern over Kent's environment as MKW. The need for profits would, in BMPC's view, undoubtedly lead to higher water bills for Kent's residents.

Brenchley Parish Council

10.63. Brenchley Parish Council was totally opposed to a take-over by GU and SAUR and urged that the MMC recommend that the bid be prohibited.

Broomfield & Kingswood Parish Council

10.64. Broomfield & Kingswood Parish Council (BKPC) considered that service from MKW had been, and still was, more than satisfactory. There had been no hose-pipe bans in the area, although neighbouring supply companies had had such bans in force. BKPC fully approved of MKW's operational policies, including its investment plans and environmental approach. BKPC, therefore, felt strongly that the proposed take-over should be refused.

Doddington Parish Council

10.65. Doddington Parish Council (DPC) urged rejection of the proposed take-over bid. MKW had served customers in its area well. There had been no hose-pipe ban in 1996. DPC understood that MKW's investment in water resources would enable this state of affairs to continue. This was particularly important to local strawberry growers who had irrigation systems in place. DPC was also worried that if the proposed take-over were successful, water would be taken to improve the situation in other areas leaving MKW customers with shortages.

Ditton Parish Council

10.66. Ditton Parish Council expressed concern regarding the proposal for the take-over of MKH by GU and SAUR. It had always been totally satisfied with the services provided by MKW and could not understand the necessity for any take-over.

Egerton Parish Council

10.67. Egerton Parish Council had considered a submission to it from MKH and supported MKH's contention that the proposed take-over should not and need not happen. As an independent company, MKH had demonstrated success in maintaining water resources and supplies and in achieving high standards of service. It made no sense to eliminate this company or to merge it with companies which had not matched MKW's achievement in avoiding supply shortages this year.

Parish Council of Farningham

10.68. The Parish Council of Farningham (PCF) wrote to express its concerns at the proposed take-over. PCF supported MKH's reasoning in objecting to the proposals. It further stated its concern about companies taking over and exploiting facilities which were an integral part of MKW's infrastructure, with the possibility that these facilities would be run down as a result of a gradual reduction in the necessary investment.

Great Chart with Singleton Parish Council

10.69. The Great Chart with Singleton Parish Council (GCSPC) believed there was no need for the proposed take-over. It would eliminate an independent comparator, making it harder for the DGWS to set stringent price controls and service standards. In GCSPC's view the proposed take-over was not required to achieve improved water supplies or service standards. This was achieved by taking bulk supplies, as MKW had done, and by effective resource management. GCSPC also made the point that MKW had invested more than twice as much per head on water resources as FDWS or SEW between 1990 and 1995.

Lenham Parish Council

10.70. Lenham Parish Council considered that MKW should continue to remain under the ownership of MKH. The Council urged that the proposals be looked at very closely as the present situation was of benefit to the people of Kent.

Plaxtol Parish Council

10.71. Plaxtol Parish Council (PPC) urged that the proposed acquisition of MKH be disallowed. It was concerned that:

(a) the continued supply of water during dry summers would be prejudiced if the two adjoining areas took too much water from the MKW area following a take-over;

(b) the village community needed to be reassured that they would not be called upon to subsidize the improvements which the bidders would need to make in their areas; and

(c) value for money and efficiency would suffer. In recent years MKW had substantially improved its efficiency and customer service and had reduced leakage from the system.

River Parish Council

10.72. River Parish Council (RPC) had considered the possible effect of the take-over bid and did not feel that the break-up of MKW would be in the best interests of the people of Kent or of the natural environment. There was no doubt, in RPC's view, that the Broad Oak reservoir scheme which was considered in the 1980s should have gone ahead to ensure adequate supplies overall for the county; it was discontinued because of the fragmentation of the water companies even before privatization. RPC could not agree with MKW's view that the additional reservoir capacity would not be needed until 2010. But in any event what was needed most in the interests of the county as a whole was to avoid the distraction of take-over bids and wasteful competition between the various water bodies, and to encourage greater co-operation and working together.

Rolvenden Parish Council

10.73. Rolvenden Parish Council said that it agreed with the case against the proposed acquisition presented by MKH, and thus opposed the take-over proposed by GU and SAUR.

Sholden Parish Council

10.74. Sholden Parish Council supported MKH's wish to remain an independent company, and felt that the proposed take-over bid was not in the best interests of the county as a whole. Whilst other water companies in the area had imposed hose-pipe bans, MKW appeared, with the help of supplies of surplus water purchased from SWS, to have managed its own resources more successfully.

Smeeth Parish Council

10.75. Smeeth Parish Council objected to the proposed take-over because MKW was giving an excellent service, particularly in respect of the amount being put back into resources to improve their management. A take-over was not needed to improve water supplies or service standards. Indeed, it would eliminate an independent comparator, making it more difficult for the DGWS to set stringent price controls and service standards.

Westbere Parish Council

10.76. The hostile take-over of MKH by GU and SAUR was of great concern to Westbere Parish Council (WPC) and its parishioners. The services enjoyed in Westbere over recent years from MKH had been of a high standard and at reasonable cost; and more particularly, through quality management and investment in the infrastructure, rationing by way of hose-pipe bans had been avoided unlike in neighbouring companies' areas. The proposed merger was designed to dissipate well-managed resources to areas with inferior facilities and could only be to the disadvantage of the customers of MKW.

Other public bodies

English Nature

10.77. English Nature said that the proposed merger did not raise any particular concerns, provided that the new owner of MKW carried out its function of managing land and water resources with due regard to the general principles of sustainability and with full regard to its duty to further nature conservation as required by the Water Resources Act 1991. As an owner of land designated as sites of special scientific interest, MKH had a statutory responsibility to consult the local authority, the Secretary of State for the Environment and English Nature if proposing to carry out any operation which was potentially damaging on that land. English Nature felt it was important that this statutory obligation should be brought to the attention of any prospective owner of such land.

East Kent Health Authority

10.78. East Kent Health Authority considered it important to draw the MMC's attention to the need to ensure that the health authority and its officers, in particular the Consultant in Communicable Disease Control (CCDC) who was also appointed as 'proper' officer to the local authorities in East Kent, continued to have the active co-operation of the water companies on issues of public health. It was a statutory requirement for regular liaison meetings to be held between the water companies and the CCDC.

10.79. Recent examples where it had been important to have full co-operation were:

— investigation of cases of cryptosporidium;
— safety of effluent from rendering plant;
— discharge of sewage into the sea;
— monitoring nitrate levels;
— protection of renal dialysis patients; and
— water contamination with sewage.

Brighton Health Care NHS Trust

10.80. Brighton Health Care NHS Trust, while not as yet directly affected by the proposed merger, felt that the trend towards combination of water companies must be of concern to clients because it affected the number of alternative pricing regimes available, and influenced the water supply strategy for the future. Combinations must inevitably alter the relationship of power between the DGWS, the customer and the companies. On balance, it was in the interest of the customer, and therefore of the Trust, to maintain the balance in favour of the DGWS. The Trust would not encourage a combination of water or utility companies.

Eastbourne & County Healthcare

10.81. Eastbourne & County Healthcare, an NHS Trust, said that it had no objection to the proposed merger and would rely on the current regulatory bodies and market forces to ensure that consumer services and associated costs were not adversely affected.

South Kent Hospitals NHS Trust

10.82. South Kent Hospitals NHS Trust said that while it did not wish to comment on whether the proposed acquisition of MKW by GU and SAUR was against the public interest, it noted that the services of a number of local water companies varied in quality and cost. It did not regard all services provided by MKW as being outstanding value for money, and would welcome a new management structure which might reduce existing prices and introduce a more competitive pricing regime.

Business and consumer organizations

The Water Group, Canterbury Friends of the Earth

10.83. The Water Group, Canterbury Friends of the Earth (the Water Group), wrote to the MMC and attended a hearing.

10.84. The Water Group was a sub-committee of the Canterbury Friends of the Earth. It was originally set up to consider a proposal from the Southern Water Authority and the then Mid Kent Water Company to build a reservoir at Broad Oak. The Water Group successfully opposed this and had subsequently kept a watch on water-related matters in the area.

10.85. The Water Group had a number of reasons for rejecting the proposed merger. MKW was primarily a Kent company, most of whose customers, employees and shareholders lived in Kent. MKW had very close local connections. This 'intimacy' would be lost if the proposed acquisition were successful. In this respect the proposal was against the public interest. The acquiring companies' headquarters were outside this country, remote from the concerns and interests of the local customers and employees.

10.86. MKH had improved its environmental record significantly. It had won acclaim for restoring Chilham Mill, and there were other areas where it had made environmental improvements. It was to be doubted whether a larger combined organization that would result from the take-over would take so much interest in such concerns.

10.87. The Water Group believed that SEW and FDWS had not co-operated with other water companies in sharing water resources. MKW had substantial partnership on water resources matters and developments, such as at Bewl, with SWS. If MKW were taken over, the legal relationship between the new companies and SWS would be in jeopardy, to the detriment of both SWS and MKW customers. MKW had come from being the company with the highest standing charges in England to being among the lowest. That was a significant and major step and was particularly important when the EA was trying to ensure the efficient use of water. Low standing charges ensured that the cost of water reflected actual use and hence encouraged economy.

10.88. The cost of the take-over would have to be recouped from somewhere. This cost was likely to come from the customers or staff, and hence was likely to be against the public interest. There would also be the incentive to sell more water (to generate more income) to help recoup the costs, and this would also be an undesirable effect. It was likely that, if the companies remained as they were, a Broad Oak reservoir would only be developed when essential, because the companies would not co-operate unless they had to. One large company would be in a more powerful position and able to push a development through sooner. The customers would have to pay the extra costs involved. The Water Group's major concern about this proposed merger was that the present separate arrangement was fairly straightforward for the DGWS and the EA to manage. With one large organization it would become much more difficult, and this would be significantly damaging to the public interest.

10.89. Accordingly, the Water Group considered the proposed acquisition to be against the public interest. Were it allowed to proceed, this should only be on condition that various offsetting public interest improvements were made, especially on the environmental side (for example, reductions in abstractions, re-using water, improving water quality and reliability of water supply). While a price reduction would be beneficial economically for customers, it might be detrimental environmentally, if reduced costs reduced the incentive to save water. On the other hand, the Water Group emphasized the need for any conditions attached to agreement to the merger to include making leakage reductions the top priority, and making sure that demand management did not just mean 'more metering' and nothing else.

The Chartered Institution of Water and Environmental Management

10.90. The Chartered Institution of Water and Environmental Management said that it wished to express its concern that the high level of professionalism in the science, engineering and management of MKW's service to customers was maintained.

Kent Chamber of Commerce & Industry

10.91. The Kent Chamber of Commerce & Industry (KCCI) said that it had taken written evidence from both FDWS and MKW.

10.92. The fundamental case advanced by FDWS was that an unequal distribution of natural resources as between the companies could and should be addressed through a corporate take-over. KCCI accepted that there was an unequal distribution of natural resources. However, it believed that the shortage of water resources in the Folkestone and Dover area could satisfactorily be met by a BST agreement with MKW, particularly from the Barham source (close to the border between the two areas). The price charged (if an issue) could be arbitrated upon by the regulator. Penalties could be attached to any failure to honour agreements to supply. On this basis, the stated objectives of FDWS could be met without the need for a take-over. KCCI had offered to arrange a meeting between FDWS and MKW to discuss a suitable BST arrangement and to act as an 'honest broker' at any stage, if that were thought to be helpful and if both parties agreed.

10.93. MKW appeared to the business community to be an increasingly well-managed, locally-directed company, which had shown great commitment over a number of years to the local community, perhaps particularly the business community. Its independent presence also enabled better comparisons of performance between companies in the region. A take-over would put this comparator role at risk. In saying this, KCCI did not in any way wish to detract from the undoubted quality of FDWS's operation within its own area, and there were a wide range of issues that it was not in a position to weigh.

Maidstone and Mid-Kent Chamber of Commerce and Industry

10.94. Maidstone and Mid-Kent Chamber of Commerce and Industry (MMKCCI) said that it would find it astonishing if the proposed merger received the blessing of the MMC. Not only was MKW one of the few truly independent water companies still existing but one of the few successful ones. It had an excellent record of supply to Mid Kent and a good image in the eye of the consumer.

Shepway Chamber of Commerce & Industry

10.95. Shepway Chamber of Commerce & Industry (SCCI) wrote to give its full support for the proposed acquisition of MKH. In coming to this conclusion SCCI had taken many issues into account:

(a) The proposals appeared to include the guarantee of a grid system from within the existing price limits to provide relief from existing and future water shortages. Both the grid system and the jobs generated by the investment would benefit the Kent customer.

(b) The MKH suggestions that bulk supplies might be available from area to area did not seem to offer the grid system which would be needed to transfer the bulk supplies.

(c) MKH had circulated a number of letters and articles which were, at best, misleading. The anti-French comments made were very damaging to the image and economic interests of Kent.

(d) The problems of water supply in the south of Kent were real and acute. GU and SAUR had a proven record of investment and were world leaders in water resource management.

(e) The commitment of GU to Kent and to east Kent in particular was genuine and to be welcomed.

(f) Four water supply companies currently served the region and the system was undoubtedly fragmented. This arrangement was in sharp contrast to much of Great Britain where water supply was provided by one company on a regional basis, enabling strategic management of the resources available. It was hard to see how the water supply arrangements in Kent could be optimized without some merging of the fragments.

(g) GU and SAUR provided the only viable, long-term solution to developing a sustainable water supply. Their plans also fitted well with the EA's wish to see greater co-operation to solve Kent's supply problems.

(h) The acquisition would defer the need for the construction of any additional surface reservoirs, would enable long-term planning of resources and would ensure a sustainable water supply now and in the future.

Business Link (Kent) Limited

10.96. Business Link (Kent) Limited (Business Link) felt that if there was a merger in being, such a merger would reduce competition in the water supply industry and would make it much more difficult for the DGWS to make comparisons. Secondly, the take-over of a company with a comparatively good track record in resource management by organizations with a less comparatively good track record seemed to Business Link to defy logic. For these reasons, the consumer would not be well served.

10.97. Business Link pointed out that it shared the same Chairman as MKH. However, the Chairman had not solicited, or contributed to, Business Link's views in any way.

10.98. As far as the proposed merger was concerned, it was the view of Business Link executive officers that the bid was not in the public interest. Business Link's catchment area consisted largely of the territories of all three companies. It believed the take-over would have a negative impact on the economic development of the sub-region. Major local investment decisions of the near future could well rest on availability and cost of water.

10.99. The bidding consortium had explicitly stated that they did not intend to undertake major investment in the foreseeable future, whereas MKW had invested consistently over the last few years. This had resulted in a small surplus of resources and no hose-pipe or other user constraints. This had not been the case in the neighbouring authorities.

10.100. It was clear that the consortium was looking to acquire MKH as a means at least to defer, if not avoid, major investment in their respective areas at the expense of users in the Mid Kent catchment. MKW prices were lower than those in Folkestone and its surrounds by approximately 20 per cent. It seemed inevitable that the consortium's comparative water shortage and consequential high prices could cause MKW prices to rise if the take-over proceeded.

10.101. It was Business Link's understanding that, should such a take-over take place, there was no expectation that the industry would become more efficient or that there would be more effective additional investment.

The Kent Dimension

10.102. The Kent Dimension is a local purchasing initiative, supported by KCC and Business Link. It said that MKW was one of the first major buyers in Kent to join this initiative and had continually worked with The Kent Dimension to ensure maximum sourcing in Kent. It said that MKW's participation in the programme had undoubtedly had a significant favourable impact on the local economy in creating local business and jobs and The Kent Dimension was concerned that this local benefit could well be lost through GU's and SAUR's centralized buying policies, if the proposed merger was allowed.

Kent County Agricultural Society

10.103. Kent County Agricultural Society (KCAS) was opposed to the proposed acquisition as it felt that the excellent standard of service offered at present by MKW would deteriorate. Through MKW's good management of its resources there was not a hose-pipe ban in operation. The two GU and SAUR companies on either side of MKW were unable to satisfy customers' needs. MKW had invested heavily in resources. Leakage had been brought down substantially and there was an ongoing programme to reduce this further.

10.104. KCAS felt that if the proposed take-over went ahead the forward planning and investment made by MKW would be halted and resources poured into neighbouring areas. As there was no direct competition in the water and sewerage industry, it was essential that there was a diversity of water suppliers to provide comparative prices for the DGWS.

Stour Fishery Association

10.105. Stour Fishery Association (SFA) wished to submit the strongest possible representation against the proposed acquisition of MKH. The proposed take-over was a threat to the ability to make comparison between various companies. It would eliminate, to a large extent, any comparison between companies, making it harder for the DGWS to set price controls and service standards. The proposed take-over would also detract from improvements in water supplies, with which a very high proportion of MKW customers were satisfied. MKW had invested more than twice as much per head on water resources as FDWS and SEW.

10.106. MKW had been providing fresh water supplies of the highest quality since at least the turn of the century. By its careful husbanding of resources and by planning well ahead, despite the almost continual drought for the last five years except for the winter of 1994/95, MKW did not have a hose-pipe ban. Each year MKH channelled its profits back into the water company to increase efficiency, reduce leakage, improve the supply of water to the many towns within its area and improve the pipelines supplying these towns. Unlike some other companies, it had not simply handed out profits to shareholders and its senior management.

10.107. Further, MKW was doing all it possibly could to increase metering. As a result of the efficient retention of supplies, it had been able to offer BSTs to two companies in the region. SFA was particularly worried at the suggestion that MKW's water resources would go to adjacent water companies. It would create considerable strain in the present MKW area. The Kentish Stour, the last surviving chalk stream in south-east England, was already abstracted to the absolute limit.

Trade unions

UNISON

10.108. UNISON, the principal trade union in the water industry with approximately 30,000 members, said that some 500 of its members had a direct interest in the proposed merger. It was represented on both European Works Councils established by CGE and SAUR. And within the UK water subsidiaries of these two companies, the union enjoyed robust and effective industrial relations. However, the position in MKH was different in that the company had decided not to recognize trade unions with effect from 1994.

10.109. UNISON's reaction to the present take-over proposal was conditioned by the policies it had developed on the future of the water industry. In 1996 UNISON had published a report, *Plan for Water*, which presented a number of options for the future. The union said that fundamental to UNISON's approach was the fact that water was a natural monopoly vital to the nation's health and its environment.

Therefore it should not be subjected to the turbulence of unbridled market forces. This was recognized to a limited extent by the putting in place of various regulatory/supervisory bodies.

10.110. UNISON believed that the regulatory bodies including the DGWS and the MMC should strike a better balance of interest between the various stakeholders in the industry, employees, consumers and shareholders. In the regulated water industry, apart from market pressures, there were also the price pressures emanating from the DGWS. Taken together these put pressure on a company to achieve greater levels of efficiency. All too often this manifested itself in an attack on jobs. UNISON said that it was particularly concerned about potential job losses because it understood that MKH would be broken up and absorbed into FDWS and SEW. It urged the MMC to make it a condition of any agreed take-over that the new company must fully discuss any restructuring proposals with UNISON with a view to reaching an agreement.

10.111. The MKH derecognition of unions had, in UNISON's view, marked a wide-ranging attack on employees' contracts of employment. The company had unilaterally imposed a job evaluation scheme and pay system, and the provisions for hours of work, sickness benefits and redundancy terms were rewritten. And the company had given further indications of its anti-trade union stance which, in UNISON's view, was totally without justification.

10.112. Hence, in the event of the proposed take-over being approved by the MMC, it should be on condition that the new company or companies should recognize the appropriate trade unions (including UNISON) for the purposes of collective bargaining and should negotiate with these trade unions on the establishment of relevant and suitable provisions and mechanisms for joint negotiating and consultation.

Businesses (including major water users)

Ashworth Frazer (Home Counties) Ltd

10.113. Ashworth Frazer (Home Counties) Ltd said that it had been a supplier to MKW for 12 years during which time it had built up a close working relationship. It asked that the MMC consider the possible adverse consequences to its business should the proposed merger be allowed.

Aylesford Newsprint Ltd

10.114. Aylesford Newsprint Ltd (AN) said that the company did not support the proposed take-over. MKW, although within one of the driest parts of the UK, had achieved something in the past 12 months that very few other water companies had been able to. It had secured sufficient volume of water to meet immediate needs and had lifted its hose-pipe ban. This had been achieved through good management and planning. The company was convinced that it would be a retrograde step for MKH to lose its independence.

10.115. AN was a major industrial water user employing 450 people. It was considering expanding the capacity of its newspaper recycling plant. It said that it relied on having an uninterrupted supply of water and was most anxious about losing MKW as its water supplier. AN noted that MKW management had achieved some notable successes over the past years to the benefit of its customers. This had included a high rate of investment, for example £34.3 per head of population in resources, and substantial reductions in leakage. These successes, together with a good business performance and the avoidance of hose-pipe bans in 1996, indicated a company that was performing well.

10.116. MKW's husbandry of resources had allowed it to offer bulk water supplies to the other two companies in the region. This, therefore, indicated that the GU and SAUR bid was much more to do with acquiring resources than with improved service and efficiencies for MKW's customers.

Babtie Group Ltd

10.117. Babtie Group Ltd, which had been retained by MKW as its independent engineering adviser with respect to the proposed GU and SAUR acquisition, submitted a statement recommending BSTs as an alternative to the proposed merger.

Belmont International Limited

10.118. Belmont International Limited (BI) said that the company and the majority of its 28 employees benefited from the superior services of MKW both at work and at home. The take-over bid should be rejected. MKW had been exemplary in its management of water resources. The performance of the GU and SAUR companies had fallen well short of those of MKW. With the continuance of MKH as an independent company the DGWS would be better placed to control price and services standards for the benefit of all water users.

Brettel Bros

10.119. Brettell Bros said that it was a small family business which currently had a framework agreement with MKW to manufacture and supply steel manhole covers and frames. It saw the business it did with MKW, which constituted a major part of its annual turnover, as essential to its survival, and that of its suppliers and workforce, as it believed that neither GU nor SAUR, both large companies, would deal with small firms such as itself.

P J Burke (Kent) Ltd

10.120. P J Burke (Kent) Ltd said that it was a small family firm employing local labour. Half its annual turnover was work carried out for MKW. It was very concerned for the future of its company and employees should the take-over go ahead. A larger utility could well use large national companies for laying mains, and small local firms would not have the opportunity to tender for the work.

Eternit UK Ltd (Pipes Division)

10.121. Eternit UK Ltd (Pipes Division) (Eternit) told us that it was principally a supplier of asbestos-cement pipes and fittings but also supplied leak noise correlation equipment and services. Its customer base consisted mainly of water utilities. On the proposed acquisition of MKH, Eternit felt that the bigger the client organization, the less likely it was that it would be considered as a supplier.

10.122. Eternit said it believed that, in the case of mergers, the economies came from job losses in the subsumed company. A merger in this case would create financial difficulties, job losses and even closures in small suppliers such as itself. It did not believe it was alone in this view. A great deal of nervousness prevailed amongst other small supply companies. Eternit believed that if the proposed merger were allowed to proceed it would constitute a signal for other predatory bids against the remainder of its client base. The very existence of such bids was harmful to businesses such as itself where cash flow and profitability had been very difficult in the years since privatization of the water industry.

Eurotunnel

10.123. Eurotunnel said that it was a substantial industrial and transport enterprise in east Kent. Although it had no premises in MKW's territory it was concerned and knowledgeable about the subject of water supply in Kent. It said that it had been in discussion with FDWS concerning a proposal to bring water from the Continent to Kent through the tunnel cooling system, a scheme taken into consideration during the design and construction of the tunnel.

10.124. Eurotunnel said it had little doubt that water supply within the Kent region would be inadequate in the future. It was pessimistic about the long-term outlook and felt that the MMC should attempt to arrive at an answer that would improve water resource prospects for the whole of Kent and East Sussex.

Fleet Cost Management

10.125. Fleet Cost Management said that it had been a supplier of a wide range of vehicle-related services to MKH since 1990. The introduction of a new parent company would lead to a review of all suppliers bringing into jeopardy a long-standing relationship.

Ford Motor Company Limited

10.126. The Ford Motor Company Limited (Ford) business centre at West Byfleet told the MMC that it understood that, potentially, its established link with MKH could disappear were the proposed bid from GU and SAUR to proceed. Ford could lose approximately £375,000 a year should the merger occur and this would have an impact on its business within Kent.

10.127. Ford thrived in a very competitive market-place and believed that the competitive element should be in place in all industries. The merging of the three companies would, therefore, not seem appropriate.

Hays Chemical Distribution Ltd

10.128. Hays Chemical Distribution Ltd (Hays) told the MMC that it had had an excellent working relationship with MKW for a number of years and this had recently grown significantly both in terms of the strength of the supplier/customer relationship and in its financial importance to Hays. It viewed with disappointment the prospect of years of hard work and relationship-building being wasted and having to start again with new organizations with different views and principles.

Invicta Trucks Ltd

10.129. Invicta Trucks Ltd (Invicta), a supplier of vans and heavy commercial vehicles, said that there had been a trend towards company mergers with the result that purchasing was conducted centrally on a larger scale. This had adversely affected Invicta. It was opposed to the proposed merger for this reason. Invicta felt that reciprocal business within local areas promoted many of the qualities that were missing in business today, such as loyalty, trust and quality. MKW was one of the few remaining utilities in Kent to which Invicta had been able to supply vehicles and associated services. The loss of this trade would be detrimental to its business in many ways. Invicta believed there could be significant reductions in work levels which would contribute to job losses.

JKN Polymers Ltd

10.130. JKN Polymers Ltd (JKN) said that MKW had become the largest user of its products in the UK, although it had since supplied many other water companies. Being adopted as a supplier and having its innovative product used by MKW afforded JKN high status in terms of the quality standards necessary to be acceptable as a supplier to the water industry. This had been achieved through close consultation with MKW. It felt it had made these achievements as a result of MKW affording small and concept companies like JKN the opportunity to supply and service a need with a truly environmentally-aware attitude. It considered SAUR's approach to choosing suppliers to be very different. The assistance and visionary encouragement of MKW had not been afforded to JKN by the larger merged water companies with the exception of Thames Water and Lyonnaise. Due to their size, the larger companies generally lacked the focus on long-term priorities at which MKW excelled.

10.131. JKN said that MKW was not just a water supply company or another commercially-motivated company. Although it was good at both, it was more importantly perceived locally as a company that put back more than it took out. It felt this benefit would be lost should the merger go ahead.

Kentec Tool Hire (Medway Handling Engineers Ltd)

10.132. Kentec Tool Hire (Medway Handling Engineers Ltd) (Kentec) said that it had taken some 13 years to develop and maintain the successful business it had now become. It had reinvested profits so as to give the company a solid foundation from which to expand. During that time it had worked very closely with some of its more important clients among which MKW and its subsidiaries ranked highly.

10.133. Kentec said that MKH was probably one of the largest buying powers in the area. If MKH were lost, there would be redundancies and the closing down of several small businesses. More importantly, Kent would lose one of the institutions which had done so much for the economic development of Kent businesses as well as spearheading many worthwhile local charity events. Kentec doubted whether GU or SAUR would do this.

Kent Technical & Draughting Services

10.134. Kent Technical & Draughting Services (KTDS) said that it had for some considerable time been providing technical assistance to MKW, and now Halcrow Engineering. Its close association with MKW and the reasonably constant flow of orders had helped it to expand its company and to invest several thousand pounds in up-to-date technology and equipment. This had permitted KTDS to continue to maintain the high quality of service it provided.

10.135. If the merger were to proceed it would be inevitable that MKW's technical services would be relocated elsewhere, leading to redundancies in KTDS. It would also similarly affect small businesses all over the south-east of England.

MCS Cleaning Contractors Ltd

10.136. MCS Cleaning Contractors Ltd (MCS) said that it had provided quality services for MKW since 1972 and feared that the loss of such a customer could result in job losses. Becoming and remaining a quality supplier to MKW had taken much time and effort. MCS believed MKW had been very active in the economic development of Kent and that businesses would suffer if MKW ceased to exist.

Medway Travel Limited

10.137. Medway Travel Limited (Medway) said that MKH had played an important role in supporting local industry and in placing business in an area which had a high level of unemployment. It understood that in an earlier inquiry the MMC had concluded that if MKW were absorbed by a larger water company it would become less useful as an independent comparator and that this would have an adverse impact on the public interest—a view which Medway supported. Medway believed that competition resulted in diversity of approach and the development of new concepts in technology and service. The merging of the three companies under consideration would negate this advantage in the Kent area.

Sabre Security

10.138. Sabre Security (Sabre) said that it was a regional security company based in Whitstable and provided the security requirements of MKW at its Paddock Wood, Ashford and Snodland depots.

10.139. MKW was one of Sabre's main customers, and the loss, or potential loss, of its business would have a significantly adverse effect on Sabre. Sabre had spent many years building up a close relationship, and felt that the proposed acquisition would undermine its hard efforts. Sabre was, therefore, of the opinion that the benefits of competition within the water industry would be clearly damaged should the merger proceed. There would also be a loss of a comparator.

Safeway Stores plc (Directorate of Engineering)

10.140. Safeway Stores plc (Safeway) said that its Directorate of Engineering considered that the proposed acquisition would constitute a monopoly of the water supply covering the area of the present three companies, and that the merger could be expected to operate against the public interest. Such a merger would clearly prejudice the ability of the DGWS to make comparisons between different water enterprises as these would have merged into a monopolistic supply.

10.141. Safeway added that if the merger took place, it would clearly be prudent for the company to budget for additional water charges for the area, as without competition there could be price pressure on the consumer. It believed such a take-over would be detrimental to the public interest.

SCA Packaging Limited

10.142. SCA Packaging Limited (SCA) said that it was a major industrial water user in Aylesford employing 485 people in the manufacture of corrugated cases and paper from recycled material. It relied on having an uninterrupted supply of water in order to conduct its business efficiently. SCA said that it would be most anxious about losing MKW as its supplier of water, especially as it was the only one of the three companies involved in the merger discussions not to have imposed any water restrictions on its customers.

10.143. SCA also said that it was important for it to be able to enjoy the benefits yielded by competition in the water industry. By losing MKW as an independent business, the number of water companies serving Kent would be reduced with, consequently, less competition in the region.

Sensus Metering Limited

10.144. Sensus Metering Limited (Sensus) said that it was a world-leading water metering equipment and system supplier. MKW was one of Sensus' principal UK customers, purchasing water meters, electronic reading systems and software. It made the following main points:

(a) Sensus' experience of working with MKW had shown it to be one of the leading water utilities in the UK in the implementation of new and innovative ways of optimizing operating methods, both in the supply and distribution of water.

(b) MKW operated fair but thorough selection of suppliers, making its choice on life cost, value, quality, availability and many other aspects. Conversely, the GU and SAUR companies did not appear to operate in this way.

(c) Sensus was under no illusion that the acquisition of MKH would in all probability result in cessation of contracts with the company. There was a significant risk of its investment being wasted.

(d) Allowing the acquisition of MKH by two utilities which currently controlled a significant proportion of the UK and French water industries did not appear to be in concert with the aim of increasing market competition.

Shepherd Neame

10.145. Shepherd Neame believed that the proposed acquisition of MKH would not produce economies of scale in relation to the production of water. It was particularly concerned at the proposals because the company relied on the quality of well water for the production of beer. The company was the only brewery remaining in Kent. Shepherd Neame believed that if there was a considerable increase in the extraction of water this could lead to an imbalance in the constituents of its water supply; it was particularly reliant on a fine balance of mineral salts. The company also thought that if the water companies were now to be grouped together, the water from local sources could easily be transferred elsewhere, and that this could restrict the availability of water within the area. That in turn could lead to a slowing down in any potential development in east Kent.

G Stow PLC

10.146. G Stow PLC (Stow) said that it was a principal waterworks contractor for MKW which it believed to be efficient and well managed while having some of the most difficult water resource problems of any area of the UK.

10.147. Stow was opposed to the proposed merger. MKW had operated a very efficient in-house geological and hydrogeological unit and carried out its own water resources work. Unlike many other water undertakings, it had always had an ongoing repair and renewal programme.

Swale Business Supplies

10.148. Swale Business Supplies said that it had been a preferred supplier to MKW for some 16 years. Should it lose MKW as a much-valued customer there was a very real likelihood of job losses.

T M Products Ltd

10.149. T M Products Ltd (TMP) viewed with concern the increasing monopolization of the water industry by large operators. It considered the proposed merger as disadvantageous for the following reasons:

(a) One of the intentions of privatizing the pre-1989 water authorities was to increase competition and customer focus in the former public sector bodies. The proposed merger would erode the diversity of the market. It would place control of key enterprises in the market outside the UK. It would also reduce local accountability of a highly visible service to the public.

(b) TMP was specifically concerned by the bid because where SAUR had taken control of other small water companies TMP had generally lost business to foreign competitors providing a technically inferior product at marginally lower cost. Because of the fixed size of the UK water market TMP had not been able to replace this business.

(c) MKW had generally been more discerning in expectations of performance from its suppliers than most of the water industry.

(d) Previous MMC investigations in 1991 had noted the value of MKW as an independent comparator. Further take-overs since then had surely strengthened the case.

T N Printers Ltd

10.150. T N Printers Ltd (TNP) said that it had spent the last six years supplying MKH and its subsidiaries with most of its business stationery. To lose this important customer could present extreme difficulties for the company. There was very little opportunity to replace such an account. The result would be a downward trend in business and inevitable redundancies.

Truck Crane Services Ltd

10.151. Truck Crane Services Ltd (TCS) said that it was a small business which had become a quality supplier to MKW after expending much time and effort to meet demands and maintain the service it required. The loss of MKW as a customer could well result in job losses within TCS since finding business opportunities in such a competitive area was very difficult. MKW had been very active in the economic development of Kent; and TCS and many other small businesses would suffer were MKW to be taken out of the market-place. It considered that there should be competition in all industries, not least the water industry, and it did not wish the merger to proceed.

Uponor Ltd

10.152. Uponor Ltd (Uponor) said that it was the major supplier of distribution pipeline materials to MKW. It felt its relationship with MKW was a mutually beneficial partnership. Uponor also believed itself to be the sole supplier of pipeline materials to GU and SAUR. Uponor did not believe the proposed merger would promote greater competition in the water industry, and questioned whether in the long term it was in the public's best interest to have fewer service providers.

Members of Parliament and Members of the European Parliament

10.153. Sir Keith Speed (declaring an interest as a director of FDWS) conveyed his support for the proposed acquisition. David Shaw (Dover) wrote to support the proposal mainly on the grounds that it would result in a more effective corporate entity in the Dover and surrounding area. He also asked that consideration be given to the support from a constituent society, the Dover Society, for the merger proposals on the grounds of reducing industry fragmentation and (through the proposed 'mini-grid') of securing more efficient use and distribution of water.

10.154. The following 11 Members of Parliament, however, wrote expressing their own concerns, or the concerns of interested parties and constituents, at the proposed merger for a number of reasons, including its likely detrimental effects on competition in the region and service levels for MKW customers: Sir Andrew Bowden (Brighton, Kemptown and a consultant to SWS), Julian Brazier (Canterbury), Dame Peggy Fenner (Medway), David Rendel (Newbury), Rt Hon Sir John Stanley (Tonbridge & Malling), Matthew Taylor (writing as Liberal Democrat Environment spokesman), Sir Teddy Taylor (Southend East), Ann Widdecombe (Maidstone) and Mark Wolfsen (Sevenoaks).

10.155. Jonathan Aitken (Thanet South) and Roger Gale (Thanet North) also stressed the problems for their constituents which the proposal would cause, as a result of water being transferred to the areas, adjacent to MKW, already controlled by other GU and SAUR companies. It appeared to Mr Gale to be abundantly plain that the purpose of the proposed 'mini-grid' would be to remove water currently available to his constituents in order to redress the shortage in Folkestone, Dover and the south-eastern area, and he wished to resist any proposal that was likely to diminish still further supplies that were already likely to be inadequate to meet local needs.

10.156. Two Members of the European Parliament (MEPs), Sir Jack Stewart-Clark (East Sussex and Kent South) and Peter Skinner (Kent West), also wrote to express concern.

Private Individuals

10.157. One-hundred and forty private individuals and local councillors sent letters expressing concern at the proposed merger.

D G GOYDER *(Chairman)*

N F MATTHEWS

K M H MORTIMER

M R PROSSER

G H STACY

P A BOYS *(Secretary)*

9 December 1996

APPENDIX 1.1
(referred to in paragraphs 1.4, 1.5 and 2.20)

The reference and background

1. On 23 May 1996 the Department of Trade and Industry sent the MMC the following reference:

Whereas it appears to the Secretary of State that it is or may be the fact that—

(A) arrangements are in progress which, if carried into effect, will result in:

(a) mergers of two or more water enterprises (as defined in section 35(1) of the Water Industry Act 1991) in that water enterprises carried on by or under the control of Mid Kent Holdings plc will cease to be distinct (within the meaning of Part V of the Fair Trading Act 1973) from water enterprises carried on by or under the control of General Utilities plc and water enterprises carried on by or under the control of SAUR Water Services plc; and

(b) mergers of two or more water enterprises in that—

(i) water enterprises carried on by or under the control of General Utilities plc will cease to be distinct (within the meaning of Part V of the Fair Trading Act 1973) from water enterprises carried on by or under the control of Mid Kent Holdings plc; and

(ii) water enterprises carried on by or under the control of SAUR Water Services plc will cease to be distinct (within the meaning of Part V of the Fair Trading Act 1973) from water enterprises carried on by or under the control of Mid Kent Holdings plc; and

(B) in each case, the value of the assets to be taken over would exceed £30 million and a water enterprise already belonging to the person making the takeover has assets the value of which exceeds £30 million;

Now, therefore, the Secretary of State, in exercise of his duty under section 32 of the Water Industry Act 1991, hereby refers to the Monopolies and Mergers Commission, for investigation and report within a period ending on 30th September 1996 the following questions:

(1)(i) whether arrangements (as described in paragraph (A) above) are in progress which, if carried into effect, will result in the creation of one or more such mergers of two or more water enterprises as are required by section 32 of the Water Industry Act 1991 to be the subject of a merger reference; or

(1)(ii) if events so require, whether the actual results of those arrangements are the creation of one or more such mergers; and

(2) if so, whether the creation of each such merger may be expected to operate or (if events so require) operates against the public interest.

23 May 1996

(signed) ARTHUR PRYOR
*An official of the
Department of Trade and Industry*

2. On 13 September 1996 the Department of Trade sent the MMC the following variation to the reference:

The Secretary of State, in exercise of the powers conferred by section 71 of the Fair Trading Act 1973, as applied by section 34 of the Water Industry Act 1991 hereby makes the following variation to the reference dated 23 May 1996 by which he referred to the Monopolies and Mergers Commission, for investigation and report, questions relating to arrangements involving water enterprises of Mid Kent Holdings plc, General Utilities plc and SAUR Water Services plc respectively:

after paragraph (2) there shall be inserted:

"(3) whether a merger of water enterprises belonging to Mid Kent Holdings plc, General Utilities plc and SAUR Water Services plc respectively, being such a merger of two or more water enterprises as is required by section 32 of the Water Industry Act 1991 to be the subject of a merger reference, has take place otherwise than as a result of the carrying into effect of arrangements that have been the subject of a reference by virtue of section 32(1)(a) of that Act; and

(4) if so, whether that merger operates or may be expected to operate against the public interest."

13 September 1996

(signed) ANN EGGINGTON
An official of the
Department of Trade and Industry

3. The composition of the Group of members responsible for the present investigation and report is indicated in the list of members in the preface.

4. Notices inviting interested parties to submit evidence to the MMC were placed in:

The Evening Standard *Kent and Sussex Courier*
Water Bulletin *Kentish Gazette*
Kent Messenger *Isle of Thanet Gazette and Times*
Kent Today *Herne Bay Gazette*
East Kent Gazette Group *Whitstable and Herne Bay Times*
Sevenoaks Chronicle

5. In addition evidence was sought from the DoE, the EA, the DGWS, the Southern Customer Service Committee, water-only companies, water and sewerage companies, local authorities, trade unions, trade and consumer organizations, major users of services provided by MKW and other interested parties. Written evidence was received from 245 of these parties, including 13 Members of Parliament, two Members of the European Parliament and 140 private individuals.

6. Three sets of hearings were held with GU and SAUR, and three hearings with MKH.

7. Submissions were received from, and hearings held with, the DGWS, the EA, OFWAT's Southern Customer Service Committee, SWS and the Water Group of the Canterbury branch of Friends of the Earth. The DoE submitted a note on the legal framework for the water industry—see Appendix 4.1. A written submission was also made by UNISON.

8. Members of the Group, accompanied by staff, visited the headquarters and operations of MKW, FDWS and SEW.

9. Some of the evidence obtained in the course of our inquiry was of a commercially confidential nature and the report contains only such information as is considered necessary for a proper understanding of its conclusions.

10. The MMC's thanks are due to all those who helped in the inquiry, particularly to GU, SAUR, MKH, and to the DGWS, and the EA.

APPENDIX 1.2

(referred to in paragraphs 1.4 and 2.126)

Statutory provisions governing
a) Mergers between water enterprises and (b) Bulk supply transfers

(a) The Water Industry Act 1991—sections 32 to 34
(as amended by the Competition and Services (Utilities) Act 1992 and the Water Enterprises (Merger) (Modifications) Regulations 1994 (SI 1994/73))

Duty to refer merger of water or sewerage undertakings.

32.—(1) Subject to the following provisions of this section and to section 33 below, it shall be the duty of the Secretary of State to make a merger reference to the Monopolies Commission if it appears to him that it is or may be the fact—

(a) that arrangements are in progress which, if carried into effect, will result in a merger of any two or more water enterprises; or

(b) that such a merger has taken place otherwise than as a result of the carrying into effect of arrangements that have been the subject of a reference by virtue of paragraph (a) above.

(2) [inapplicable]

(3) [inapplicable]

Exclusion of small mergers from duty to make merger reference.

33.—(1) The Secretary of State shall not make a merger reference under section 32 above in respect of any actual or prospective merger of two or more water enterprises if it appears to him—

(a) that the value of the assets taken over does not exceed or, as the case may be, would not exceed £30 million; or

(b) that the only water enterprises already belonging to the person making the take over are enterprises each of which has assets the value of which does not exceed or, as the case may be, would not exceed that amount.

(2) In relation to a merger of two or more water enterprises—

(a) the value of the assets taken over shall, for the purposes of subsection (1) above, be determined in accordance with section 67 of the 1973 Act by reference only to assets employed in or appropriated to a water enterprise; and

(b) the value of the assets of a water enterprise belonging to the person making the take over shall be taken for those purposes to be the value of such assets employed in or appropriated to that enterprise as by virtue of the exceptions in paragraph (a) of subsection (2) of that section are disregarded in determining the value of the assets taken over;

and paragraph (b) of that subsection shall apply for determining the value of the assets referred to in paragraph (b) above as it applies in relation to the assets taken over.

(3) For the purposes of this section and of any determination in accordance with this section—

(a) the assets treated as employed in or appropriated to a water enterprise carried on by a company holding an appointment under Chapter 1 of this Part shall include all the assets for the time being of that company;

(b) every water enterprise any of whose assets fall to be disregarded as mentioned in subsection (2)(b) above shall be treated as belonging to the person making the take over;

(c) the enterprises mentioned in paragraph (b) above shall be treated as separate enterprises in so far as they are carried on by different companies holding appointments under Chapter 1 of this Part: and

(d) subsections (3) and (4) of section 67 of the 1973 Act (assets treated as appropriated to an enterprise and mergers over a period) shall apply as they apply for the purposes of, and of any determination in accordance with, subsection (2) of that section.

(4) If the Secretary of State considers that it is appropriate—

(a) for subsection (1) above to have effect with a reference in paragraph (a) to a different amount; or

(b) for the condition set out in that paragraph to be modified in any other respect, he may, in relation to mergers after the coming into force of the regulations, by regulations make such modifications of that paragraph and, for that purpose, of the other provisions of this section as may be prescribed.

References with respect to water enterprise mergers.

34.—(1) Subject to subsections (2) to (4) below, the 1973 Act shall have effect in relation to any reference under section 32 above as if—

(a) any such merger of two or more water enterprises as is required to be the subject of such a reference were a merger situation qualifying for investigation; and

(b) a reference under that section were made under section 64 of that Act or, as the case may be, under section 75 of that Act (references in anticipation of a merger).

(2) Nothing in subsection (1) above shall have the effect in relation to any reference under section 32 above of applying—

(a) so much of Part V of the 1973 Act as requires the Monopolies Commission to consider any of the matters set out in subsection (1) of section 64 of that Act; or

(b) the provisions of sections 69(2) to (4) and 75(3) of that Act (power to restrict matters referred).

(3) In determining on a reference under section 32 above whether any matter operates, or may be expected to operate, against the public interest the Monopolies Commission—

(a) shall have regard to the desirability of giving effect to the principle that the Director's ability, in carrying out his functions by virtue of this Act, to make comparisons between different water enterprises should not be prejudiced; and[1]

---

[1] Amended by Competition and Services (Utilities) Act 1992.

(b) shall have regard to the desirability of achieving any other purpose so far only as they are satisfied—

(i) that that other purpose can be achieved in a manner that does not conflict with that principle; or

(ii) that the achievement of that other purpose is of substantially greater significance in relation to the public interest than that principle and cannot be brought about except in a manner that conflicts with that principle.

(4) No order shall be made under Part V of the 1973 Act in consequence of any merger reference made under section 32 above in respect of an actual merger unless the reference was made within the period of six months beginning with whichever is the later of—

(a) the day on which the merger took place; and

(b) the day on which the material facts about the transactions which resulted in the merger first came to the notice of the Secretary of State or the Director General of Fair Trading or were made public within the meaning of section 64 of the 1973 Act;

and if on such a reference the Monopolies Commission are satisfied that the reference was not made within that period their report on the reference shall state that fact and nothing else.

(b) The Water Industry Act 1991—sections 40 and 40A
(as replaced by the Competition and Services
(Utilities) Act 1992 and amended by the Environment Act 1995)

Bulk supplies.

40.—(1) Where, on the application of any qualifying person—

(a) it appears to the Director [General of Water Services] that it is necessary or expedient for the purposes of securing the efficient use of water resources, or the efficient supply of water, that the water undertaker specified in the application ("the supplier") should give a supply of water in bulk to the applicant, and

(b) the Director is satisfied that the giving and taking of such a supply cannot be secured by agreement,

the Director may by order require the supplier to give and the applicant to take such a supply for such period and on such terms and conditions as may be provided in the order.

(2) In this section "qualifying person" means—

(a) a water undertaker; or

(b) a person who has made an application for an appointment or variation under section 8 above which has not been determined.

(3) Where the application is made by a person who is a qualifying person by virtue of subsection (2)(b) above, an order made under this section in response to that application shall be expressed not to come into force until the applicant becomes a water undertaker for the area specified in the order, or for an area which includes that area.

(4) Subject to subsection (3) above, an order under this section shall have effect as an agreement between the supplier and the applicant.

(5) The Director shall not make an order under this section unless he has first consulted the Environment Agency.

(6) In exercising his functions under this section, the Director shall have regard to the desirability of—

    (a) facilitating effective competition within the water supply industry;

    (b) the supplier's recovering the expenses of complying with its obligations by virtue of this section and securing a reasonable return on its capital;

    (c) the supplier's being able to meet its existing obligations, and likely future obligations, to supply water without having to incur unreasonable expenditure in carrying out works;

    (d) not putting at risk the ability of the supplier to meet its existing obligations, or likely future obligations, to supply water.

Variation and termination of bulk supply agreements.

40A.—(1) This section applies where, on the application of any party to a bulk supply agreement—

    (a) it appears to the Director that it is necessary or expedient for the purpose of securing the efficient use of water resources, or the efficient supply of water, to vary the agreement or to terminate it, and

    (b) the Director is satisfied that that cannot be achieved by agreement between the parties to the agreement.

(2) The Director may by order—

    (a) vary the agreement by—

        (i) varying the period for which the supply of water is to be given; or

        (ii) varying any of the terms or conditions on which that supply is to be given; or

    (b) terminate the agreement.

(3) Before making any order under this section the Director shall consult the Environment Agency.

(4) Where an order is made under this section the agreement concerned shall have effect subject to the provision made by the order or (as the case may be) shall cease to have effect.

(5) An order under this section may require the payment of compensation by any party to the agreement to any other party.

(6) The obligations of a water undertaker under subsection (5) above shall be enforceable under section 18 above by the Director.

(7) In exercising his functions under this section, the Director shall have regard to the expenses incurred by the supplier in complying with its obligations under the bulk supply agreement and to the desirability of—

    (a) facilitating effective competition within the water supply industry;

(b) the supplier's recovering the expenses of complying with its obligations by virtue of this section and securing a reasonable return on its capital;

(c) the supplier's being able to meet its existing obligations, and likely future obligations, to supply water without having to incur unreasonable expenditure in carrying out works;

(d) not putting at risk the ability of the supplier to meet its existing obligations, or likely future obligations, to supply water.

(8) In this section—

"bulk supply agreement" means an agreement between one or more water undertakers for the supply of water in bulk and includes—

(a) an order under section 40 above which is deemed to be an agreement by virtue of subsection (4) of that section; and

(b) any agreement which has been varied by order under this section; and

"supplier", in relation to a bulk supply agreement, means any water undertaker which is required by the agreement to provide a bulk supply of water.

APPENDIX 2.1

(referred to in paragraphs 1.3, 2.15, 3.3 and 6.3)

Synopsis of GU/SAUR proposals as finally presented to us

Stage 1

GU and SAUR acquire the entire issued share capital of MKH through a new company (Newco) which is to be specially formed for the purpose of the bid. GU and SAUR announced their intention to proceed in this manner, subject to regulatory clearance, in a joint statement issued on 21 December 1995.

Stage 2

Once Newco has acquired control of MKH, GU and SAUR intend to restructure the business of Mid Kent Water. Apart from certain water resource assets (described below) the business would be divided into approximately equal halves determined by value. The boundary line has not been precisely defined but would probably run within the corridor hatched on the map at Figure 1. The business conducted in the area to the west of the boundary line would be amalgamated with SEW and the business in the area to the east with FDWS.

All MKW's existing water abstraction rights, including necessary rights of access to land, and rights to receive supplies of water from third parties, and all new abstraction licences applied for within the former MKW area, and the rights and licences associated with any major new resource development, for example a reservoir at Broad Oak, would be held by a joint venture company, the JRC owned equally by SEW and FDWS. Any such major development would be effected through a JVA or other similar arrangement under which SEW and FDWS would jointly procure, construct, operate and maintain it, possibly with the participation of other water undertakers.

FIGURE 1

GU/SAUR proposed division of Mid Kent

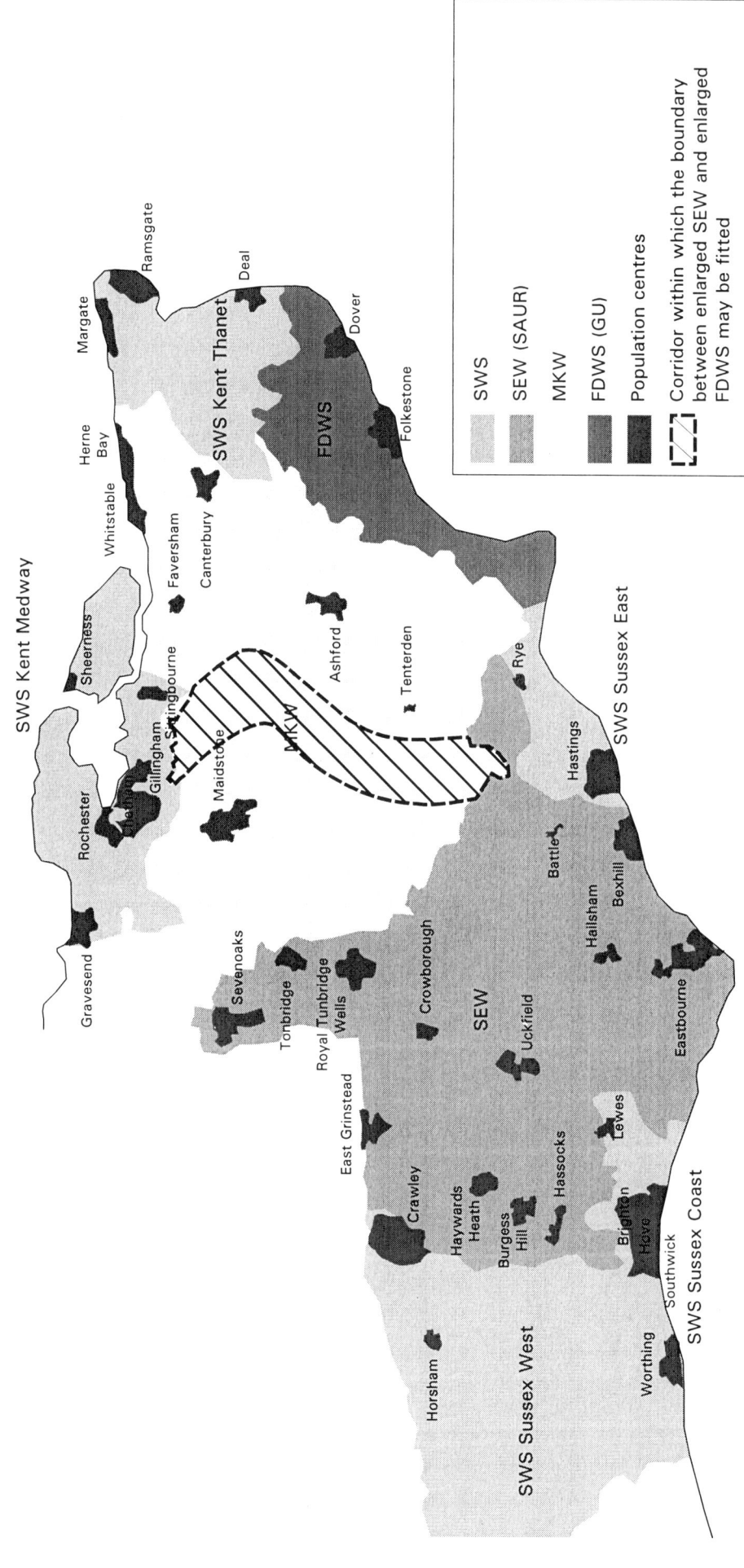

Source: GU/SAUR.

APPENDIX 3.1
(referred to in paragraphs 3.11, 6.67, 6.84 and 7.62)

Chronology of main events involving GU, SAUR and Mid Kent

Activity	Date
SAUR initially acquired 4.56 per cent voting stock in MKW.	April/May 1988
GU initially acquired a 14.61 per cent holding in MKW.	June 1988
MKH incorporated as a limited company.	August 1988
GU announced offers for FDWS (then Folkestone and District WC).	December 1988
GU acquired 73 per cent of the voting shares of FDWS.	January 1989
SAUR Water Services acquired Eastbourne Water Services, Mid Sussex Water and West Kent Water.	February 1989
MKH registered as a public limited company (3 March 1989). Stockholders of MKW shares were offered MKH shares in exchange for their MKW stock. At the same time there was a rights issue and an offer of shares to investors and employees.	March–August 1989
GU's share of MKH voting stock increased to 29.8 per cent and SAUR's to 15.8 per cent.	March 1989
SAUR's share of MKH voting stock increased to 19.5 per cent.	November 1989
GU/Mid Kent merger reference to MMC.	January 1990
Resulting from MMC report, GU was required, under the FTA, to undertake to the Secretary of State for Trade and Industry *inter alia* to reduce its shareholding in MKH to not more than 19.5 per cent by 30 June 1992.	March 1991
SEW formed out of merger of Eastbourne, West Kent and Mid Sussex (ordinary share capital is not listed on the Stock Exchange).	May 1991
On 30 June GU disposed of 9.38 per cent of MKH's share capital by way of a sale of preference shares to Morgan Grenfell, reducing its holding to 19.5 per cent (which later fell to 19.45 per cent as MKH's total issued share capital increased).	June 1992
Folkestone and District (GU) became FDWS and was incorporated as a private company under the Companies Act 1985 and its ordinary and preference shares delisted.	June 1992
SAUR unsuccessfully sought representation on the Board of MKH.	June 1993
GU and SAUR signed a JVA embodying intention to make bid for MKH (followed by announcement).	20 December 1995
GU and SAUR signed a supplemental agreement agreeing to complete implementation of the proposed restructuring of MKH.	12 February 1996

MKH asked the High Court for declarations that, among other things, GU's undertakings not to increase its shareholding in MKH above 19.5 per cent had been breached by the arrangements for the bid made with SAUR.	2 April 1996
The High Court (Mr Justice Knox) decided that MKH did not have the right to enforce the undertakings obtained under the FTA.	30 April 1996
GU and SAUR/MKH proposals referred to MMC (reporting date 30 September).	23 May 1996
At MKH's AGM, GU voted unsuccessfully against resolution 4 (ordinary) and successfully against 5 (special) with SAUR abstaining on each; SAUR voted successfully against resolution 6 (special) with GU abstaining. Both voted successfully against MKH's proposed performance share plan (ordinary) at the EGM the same day.	18 July 1996
Variation of reference to MMC to cover the possibility of a merger in being (reporting date 9 December).	13 September 1996

Source: MMC.

Note: Corrall-Montenay, which is 50 per cent owned by CGE (GU's parent), acquired about 2 per cent of MKW stock in December 1986, which it sold in June 1992.

APPENDIX 3.2
(referred to in paragraph 3.26)

CGE financial information

TABLE 1 **CGE HCA group balance sheet summary**

£ million

As at 31 December

	1991	1992	1993	1994	1995
Total assets	20,607	22,728	25,321	27,082	28,098
Tangible fixed assets and trade investments	6,567	7,553	8,804	10,322	11,220
Stocks and debtors less current creditors (other than borrowings)	2,224	2,922	3,161	2,445	1,195
Net assets used in the business	8,791	10,475	11,965	12,767	12,415
Cash assets less borrowings	(5,247)	(6,286)	(7,029)	(7,166)	(7,309)
Provisions for liabilities and charges	(2,931)	(3,152)	(3,374)	(3,775)	(4,108)
Net tangible assets	613	1,037	1,562	1,826	998
Goodwill and intangible assets	1,975	2,329	2,766	3,118	3,393
Net assets	2,588	3,366	4,328	4,944	4,391
Share capital and reserves	2,226	2,906	3,832	4,176	3,658
Minorities	362	460	496	768	733
	2,588	3,366	4,328	4,944	4,391

Source: GU/MMC analysis.

Note: Figures have been translated at FF8.25 = £1.

TABLE 2 **CGE HCA profit and loss summary**

£ million

As at 31 December

	1991	1992	1993	1994	1995
Turnover	16,354	17,380	17,892	18,928	19,753
Operating profit	680	668	559	238	(117)
Exceptional items	12	15	29	429	102
Net interest and financial income	(213)	(257)	(184)	(264)	(412)
Profit before tax	479	426	404	403	(427)
Tax	(139)	(108)	(96)	(108)	(174)
Profit after tax	340	318	308	295	(601)
Minority interest	(23)	33	80	111	154
Dividends	(94)	(111)	(130)	(147)	0
Retained profit	223	240	258	259	(447)
Operating profit as % of turnover (%)	4.2	3.8	3.1	1.3	−0.6
Goodwill amortization included in operating profit above	(49)	(56)	(76)	(93)	(124)

Source: GU/MMC analysis.

Note: Figures have been translated at FF8.25 = £1.

TABLE 3 **CGE HCA financial statistics**

As at 31 December

	1991	1992	1993	1994	1995
Average net operating assets (£m)	8,113	9,633	11,220	12,366	12,591
Operating profit (£m)	741	739	664	759	1,005
Return on net operating assets (%)	9.1	7.7	5.9	6.1	8.0
Average shareholders' funds and minorities (£m)	2,405	2,977	3,846	4,635	4,667
Profit on ordinary activities before tax (£m)	479	426	404	403	(427)
Return on average shareholders' funds and minority interests (%)	20	14	11	9	−9
Earnings per ordinary share (£)	3.59	3.84	3.82	3.65	(3.78)

Source: GU/MMC analysis.

Notes:
1. Figures have been translated at FF8.25 = £1.
2. Averages for assets and shareholders' funds are arithmetic means of the figures at the beginning and end of each year.
3. Return on net operating assets is operating profit and exceptional items before deduction of goodwill amortization.
4. Profit before tax is after exceptional items.

APPENDIX 3.3

(referred to in paragraphs 3.31 to 3.34, 3.54 and 10.17)

The WaSCs and WoCs

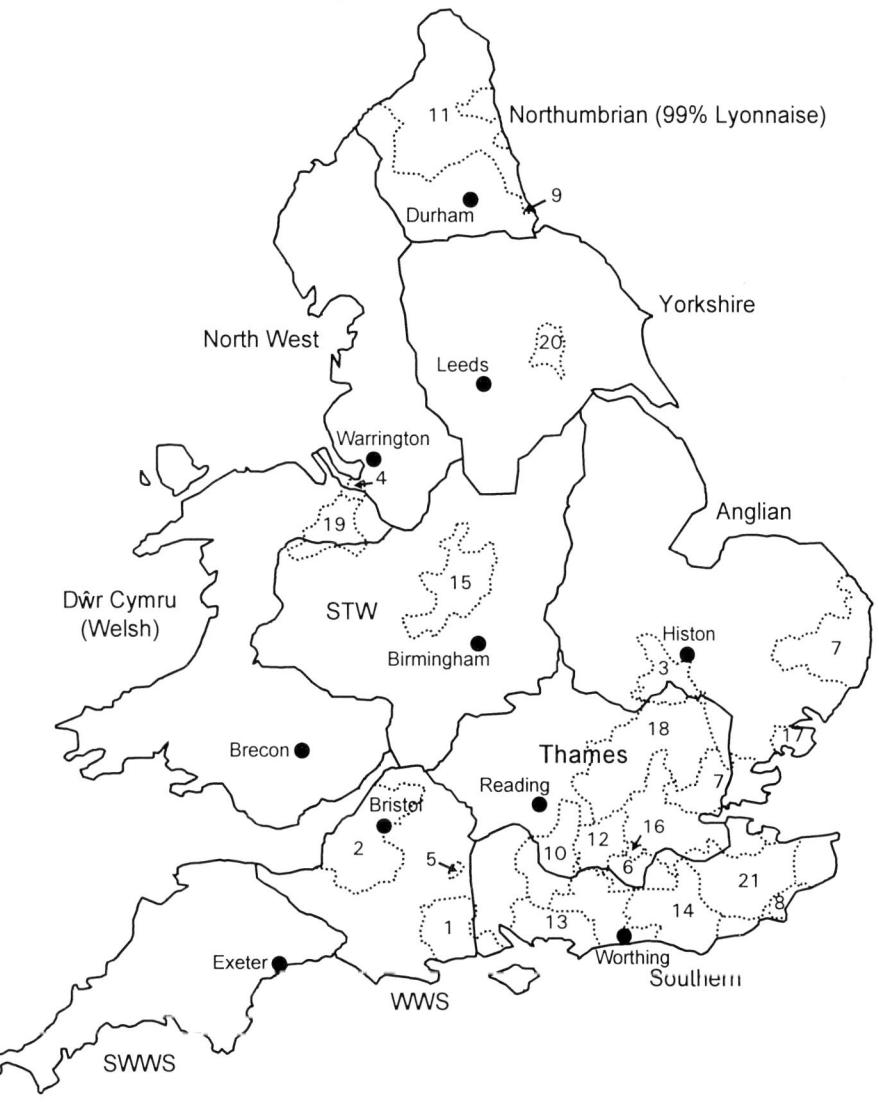

The areas served by WaSCs are defined by solid lines and their headquarters are named.
The WoCs are numbered as below and their areas of operation shown by dotted lines.

1. Bournemouth & West Hampshire Water PLC
2. Bristol Water plc (25.0% GU)
3. Cambridge Water Company
4. Chester Waterworks Company
5. Cholderton & District Water Company Limited
6. Sutton and East Surrey Water plc*
7. Essex & Suffolk Water Plc (98.8% Lyonnaise)
8. Folkestone and Dover Water Services Ltd (74.1% GU)
9. Hartlepool Water PLC
10. Mid Southern Water plc (99.44% SAUR)
11. North East Water PLC†
12. North Surrey Water Ltd (98.9% GU)
13. Portsmouth Water plc
14. South East Water Limited (100% SAUR)
15. South Staffordshire Water Plc (27.8% GU)
16. Sutton District Water Plc‡
17. Tendring Hundred Water Services Ltd (99.1% GU)
18. Three Valleys Water PLC (100% GU)
19. Wrexham Water plc
20. York Waterworks Plc
21. Mid Kent Water PLC

Sources: OFWAT and GU/SAUR.

*Owns 14 per cent of the shares in the holding company for Portsmouth Water.
†Now merged with Northumbrian.
‡Now merged with East Surrey Water to form Sutton and East Surrey Water plc.

APPENDIX 3.4
(referred to in paragraph 3.39)

FDWS financial information

TABLE 1 **FDWS CCA balance sheet summary**

£ million

As at 31 March

	1992	1993	1994	1995	1996
Total assets	101.9	103.8	107.2	111.3	160.2
Tangible fixed assets and trade investments	100.5	102.4	105.7	109.5	158.6
Stocks and debtors less current creditors (other than borrowings)	(0.1)	(1.2)	(1.8)	(2.7)	(3.6)
Net assets used in the business	100.4	101.2	103.9	106.8	155.0
Cash assets less borrowings	(3.5)	(3.9)	(4.6)	(5.3)	(4.7)
Provisions for liabilities and charges	(0.6)	(0.6)	(0.6)	(0.7)	(0.7)
	96.3	96.7	98.7	100.8	149.6
Share capital	3.0	3.0	3.0	3.0	3.0
Current cost reserve	91.8	92.5	93.6	95.1	143.7
Profit and loss account	1.5	1.2	2.1	2.7	2.9
	96.3	96.7	98.7	100.8	149.6

Source: FDWS/MMC analysis.

TABLE 2 **FDWS CCA profit and loss summary**

£ million

Years ended 31 March

	1992	1993	1994	1995	1996
Turnover	7.6	8.6	9.6	10.2	10.5
Current cost operating costs	(5.6)	(5.9)	(5.5)	(4.9)	(5.0)
Capital costs:					
Depreciation	(1.0)	(1.4)	(1.3)	(2.2)	(2.5)
Infrastructure renewal charge	(0.5)	(0.2)	(0.1)	(0.4)	(0.5)
Other costs and adjustments	0.2	0.1	0.1	0.2	0.2
Net profit before interest	0.7	1.2	2.8	2.9	2.7
Net interest	(0.3)	(0.4)	(0.4)	(0.5)	(0.4)
Exceptional item	0.1	0.0	0.0	0.0	0.0
Profit before tax	0.5	0.8	2.4	2.4	2.3
Tax	(0.0)	(0.0)	(0.3)	(0.5)	(0.5)
Dividends	(0.2)	(1.2)	(1.1)	(1.4)	(1.6)
Retained current cost profit	0.3	(0.4)	1.0	0.5	0.2

Source: FDWS/MMC analysis.

TABLE 3 **FDWS CCA financial ratios**

Years ended 31 March

	1992	1993	1994	1995	1996
Net operating assets (£m)	98.5	100.8	102.6	105.4	130.9
Operating profit (£m)	0.6	1.2	2.6	2.7	2.6
Return on average net operating assets (%)	0.6	1.2	2.6	2.6	2.0
Average shareholders' funds (£m)	94.5	96.5	97.7	99.8	125.2
Profit on ordinary activities before tax (£m)	0.5	0.8	2.4	2.4	2.3
Return on average shareholders' funds (%)	0.5	0.9	2.4	2.5	1.9
Debt:equity (%)	3.7	4.1	4.7	5.2	3.2
Interest cover (times)	2.4	3.3	6.9	6.2	6.4

Source: FDWS/MMC analysis.

APPENDIX 3.5
(referred to in paragraph 3.52)

SAUR Group financial information including the results of associated companies

TABLE 1 **SAUR SA HCA consolidated balance sheet summary**

£ million

	1991	1992	1993	1994	1995
Total assets	1,143	1,358	1,457	1,395	1,457
Tangible fixed assets and trade investments	339	349	402	384	454
Stocks and debtors less current creditors (other than borrowings)	3	14	(6)	(15)	(34)
Net operating assets	342	363	396	369	420
Cash less borrowings	(347)	(350)	(379)	(328)	(383)
Associated company investments	139	169	180	210	152
Provisions for liabilities and charges	(96)	(103)	(113)	(121)	(130)
Net tangible assets	38	79	84	130	59
Intangible assets	42	46	59	58	57
Goodwill	51	146	136	125	107
Net assets	131	271	279	313	223
Share capital and reserves	118	118	124	149	98
Minorities	13	153	155	164	125
Shareholders' funds	131	271	279	313	223

Source: SAUR/MMC analysis.

Notes:
1. A change in the method of consolidating associated companies in 1992 increased shareholders' funds from FF1,164 million to FF2,234 million.
2. Figures have been translated at FF8.25 = £1.

TABLE 2 **SAUR International HCA consolidated balance sheet summary**

As at 31 December

£ million

	1991	1992	1993	1994	1995
Total assets				831	913
Tangible fixed assets and trade investments				272	330
Stocks and debtors less current creditors (other than borrowings)				(34)	(48)
Net operating assets				238	282
Cash less borrowings		Company did not exist		(161)	(197)
Associated company investments				9	10
Provisions for liabilities and charges				(11)	(15)
Net tangible assets				75	80
Intangible assets				262	259
Goodwill				18	29
Net assets				355	368
Share capital and reserves				336	349
Minorities				19	19
Shareholders' funds				355	368

Source: SAUR/MMC analysis.

Note: Figures have been translated at FF8.25 = £1.

TABLE 3 **SAUR SA HCA consolidated profit and loss summary**

£ million
Years ended 31 December

	1991	1992	1993	1994	1995
Turnover	816	865	929	889	996
Operating profit	41	27	40	43	60
Exceptional items	0	13	5	74	2
Goodwill amortization	(3)	(9)	(8)	(8)	(20)
Profit before interest	38	31	37	109	42
Net interest and financial income	(33)	(28)	(25)	(36)	(25)
Associated companies	5	16	9	8	(53)
Profit before tax	10	19	21	81	(36)
Tax	(1)	(1)	(4)	(16)	(10)
Profit after tax	9	18	17	65	(46)
Minority interests	(1)	(6)	(6)	(5)	13
Distributable profit	8	12	11	60	(33)
Operating profit as % turnover	5.0	3.1	4.3	4.9	6.0

Source: SAUR/MMC analysis.

Notes:
1. A change in the method of consolidating associated companies in 1992 increased profits after tax from FF106 million to FF151 million.
2. The exceptional item in 1994 was largely profit on disposal of fixed assets.
3. Figures have been translated at FF8.25 = £1.

TABLE 4 **SAUR International HCA consolidated profit and loss summary**

£ million
Years ended 31 December

	1991	1992	1993	1994	1995
Turnover				295	366
Operating profit				30	38
Exceptional items				(3)	(0)
Goodwill amortization				(1)	(2)
Profit before interest				26	36
Net interest and financial income				(10)	(15)
Associated companies		Company did not exist		1	1
Profit before tax				17	22
Tax				(3)	(4)
Profit after tax				14	18
Minority interests				(1)	(2)
Dividends				0	0
Retained profit				13	16
Operating profit as % turnover				10.2	10.3

Source: SAUR/MMC analysis.

Note: Figures have been translated at FF8.25 = £1.

TABLE 5 **SAUR SA HCA consolidated financial statistics**

Years ended 31 December

	1991	1992	1993	1994	1995
Average net operating assets (£m)	314	352	379	382	395
Return on average net operating assets (£m)	40.8	39.7	44.8	117.3	61.6
Return on average net operating assets (%)	13.0	11.3	11.8	30.7	15.6
Average shareholders' funds and minorities (£m)	112	201	275	296	268
Profit before tax (£m)	9.7	19.1	21.0	80.6	(35.6)
Return on average shareholders' funds and minorities (%)	8.7	9.5	7.6	27.2	(13.3)
Debt:equity (%)	918	447	452	253	643
Interest cover (times)	1.3	1.4	1.7	3.3	2.5

Source: SAUR/MMC analysis.

Notes:
1. Return on average net operating assets is operating profit and exceptional items before goodwill amortization and tax.
2. Averages for assets and shareholders' funds are arithmetic means at the beginning and end of each year.
3. Figures have been translated at FF8.25 = £1.

TABLE 6 **SAUR International HCA consolidated financial statistics**

Years ended 31 December

	1991	1992	1993	1994	1995
Average net operating assets (£m)				238	260
Return on average net operating assets (£m)				27.2	37.4
Return on average net operating assets (%)		Company did not exist		11.4	14.4
Average shareholders' funds and minorities (£m)				355	362
Profit before tax (£m)				17.6	22.1
Return on average shareholders' funds and minorities (%)				5.0	6.1
Debt:equity (%)				214	245
Interest cover (times)				2.8	2.5

Source: SAUR International accounts/MMC analysis.

Notes:
1. Debt:equity is based on net debt and net tangible assets.
2. Interest cover is operating profit plus exceptional items divided by net financial expense.
3. Averages for 1994 are not available and year-end figures have been used.
4. Figures have been translated at FF8.25 = £1.

APPENDIX 3.6
(referred to in paragraph 3.58)

SEW financial information

TABLE 1 **SEW CCA balance sheet summary**

£ million

Years ended 31 March

	1992	*1993*	*1994*	*1995*	*1996*
Total assets	789.7	809.4	835.2	866.5	898.7
Tangible fixed assets and trade investments	782.6	801.4	824.6	857.8	891.2
Stocks and debtors less current creditors (other than borrowings)	(2.4)	(0.2)	(3.9)	(4.0)	(9.9)
Net operating assets	780.2	801.1	820.7	853.8	881.3
Cash assets less borrowings	(53.1)	(51.3)	(48.2)	(46.7)	(47.8)
Provisions for liabilities and charges	0.5	(2.0)	(1.0)	(0.6)	(0.7)
	727.6	747.8	771.5	806.5	832.8
Share capital	9.0	12.9	12.9	12.9	6.1
Current cost reserve	717.8	731.6	748.8	775.0	796.7
Profit and loss account	0.8	3.3	9.8	18.6	30.0
	727.6	747.8	771.5	806.5	832.8

Source: SEW/MMC analysis.

TABLE 2 **SEW CCA profit and loss summary**

£ million

Years ended 31 March

	1992	*1993*	*1994*	*1995*	*1996*
Turnover	44.3	48.0	50.4	50.9	53.6
Current cost operating costs	(22.4)	(24.0)	(23.6)	(22.7)	(21.9)
Capital costs:					
Depreciation	(8.5)	(9.3)	(8.6)	(7.2)	(8.1)
Infrastructure renewal charge	(4.7)	(4.9)	(5.1)	(5.3)	(4.0)
Other costs and adjustments	1.8	1.8	1.9	2.7	2.4
Net profit before interest	10.5	11.6	15.0	18.4	22.0
Net interest	(7.6)	(8.3)	(6.7)	(7.0)	(7.4)
Profit before tax	2.9	3.3	8.3	11.4	14.6
Tax	(1.0)	(0.1)	(0.8)	(1.4)	(2.1)
Dividends	(0.6)	(0.7)	(1.0)	(1.1)	(1.2)
Retained current cost profit	1.3	2.5	6.5	8.9	11.3

Source: SEW/MMC analysis.

TABLE 3 **SEW CCA financial statistics**

Years ended 31 March

	1992	1993	1994	1995	1996
Net operating assets (£m)	777	791	811	837	868
Return on net operating assets (£m)	8.3	10.6	13.8	16.6	19.8
Return on net operating assets (%)	1.1	1.3	1.7	2.0	2.3
Average shareholders' funds (£m)	713	738	760	789	820
Profit on ordinary activities before tax (£m)	2.9	3.3	8.3	11.4	14.6
Return on average shareholders' funds (%)	0.4	0.4	1.1	1.4	1.8
Debt:equity (%)	7.3	6.9	6.2	5.8	5.7
Interest cover (times)	1.4	1.4	2.2	2.6	3.0

Source: SEW/MMC analysis.

Note: Capital employed and shareholders' funds in 1992 are year-end figures because opening balance sheet figures were not available.

APPENDIX 3.7
(referred to in paragraphs 2.7, 3.66 and 10.35)

Significant interests in the share capital of MKH at 30 September 1996

The preference shares carry voting rights ranking *pari passu* with ordinary shares but are due for redemption by no later than 31 March 1997. Following redemption, the percentage shares of the main shareholders will be those shown in the 'Ordinary Shares' column below (subject to any further shares being issued or changes in shareholdings).

	Ordinary shares (% of class)	10% redeemable preference shares 1997 (% of class)	% of total issued capital
Compagnie Générale des Eaux	4,150,456 (24.24)	541,000 (7.73)	19.45
SAUR Water Services plc	2,474,103 (14.45)	2,203,000 (31.47)	19.39
Prudential Corporation plc	1,681,900 (9.82)	1,375,900 (19.66)	12.68
Morgan Grenfell & Co Limited	- -	2,256,000 (32.23)	9.35
Axa Equity & Law Life Assurance Society plc	1,491,985 (8.71)	- -	6.18
Sun Life Trust Management Ltd	812,500 (4.74)	- -	3.37
AMP Asset Management plc	542,847 (3.17)	200,000 (2.86)	3.08
Equitable Life Assurance Society	725,000 (4.23)	- -	3.01
Royal London Mutual Insurance Society Limited	628,672 (3.67)	- -	2.61
Total number of shares in issue at 30 September 1996 ('000)	17,123	7,000	

Source: MKH.

There are warrants in issue to subscribe for 1,861,987 ordinary shares at 600p exercisable between 1996 to 1999, and options to subscribe for 390,062 ordinary shares at prices between 222p and 365p variously exercisable on various dates up to 2005.

APPENDIX 3.8
(referred to in paragraph 3.81)

MKW financial information

TABLE 1 **MKW CCA balance sheet summary**

£ million
Years ended 31 March

	1992	1993	1994	1995	1996
Total assets	569	589	609	505	523
Tangible fixed assets and trade investments	568	586	607	506	522
Stocks and debtors less current creditors (other than borrowings)	(7)	(8)	(10)	(12)	(14)
Net assets used in the business	561	578	597	494	508
Cash assets less borrowings	(12)	(20)	(25)	(21)	(17)
Provisions for liabilities and charges	(2)	(1)	(2)	(4)	(4)
	547	557	570	469	487
Share capital	19	19	19	19	19
Current cost reserve	510	520	532	426	439
Profit and loss account	18	18	19	24	29
	547	557	570	469	487

Source: MKW/MMC analysis.

TABLE 2 **MKW CCA profit and loss account summary**

£ million
Years ended 31 March

	1992	1993	1994	1995	1996
Turnover	28.7	30.5	31.2	32.5	34.7
Current cost operating costs	(18.6)	(21.2)	(18.5)	(17.3)	(15.5)
Capital costs:					
Depreciation	(3.3)	(3.6)	(4.0)	(3.7)	(4.0)
Infrastructure renewals charge	(2.3)	(1.9)	(2.2)	(2.2)	(2.6)
Other costs and adjustments	0.7	0.1	(0.3)	1.3	1.0
Net profit before interest	5.2	3.9	6.2	10.6	13.6
Net interest	(0.6)	(1.0)	(2.0)	(2.0)	(1.6)
Exceptional item	0.0	0.0	0.0	0.0	(2.3)
Profit before tax	4.6	2.9	4.2	8.6	9.7
Tax	(0.6)	(0.5)	(0.7)	(1.2)	0.1
Dividends	(2.6)	(2.3)	(2.5)	(2.7)	(4.7)
Retained current cost profit	1.4	0.1	1.0	4.7	5.1

Source: MKW/MMC analysis.

TABLE 3 **MKW CCA financial ratios**

Years ended 31 March

	1992	1993	1994	1995	1996
Average net operating assets (£m)	545	569	588	546	501
Operating profit (£m)	4.6	3.5	5.6	9.4	12.7
Return on average net operating assets (%)	0.8	0.6	0.9	1.7	2.5
Average shareholders' funds (£m)	532	552	564	520	478
Profit on ordinary activities before tax (£m)	4.6	2.9	4.2	8.6	9.7
Return on average shareholders' funds (%)	0.9	0.5	0.7	1.6	2.0
Debt:equity (%)	2.1	3.6	4.4	4.5	3.5
Interest cover (times)	9.3	3.9	3.0	5.2	7.3

Source: MKW/MMC analysis.

Note: Interest cover is calculated on actual figures rather than the rounded figures shown.

APPENDIX 3.9
(referred to in paragraphs 2.59 and 3.87)

Assets test

Historical cost summarized balance sheets of the companies shown as at 31 March 1996.

	FDWS	Three Valleys	MKW	£ million SEW
Fixed assets	19.0	238.6	93.3	484.7
Current assets:				
Stocks	0.2	1.8	0.7	0.5
Debtors	1.7	14.4	4.5	8.1
Cash	0.5	1.8	1.3	0.0
Total current assets	2.4	18.0	6.5	8.6
Total assets	**21.4**	**256.6**	**99.8**	**493.3**
Creditors due within one year	(5.8)	(78.0)	(29.2)	(48.4)
Creditors due after one year	(4.4)	(88.0)	(7.8)	(56.5)
Provisions for liabilities and charges	(0.3)	0.0	(3.7)	(3.9)
Net assets	10.9	90.6	59.1	384.5
Represented by:				
Share capital and reserves	3.0	44.3	18.7	343.8
Profit and loss account	7.9	46.3	40.4	37.1
Minorities	0.0	0.0	0.0	3.6
Shareholders' funds	10.9	90.6	59.1	384.5

Source: The companies' accounts.

APPENDIX 4.1

(referred to in paragraphs 2.62, 2.126, 4.2, 5.23, 8.47, 9.3 and 10.2)

Legal framework for the water industry and for water resource management (BSTs and abstraction licensing): Note by the DoE

1. The legal framework for the water industry which was constructed by the Water Act 1989 (subsequently consolidated into the 1991 Act and the Water Resources Act 1991) incorporates two[1] regulatory bodies to whom the proposed merger is of significance in terms of their duties and functions. These are the DGWS and the EA.

Director General of Water Services

2. The DGWS is appointed by the Secretary of State under section 1 of the 1991 Act. The DGWS or, as the case may be, the Secretary of State is required by section 2(2) of that Act to exercise his powers and duties relating to the regulation of water undertakers in 'the manner which he considers is best calculated to secure that the functions of a water undertaker ... are properly carried out' and, without prejudice to that generality, to secure that water undertakers are 'able (in particular, by securing reasonable returns on their capital) to finance the proper carrying out of [their] functions'.

3. Subject to these primary requirements, the DGWS or, as the case may be, the Secretary of State is also required, amongst other provisions of section 2(3) of the Act, to:

(a) ensure that customers' interests are protected in respect of charges, and in particular that customers in rural areas are protected and that there is no undue preference or discrimination in the fixing of charges;

(b) ensure that customers' interests are protected in respect of the terms on which services are provided and the quality of those services;

(c) promote economy and efficiency on the part of water undertakers carrying out their functions; and

(d) facilitate effective competition between companies holding or seeking appointments as water undertakers.

4. The powers and duties of the DGWS range widely in respect of the activities and standards of performance of water companies. The DGWS operates independently of the Secretary of State, except to the extent that the exercise of his duties might lead him to recommend to the Secretary of State consideration of legislative changes, or in respect of certain duties on water undertakers for which only the Secretary of State can initiate enforcement action. The DGWS is required, by section 193 of the 1991 Act, to make to the Secretary of State a report on his activities each year.

Environment Agency

5. The EA is a body corporate established under section 1 of the Environment Act 1995. Under section 6(2) of the Act it has the duty:

> to take all such action as it may from time to time consider, in accordance with any directions given by Ministers under section 40 of the Act to be necessary or expedient for the purpose—

---

[1] There is a third, the DWI, which is the regulator for drinking water quality for whom the proposed merger is not of significance.

(a) of conserving, redistributing or otherwise augmenting water resources in England and Wales; and

(b) of securing the proper use of water resources in England and Wales.

6. Section 20 of the Water Resources Act 1991 gives the EA the duty

so far as is reasonably practicable to enter into and maintain such arrangements with water undertakers for securing the proper management or operation of—

(a) the waters which are available to be used by water undertakers for the purposes of, or in connection with, the carrying out of their functions; and

(b) any reservoirs, apparatus or other works which belong to, are operated by or are otherwise under the control of water undertakers for the purposes of, or in connection with, the carrying out of their functions,

as the Agency from time to time considers appropriate for the purposes of carrying out its functions ...

7. Although section 20(2)(c) of that Act requires questions arising under such arrangements once made to be referred for determination to the Secretary of State or the DGWS, there are currently no powers under which the EA can compel water companies to enter into new arrangements. Obligations upon water companies under such arrangements are enforceable by the Secretary of State under section 18 of the 1991 Act.

8. As indicated in section 6(2) of the Environment Act 1995, Ministers have the power to give the EA directions of a general or specific character with respect to the carrying out of its functions. Ministers may also, under section 51 of the Environment Act 1995, require the EA to furnish such information relating to its responsibilities and conduct of its functions as they may reasonably require. The EA is required, by section 52 of the Environment Act 1995, to provide an annual report on its activities to Ministers. Otherwise, the EA, like the DGWS, operates independently of the Secretary of State.

Regulators and the proposed merger

9. Thus of the benefits claimed for the proposed mergers by GU and SAUR in their announcement on 21 December 1995, those concerning the better use of existing resources, the more effective development of large-scale resources and an improved match between supply and demand fall—to varying extents—within the regulatory remits of both the EA and the DGWS, while that concerning the creation of improved comparators lies within the remit of the DGWS alone.

Water resource management

10. Two main mechanisms exist for redistribution of existing water resources—bulk transfers of raw or treated water between companies, and redistribution of existing licensed abstractions.

Bulk supply of water between companies

11. Bulk supply arrangements can be made by order under section 40 of the 1991 Act as substituted by section 44 of the Competition and Service (Utilities) Act 1992 and enable the DGWS, on application of a water undertaker, to make an order requiring another water undertaker to give a bulk supply to the applicant on whatever terms and conditions are specified in the order.

12. In making the order, it has to appear to the DGWS that the application is necessary or expedient for the purposes of securing the efficient use of water resources or the efficient supply of water, and the DGWS has to consult the EA in view of the latter's duties (see paragraph 5 and following). The DGWS

also has to consider the effect of the application on the supplying company's ability to meet its existing and likely future obligations to supply water, and to have regard to the desirability of facilitating effective competition with the water supply industry.

13. Bulk supply arrangements do not have to be made by order; the supplier and recipient may make an agreement in the ordinary course of events, featuring whatever financial or other conditions they mutually consider appropriate. Indeed, in making an order, the DGWS has first to be satisfied that a bulk supply cannot be secured by agreement.

14. A bulk supply made by order can be varied or terminated on application to the DGWS by any party to it. Variation or termination has to appear to the DGWS as necessary or expedient for securing the efficient use of water resources, and he has to be satisfied that an order is appropriate because the change cannot be agreed between the parties. As with the initial making of an order, the DGWS has to consult the EA and to apply the other considerations described in paragraph 12. In making an order for variation or termination, the DGWS may require the payment of compensation by any party to the bulk supply order to any other party.

15. The powers of the DGWS in relation to variation or termination of bulk supply orders would appear to provide considerable protection against any commercially or operationally unreasonable proposed action by any party to an order once it is made. However, it should be noted that the current legislation does not provide for an order to be sought by any 'person' other than a water undertaker or a 'person' seeking that status; neither the DGWS nor the EA may compel application, although they are free to offer advice and encouragement as appropriate.

Licences for abstraction of water

16. Abstraction licences are required for all significant abstractions from ground or surface water resources and are administered by the EA. Section 49 of the Water Resources Act 1991 provides for the succession of licences when there is change in the occupation of the whole of the land specified in the licence as the land on which the abstracted water is to be used; provided the new occupier gives notice to the EA within 15 months of the change in occupation the licence passes to that new occupier. Section 50 of the Act provides for succession where there is a change in occupation of only part of the relevant land.

17. Provision exists, under section 52 of the Water Resources Act 1991, for the modification or revocation of licences by the EA. The Secretary of State may also issue a direction to the EA to formulate proposals for modification or revocation if he considers such a step to be appropriate, whether or not because of representations made to him. Provision is made for objections to modification or revocation from the licence-holder or any other person to be heard or to be referred to a local inquiry.

18. The facility for modification or revocation of abstraction licences may provide opportunity for a redistribution of water resources, by those means followed by the granting of a new licence to the intended beneficiary. However, unless the existing licence-holder has voluntarily sought revocation, has failed to abstract any water for at least seven years, is in breach of licence conditions, or is otherwise content not to seek it, compensation for revocation or modification is payable by the EA. Any such revocation and issue of a new licence would have to be for the purposes of discharging the EA's duties in respect water resource management (see paragraph 5).

APPENDIX 4.2
(*referred to in paragraphs 2.62, 4.2, 5.23 and 9.3*)

The operation of the current statutory regime: Note by OFWAT

Section 1: The regulatory bodies and their functions

1. The Water Act 1989 withdrew the former Water Authorities' regulatory and environmental functions and, in so doing, divorced the supply of clean water and the treatment and disposal of sewage from the regulation and management of water resources and waterways. It provided the framework for the dissolution of the water authorities, the creation of the new Water Service PLCs and their subsidiaries, which were the appointed water and sewerage undertakers, and provided for the regulation of the industry.

2. The current arrangements for the water industry were put in place by the Water Act 1989. Consolidation in 1991 led not only to the 1991 Act but also to the Water Resources Act 1991. The 1991 Act contains the constitution and functions of the DGWS and the DWI. The Water Resources Act 1991 deals with the constitution and functions of the NRA, now the EA. The Statutory Water Companies Act 1991 contains constitutional provisions about WoCs and the Water Consolidation Act 1991 amends general legislation to match the regime of privatized water and sewerage services. Further provisions result from the Competition and Services (Utilities) Act 1992, and from the Environment Act 1995 which, amongst other things, established the EA.

The role of the Secretaries of State

3. The Secretaries of State for the Environment and for Wales are required to fulfill specific duties under the terms of the 1991 Act. Each has a continuing role in relation to the overall supervision of the industry and the setting of standards with respect to water quality (which are supervised and enforced by the DWI). Each has authorized the DGWS to appoint a new licensee for the whole or any part of an existing company's area of appointment, provided the latter agrees.

4. In setting the initial price limits for each water and sewerage undertaker at privatization, the Secretary of State took account of the need to provide a reasonable return to investors, the impact of charges on both domestic and non-domestic consumers, the need to finance quality improvements and the need to provide a framework for setting price limits which were capable of accommodating subsequent changes imposed upon the industry.

5. The licences (at Condition B) enable price limits to be revised by the DGWS at five- or ten-yearly intervals (Periodic Reviews) and between them, by interim determinations, which enable account to be taken of the impact of, for example, new legal obligations imposed on an undertaker, or its failure to achieve an output for which funding had previously allowed.

6. In order to protect the consumer from monopoly abuse and ensure the maintenance of standards of performance, the 1991 Act empowers the Secretary of State, or with his consent the DGWS, to terminate appointments, to vary the area of appointments and to make replacement appointments in defined circumstances. The Secretary of State also has powers to set and enforce standards of performance in connection with water supply and sewerage services. He has the power to approve codes of practice (as does the DGWS under the licences) and to ensure that where enterprises contravene regulations concerning specified levels of service compensation is paid to customers.

The Director General of Water Services

7. The DGWS is appointed by the Secretary of State. Under the 1991 Act, the DGWS has a primary duty to act in the manner he considers best calculated to ensure that the functions of water and sewerage

undertakers are properly carried out and that the appointed companies are able to finance those activities, in particular by securing reasonable returns on their capital.

8. Subject to this requirement, the DGWS also has a duty under the Act to exercise his powers in the manner best calculated to protect the interests of customers, to promote economy and efficiency on the part of the appointed companies in carrying out their water and sewerage functions, and to facilitate effective competition between persons holding or seeking those appointments.

9. The DGWS carries out his duties through each undertaker's Instrument of Appointment (licence) which describes the area of appointment and includes detailed regulations relating to the restriction of charges, tariff arrangements, the form of accounts, ring-fencing of the appointed business, levels of service targets, and provisions relating to disposals of land (see section 2 of this appendix, which starts at paragraph 44).

10. The licence also provides for the delivery of certain accounts and other information to the DGWS. This information enables him to carry out his functions and exercise his powers which relate (amongst other things) to replacement appointments in specified circumstances, the modification of appointment conditions, the application of competition legislation and the review of each company's price limits.

11. The DGWS may, on application, by order require an undertaker to provide the applicant with a supply of water in bulk. It must appear to the DGWS that the order is necessary to secure the efficient use of water resources or supply of water and that the supply cannot be arranged by agreement. The DGWS shall not make an order which he considers will affect the EA's ability to carry out its functions, without prior consultation.

12. There is provision in the 1991 Act for the introduction of competition in the water and sewerage industries on a greenfield site, or for supplying an existing, large customer. The Secretaries of State have authorized the DGWS to make an appointment or variation covering part of an existing area (an inset appointment).

13. The DGWS may modify appointment conditions. Where this or any other modification is not accepted by an undertaker, the DGWS may refer the matter to the MMC to investigate and report on whether any matter which relates to the carrying out of any function operates or may be expected to operate against the public interest.

14. If requested by the DGFT the DGWS exercises the function of the DGFT under Part III of the FTA, which relates to the interests of customers. The functions of the DGFT in relation to monopoly situations relating to commercial activities concerning the supply of water or provision of sewerage services are exercisable concurrently by the DGWS and the DGFT. The DGWS may also exercise the functions of the DGFT under the Competition Act 1980 in relation to courses of conduct 'which have or are intended to have or are likely to have the effect of restricting, distorting, or preventing competition in connection with the supply of water or securing a supply of water or with the provision or securing of sewerage services'.

15. The 1991 Act also requires that any merger of two or more water enterprises (water or sewerage undertakers) and which pass the £30 million assets test is referred to the MMC for investigation and report. Other cases may be referred under the FTA if the value of assets taken over exceeds £70 million, or if the 25 per cent market share test applicable to the UK (or a substantial part of it) is satisfied.

Quality and environmental regulation

The current regime

16. Responsibility for setting the drinking water quality and environmental standards, with which undertakers must comply, lies with the Secretary of State for the Environment (or for Wales as appropriate).

17. The Water and Land Directorate (the Directorate) of the DoE provides policy advice to the Secretary of State on all matters relating to the water environment and its remit accordingly extends from

groundwater, rivers, lakes, coastal waters and the oceans, to water supply including drinking water and waste water matters. Its policy advice relates to the exercise of the powers and duties of the Secretary of State as set out in statute and, so far as that is applicable, common law. The Directorate also oversees the legal framework within which the activities of the regulators in this area, and the water and sewerage undertakers, are conducted. The two principal quality regulators are the EA and the DWI. Their roles are described in paragraph 20 onwards.

18. The Directorate advises ministers on drinking water and environmental standards. Many of these standards derive from EC Directives. The Directorate negotiates on behalf of the UK in this forum and advises in relation to the implementation of EC Directives in UK law; as necessary, it also defends the UK in infraction proceedings brought by the European Commission in the European Court of Justice.

19. Although the application of the quality standards on the ground is essentially the responsibility of the DWI and the EA, the Directorate nevertheless has a role in this area. First, the Secretary of State can hear appeals against refusals of, or the conditions of, discharge consents and abstraction licences. Secondly, where an application for a discharge consent or abstraction licence has been made, the Secretary of State can call in that application for his own decision. Thirdly, section 6(2) of the Environment Act 1995 confers on the Secretary of State powers to give general or specific directions to the EA with respect to a number of matters, including discharge consents; in particular, he may give directions to the EA so as to enable the UK to give effect to EC legislation. Finally, the Secretary of state can influence the conduct of the EA through statutory guidance which the EA then takes into account in determining particular cases.

The Environment Agency for England and Wales

20. The EA is a body corporate established under section 1 of the Environment Act 1995. The EA began operation on 1 April 1996, when all of the NRA's functions described in the 1991 Act were transferred to it. The functions of Her Majesty's Inspectorate of Pollution, the Waste Regulation Authorities and some central functions from the DoE were also transferred to it. The EA's functions relate to England and Wales and include the duty of conserving, redistributing and augmenting water resources and securing their proper use. Its functions also cover other matters including the quality of inland and coastal waters, water pollution, navigation, fisheries and flood defence. It is the abstraction licensing authority for all water sources and determines and collects the charges in relation to licensing (known as abstraction charges). It is also responsible for controlling sewerage undertakers' discharges into receiving water and for collecting charges in respect of consents to discharge.

21. In certain instances the Environment Act 1995 and the 1991 Act require the approval by the Secretary of State for EA decisions, and give powers to the Secretary of State to give guidance and general and specific directions to the EA. For example, the Secretary of State may give specific directions to the EA so as to enable the UK to give effect to European legislation.

22. The EA is funded by a combination of Government grants, grant-in-aid, and self-generated income from its charging schemes. Charging schemes generate about three-quarters of its funding; an example is the charge on licensed abstractors under a scheme of abstraction charges approved by the Secretary of State. In the 1996/97 financial year, the EA has a budget of about £550 million and will employ about 9,000 staff.

23. The EA's primary relationship with the water and sewerage undertakers is in the areas of water quality and water resource matters.

24. The EA is organized into eight regions, with its head office in Bristol. Those eight regions are further subdivided into 26 areas covering England and Wales. There is a national Board, and each region has three statutory committees: the Regional Flood Defence Committee, which has executive powers, and two advisory committees, one on fisheries and one called the Regional Rivers Advisory Committee, which covers the remainder of its functions.

25. As the licensing authority for water abstraction, the EA is responsible for the issuing of abstraction licences to both WOCs and WaSCs. New licences to abstract will be granted only if the EA

is satisfied of the need for new resources following a thorough analysis of demand, including the scope for demand management, and that the environmental impacts are acceptable. Abstractors have a right of appeal to the Secretary of State against an EA decision with respect to the granting or refusal of a licence. The EA has the power to prosecute for breach of a licence condition.

26. Abstraction licences are determined after discussion with the companies and consideration of representations from relevant parties. Abstractors are charged on a cost recovery basis; there is a standard charging system across the country, but the unit charge itself will vary region by region to reflect the differing circumstances and hence different costs in the various regions. However, the relative charges for a water company compared, for example, with a fish farmer or spray irrigator will be the same across the country as a whole.

27. The EA is responsible for giving consents to discharge to sewerage undertakers. Here, the EA's jurisdiction extends to controlled waters, which for the general purposes of sewerage undertakers' discharges means any waters into which those discharges are made; the EA has a responsibility to control those discharges and to monitor the receiving waters. Consents to discharge impose various conditions to which the discharger has to adhere; in this way, by controlling the quality of the discharge, the EA ensures river and coastal water quality.

28. As with abstraction licences, consents to discharge are charged on a cost recovery basis. The charges are based on the EA's assessment of three elements of cost, namely the volume of the discharge, the quality and nature of the discharge and the receiving water into which that discharge is made. The costs associated with these elements will vary according to the difficulty involved in, for example, obtaining samples from coastal waters as opposed to an inland site.

29. By and large, consents to discharge are imposed after discussion with the undertakers. Dischargers have a right of appeal to the Secretary of State against an EA decision with respect to the granting or refusal of a consent. A consent to discharge is a defence against a charge of causing pollution. However, if a discharger exceeds the conditions of his consent to discharge, the EA has the power to prosecute.

The Drinking Water Inspectorate

30. The DWI is part of the DoE. It was established on 1 January 1990 and acts under section 86 of the 1991 Act as technical assessor on behalf of the Secretary of State in relation to his powers and duties in respect of the quality of drinking water supplies. These powers and duties relate principally to the duties of water undertakers with respect to water quality, regulations for preserving water quality, the offence of supplying water unfit for human consumption, and standards of wholesomeness of water supplies. The Secretary of State is able to determine its policy and actions.

31. The main tasks of the DWI are to:

(a) carry out the technical audit of water undertakers;

(b) advise the Secretary of State on the steps required to enforce obligations under the relevant legislation;

(c) investigate incidents which affect drinking water quality adversely;

(d) advise the Secretary of State of the prosecution of water undertakers if water has been supplied which is unfit for human consumption;

(e) provide technical and scientific advice to Ministers and officials of the DoE and the Welsh Office on drinking water policy issues;

(f) identify and assess new issues or hazards relating to drinking water quality and initiate research as required;

(g) assess and respond to consumer complaints when local procedures have been exhausted;

(h) assess chemicals and materials used in the provision of water supplies; and

(i) provide authoritative guidance or analytical methods used in the monitoring of drinking water.

32. The outcome of the technical audit process, together with a summary of performance of the DWI's other tasks, is reported each year by the Chief Inspector to the Secretaries of State.

33. Under the 1991 Act, 'wholesomeness' in relation to water is defined by reference to standards and other requirements set out in the Water Supply (Water Quality) Regulations 1989, which have been amended slightly by the Water Supply (Water Quality) (Amendment) Regulations 1989 and 1991 (the regulations). Water supplied for the domestic purposes of drinking, washing and cooking or for the purpose of food production will be regarded as wholesome provided that it satisfies three criteria: first, that it meets the standards prescribed in the regulations for the particular properties, elements, organisms or substances; secondly, that the hardness or alkalinity of water which has been softened or desalinated is not below the prescribed standards; and thirdly, that it does not contain any element, organism or substance, whether alone or in combination, at a concentration or value which would be detrimental to public health.

34. The regulations incorporate all the standards (maximum admissible concentrations and minimum required concentrations) set out in the EC Drinking Water Directive 1980 (80/778/EEC) and they also include 11 national standards. In addition to these standards applying to water at the time of supply, a number of standards apply to water issuing from treatment works and to water held in service reservoirs within the distribution system. The Secretary of State has powers to authorize the relaxation of a standard, but only in particular circumstances and not to the extent that public health could be endangered.

35. Statutory responsibility for monitoring the quality of water supplies is placed upon the water undertakers by the requirements of the regulations. This 'self-monitoring' role for the water undertakers is subject to checks by local authorities and by the DWI. The basic unit for monitoring is the water supply zone. This is an area designated by a water undertaker, usually by reference to a source of supply, in which not more than 50,000 people reside.

36. The Secretary of State is required under section 18 of the 1991 Act to take enforcement action to secure compliance when he is satisfied that an appointed water undertaker is contravening, or has contravened and is likely to contravene again, any statutory requirement enforceable under the section. Enforcement action can be taken for contravention of wholesomeness, monitoring and treatment requirements under the regulations, and also for contravention of the records and information requirements of the regulations. The Secretary of State can also institute prosecution proceedings under section 70 of the 1991 Act for the offence of supplying water unfit for human consumption.

37. Enforcement action usually begins with a 'notice of intention to enforce' being served on the company. This usually results in the company giving a legally binding undertaking to carry out a programme of work to secure or facilitate compliance with the required standards for drinking water quality within a given time-scale. It may sometimes be appropriate to make a provisional or a final order for the purposes of securing compliance, but circumstances have not yet arisen in which such steps have been necessary.

38. The DWI will initiate enforcement action on behalf of the Secretary of State in the following circumstances:

(a) when a water quality standard set by regulation 3 of the regulations has been breached and the breach is not trivial and is likely to recur;

(b) when a breach of one of the other enforceable regulations, such as those covering sampling, analysis, water treatment or information requirements, has been identified; or

(c) when existing undertakings or time-limited relaxations, authorized under regulation 4 of the regulations, expire before the required improvements have been completed.

The DWI will not initiate enforcement action when a company, after becoming aware of a breach of a regulatory requirement, takes immediate remedial action and demonstrates that compliance has been achieved.

Drinking Water Standards

39. As noted above, quality standards for water supply were formalized by the 1989 Regulations which apply the requirements of the Drinking Water Directive 1980 (80/778/EEC) in the law of England and Wales and include some national standards. The regulations specify the prescribed concentrations or values for a range of parameters which must not be breached, although provision is made for authorized relaxation in respect of some parameters in certain circumstances. The aesthetic quality of the water, resulting from parameters which affect water quality in the distribution system such as iron and manganese, will have required the greatest expenditure, while pesticides have had the highest public profile.

Customer protection and representation: Customer Service Committees

40. The DGWS has a secondary duty to protect the interests of customers. A feature of the regulatory regime is the existence of ten regional CSCs appointed by the DGWS to help him in this duty. The role of the CSCs is set out in the 1991 Act.

41. The Chairmen of the CSCs and the Director form the OFWAT National Customer Council (ONCC). This is a non-statutory body set up with the support of the President of the Board of Trade, who has parliamentary responsibility for customer representative bodies, and the Secretaries of State for the Environment and for Wales. The ONCC complements the work of the CSCs and strengthens the representation of water customers' interests nationally. The ONCC and the CSCs publish annual reports which describe their activities in representing water customers.

42. The DGWS sought to involve customers in the setting of revised price limits in a number of ways, but primarily through the ONCC and the CSCs. He and the Chairmen of the CSCs believe that the interests of customers have been better served in the Periodic Review as a consequence of these links between customer representation and economic regulation.

43. The Chairmen of the relevant CSCs have given evidence to the MMC on recent inquiries into the price limits set for South West Water and Portsmouth Water and also the take-over of Northumbrian Water by Lyonnaise.

Section 2: The licence

44. Each of the WaSCs and the WoCs holds a licence as a water and sewerage or water undertaker. These appointments are open-ended commencing 1 September 1989. They may be terminated by the Secretary of State for the Environment (or for Wales as appropriate), provided that at least ten years' prior notice has been given and that the notice expires no earlier than 25 years after the original appointment. The conditions of appointment may be varied (after public consultation) by agreement between the appointee and the DGWS subject to the Secretary of State's power in certain circumstances to require a reference to the MMC. If the DGWS considers at any time that an appointee, when carrying out its functions, is operating in a manner that is against the public interest, he can require the MMC to investigate and report on the matter, and to consider whether the effects could be remedied by modification to the licence.

45. The licences impose new obligations upon water undertakers. The general obligations include the following:

   (a) to limit increases in standard charges by reference to movements in the RPI plus an adjustment factor (K), and to comply with the detailed procedures and calculations specified in the Instrument of Appointment, including interim and periodic reviews of the price limits (Condition B);

(b) to limit infrastructure charges for the initial connection of domestic water or sewerage to an amount based on a standard amount, adjusted by the RPI and relevant multiplier as specified (Condition C);

(c) to issue a charges scheme setting out standard tariffs for supplies of water for domestic purposes (Condition D);

(d) to prepare, within two months of appointment, codes of practice for domestic customers covering general information for customers, procedure for disconnection of supplies and procedure on leakage from metered supplies;

(e) to avoid undue discrimination between classes of customer in setting charges (Condition E);

(f) to comply with detailed accounts and accounting information requirements, including the provision of information on transactions entered into by the undertaker with or for the benefit of associated companies, together with details of the bases used for allocations and apportionments (Condition F);

(g) to provide information on levels of service delivered and, if required, to set levels of service targets enabling the DGWS to monitor the levels attained and to intervene if services are not carried out properly (Condition J); and

(h) to draw up long-term plans for the maintenance of, and investment in, water distribution systems so that the DGWS can be sure that standards will be maintained.

46. Since they were granted, the DGWS has secured the companies' agreement to a number of amendments. For example, the provisions in Condition B about interim determinations have been simplified. There are now fewer triggers for such action and the method of calculating revised Ks has been made more quantitative and less judgmental. Companies were allowed to choose whether the amended licence would require the DGWS to take account of a cost of capital appropriate to the financing of expenditure solely by borrowing, or a weighted average cost of capital, assuming a mixture of equity and debt funding.

47. Finally, Condition B originally entitled each company to ask for a revision of Ks, if it faced some misfortune which had a significant adverse effect upon its affairs. Some companies chose to delete that altogether, but others agreed to retain a revised version, which gave to the DGWS a reciprocal right to revise Ks if the company enjoyed some unforeseen windfall.

48. Other important changes were made to Condition C relating to infrastructure charges, which are payments made for the connection of premises which are to receive, for the first time, water or sewerage services for domestic purposes. The changes enable the charges to be calculated more appropriately in relation to hotels, blocks of flats and converted buildings.

49. Condition F contains the machinery for the DGWS's financial scrutiny of each company's licensed business. It was amended, following the Competition and Service (Utilities) Act 1992, to prohibit cross-subsidy between the licensed business and other businesses owned by the company or members of its group.

50. The DGWS was empowered to issue accounting guidelines, requiring the companies to provide regulatory accounting information about these intra-group transactions. They were published in March 1994 in a letter from the DGWS to the regulatory directors of the companies.

51. Condition F had earlier been amended to place a duty upon each company's directors, to certify (at least annually) the adequacy of financial and management resources for the conduct of the licensed business. The directors are now required to renew that certificate whenever the company or a member of its group embarks on a new business venture, which, in the directors' opinion, is likely to affect the financial resources available to the company for use in the licensed business.

APPENDIX 4.3

(referred to in paragraphs 2.97, 2.145 and 4.23)

Customer service levels

1. The parties made a number of statements about their levels of customer service and how these had changed over time. We asked OFWAT to provide data on this topic. The data are set out in Table 1.

TABLE 1 Changes in the DG levels of service indicators between 1992/93 and 1995/96

per cent

	1992/93	1993/94	1994/95	1995/96
Properties likely to experience low pressure (DG2)*				
MKW	2.17	1.56	1.29	1.50
FDWS	2.17	2.02	0.94	0.09
SEW	0.79	0.49	0.31	0.17
National average†	1.26	1.02	0.81	0.78
Properties which experienced 12-hour interruptions to supply (DG3)*				
MKW	0.11	0.17	0.00	0.02
FDWS	0.00	0.08	0.01	0.00
SEW	0.11	0.16	0.05	0.03
National average†	0.38	0.35	0.26	0.58
Response to billing queries (DG6)*‡	Categories			
MKW	Good	Poor	Very poor	Very good
FDWS	Poor	Moderate	Moderate	Very good
SEW	Poor	Very good	Very good	Very good
Response to written complaints (DG7)*‡				
MKW	Very poor	Very poor	Poor	Very good
FDWS	Poor	Good	Good	Very good
SEW	Moderate	Very good	Very good	Very good

Source: OFWAT.

*A description of these service levels is given in paragraphs 4 to 15.
†Weighted average of all companies.
‡A description of the categories is given in Tables 2 and 3.

2. Table 1 shows the companies' performance against four of OFWAT's DG levels of service indicators (see paragraph 4.23). Comparisons of performance over time against DG8 and DG9 are not possible as these two indicators were only introduced in 1995/96. The DGWS told us that OFWAT did not compare performance between companies against DG1 and DG4 as these measures could be influenced by climate and weather patterns. Performance against DG5 was not carried out as these three companies are WoCs.

3. The DGWS pointed out that comparing annual results over such a short time period could give misleading results. Broadly speaking the performances of the three companies for DG3, DG6 and DG7 have improved over the period and the companies' levels were similar in 1995/96. The companies' performance against DG2 has improved during the period but the improvement by MKW is less than that of FDWS and SEW and in 1995/96 MKW's performance was higher than the national average.

Description of customer service indicators in Table 1

DG2: *Pressure of mains water*

4. This indicator shows the number of domestic properties which are at risk of receiving a pressure below the reference level due to deficiencies of the supply and distribution system.

5. The reference level of service is defined as 10 metres head of pressure[1] at the boundary stop tap with a flow of 9 litres a minute. This should be sufficient to fill a 1 gallon (4.5 litre) container in 30 seconds from a ground-floor kitchen tap.

6. There are a number of exceptions to this, to allow for circumstances beyond a company's control. Many pressure problems, for example, are caused by a customer's own plumbing.

7. Since it is impractical to measure the pressure and flow at the boundary of every customer's property, companies are allowed to report against an alternative reference level of 15 metres head of pressure in the distribution main supplying the property. This is a sufficiently high pressure, even allowing for the connection from the water main to the property boundary.

8. Companies are expected to maintain registers which identify the properties at risk of receiving low pressure.

DG3: Interruptions to supply

9. This indicator shows the number of properties experiencing interruptions to their supply of greater than 12 hours' duration which are the responsibility of the water company but which are not planned and not warned.

10. Incidents of supply interruptions are excluded if:

— they are caused by a third party; or

— they are as a result of planned maintenance work and customers have been given reasonable advance warning.

11. Companies are required to maintain registers that identify those properties affected by supply interruptions.

DG6: Billing queries (written and telephone)

12. This indicator shows the total number of written and telephone billing queries received and the number dealt with in 2, 5, 10, 20 and more than 20 working days.

13. A billing query is any enquiry regarding a bill—for example, an account query, change of address, request for alternative payment arrangements—which is not a complaint (see DG7 below).

DG7: Written complaints

14. This indicator shows the total number of written complaints received and the number dealt with in 2, 5, 10, 20 and more than 20 working days.

15. A written complaint is any letter, however mildly worded, that draws attention to any service provided by or action by the company or its representatives which falls short of the expectation of the correspondent. All complaints, including those about general levels of charging or other policy issues and complaints which are not justified, must be included.

16. Tables 2 and 3 show a description of categories in DG6 (written and telephone billing queries) and in DG7 (written complaints) respectively.

---

[1]This is a pressure sufficient to raise water to a height of 10 metres.

TABLE 2 Description of categories in DG6: written and telephone billing queries

Categories	Criteria
Very good	More than 70 per cent of responses dealt with within two days, together with less than 5 per cent of responses outstanding after 20 days.
Good	More than 60 per cent of responses dealt with within two days, together with less than 10 per cent of responses outstanding after ten days, together with less than 3 per cent of responses outstanding after 20 days.
Moderate	More than 50 per cent of responses dealt with within two days, together with less than 15 per cent or responses outstanding after ten days, together with less than 5 per cent of responses outstanding after 20 days.
Poor	More than 40 per cent of responses dealt with within two days, together with less than 20 per cent of responses outstanding after ten days, together with less than 8 per cent of responses outstanding after 20 days.
Very poor	Does not meet the minimum for the poor category.

Source: OFWAT.

TABLE 3 Description of categories in DG7: written complaints

Categories	Criteria
Very good	More than 60 per cent of responses dealt with within five days, together with less than 10 per cent of responses outstanding after ten days, together with less than 1 per cent of responses outstanding after 20 days.
Good	More than 50 per cent of responses dealt with within five days, together with less than 15 per cent of responses outstanding after ten days, together with less than 3 per cent of responses outstanding after 20 days.
Moderate	More than 40 per cent of responses dealt with within five days, together with less than 20 per cent or responses outstanding after ten days, together with less than 5 per cent of responses outstanding after 20 days.
Poor	More than 30 per cent of responses dealt with within five days, together with less than 30 per cent of responses outstanding after ten days, together with less than 8 per cent of responses outstanding after 20 days.
Very poor	Does not meet the minimum for the poor category.

Source: OFWAT.

APPENDIX 4.4
(referred to in paragraphs 2.79 and 4.34)

The DGWS's view of the status of water companies[1,2]

	WaSCs		WoCs	
Independent	Anglian		Bournemouth & W Hants	
	Dŵr Cymru		MKW	
	North West		East Surrey & Sutton*	
	Severn Trent		Cambridge	
	SWS		Portsmouth	
	South West			
	Thames			
	Wessex			
	Yorkshire			
GU†			Three Valleys	(100)
			Tendring Hundred	(99.1)
			North Surrey	(98.9)
			FDWS	(74.1)
			South Staffordshire	(27.8)
			Bristol	(25.0)
SAUR†			SEW	(100)
			Mid Southern	(99.4)
Lyonnaise	Northumbrian	(99.0)		
			Essex and Suffolk	(98.8)

Source: OFWAT.

*Owns 14 per cent of the shares in the holding company for Portsmouth Water.
†Percentage of shareholdings shown in brackets.

---

[1]Companies which have asset values below the threshold for reference to the MMC of £30 million set out in the 1991 Act are Hartlepool, Wrexham, York, Chester and Cholderton.

[2]Shareholdings outside the water industry are not shown.

APPENDIX 4.5

(referred to in paragraphs 4.40, 4.42 and 8.27)

The DGWS's approach to valuing the loss of a leading comparator

1. During the Lyonnaise/Northumbrian merger inquiry, the DGWS told us about work on the impact that the loss of the leading water service comparator in his 1992/93 analysis might have had on the tightness of the operating cost targets set in the Periodic Review. Given a number of assumptions, this work suggested that the loss of the leading comparator for operating expenditure could have led to water service price limits some £50 million a year higher (for England and Wales as a whole). No estimate was made of the effect of losing a comparator for the sewerage service.

Outline of the current simulation work

2. Subsequently the DGWS has developed a more generalized simulation analysis of the effect of losing a leading comparator. The DGWS told us that he had used this analysis to estimate the increase in the costs that he might have to allow for in setting price limits in England and Wales, if he lost a leading comparator. The work to date had been focused on water service operating expenditure but was capable of being extended to the sewerage service and to capital expenditure.

3. His analysis assumed that, at some time in the future, the hypothetical lost comparator (the target) would have become a frontier company in a major part of its activities (in this example, operating efficiency in the water service). The DGWS used a series of standard rules, similar to those he had applied in the 1994 Periodic Review, to calculate the overall savings that might have been incorporated into the price determinations for all companies, on the assumption that the target was the frontier company. The implications of losing the frontier company were then simulated by moving it down the 'league table' and generating a revised profile of potential savings using the same rules. The difference between the two profiles illustrated the possible value that could be ascribed to this aspect of losing the leading comparator. By carrying out a large number of simulations, the DGWS derived a range of potential losses which would apply to different-sized companies.

Detail of the method used

4. The approach relied on a number of key assumptions. All companies were treated as equivalent anonymous building blocks, numbered 1 to 28, in the model. They were divided into 9 size bands and 11 efficiency bands. The numbers of companies in each band, for both sets of bands, were based on the current frequency distributions of the companies' turnovers and water service operating costs. The simulations then assumed that these distributions would remain unchanged at future Periodic Reviews,[1] although the positions of the companies within them would change.

5. Table 1 shows the company size bands used in the model.

TABLE 1 Company size bands used in the simulation model

Band	Description	Turnover range	Number of companies
1	Small local company	£25m or less	9
2	Medium local company	£26m to £50m	4
3	Large local or smaller regional company	£51m to £75m	4
4	Very large local or medium regional company	£76m to £100m	2
5		£101m to £125m	2
6		£126m to £150m	1
7	(Vacant band)	£151m to £200m	0
8	Large regional company	£201m to £250m	2
9		£251m to £300m	1
10	Huge regional company	£301m and over	3

Source: OFWAT.

---

[1] That is, that there would be no 'bunching' in the companies' performance.

6. Table 2 shows the relative efficiency bands used in the simulation model.

TABLE 2 Company efficiency bands used in the simulation model

Band	Description	Number of companies
1	Frontier company	1
2	Within 5% of frontier	1
3	Between 5% and 10% from frontier	1
4	Between 10% and 15% from frontier	4
5	Between 15% and 20% from frontier	6
6	Between 20% and 25% from frontier	5
7	Between 25% and 30% from frontier	4
8	Between 30% and 35% from frontier	3
9	Between 35% and 40% from frontier	1
10	Between 40% and 45% from frontier	1
11	More than 45% from frontier	1

Source: OFWAT.

7. Simulation runs were carried out for each possible size of frontier company. The model first created a simulated 'league table' of companies. Each remaining building block in turn was randomly allocated to a size band and an efficiency band according to the fixed frequency distributions. An industry bench-mark was then set at a level equalled or bettered by 3 per cent of the simulated industry by turnover (see paragraph 14).

8. Having set the bench-mark, the model then estimated each building block's scope for efficiency savings. It was assumed that each building block could make savings on costs amounting to half the average turnover in each size band. The model calculated these savings as half the gap between the building block's performance and the bench-mark and phased them over the five years of the price determination. It also made an appropriate adjustment for the time-lag between the date of the cost data and the commencement of the regulatory period.

9. The next stage of the simulation was to repeat the analysis with the frontier company removed by downgrading its performance into a lower efficiency band whilst leaving the other building blocks unchanged. The model then calculated a revised 'league table' and bench-mark and reassessed the building blocks' scope for cost savings.

10. This analysis produced two profiles of potential savings, with and without the frontier company. The model next calculated the difference and determined its NPV, using a 6.5 per cent discount rate.

11. The model then repeated the various steps above to generate a random sample of about 50 simulations for this size of leading comparator. This process was then repeated, assuming that the frontier company was in a different size band, until results had been obtained for all the size bands.

Results of the simulations

12. The results of the simulations are summarized in Table 3. The simulations produced relatively large costs within a wide range of possible estimates of the cost of losing a target company of a particular size, even with the conservative assumptions used.

TABLE 3 Impact of loss of a leading water service comparator at the next Periodic Review

Target company	Typical company*	Average loss (and range) £m (NPV) (rounded to nearest ten)
Small local company (band 1)	BWH, CAM, HPL, NSY FDWS, WRX, THD, YRK, CHR	25 (10–290)
Medium local company (band 2)	MKW, PRT, MSN, SES	120 (20–590)
Large local or smaller regional company (band 3)	BRL, SEW, SST, WWS	200 (40–600)
Very large local or medium regional company (bands 4, 5, 6)	SWWS, ESK, TVW, SWS, NNE	500 (200–770)
Large regional company (bands 8, 9)	YKS, WSH, ANG	570 (280–810)
Huge regional company (band 10)	TMS, NWT, STW	620 (340–850)

Source: OFWAT.

Note: These numbers illustrate the possible impact of the loss of a leading comparator only in so far as it affects the price limits set at the next Periodic Review. Other aspects of a loss of comparator are not included in these numbers.

13. For companies in the same size range as MKW, the derived range of costs was £20 million to £590 million, with an average £120 million.

14. Small and medium-sized local companies at the forefront of efficiency were not felt to provide sufficient evidence for the DGWS to set the industry bench-mark at their level of performance. For the purposes of the simulation, he had therefore assumed that 3 per cent of the industry by turnover[1] was needed to set a robust cost bench-mark. The results of the modelling highlighted its sensitivity to this assumption and the importance of companies at or around the 3 per cent level, that is in size bands 3 and 4. This effect also explains the low cost of losing companies below this size shown in Table 3.

15. These estimated losses only related to water service operating costs. If the target company were also to be at the frontiers for sewerage operating efficiency and for capital investment procurement for both services, the harm would have been substantially greater (possibly as much as twice the costs generated by the simulations when operating and capital costs are included for water services).

Timing of becoming the leading comparator

16. The DGWS had also looked at the likelihood of companies of different efficiency levels becoming the leading comparator at a future review. Recent relative performance of companies compared with their positions in the 1992/93 analysis had demonstrated the scale of 'leap-frogging' (poorly-performing companies moving rapidly up the league table). This evidence could be used to guide a judgment as to the first Periodic Review at which a particular type of company could be expected to be a contender for 'pole position'. Companies currently in the upper quartile of efficiency might be contenders for the frontier in 1997/98 (in time to influence bench-marks in a 1999 Periodic Review), companies in the second quartile might be able to reach this position in 2002/03 (in time for the 2004 Periodic Review) and so on through to the prospective Review in 2014.

17. Table 4 shows the factors which might be applied to discount the costs in Table 3 to reflect delays in the date of the Periodic Review at which a threatened company could be judged to become a serious contender for the leading comparator, caused by its current performance.

---

[1] A level above the individual turnover of MKW, SEW and FDWS.

TABLE 4 **Possible current performance factors**

Achievement of leading comparator status in ...	Current relative efficiency of target company	Proportion of average loss (and range) given in Table 3 (%)
1997/98	Upper quartile	100
2002/03	Second quartile	72
2007/08	Third quartile	51
2012/13	Bottom quartile	36

Source: OFWAT.

Key limitations of the work

18. The DGWS told us that, as his analysis was relatively complex, it was important to recognize what his work did not purport to do, as much as what it did illustrate:

(a) The analysis was concerned with the impact of losing a leading comparator only in so far as it might affect the setting of price limits at a future Periodic Review. Very valuable comparisons were made at other times across the whole range of company activities. These represented additional unquantifiable losses.

(b) It did not cover the sewerage service. The approach could be applied to the sewerage service but it would be expected to produce different results.

(c) As the analysis assumed that the company lost had become the leading comparator, it was necessary to make a subjective assessment of the probability of the particular company concerned achieving this.

(d) The focus was on the lost comparator, not on the effect on the acquiring company and the consequent change in the structure of the industry.

(e) The analysis took no account of the progressive damage to comparative competition through successive losses of comparators.

(f) It had assumed that the DGWS would adopt the same methods in future Reviews as he did in the 1994 Periodic Review. In particular that, to maintain incentives, the DGWS would assume in future price limits that companies would only move halfway to the industry bench-mark over the period of the future price limits.

19. In view of the above limitations, the DGWS considered that his analysis significantly underestimated the total damage to comparative competition through the loss of a leading comparator. MKH had also estimated the loss associated with the reduced robustness of the DGWS's econometric models to be in the range of £33 million to £72 million (see Appendix 4.6). The DGWS felt that this detriment was distinct and additional to that estimated in his simulation analysis as was the damage associated with the reduced effectiveness of other unquantified aspects of comparative competition. Both pieces of work illustrated the importance to good regulation of preserving the number of comparators and the substantial scale of the public interest detriment associated with water company mergers.

Implications

20. The DGWS considered it crucial to be clear about the purpose of his simulations. The work did not give definitive answers but acted as a guide to the potential damage to the DGWS's ability to regulate the companies in England and Wales as a whole that would result from a single aspect of losing a comparator. On any scale he considered the resulting costs to be substantial public interest detriments.

APPENDIX 4.6

(referred to in paragraphs 4.40 and 4.44)

MKH's approach to valuing the loss of a comparator

1. MKH defined the cost of losing a comparator in terms of the overall long-term impact which the reduction in the information available to the DGWS would have on the prices which customers paid for their water services.

2. MKH told us that as the number of comparators declined, the DGWS would become less well placed to use comparative information to identify the relative efficiency of companies. If less information was available to the DGWS, the precision of his estimates of relative efficiency would become weaker. As MKH would expect him to be forced to err on the side of caution in determining efficiency targets, it would expect there to be a tendency for price limits to be set higher that they might otherwise have been.

3. In MKH's view there was insufficient information to establish a precise value of the loss of a comparator. It told us, however, that it was possible to establish a minimum value for the loss, in terms of what the effect on the last Periodic Review might have been, and then to take into account the unquantifiable factors that would influence the total value of losing a comparator.

4. MKH's estimates were expressed as NPVs over a 20-year time period. It told us that given that the exercise discounts additional post-tax costs to consumers, and real post-tax interest rates for most consumers are around 5 per cent (plus or minus 3 per cent), depending on whether one is a net borrower or a net lender, it used a 5 per cent real discount rate for its mid-point estimate, 8 per cent for its lower bound estimate and 2 per cent for its upper bound estimate. Its estimates were based on operating costs only.

5. MKH modelled the potential impact of losing MKW on operating cost efficiency targets by considering the effect that its loss would have on the statistical confidence intervals around the estimates of each target. To do this, it used the most recent available data to estimate econometric models for water services similar to that used by the DGWS. The water service model had three explanatory variables and was very similar to that used by the DGWS. Table 1 shows the models estimated by MKH.

TABLE 1 **Clean water model: estimation results**

Variable	Coefficient	Standard error
Dependent variable:		
Ln(Adjusted Opex)*†		
Explanatory variables:		
Constant	3.867	0.336
Ln(WDELC)*‡	0.617	0.096
Ln(LEN)*§	0.348	0.094
PMNH¶	−0.959	0.325
R^2	0.99	

Source: MKH.

*Ln( )—natural logarithm.
†Operating expenditure less exceptional items, rates, third party services, abstraction charges and expected pumping costs.
‡WDELC—water delivered (company estimate).
§LEN—length of mains.
¶PMNH—proportion of water delivered to measured non-households.

6. The widths of the confidence intervals with and without MKW in the sample were compared to provide a measure of the increase in the regulatory uncertainty that would result from the loss of MKW. This approach produced a unique result for the loss of MKW rather than a general estimate of the effect of losing a comparator. Table 2 shows the resulting changes in the confidence intervals for the water service.

TABLE 2 Change in confidence intervals after the loss of MKW: water service

per cent

Company	MKW in sample Range of confidence interval as a proportion of predicted costs	MKW excluded from sample Range of confidence interval as a proportion of predicted costs	Difference*
Anglian	20.2	20.4	0.2
Bristol	11.6	11.6	0.1
Bournemouth & W Hants	26.1	26.1	0.0
Cambridge	17.7	18.2	0.5
Chester	20.2	20.3	0.1
Essex & Suffolk	14.2	14.2	0.0
East Surrey	15.8	16.0	0.2
Folkestone & Dover	16.1	16.2	0.2
Hartlepool	38.5	38.5	0.0
Mid Southern	13.2	13.4	0.1
Northumbrian	17.8	17.9	0.1
North East	11.0	11.2	0.2
North Surrey	12.9	13.0	0.1
North West	19.6	19.6	0.0
Portsmouth	13.4	13.4	0.0
South East	14.4	14.7	0.3
Southern	14.4	14.4	0.0
South Staffs	15.2	15.2	0.0
Sutton	27.3	27.3	0.0
Severn Trent	18.9	19.0	0.0
South West	22.9	23.4	0.5
Tendring Hundred	23.7	24.1	0.4
Thames	29.3	29.4	0.1
Three Valleys	20.3	20.3	0.0
Wrexham	22.4	22.9	0.5
Dŵr Cymru	18.6	18.9	0.3
Wessex	19.6	20.0	0.4
Yorkshire	18.0	18.1	0.1
York	16.2	16.4	0.2
Average	18.95	19.11	0.16

Source: MKH.

*Column 3 less column 2. All figures are subject to rounding differences.

7. MKH's resulting estimates of the effect of losing MKW as a comparator showed that the width of the confidence intervals for the estimation of each company's efficiency target had increased, on average, by 0.16 per cent for water services. It then calculated revised efficiency targets on the basis that companies would be given the benefit of the doubt for this increased uncertainty in the estimates. Water efficiency targets were set 0.032 per cent a year lower on average (0.16 averaged over the five-year review period). MKH then converted its estimates of the reduced efficiency targets into annual amounts and their impact was assessed using an industry model.

Total effect of increased uncertainty

8. Table 3 shows the effect of losing MKW as a comparator based on operating costs. From this analysis, MKH took its estimate of this aspect of the cost of losing MKW as a comparator as being between £33 million and £72 million with a central estimate of £48 million.

TABLE 3 Cost of increased uncertainty in efficiency comparisons caused by the loss of MKW

£ million, 1994/95 prices

	Mid-point estimate	*Lower bound*	*Upper bound*
Operating efficiency			
Water service*	48	33	72

Source: MKH.

---

*MKH's estimates relate to the loss of MKW as a comparator. Its estimates are based on operating costs of water services only. The lower bound uses a discount rate of 8 per cent, the mid-point uses a discount rate of 5 per cent and the upper bound a discount rate of 2 per cent. All estimates use a time horizon of 20 years.

Other factors

9. MKH considered the above costs to be minimum estimates of the cost of losing MKW as a comparator, given the likely effect of other factors which it had not been able to quantify in this analysis and potential developments in the use of comparators. These included capital costs, the allowed rate of return, the financial profile, capital maintenance, quality of service and dynamic effects. In general terms, MKH's view was that the loss of a comparator would also increase uncertainty for the DGWS when he carried out comparative analysis in these areas.

APPENDIX 5.1
(referred to in paragraph 5.13)

Key water resource schemes—Southern Region

Scheme name	Operating undertaker	Other key beneficiaries	Type of scheme	Date completed
Powdermill	Southern Water Services		Reservoir Reliable yield 2.1 Ml/d Capacity 856 Ml gross 808 Ml net	1933
Darwell	Southern Water Services		Reservoir Reliable yield 19.0 Ml/d Capacity 4,460 Ml net	1950
Weir Wood	Southern Water Services	South East Water	Reservoir Reliable yield 13.5 Ml/d Capacity 5,623 Ml gross	1954
Barcombe	South East Water		Reservoir (Bankside Storage) Reliable yield—see Ardingly Capacity 546 Ml	1966
Arlington	South East Water		Reservoir Reliable yield 198 Ml/d Capacity 3,750 gross 3,500 net	1970
Bough Beech	East Surrey Water		Reservoir Reliable yield 23.0 Ml/d Capacity 8,630 Ml gross	1971
Eccles Lake	Southern Water Services		Reservoir Reliable yield—see Bewl Capacity 409 Ml	1972
Bewl	Southern Water Services	Mid Kent Water An undertaker other than SWS	Reservoir and river augmentation Reliable yield 103 Ml/d Capacity 31,367 Ml gross	1976

Scheme name	Operating undertaker	Other key beneficiaries	Type of scheme	Date completed
Ardingly	South East Water		Reservoir and river augmentation Reliable yield 36.5 Ml/d (with Barcombe) Capacity 4,770 Ml gross 4,320 Ml net	1977
North Kent Aquifer	Southern Water Services	Mid Kent Water	Groundwater scheme	1989/90
South Downs	Southern Water Services		Groundwater scheme	Early 1970s
Isle of Wight	Southern Water Services		Groundwater augmentation and transfer	1991
River Itchen Augmentation Scheme (Candover)	NRA	River Environmental Support Southern Water Services Portsmouth Water	Groundwater augmentation	1980
River Itchen Augmentation Scheme (Alre)	NRA	River Environmental Support Southern Water Services Portsmouth Water	Groundwater augmentation	1994

Source: EA.

APPENDIX 5.2
(referred to in paragraph 5.50)

NRA Southern regional strategy—future resource balance

TABLE 1 **Low forecast: average demand**

Ml/d

Company	Zone	Yields 1992	Resource balance to 2021 (+ indicates a resource surplus)						
			1992	1996	2001	2006	2011	2016	2021
Folkestone & Dover	Total:	49	−3	1	4	3	2	0	−2
South East	Total:	179	22	26	19	15	9	2	−5
Mid Kent	Total:	171	19	44	43	48	43	38	32
Southern (E Sussex and Kent)									
	Kent Medway	158	35	69	68	66	63	59	56
	Kent Thanet	66	10	22	21	26	24	23	22
	Sussex East	25	−3	0	−1	−2	−3	−4	−6
	Total	249	45	91	88	90	84	78	72
Southern (total inc Hants and Sussex Coast)		817	190	265	263	252	232	209	188

TABLE 2 **High forecast: average demand**

Ml/d

Company	Zone	Yields 1992	Resource balance to 2021 (+ indicates a resource surplus)						
			1992	1996	2001	2006	2011	2016	2021
Folkestone & Dover	Total:	49	−3	−5	−6	−9	−12	−16	−19
South East	Total:	179	22	13	1	−9	−20	−31	−42
Mid Kent	Total:	171	19	23	18	16	7	−2	−11
Southern (E Sussex and Kent)									
	Kent Medway	158	35	53	47	41	34	27	21
	Kent Thanet	66	10	15	12	15	12	9	6
	Sussex East	25	4	−3	−5	−7	−9	−11	−12
	Total	249	49	65	54	49	37	25	15
Southern (total inc Hants and Sussex Coast)		817	197	191	160	127	90	51	18

TABLE 3 **Low forecast: peak demand**

Ml/d

Company	Zone	Yields 1992	Resource balance to 2021 (+ indicates a resource surplus)						
			1992	1996	2001	2006	2011	2016	2021
Folkestone & Dover	Total:	56	−8	−3	1	0	−2	−5	−7
South East	Total:	231	29	31	22	18	10	1	−10
Mid Kent	Total:	204	7	38	44	55	48	41	33
Southern (E Sussex and Kent)									
	Kent Medway	197	51	86	86	85	81	76	71
	Kent Thanet	72	−6	8	8	6	4	1	−1
	Sussex East	33	−4	0	−1	−2	−4	−6	−7
	Total	302	41	94	93	89	81	71	63
Southern (total inc Hants and Sussex Coast)		947	133	222	221	206	1,762	143	112

TABLE 4 High forecast: peak demand

Ml/d

Company	Zone	Yields 1992	Resource balance to 2021 (+ indicates a resource surplus)						
			1992	1996	2001	2006	2011	2016	2021
Folkestone & Dover	Total:	56	−8	−10	−12	−16	−20	−24	−29
South East	Total:	231	29	14	−4	−19	−33	−48	−64
Mid Kent	Total:	204	7	15	12	12	−1	−13	−26
Southern (E Sussex and Kent)									
	Kent Medway	197	51	69	61	52	44	36	27
	Kent Thanet	72	−6	−1	−5	−10	−14	−19	−23
	Sussex East	33	−4	−4	−7	−9	−12	−15	−17
	Total	256	64	76	73	70	65	59	53
Southern (total inc Hants and Sussex Coast)		947	133	135	89	35	−19	−74	−120

Source: EA.

APPENDIX 5.3
(referred to in paragraph 5.59)

Local resource developments identified by the NRA Southern Region 1994

			Yield Ml/d	
Company	Source	Year	Average	Peak
Folkestone & Dover	Abstraction at coastal site to replace Stonehall*	2001	2	2
SWS Medway	Northfleet Higham, Selling Three Crutches	1996	2	2.5
SWS Medway	Yalding†	1996	21.75	21.75
SWS Sussex West	Smock Alley, Nutbourne	1996	6.7	9.8
SWS Sussex West	Hardham	2001	19	19
SWS Sussex East	Buckshole	1996	0.5	0.5
SWS Sussex East	Net gain by transfer from Bewl reservoir to Darwell reservoir	1996	2	2
SWS Sussex Coast	Groundwater	1996	0	8
SWS Thanet	Plucks Gutter, Fleming, Sutton, Martin Mill	1996	6.3	8.7
SWS Thanet	Abstraction from North and South streams to replace Wingham*	2005	5	−1.4
Mid Kent	Groundwater not conflicting with NRA policy	2006	12.8	30.7
Mid Kent	Abstraction from West Stourmouth to replace Barham*	2005	4	4
Mid Kent	Yalding†	1996	7.25	7.25
South East Water	Powdermill	1994/95	1.5	1.5
Portsmouth	None			
Total	‡		72.8	98.3

Source: EA.

*Possible alternatives to low flow catchment abstractions, not agreed by water companies.
†Operational 1995.
‡Allowance made in resource/demand balance for 18.2 Ml/d extra resources at Fawley for SWS Hampshire zone.

APPENDIX 6.1

(referred to in paragraph 6.17)

Extract from Martin Smith's affidavit in the course of proceedings before Mr Justice Knox in April 1996

The proposal involves the proposed merger of part of Mid Kent Water's operations with those of Folkestone and Dover and the proposed merger of the other part of Mid Kent Water's operations with South East Water. This necessarily gives rise to a very different type of merger situation from the one which was the subject of the 1990 inquiry and which led to the giving of the Undertakings. First, it would involve a take-over of Mid Kent which would give General Utilities and SAUR Water Services full ownership and control over Mid Kent. Secondly, General Utilities and SAUR Water Services propose a radical restructuring of Mid Kent Water's operations in the manner I have just described. Thirdly, General Utilities and SAUR Water Services believe that the acquisition of Mid Kent Water and merger of its eastern operations with those of Folkestone and Dover and its western operations with South East Water will offer the range of benefits summarised in their press release of 21 December 1995 under the heading 'Reasons for the Proposed Offer' (page 10-12 of 'GLB1').

The benefits listed in the press release of 21 December 1995 and which in my view make clear that this is a completely different proposal from the merger situation which the MMC considered in 1990 are as follows:

- better use of existing water resources, which will protect customer supplies into the future and help avoid the water shortage problems which affected the areas in question (that is to say, the supply areas of Folkestone and Dover, Mid Kent and South East Water) last year (ie, 1995) and in previous years;

- more effective development of new large scale water storage resources;

- an improved match between demand and supply in the enlarged areas to which better demand management, including leakage reduction, will contribute;

- General Utilities and SAUR Services have a proven track record of customer service; and

- the merger will create improved comparators and thereby enhanced the DGWS's ability to compare effectively the performance of supplies in the region.

None of these benefits could be achieved through a minority holding of the kind which was the subject of the 1990 inquiry.

I am informed by General Utilities that there is a substantial imbalance in the allocation of water resources between the water companies in the Southern Region. General Utilities believes that this is detrimental both to customers and the process of comparative competition. It believes that the proposed acquisition of Mid Kent and its subsequent restructuring in the manner I have described would:

- eliminate this detriment;

- improve distribution within the current area of supply of Mid Kent;

- enable the parties to connect the supply systems of Folkestone and Dover, Mid Kent and South East Water, optimising resource usage and improving security of supply for customers of each of them;

- involve creative measures of demand management and water conservation;

- enable long-term resource planning development on a regional basis; and

- postpone the need for a major new regional water storage resource.

These are all matters which are properly within the remit of the MMC.

The public interest benefits which General Utilities and SAUR Water Services believe the proposed joint offer will deliver are, as I have said, very different both in nature and scale form those considered in the 1990 inquiry. Clearly those public interest benefits will need to be evaluated. The appropriate body to evaluate them, and the one charged with that responsibility under sections 32 to 34 of the Water Industry Act 1991, is the MMC.

APPENDIX 6.2

(referred to in paragraphs 3.62 and 6.63)

Undertakings by GU to the Secretary of State for Trade and Industry

Following the report of the Monopolies and Mergers Commission (Cm 1125) on the reference, dated 4 January 1990, concerning the water enterprises carried out by General Utilities PLC and the Mid-Kent Water Company, these undertakings are given by General Utilities PLC to the Secretary of State for Trade and Industry.

1. Definitions

'Associated Persons' are those who are associated with GU or any Group Company, as defined in Section 77(4) of the Fair Trading Act 1973;
'the Appointment' means MKW's Licence, dated August 1989, issued by the Secretary of State for the Environment, under S11 of the Water Act 1989;
'the Appointment Business' has the same meaning as in condition A in schedule 2 of the Appointment;
'the Director' means the Director General of Water Services;
'GU' means General Utilities PLC;
'MKH' means Mid Kent Holdings plc;
'MKW' means Mid Kent Water plc;
'Group Company' means any Subsidiary of GU and any Subsidiary of any Holder of GU;
'the GU holding in MKH' means the aggregate of the Stock of MKH held, directly or indirectly, from time to time by GU and any Group Company, or in which, directly or indirectly, any of them has an Interest;
'Interest' in relation to any Stock includes an entitlement, by a person not being a registered holder, to exercise any right conferred by that holding or an entitlement to control the exercise of that right;
'the Relevant Date' means the date on which the GU holding in MKH is reduced to or below the level specified in 2 or the date specified in 2, whichever happens first;
'Stock' means all of the ordinary, preference and redeemable preference shares of MKH and includes any class of share or stock, carrying any voting rights, which may replace any of the Stock;
'Subsidiary' has the same meaning as in section 736 of the Companies Act 1985, as substituted by section 144(1) of the Companies Act 1989;
'Transaction' means a transaction between MKW and GU or a Subsidiary of GU of a description specified in the first column of the Appendix to condition F or the Appointment, but as if each reference to Associated Company were a reference to GU or a Subsidiary of GU;
'Holder', in the definition of Group Company, means a holding company, as defined in the same version of S736.

2. The Undertaking to Divest

GU will procure that, before 30 June 1992, the GU holding in MKH is reduced to such a level as will confer upon its holders (when aggregated with any Stock which is held directly or indirectly by Associated Persons or in which any of the latter has an Interest) the right to exercise in aggregate not more than 19.5 per cent of the total number of votes exercisable, upon any matter, at general meetings of MKH.

3. Undertakings in support of the divestment undertaking at 2 above

GU will procure that, after the Relevant Date:

    (a)   the GU holding in MKH does not exceed that required in 2; and

(b) neither it nor any Group Company will enter into or carry out any agreement or arrangement which may result in any Associated Person acquiring, directly or indirectly, any Stock or any Interest, if the aggregate of the voting rights, in respect of that Stock or Interest and those in respect of the GU holding in MKH, would exceed the percentage specified in 2.

Provided that this undertaking shall not require any further action, on the part of any person referred to in *(b)* if, as a result only of anything done by MKH including, without limitation, any redemption or re-purchase of Stock, the GU holding in MKH again exceeds that required in 2.

4. Undertakings to apply until the Relevant Date.

GU will procure that until the Relevant Date:

(a) the GU holding in MKH does not at any time exceed 29.8 per cent;

(b) neither it nor any Group Company will enter into or carry out any agreement or arrangement which may result in any Associated Person acquiring, directly or indirectly, any Stock or any Interest; and

(c) voting rights attached to the GU holding in MKH will not be exercised on any occasion to the extent that they would (when aggregated with those exercisable by any Associated Persons) amount to more than 19.5 per cent of the the total votes attaching to the Stock.

5. Other Continuing Undertakings:

(a) (1) GU will (and will procure that its Subsidiaries will) if requested by the Director, provide to him information of the types and in the form he may require about completed Transactions; and

(2) GU will use all reasonable endeavours to procure that Compagnie Generale des Eaux and its Subsidiaries comply with (1) as if they were Subsidiaries of GU.

Provided that nothing in this undertaking 5*(a)* shall impose on GU, CGE or any of their respective Subsidiaries, obligations which are more onerous (whether in terms of the type of information required to be disclosed or the frequency or timing of disclosure or otherwise) than those imposed under paragraph 6 of condition F of the Appointment, in respect of the disclosure by MKW of information about transactions with Associated Companies.

(b) GU will not obtain (or if offered, accept) from MKH or any Subsidiary of MKH any financial or accounting information about the Appointed Business of MKW which has not been made available, on the same footing, to all other owners of Stock; and

(c) GU will not seek (or if offered, accept) the opportunity to nominate any person to serve as a director of MKH or MKW.

21 March 1991

Signed for and on behalf of
General Utilities PLC

APPENDIX 6.3

(referred to in paragraphs 2.30, 6.67, 7.62 and 10.36)

Notice of Annual General Meeting

Notice is hereby given that the 1996 Annual General Meeting of Mid Kent Holdings plc will be held at 11.00 am on Thursday 18 July at the Great Danes Hotel, Hollingbourne, Kent, to receive the Report and Accounts for the year ended 31 March 1996 and for the following business:

Ordinary business

1. To declare a final ordinary dividend.
2. To re-elect Mr T I Perkins a director.
3. To re-appoint Arthur Andersen auditors and authorise the directors to determine the auditors' remuneration.

Special business

4. To consider and, if thought fit, pass the following resolution as an ordinary resolution:

    That the directors be and are hereby authorised, generally and unconditionally for the purposes of Section 80 of the Companies Act 1985, to allot relevant securities (as defined in Section 80(2) of that Act) up to a maximum aggregate nominal amount of £5,707,789 provided that:

    (a) this authority shall expire at the conclusion of the Annual General Meeting held next after the passing of this resolution or 15 months after the passing of this resolution (whichever is the earlier); and

    (b) the Company may before such expiry make any offer, agreement or other arrangement which would or might require relevant securities to be allotted after such expiry and the directors may allot relevant securities pursuant to any such offer, agreement or other arrangement as if the authority hereby conferred had not so expired.

5. To consider and, if thought fit, pass the following resolution as a special resolution:

    That the directors be and are hereby empowered, pursuant to Section 95 of the Companies Act 1985, for the period commencing on the date of the passing of this resolution and expiring at the conclusion of the Annual General Meeting of the Company held next after the passing of this resolution or 15 months after the passing of this resolution (whichever is the earlier) and at any time thereafter pursuant to any offer, agreement or other arrangement made by the Company before the expiry of this power, to allot for cash, out of any relevant securities (as defined in Section 80(2) of that Act) that they are from time to time authorised to allot, and as if Section 89(1) of that Act did not apply to such allotment:

    (a) equity securities as so defined in Section 94(2) of that Act in connection with any rights issue to holders of ordinary shares, and/or redeemable preference shares and/or warrants to subscribe for ordinary shares (other than those holders with registered addresses outside the United Kingdom to whom an offer would, in the opinion of the directors, be impracticable or unlawful in any relevant jurisdiction), in proportion to their respective entitlements (inter se) to such securities (subject to such exclusions or arrangements as the directors shall deem necessary or expedient to deal with fractional entitlements or legal problems under the laws of any territory or the requirements of any recognised regulatory body or other stock exchange in any territory);

(b) any number and amount of equity securities otherwise than pursuant to (a) above up to a maximum aggregate nominal amount of £856,168.

6. To consider and, if thought fit, pass the following resolution as a special resolution:

That, subject to the consent of the holders of its 10 per cent redeemable cumulative preference shares 1997 of £1 each in separate general meeting, the Company be and is hereby generally and unconditionally authorised to make market purchases (within the meaning of Section 163 of the Companies Act 1985) of ordinary shares of £1 each in the capital of the Company ('Ordinary Shares') subject to the following restrictions and provisions:

(a) the maximum number of Ordinary Shares hereby authorised to be purchased is 1,712,336;

(b) the minimum price which may be paid for an Ordinary Share is £1;

(c) the maximum price which may be paid for an Ordinary Share is an amount equal to 105 per cent of the average of the middle market quotations for an Ordinary Share derived from the London Stock Exchange Daily Official List for the 10 business days immediately preceding the day on which the Ordinary Share is contracted to be purchased;

(d) the minimum and maximum prices per share referred to in sub-paragraphs *(b)* and *(c)* above are in each case exclusive of any expenses and advance corporation tax (if any) payable by the Company;

(e) this authority shall expire at the conclusion of the Annual General Meeting held next after the passing of this resolution or 15 months after the passing of this resolution (whichever is the earlier); and

(f) the Company may make a contract to purchase Ordinary Shares under this authority before the expiry of such authority which will or may be executed wholly or partly after the expiry of such authority, and may make a purchase of Ordinary Shares pursuant to any such contract.

By Order of the Board
D W Walker
Secretary

18 June 1996

Shareholders may appoint one or more proxies, who need not be shareholders, to attend and vote on their behalf. The instrument appointing a proxy must reach the Company's registered office not less than 48 hours before the time fixed for the Meeting.

Copies of directors' service contracts of more than one year's duration will be available for inspection at the Company's registered office during normal business hours on any weekday (Saturdays and public holidays excepted) from today until the Annual General Meeting. They will also be available for inspection at the place of the Annual General Meeting during and for fifteen minutes immediately before the Meeting.

MID KENT HOLDINGS PLC

Notice of Extraordinary General Meeting

Notice is hereby given that an Extraordinary General Meeting of Mid Kent Holdings plc will be held at 11.30 am on Thursday 18 July 1996 (or so soon thereafter as the Annual General Meeting of the

Company convened for the same day shall have been concluded or adjourned, save that if such conclusion or adjournment shall be after 12.30 pm so soon thereafter as the Separate General Meeting of the holders of the 10 per cent redeemable cumulative preference shares 1997 of £1 each convened for the same day shall have been concluded or adjourned) at the Great Danes Hotel, Hollingbourne, Kent, to consider and, if thought fit, to pass the following resolution as an ordinary resolution:

> THAT the Mid Kent Holdings Performance Share Plan to be constituted by the Rules produced in draft to this Meeting marked 'A' and for the purpose of identification signed by the Chairman of the Meeting, the principal terms of which are summarised in the circular to shareholders dated 1 July 1996 accompanying the Notice of this Extraordinary General Meeting, be and is hereby approved and the directors be and are hereby authorised to cause such Rules to be adopted in the form of such draft (with such modifications (if any) as they consider necessary or desirable) and to do all such acts and things that they may consider necessary or desirable for implementing and giving effect to the same; AND THAT the Mid Kent Holdings Employee Benefit Trust (the 'Trust') to be constituted by a Trust Deed produced in draft to this Meeting marked 'B' and signed for the purpose of identification by the Chairman of the Meeting, the principal terms of which are summarised in the circular to shareholders dated 1 July 1996 accompanying the Notice of this Extraordinary General Meeting, be and is hereby approved and the directors be and are hereby authorised to cause the Trust to be established in the form of such draft (with such modifications (if any) as they consider necessary or desirable) and to do all such acts and things that they may consider necessary or desirable for implementing and giving effect to the same.

By Order of the Board
D W Walker
Secretary

1 July 1996

Registered Office:
High Street
Snodland
Kent ME6 5AH

Shareholders may appoint one or more proxies, who need not be shareholders, to attend and vote on their behalf. The instrument appointing a proxy must reach the Company's registered office not less than 48 hours before the time fixed for the Meeting.

MID KENT HOLDINGS PLC

NOTICE IS HEREBY GIVEN that a SEPARATE GENERAL MEETING of the holders of the 10 per cent redeemable cumulative preference shares 1997 of £1 each will be held at 12.30 pm on Thursday 18 July 1996 at the Great Danes Hotel, Hollingbourne, Kent, and if a quorum for the Separate General Meeting is not present the meeting will be adjourned to 12.30 pm on Friday 19 July 1996 at the Company's registered office, High Street, Snodland, Kent, FOR THE PURPOSE OF considering and, if thought fit, passing the following Resolution which will be proposed as an Extraordinary Resolution:

EXTRAORDINARY RESOLUTION

THAT this meeting of the holders of the 10 per cent redeemable cumulative preference shares 1997 of £1 each (the 'Preference Shares') hereby sanctions and consents to:

(i) the passing, as a special resolution of the Company, of resolution numbered 6 contained in the notice of Annual General Meeting of the Company dated 18 June 1996 and the carrying into effect of such resolution; and

(ii) any variation (including any deemed variation) or abrogation of the rights attached to the Preference Shares which will or may result from the passing as a special resolution and the carrying into effect of such resolution and the purchase of ordinary shares of £1 each in the terms authorised by such resolution.

By Order of the Board
D W Walker
Secretary

18 June 1996

Registered Office:
High Street
Snodland
KENT ME6 5AH

Shareholders may appoint one or more proxies, who need not be shareholders, to attend and vote on their behalf. The instrument appointing a proxy must reach the Company's registered office not less than 48 hours before the time fixed for the Meeting.

APPENDIX 8.1

(referred to in paragraphs 2.62, 4.3, 8.9. 8.10 and 8.16)

The use of comparators in the water industry and effects of losing them: Note from the DGWS

Use of comparators and effects of losing them

Introduction

1. As appears from the following sections, comparisons between companies play an essential role not only in the determination of price controls but throughout the DGWS's performance of his functions. Their uses, and the potential consequences of reduction in the number of comparators, are described below in relation to the various elements of the analysis made for price control purposes in the Periodic Review (paragraphs 7 to 81 and 127 to 138) and also in relation to other aspects of ongoing regulation such as customer service standards and tariff structures (paragraphs 82 to 126 and 139 to 160).

2. So far as concerns the use of comparisons in the Periodic Review, it may be helpful by way of introduction first briefly to describe the DGWS's approach to the Periodic Review (which is described more fully in his publications *Setting Price Limits for Water and Sewerage Services*, of November 1993, and *Future Charges for Water and Sewerage Services: The Outcome of the Periodic Review*, of July 1994.

3. During the Periodic Review the DGWS developed a structure for information analysis and judgments based on a matrix of purpose and cost categories. As can be seen from Table 1, the purpose categories comprise:

— base service provision: the maintenance of existing levels of service;

— enhanced service levels: the improvement in standards of service not driven by legal obligations;

— supply/demand balance: programmes for system expansion, control of leakage or demand management measures to meet any shortfall between forecast demand and existing capacity; and

— quality enhancements: obligatory improvements to water and waste water discharges to meet drinking water and environmental quality standards.

4. Within each of those purpose categories, three main cost categories were considered (again as shown in Table 1), namely operating costs, capital expenditure and the return on capital.

5. The first three purpose categories and their associated costs are grouped as base utility service. The expectation at the Periodic Review was that for the base utility service price limits would reflect a reduction in real terms (as with other utilities with the RPI−X formula); only the fourth purpose category, quality, might result in a positive element in price limits, leading to a real price rise. Thus the price control formula of RPI ± K could be regarded as RPI−X + Q (for quality).

TABLE 1   Strategic business plan matrix of purpose and cost categories

			Operating costs %	Capex (inc capital) maintenance %	Return on capital
Base utility service	RPI − X	Base service provision	89	45	N/A
		Enhanced service levels	0	2	N/A
		Supply and demand balance	2	8	N/A
Quality	+ Q	Quality enhancements	9	45	N/A

Source: OFWAT.

6. In Table 1 the percentages shown in the operating cost and capital expenditure columns of the matrix are the proportions of the ten-year industry totals for the cost category (water and sewerage services combined) accounted for by each purpose category within the provisions made in the DGWS's determinations. The percentages provide a rough weighting as a guide to the importance of the comparisons referred to in the following sections.

Base service provision—operating cost comparisons

Summary

7. Comparisons of companies' performance and relative operating efficiency in the base year (1992/93) were important and very effective in the DGWS's determinations. The comparative work over the period from early 1990 right up to the summer of 1994 enabled the DGWS to set price limits on the assumption of continuing savings in base operating costs. Efficiency assumptions were made that varied according to relative efficiency as identified through the comparisons. The currently most efficient companies were assumed to achieve savings of 0.5 per cent a year on base operating costs; for the currently most inefficient companies target savings of 3.5 per cent a year for the water service and 3.4 per cent for the sewerage service were assumed. The company-specific assumptions are equivalent to a real average reduction in operating costs of 3 per cent over the period 1995 to 2000 for the industry as a whole. In cash terms this equates to average reductions of £75 million a year for the industry as a whole.

The approach

8. The unit operating costs (expressed in terms of pence per cubic metre of water delivered to customers or sewage collected from customers) vary considerably across the companies. Such comparisons have been made and published for a number of years by the DGWS as a spur to greater transparency and also to help in understanding the extent to which these figures provide an effective measure of relative efficiency (most recently reported in the 1994/95 Report on *The Cost of Water Delivered and Sewage Collected*—OFWAT, November 1995). The DGWS has concluded that differences in unit costs do not in themselves directly reflect differences in companies' relative efficiency. Each company has a different operating environment and company-specific circumstances which may be beyond management's control, particularly in the short term. These factors appear to influence the company's costs irrespective of relative efficiency.

9. For the 1994 Periodic Review the DGWS sought to make comparisons of companies' operating costs taking account of explanatory factors arising from their individual circumstances in order so far as possible to identify relative company efficiency. The aim was to justify the application of assumptions differing as between the companies about the scope for efficiency savings. Greater reductions could then

be assumed for companies judged to be less efficient, so as to provide them with the incentive to reduce their costs to the levels at or below those achieved by the more efficient companies.

10. Over a number of years, by applying both econometric and DEA techniques to information, of gradually improving consistency, collected from the companies it was possible to develop robust models that were used in the Periodic Review. The numbers of independent comparators in the water service provided a reasonable basis for comparative analysis at the company level. Early work on the sewerage service showed that because there were only ten companies comparisons at that level would be ineffective. The strategy in each service is described below.

Water delivered and sewage collected

11. For the comparative analyses, water delivered and sewage collected were chosen as the output measures. In each case, estimates had to be made of differing components that make up these outputs to/from customers. Detailed comparisons were made of companies' estimates of water delivered as this is an important output measure used to derive unit costs and is incorporated as an explanatory factor in the modelling. Water delivered and its components are also key statistics used in the tariff basket calculation to ensure that companies' charges are consistent with price limits and do not discriminate between different customer types. As a result of such comparisons and subsequent queries by the DGWS in the early years there was a substantial improvement in companies' submissions by 1992/93 (the base year for the Periodic Review), with a consequent improvement in the robustness of OFWAT's analyses.

Consistency of data from companies

12. Inconsistencies in data from the companies hampered the early work, although this has been improved by tightening the definitions of each data item and as a result of apparent rogue numbers being challenged both by the DGWS and by the Reporters. Nevertheless, it is accepted that there is still some way to go before the optimum level of consistency is achieved between company data returns. In the light of the relative efficiency judgments made in the Periodic Review, the companies may have incentives to manipulate data, so that there will be a need for greater vigilance on data quality in the future to maintain the effectiveness of these comparators.

Water service econometric comparisons

13. The water service modelling strategy at the company level initially involved joint development with the industry followed by widespread consultation on OFWAT's analytical results. The work was subject to expert testing, publication in research papers and scrutiny by outside experts and the companies. The comparative models were refined and updated both as data quality improved and in response to critical comment. The comparative work has received broad acceptance throughout the industry such that its use in the Periodic Review has been reasonably uncontroversial.

14. The DGWS judged the scope for individual companies to reduce operating costs mainly on econometric analyses of operating costs carried out by Professor Mark Stewart of the University of Warwick (and published in OFWAT research papers 2, 3 and 4) but updated to reflect more recent data and comments from companies. Four company level models were developed: an overall model of the water service and individual models of distribution, resources/treatment and business activities (mainly customer and scientific services). The models resulted in estimates of each company's relative operating efficiency.

Sewerage service econometric comparisons

15. For the sewerage service, the existence of only ten sewerage companies, coupled with the large number of factors which could potentially affect companies' costs, made company-wide comparisons of some activities not feasible. To overcome this problem a least worst option was adopted; this involved developing models of sewerage operations at a district level and large works at the works level combined

with secondary models of small treatment works, sludge treatment and disposal and business activities. These models themselves depended upon the collection of comparative data. The extra data to enable these comparisons to be carried out were collected in 1993.

Other relevant comparisons

16. Comparisons of companies' operating costs using DEA were also undertaken for certain activities. This alternative technique for identifying the performance of companies relative to efficient companies tended to reinforce the conclusions derived from the econometric analyses.

17. The DGWS also took into account companies' submissions on the effect of their special circumstances; individual company costs and efficiency improvements which companies had incorporated in their Strategic Business Plan submissions (March 1994) and reviews of actual operating costs in the first period were compared with actual expenditure up to 1988/89 and the projections then assumed.

18. Comparisons were also made of the levels of service achieved by companies and the steps they were taking to improve unsatisfactory service levels.

The results

19. Based on the econometric analyses and the additional indicators of efficiency referred to above, the DGWS judged that the scope for company-specific savings in operating expenditure was in the range 0 to 2.5 per cent a year for water and 0 to 2.4 per cent a year for sewerage in the quinquennium from 1995 to 2000; this was in addition to industry-wide saving of 1 per cent a year in the whole decade from 1995 to 2005. A special exception was made for two small, low-charging WoCs where the scope for future efficiency savings was assessed at 0.5 per cent a year in total.

20. In broad terms, achievement of the company-specific reductions in operating costs up to 2000 would bring most companies about halfway from their existing cost levels to the costs of the more efficient companies. This cautious approach reflects uncertainties in the data from companies and the difficulties involved in identifying an efficiency frontier at this early stage of the comparative work.

Base service provision—capital maintenance comparisons (including the cost base)

Summary

21. Capital maintenance requirements to maintain serviceability for customers of the companies' operational assets represent a major element of the substantial capital investment programmes. Historical comparisons of relative levels of capital maintenance between companies have shown significant variations in both levels of activity and expenditure. Work is continuing on comparative data to determine whether these differences represent differential efficiency or the result of special circumstances.

22. In one aspect, namely surface asset capital maintenance, the direct comparative analysis of capital maintenance levels (current and forecast) did provide the basis for capping planned expenditure for all companies to then current expenditure levels of those companies with the recognizably worst assets (giving rise to a cap of £20 per connected property a year).

23. For the underground assets, capital maintenance comparisons were not as useful as between companies. For individual companies, historical information on performance (serviceability for customers as measured by such factors and water main bursts) when compared with actual expenditure led to the conclusion that there was no general case for increases in levels of capital maintenance. This left judgments to be made on companies' general levels of capital productivity and the scope for improvements over time.

24. Unit capital costs for specimen works (standard costs) collected from companies were compared to provide a basis for judgments of relative capital efficiency. This comparative analysis provided the

basis for judgments of the differential scope for capital cost savings, ranging from 0 to 8.7 per cent, to be incorporated into price limits. These adjustments were applied to the projected cost of capital maintenance associated with base service provision and to planned capital investment in quality enhancements for the water service and in part to that required in the sewerage service.

25. In addition to these adjustments the DGWS also concluded that there was scope for a continuing improvement in capital productivity amounting to 1 per cent a year.

26. The DGWS considered that the standard cost approach developed for the 1994 Periodic Review should provide a good tool for the future provided the number of independent comparators was maintained. The analysis of standard costs highlighted concerns about the number of independent comparators since the various companies in the GU group were submitting identical standard costs.

The Cost Base approach

27. The water industry, in contrast with other utilities, is characterized by the high level of capital investment needed both to maintain serviceability to customers and to achieve the quality enhancements required by the quality regulators. It was important to extend the scope of comparisons to the whole capital investment area to see if a robust method could be developed to identify relative efficiency and so the scope for differential judgments to be taken into account in price limits.

28. In 1989 consultants working for the Secretaries of State had reviewed the then authorities' capital investment plans. Whilst identifying reasonably wide differences in unit capital costs they were unable to advise on company-specific adjustments or the scope for continuing savings. This represented a considerable gap in the armoury of the economic regulator.

29. To overcome this gap the Cost Base strategy was developed. The DGWS carefully specified standard costs across typical underground and surface asset works that were thought to characterize the companies' likely capital programmes. Some of the standard costs were unit costs of, say, laying particular sized pipes in typical conditions; in other cases they were typical capital projects, for example building a standard-sized service reservoir.

30. By setting down a series of general assumptions to be made for the derivation of standard costs, the impact of differences between companies' operating environments was reduced to a minimum. The standard costs were linked closely to a breakdown of planned investment programmes by asset types which provided a robust basis for aggregate investment weighting factors to be derived.

31. In theory the differences between companies' standard costs would show different efficiencies in the specification, design and procurement of capital works. The lowest standard costs would provide a basis for the setting of yardsticks. The gaps between company submissions and the yardsticks when aggregated (using an appropriate weighting method) would indicate the scope for savings that may be able to be assumed in setting price limits for the same level of output delivery.

32. The Cost Base approach was developed in the period leading up to the Periodic Review. Extensive consultation on the approach was carried out with the companies and their Reporters[1] in 1993. Companies suggested revisions to the draft proposals which would enhance comparability, and many of these were included by the DGWS in the final specification of standard costs.

33. Companies submitted standard costs initially in their *Cost Base Report* (October 1993) and again with their Strategic Business Plans in March 1994. The initial submissions were compared and companies were told in January 1994 of the general position of the standard costs they had submitted within the range of costs submitted by the industry. The result of comparative analysis at that stage was to hold down the costs claimed in the Strategic Business Plans below the levels claimed in October 1993.

---

[1]Independent consultants who carried out an engineering audit.

34. The Reporters confirmed that the standard costs were prepared using the same policies and practices as the capital expenditure programmes. The DGWS also employed consulting engineers to provide independent estimates for standard costs which were used to validate his choice of yardsticks.

35. A judgment was made that for the 1994 Periodic Review the standard cost yardsticks would be set at or around the lower quartile of the company submissions rather than the lowest standard cost submitted. This cautious judgment reflected the early stage of the development of the Cost Base approach to comparative capital costs.

36. The gaps between submitted standard costs and the yardsticks were weighted by asset group on the basis of company investment programmes to generate Cost Base adjustment factors for infrastructure and surface assets for each service. These factors were based on the assumption that only a quarter of the gap to the yardsticks would be targeted in price limits—a very cautious judgment linked to the early development of the comparative tool, uncertainties about the level of consistency in company submissions and the need to retain incentives. The DGWS commissioned consultants to review and validate the quality of the analysis of the standard costs.

The results

37. The comparative analysis led to the determination of a range of capital cost adjustments as indicated in Table 2.

TABLE 2 Comparative standard cost adjustments over the period 1995/96 to 2004/05

	Cost Base adjustments %
Water service investment	
Infrastructure assets	0–8.7
Non-infrastructure assets	0–7.5
Sewerage service investment	
Infrastructure assets	0.1–8.5
Non-infrastructure assets	0–5.8

Source: OFWAT.

38. As indicated above, the percentages in Table 2 are actually one-quarter of the difference between companies' weighted average unit costs and the yardstick costs. So, for example, taking the largest adjustment for water service infrastructure assets (in the top row) made for the company with the highest standard costs, although the weighted average of the yardstick cost was 34.8 per cent lower than that company's standard costs, the reduction made to that company's costs was only 8.7 per cent. If the lowest standard costs had been used as the yardsticks then the adjustment factors would have been considerably larger.

39. The calculated cost adjustments were applied to the whole of capital maintenance expenditure allowed in the final determination. The aggregate impact on companies' costs was a reduction of 4.2 per cent of water estimates (£0.26 billion) and 3.3 per cent of sewage estimates (£0.45 billion). These adjustments as noted above are only one-quarter of the difference between company estimates and the yardsticks.

40. The DGWS's approach to the Cost Base was considered to be *'broadly sound'* by the MMC in their report on the determination of adjustment factors and infrastructure charges for South West Water Services Ltd (HMSO, July 1995). The MMC were of the view that the use of a large number of schemes confidently showed general pricing trends.

The future

41. The companies did not agree with the standard cost approach to comparative capital costs. Whilst they accepted the need to develop comparisons in this area, in general they argued that all capital projects were unique and hence not comparable. The arguments raised were somewhat more compelling in relation to the surface asset areas than for the underground work on the existing networks. The strength of the companies' representations was a factor in the rather cautious judgments made in this area in the Periodic Review.

42. Development of the Cost Base comparative approach will lead to more robust analysis and larger adjustments to capital programmes in future. However, this development depends crucially upon the availability of comparators. Even the most efficient companies are not universally low cost, being better at some activities than others. The greater range of comparators available for the water service has enabled the DGWS to make a proportionately larger reduction from the companies' claimed expenditure in the case of water than for sewerage.

Resource management, supply/demand

43. Where the DGWS considered that it was appropriate to allow within price limits for expenditure to meet growth in demand to maintain a balance between supply and demand, he applied national unit cost yardsticks to the companies' demand forecasts to determine expenditure levels. The yardsticks were derived from cost estimates by various companies (for example, estimates of the unit cost of developing the next increment of resource were based on individual companies' Paying for Growth appraisals). The expenditure levels determined for the supply/demand balance by applying the yardsticks were assessed against each company's bid. Those companies whose claimed expenditure was consistent with their demand forecasts had price limits that reflected this. With regard to the capital expenditure allowed for sewerage growth, two companies received all the expenditure that they claimed; two companies received no expenditure on the basis of flat demand forecasts; and six companies received less expenditure than they requested.

44. A sufficient range of comparators is important in reaching reasoned judgments as to the level of the yardsticks to be used. Particularly in the case of expenditure on new resources to meet demand increases, only limited data were available since many companies forecast no such expenditure. Such circumstances can magnify the effect of the loss of an individual comparator.

45. In the context of supply/demand, comparative data were also used in assessing the costs claimed for metering and the effects of metering upon demand levels; in each case these were compared with the results of metering trials which were primarily carried out in the Isle of Wight.

46. Since demand forecasts are relevant in setting price limits in relation both to the expenditure necessary to maintain the supply/demand balance and also to companies' revenue projections, the use of comparators in the assessment of demand forecasts is important. Comparators can assist the DGWS to understand and possibly challenge differences between companies in respect of, for example:

— the effect of metering on household demand for water;
— forecasts of commercial demand which provide an important source of revenue; and
— the ability of each company to manage leakage and the effects of leakage control on supply.

47. As a result of the supply difficulties during the summer of 1995, OFWAT carried out a detailed analysis of companies' methodologies with respect to the various components of the water balance, including leakage and the estimation of the economic level of leakage. This work involved comparing companies' estimates of the water balance component and challenging those who appeared to be outliers, or not employing best practice.

48. The work has resulted in substantial changes to some companies' estimated leakage levels. A reduction in the number of comparators would reduce the DGWS's ability to assess individual companies within this important area of work, since it would not enable macro tendencies, such as regional factors, to be taken into account.

49. Reduction in comparative information would reduce the DGWS's ability to assess individual companies' forecasts in an area where it is already difficult to make judgments.

Drinking water quality

Management of quality enhancement up to 1995

50. When price limits were set in 1989, allowance was made for companies to comply with enhanced quality standards in relation to both specified schemes and general compliance (unless these were specifically left out of account, as 'notified items' to be revisited if and when relevant costs were incurred): When price limits were being set in the 1994 Review, companies were permitted to submit claims for retrospective funding both of relevant notified items and new quality obligations which had been 'logged up' (that is, not made the subject of an interim determination but recognized as imposing new costs on the company) to be allowed for at the next Periodic Review. The quality regulators also reported to the DGWS on company progress with the legal compliance programmes. Checks were made to ensure that companies had fulfilled the obligations funded in price limits and were not in 'shortfall'.

51. In respect of additional expenditure prior to 1995 for quality improvements that the companies claimed had not been taken into account in the 1989 price limits, eight of the WaSCs and 12 of the WoCs submitted claims for additional allowances. The number of companies submitting claims allowed comparative judgments to be made on their validity. For example, five of the WaSCs and five of the WoCs claimed for the additional costs they associated with the New Roads and Street Works Act 1991. By comparing these claims and the submissions of the other companies, it was possible to see that many companies had borne these costs in their base programme. These costs were not permitted as new obligations.

52. The comparisons allowed the fair treatment of all companies, including those not submitting claims for further price increases from customers. At 1992/93 prices claims for £830 million of capital expenditure were received and allowance was made for 56 per cent (£469 million). Extra operating expenditure of £51 million was claimed and £19 million (37 per cent) allowed.

53. Any reduction in the number of companies or groups of companies available to submit claims would weaken the effectiveness of comparisons for assessing claims.

54. Using information received from the quality regulators, checks were made to ensure that companies had complied with the legally required dates for carrying out work. It was possible to ascertain whether compliance with quality standards was generally achieved by legal due dates. The quality regulators were asked to report any shortfalls in the compliance programmes by companies in the period up to 31 March 1993—the reconciliation point for the review. Where shortfalls in compliance were identified, judgments were made on the effect on the price limits.

55. A reduction in the number of comparators and increase in the size of companies would tend to obscure the compliance levels. The differences between compliant and non-compliant companies would tend to be lost with the greater degree of averaging, making comparisons difficult in future.

Quality enhancements (water service)—operating costs and capital costs

The approach

56. During preparations for the Periodic Review and the quality debate a number of policy documents on the approach to funding the new quality standards were published including *Paying for Quality—a Political Perspective,* published by the DGWS in July 1993, and the response to it by the Secretaries of State, *Water Charges—The Quality Framework,* published in October 1993.

57. *Paying for Quality* included the total cost, estimated by individual companies, of meeting existing obligations and possible additions. The maximum potential cost of existing and imminent new obligations

for the water service was £6.2 billion in capital expenditure and £0.87 billion in operating expenditure over the ten years to 2004/05 (at 1993/94 prices).

58. The procedures for allowing for these quality enhancements at the Periodic Review were set out in *Water Charges* and further procedures drawn up during the quadripartite process between companies, the quality regulators, the DoE and OFWAT. Comparing company approaches to dealing with potential quality problems was an important element in defining the obligations to be allowed for in the Review, and had a substantial effect on limiting the final cost to the customer. Costs for quality enhancement in company Strategic Business Plans totalled £4.8 billion in capital expenditure and £1.2 billion in operating expenditure for the ten years to 2004/05. In the determination £3.9 billion in capital expenditure and £0.83 billion in operating expenditure was allowed for in price limits for water quality enhancement.

Allowances for water quality enhancement in the new price limits—treatment

59. Allowance was made in the price limits for upgrading water treatment processes. In the period to March 2000, over 120 pesticide removal plants and 30 nitrate removal plants will have been completed. Over 70 water treatment works will have been modified to reduce the risk of cryptosporidium entering the distribution system and over 100 water sources will have been treated to reduce lead take-up from lead plumbing. The need for all of these schemes had been confirmed by the DWI on a case-by-case basis consistent with the response of the Secretaries of State.

60. The treatment methods employed by companies to meet specific parameter standards varied and it was possible to calculate unit costs for the treatment plant. However, at this stage of regulatory development it was not possible to carry out yardstick comparisons as the problems were too heterogeneous. Comparisons could, however, be used to pinpoint obviously expensive companies, which were asked for more information on the work planned. In one case, a significant reduction of £13.9 million was made to the amount allowed in price limits by comparing the cost of dealing with similar problems in other companies.

61. The Strategic Business Plans included £1,300 million in capital expenditure and £900 million in operating expenditure for enhanced water treatment, of which £800 million in capital expenditure and £700 million in operating expenditure were allowed for in price limits. The judgments made leading to these reductions were facilitated by having a number of companies to compare. These reductions included the Cost Base adjustments to capital expenditure and adjustments to take account of differing operating efficiencies. These were drawn from comparisons between companies (see paragraphs 7 to 42).

62. Many of the quality problems encountered in the industry tend to be focused on particular areas of England and Wales, for example pesticides in the South and East and iron and manganese where upland water is used. The loss of independent companies in any given region would further reduce the scope for comparison between adjoining companies.

Allowances for water quality enhancement in the new price limits—distribution

63. For the whole industry, 80 per cent of the allowance in price limits for capital expenditure for quality was included to deal with problems caused by the condition of the distribution system (£3 billion over the ten years to 2004/05). The amount of work needed in the ten years was confirmed by the DWI and appropriate allowances made for funding this work. Comparisons in the cost of the activity required were drawn from the Cost Base Reports (see paragraphs 21 to 42). This led to a reduction of £122 million in the allowance made. The major need for comparators on the quality side over the next ten years will be to compare how efficient the companies have been in achieving the compliance levels that have been funded in their respective price limits.

The future

64. Drinking water quality is one of the major concerns of customers. The DWI enforces the requirement for companies to comply with the relevant water quality regulations and carry out extensive

analysis of the water supplied to customers. These include more than 50 microbiological, chemical and aesthetic parameters. This database has been developing over the last four years. In 1994 nearly 3.5 million analyses of water samples were reported to the DWI, and 99.3 per cent demonstrated compliance with the relevant water quality standards. Using this database it will be possible to compare the actual performance of companies in terms of the quality of water supplied to customers.

65. The quality of water supplied to customers is still largely driven by the position in 1989. This includes the type of raw water treated (for example, surface or ground) and the type of treatment process used. Under the current quality enhancement programme many of the treatment plants are being modified, particularly those receiving surface water at risk of pesticide contamination. The performance of companies will be assessed from water quality data. The level of compliance may depend on:

— policy on the type of treatment process to install;
— decisions on the source and quality of raw water to exploit;
— policy on disinfection procedures and the level of risk to accept; and
— style of dealing with the quality regulator.

66. The management policies developing since 1989 will take some time to be expressed in water quality data. It is necessary to maintain the separate management of companies to allow divergence in management policies to be expressed in performance. This can then be linked with efficiency comparisons and used in compiling yardsticks for the industry.

67. The loss of companies in the same region would limit the power of the regulatory regime. As the regime matures for companies in the same region, any differences in quality compliance will be a function of management and their assets rather than the local conditions. If only a few large companies remained, any extremes of compliance would be diluted. Mergers would mean the loss of outliers, both the excellent companies to use as yardsticks for the others, as well as any obviously poor companies and those with unusual operating environments.

Sewerage and sewage treatment

Quality enhancements (sewerage service)—operating costs and capital costs comparisons

Summary

68. Quality enhancements in the sewerage service are dominated by the requirements of achieving compliance with the Urban Waste Water Treatment Directive (UWWTD). The Directive requires the provision of sewage treatment facilities on coastal and estuarial discharges and upgrading of a number of existing sewage treatment works discharging to inland waters. As two sewerage companies have no coastal discharges, the number of comparators in this area is reduced to eight. The Directive also requires substantial improvements to sewerage system overflows.

69. Comparisons between companies played an important part in achieving the reduction in anticipated costs of meeting the requirements of the UWWTD. Comparisons in the sewerage service are severely hampered by the limited number of companies. As indicated in paragraphs 1.2 and 1.3, the least worst solution to these problems has been either to develop an indirect form of comparisons (*Cost Base*) or to seek to compare performance of operating units below the company level (sewerage service econometrics). In reviewing the sewerage service quality enhancements, the DGWS compared company forecast capital costs at the levels of treatment required to meet the UWWTD requirements. A model of the costs of compliance was developed using data from one company and this was applied to adjust the costs allowed for higher-cost companies. Continuing efficiency assumptions were also applied (see paragraphs 21 to 42).

70. The increases in unit operating costs associated with the UWWTD projects varied significantly between the companies. The comparative operating cost econometric models developed by Professor Stewart provided a robust basis for judgments of the increases in operating costs.

71. Between early 1993 and the 1994 determinations the costs projects for compliance with the UWWTD were reduced from around £10 billion to around £6 billion; £3 billion of the reduction can be attributed to the quality framework strategy described below.

The approach—quality framework

72. From 1992 (*Cost of Quality*—August 1992) to 1993 (*Paying for Quality*—July 1993 and *The Quality Framework*—October 1993 (DoE/Welsh Office)) the DGWS involved the Secretaries of State and the quality regulators in defining consistent quality enhancement requirements for the period 1995/96 onwards. Differing assumptions made by the companies about the implications of the UWWTD as well as differing approaches to compliance by the ten regions of the NRA were exposed during the debate.

73. The resultant formal guidelines issued by the NRA in December 1994, after scrutiny by the Secretaries of State and OFWAT, removed the scope for widely differing assumptions by companies or NRA regions. This quality framework strategy resulted in a substantial reduction in the assumed costs of meeting the UWWTD from the £10 billion figure in 1993 to around £7 billion (prior to comparative cost judgments below).

The approach—capital costs

74. The Cost Base approach (see paragraphs 21 to 42) was intended to provide a basis for testing the relative capital costs across all output areas. In the event, the method was only used for base service provision and quality enhancements. For the sewerage service quality enhancements the Cost Base was supplemented by a more direct form of comparisons arising from analysis of the Strategic Business Plan data.

75. Analysis of the unit costs of achieving compliance with the required UWWTD outputs in the Strategic Business Plans revealed wide disparities between companies. The position was similar for each of the three discharge groups (freshwater, estuarial and coastal) and for sludge disposal unit costs.

76. One company with generally low unit costs provided an audited breakdown of its capital and operating costs of meeting the UWWTD. These company data formed the basis of the yardsticks for the costs of meeting the UWWTD requirements. These yardstick data, coupled with the project-by-project data collected as part of the validation of the UWWTD programmes, permitted an overall yardstick cost to be determined for each discharge group. The DGWS considered that the high-cost companies should be able to achieve the UWWTD outputs at costs that were halfway between their costs and the yardstick cost (except where company costs adjusted by the Cost Base factors were lower in which case that figure was assumed).

77. The numbers of companies whose costs in each of the discharge groups were adjusted by reference to each of the two comparative methods are shown in Table 3.

TABLE 3 **Comparative methods used to adjust UWWTD costs**

UWWTD discharge group	Adjustment via UWWTD comparative costs	Adjustments via Cost Base comparative 'standard costs'
Freshwater discharges	1	9
Estuarial discharges	5	5
Coastal discharges (only 8 companies)	4	4
Sludge disposal (only 9 companies)	2	7

Source: OFWAT.

The approach—operating costs

78. The setting of price limits through to 2005 required judgments on the increases in operating costs associated with the running of the new UWWTD installations. Companies submitted their projections for these operating costs in their Strategic Business Plans. Comparative analysis of the company numbers revealed very substantial variations in assumed unit costs for essentially similar conventional treatment plants.

79. By extending the use of the comparative econometric models of current sewage treatment works developed by Professor Stewart (see paragraphs 7 to 20) a yardstick level of additional operating costs was derived. Given the robustness of the model and the fact that most of the additional costs would fall post-2000, a standard margin on the costs projected by the model was taken as the maximum to be allowed for in price limits.

The results

80. The DGWS considered that the use of comparisons in judging the appropriate financial provision for the sewerage service quality enhancements was a powerful example of comparative competition in action. Comparisons played a vital part in decisions on the guidelines for implementation of the UWWTD. The planned Cost Base method for comparing capital costs was used to good effect. A robust approach to comparing UWWTD costs was developed following the submission of company Strategic Business Plans. Comparative cost models derived to assess the current relative performance of companies were used as a powerful estimating tool for net additional operating costs.

81. Comparisons in this area reduced the assumed impact of the UWWTD on costs to be recovered from customers by 40 per cent over the period of the new price limits. A merger of two of the current sewerage undertakers would reduce the number of comparators and hence weaken the information available for such analysis of costs.

Customer service

The need to compare performance in delivering service

82. The DGWS told us that he must carry out his functions in the way he thinks best calculated to protect the interests of customers with respect to the quality of service they receive and the terms upon which those services are provided.

83. Individual customers generally have no choice as to the company that provides them with water and sewerage services, and little influence over the price and quality of the services received. In a competitive market customers can signal their dissatisfaction with any aspect of the price or quality of service they receive by taking their custom to another supplier. In the absence of such signals from customers, OFWAT acts as a proxy for a competitive market by:

— measuring the quality of service that companies are providing to their customers and comparing the results;

— publishing the results, identifying (wherever possible) companies that are providing better service so that customers and others (for example, Government, consumer groups, the City and the press) can see clearly which suppliers customers might *prefer* if they had a choice;

— taking account of comparative performance when assessing companies' operating efficiency at a price review;

— taking regulatory action where individual companies performance is unsatisfactory; and

— where necessary developing standards or guidelines for companies to improve their service.

84. The DGWS's preferred approach to meeting his statutory duty and protecting the interests of customers with regard to service quality is to allow acceptable standards of service to be produced by comparative competition, led by what the best companies have demonstrated can be achieved, rather than to intervene directly in the day-to-day management of companies by setting service standards. This he considered to be an arm's length approach to regulation. It corresponds to what happens in the marketplace where companies have to cope with a constantly evolving environment.

85. The DGWS, nevertheless, does have statutory powers to set performance standards for individual companies if he considers that such action is necessary to ensure that customers receive an appropriate standard of service. In deciding whether to exercise these powers, as well as in determining the standards of performance to be set, comparators are critical. They are used to identify the standards (or procedures and policies) of performance which are being achieved by companies; in addition, where possible, the standards being achieved in comparable industries are taken into account.

How does OFWAT compare performance?

86. The DGWS uses a number of sources of information to compare performance, including:

— information supplied by companies in their annual July Returns against formal measures of service defined by the DGWS (the DG Levels of Service Indicators) of which there are currently nine;

— other information supplied by companies (for example, disconnection figures and rates of disconnection per 10,000 customers, optional meter schemes and payments under the Guaranteed Standards Scheme);

— reports to the DGWS from CSCs (for example, complaint procedures; debt and disconnection; optional metering; services for customers with special needs); and

— information published by companies (for example, payment methods advertised on or with bills; customer information; services for customers with special needs).

87. The DGWS has devoted significant effort to securing information from companies on a consistent basis that allows for appropriate comparisons of service standards to be made. Over the five years since the DGWS was appointed the aspects of service kept under comparative review have been progressively developed. The DGWS has extended, in consultation with the industry, the range and scope of the quantitative measures of service to customers (DG Levels of Service Indicators) which came into effect from 1 April 1995.

The scope of service compared

88. OFWAT reviews companies' comparative performance in delivering services to customers in the following key areas:

Water supply services

— adequacy of water resources and restrictions on water use (eg hose-pipe bans);
— interruptions to supply;
— inadequate pressure.

Sewerage services

— foul flooding of properties from sewers.

Customer service

— complaint handling including the volume/rate of customer complaints received by companies and by OFWAT and the effectiveness of company complaint handling and use of financial redress;

— speed of response to customers who contact companies with billing queries and written complaints;

— payment of bills including the method of payment available to customers and procedures for handling debt;

— provision of information to customers including information required by conditions of the licence of appointment to be available to customers;

— the price, terms and conditions of optional metering schemes;

— response to telephone contact from customers (from 1995/96); and

— proportion of metered accounts based on actual meter readings (from 1995/96).

89. The DGWS's Levels of Service Report is published annually. It covers performance against the DG Levels of Service Indicators, which increased from seven to nine in the Report for 1995/96 (some indicators have more than one component). In addition the DGWS periodically publishes reports which review particular aspects of customer service, for example debt and disconnection, optional meter schemes and services for elderly and disabled customers. In 1995 the DGWS published reports on complaint handling, payment methods and customer information.

90. There is strong evidence from customer information material produced by companies, as well as discussion with companies, that companies attach considerable importance to their rankings, or the DGWS's comparative assessment, in these reports. This is particularly true on a regional basis: companies are as much concerned with performance compared with local competitors (a concern which tends to be stimulated by local scrutiny undertaken by CSCs) as with their national ranking.

Range of performance

91. Examples of the range of customer service performance by FDWS, MKW and SEW is shown in Table 4.

TABLE 4 Examples of the range of company performance in providing customer service

	Best 5 companies	FDWS	MKW	SEW	Worst 5 companies
Reliability of supply					
In 1994/95 percentage of customers experiencing an unplanned supply interruption of over 12 hours	<0.01	0.01	0	0.05	>0.32
Pressure					
Percentage of customers in 1994/95 likely to receive poor pressure	<0.14	0.94	1.29	0.31	>1.10
Response times to billing queries					
Percentage of billing queries taking more than 10 days	<0.1	12	35	4	>7
Response times to written complaints					
Percentage of complaints taking more than 10 days	<0.1	12	24	9	>11
Optional meter schemes					
Price in 1995/96 of meter installed by the company in highway/pavement (£)	£0	£0	£150	£0	£150–£182
Disconnection					
Rate of disconnection in 1994/95 per 10,000 customers	<2	7	14	0	>8
Complaint handling					
Complaints to OFWAT as a percentage of complaints to company	<6	6	18	31	>30
Complaints					
Rate of complaints to company per 10,000 customers	<14	78	35	33	>78

Source: OFWAT.

Key effects of OFWAT's use of comparators to improve services

92. The DGWS considered that the use of comparative performance had brought improvements in customer service which might not otherwise have arisen. Those companies which *want* to provide their customers with a good service (and to be seen to be doing so) have been able to identify, from the published performance of other companies, a higher level of service that they can be expected to provide.

93. The rest of this section summarizes, by way of example, the effects which the DGWS's use of comparative performance has had in improving some key aspects of customer service over the last five years.

Reliability of supply

94. In 1991/92 eight companies were able to report that 0.05 per cent of customers or less had experienced an unplanned interruption of supply lasting more than 12 hours. By 1994/95 this number had increased to 13 companies.

Low pressure

95. In 1994/95 the percentage of customers nationally likely to experience problems of low pressure was 0.89 per cent compared with 1.69 per cent in 1991/92. The number of companies achieving a very high standard (of less than 0.15 per cent of customers) was eight compared with six in 1991/92.

Complaint handling

96. Companies' complaints procedures have improved. First, the DGWS has been able to approve all companies' complaints procedures under powers given to him by the Competition and Service (Utilities) Act 1992. In very few cases could the procedures be approved without significant changes. Comparing different companies' procedures and identifying the best helped the DGWS to develop his criteria against which all procedures would be measured; it also helped in subsequently obtaining the agreement of companies to the necessary changes.

97. More effective company complaints procedures should lead to a reduction in the number of complaints that the DGWS receives and a reduction in the proportion that need to be formally investigated. The DGWS has already begun to see a reduction in the number of complaints received and the proportion of all complaints received by the DGWS's CSCs which needed investigation by CSCs, instead of being referred to the company for a direct reply, reduced in 1994 to 44 from 53 per cent in 1993/94.

98. The ability to make comparisons between companies is critical to the ongoing process of the DGWS and CSCs monitoring how individual companies apply their policies in practice and, importantly, identifying the need for and securing improvements.

Speed of response

99. Although the number of written complaints which companies receive from customers has steadily and significantly increased since 1990/91, their performance in providing responses quickly has continued to improve. In 1994/95 23 companies had a very good performance in responding to complaints; only four companies achieved this performance in 1990/91 if continuing to improve.

100. Speed of response to billing queries has also improved despite a steady increase in numbers. For example, in 1994/95 89 per cent of billing queries received a reply within five working days compared with 72 per cent in 1990/91; 19 companies had a very good performance in responding to billing queries; only three companies achieved this performance in 1990/91.

101. Importantly the desegregated information on comparative performance in this area has allowed the DGWS to identify clearly those companies which are providing customers with a poor service so that appropriate action can be taken to secure an adequate service for customers.

Compensation for service failures

102. The policy and practice of companies in providing compensation to customers who have experienced poor service has improved. The availability of comparators has been critical to achieving the improvements so far and will continue to be important to the DGWS's future work to ensure that companies approach this issue more consistently.

103. The improvements achieved by the DGWS's ability to use comparative performance in this area so far include the following:

— The procedures of all companies include a commitment to consider, in the event of a complaint, whether compensation would be appropriate.

— All companies in membership of the Water Services Association/Water Companies Association have agreed to apply a common framework of principles when deciding whether or not to make compensation payments. This framework was developed by OFWAT in light of the best company policies on this issue and the early agreement of some companies was a critical spur to obtaining the agreement of the remainder (some of which resisted strongly).

— Six companies have recently promulgated new commitments on compensation or charters which extend the Guaranteed Standards Scheme, each in different ways. In some cases these companies have adopted an improved or tighter standard against which compensation will be provided for failures or have extended automatic payments more widely across the Guaranteed Standards Scheme or have introduced new standards which are not currently covered by the legal minimum set out in the Guaranteed Standards Scheme. Not only have these developments been prompted by these companies comparing themselves with each other but they provide a spur for the rest of the industry to improve their own principles and policies in this area. The DGWS expects to see further improved schemes this year from other companies.

104. Internal guidance for CSCs on compensation 'precedents' achieved when investigating individual complaints is effective precisely because of the ability to draw on a wide range of comparators. A recent survey of 600 cases investigated by CSCs identified significant differences between companies in the extent to which they paid compensation to customers, where appropriate, and did so spontaneously, without prompting by OFWAT or the CSCs. The performance of the 12 companies which made payments in 100 per cent of cases (the industry average was 44 per cent) will be very important to the DGWS's ability to achieve further improvements.

Disconnections

105. The ability of the DGWS, CSCs and others to compare company practice on debt and disconnection has been a critical factor in bringing improvements in company procedures and a reduction in the number of disconnections.

106. An OFWAT review of company practice in 1991 led directly to the development of guidelines on procedures before disconnecting supplies. These guidelines drew significantly on the comparisons the DGWS had been able to make.

107. The DGWS's subsequent monitoring, which has measured company practice against these guidelines, has stimulated improvements in the procedures of many companies. The DGWS and CSCs have been able to identify and point to companies which have procedures which go beyond the DGWS's guideline expectations and those which have achieved a very low (or non-existent) rate of disconnection.

108. Companies report the number of disconnections for non-payment to the DGWS every six months. These are published by OFWAT and are used by the DGWS and a wide range of interested parties to identify the overall national trend in disconnections and, importantly, variations in the rate of disconnection at the level of CSC regions and companies.

109. Overall, domestic disconnections have fallen by 53 per cent since 1991/92 (the year prior to issue of the DGWS's guidelines) and the latest (1994/95) annual level of disconnection is below the pre-privatization level in 1988/89. The highest rate of disconnection (per 10,000 connections) was 76 in

1991/92; this had reduced to 36 in 1993/94 but rose to 60 in 1994/95. The DGWS believes that the process of comparing company performance, developing the guidelines, publishing the results of the comparisons made and the continued publication of the disconnection figures have been effective in reducing disconnections significantly across the industry.

Optional meter schemes

110. Company schemes for customers to opt for a meter have improved significantly since 1991 when the DGWS first reviewed and compared these schemes, developed guidelines and asked all companies to review and revise their schemes.

111. The average charge for installing a meter in 1996/97 is 54 per cent lower than it was before the DGWS's guidelines were issued in 1992. Customer choice over location and who can install the meter has progressively improved. Comparators have been important in this process, particularly over the last three years with the publication of comparative information about meter option schemes in a form which identifies clearly those companies with the best and worst schemes from a customer viewpoint.

The impact of loss of comparators

112. In general any reduction in the number of separate companies would diminish the effectiveness of the DGWS's capacity to achieve service improvements through the use of comparative performance. A critical factor in this process has been the DGWS's ability to identify a clear and wide *range* of performances on the part of companies both at the extreme and intermediate points. In many areas of service it is often only a very few companies (and in the past sometimes only one) which demonstrate what can be achieved.

113. The following examples demonstrate the limitations which reliance on comparative information at, for example, only a regional level (ten companies) could have in the areas of disconnection figures and charges for installing optional meters. In both cases the reduction of comparators to ten regional averages fails to reveal the full range of both better and poorer performance.

Impact of loss of comparators: disconnection figures

114. Table 5 shows, by number of companies and number of regions, the spread of rates of disconnection for non-payment in 1994/95, across nine bands from 0 to over 35 disconnections per 10,000 households. The table shows clearly that reducing the number of comparators towards the number of regions would disguise the wide range of rates of disconnection that can currently be seen and the proportion of separate units (or companies) with rates of disconnection in the different bands.

TABLE 5 Potential impact of reduction in number of company comparators—disconnection rates

Rate of disconnections per 10,000 households 1994/95	Regions (10)		Companies (30)	
	Number of regions	% regions	Number of companies	% companies*
0–2	7	70	11	37
2.1–5	2	20	10	33
5.1–10	1	10	6	20
10.1–15	-	-	2	7
15.1–20	-	-	1	3
20.1–25	-	-	-	-
25.1–30	-	-	-	-
30.1–35	-	-	-	-
35+	-	-	-	-
	10		30	

Source: OFWAT.

*As at 31 March 1996, excluding Cholderton and District Water Company.

Impact of loss of comparators: reliability of supply

115. Table 6 shows the number of companies whose performance against the DG3 indicator (that is, properties affected by supply interruptions of over 12 hours) falls into each of the five performance categories. It shows that a significant number of companies are at the extremes of the range with well above average or well below average performance.

116. Table 6 also shows the data on a regional basis, for the year 1994/95, calculating regional performance by aggregating performance for each of the companies in the region concerned. The performance achieved is markedly different expressed on a regional rather than company basis. The distribution is much narrower, with only one region achieving the highest level of performance. Again, this example clearly demonstrates that reducing the number of available comparators dramatically and detrimentally alters the picture of comparative performance.

TABLE 6 Potential impact of a reduction in the number of company comparators—reliability of supply

DG3 supply interruptions 1994/1995 performance band (properties affected by interruption over 12 hours)	*Regions* Number	%	*Companies* Number	%
Well above average (<0.05%)	1	10	13	43
Above average (0.05–0.10)	3	30	7	23
Average (0.10–0.20)	4	40	5	17
Below average (0.21–0.50)	1	10	3	10
Well below average (>0.50)	1	10	2	7

Source: OFWAT.

Complaints/disputes

117. The DGWS has a duty and powers to settle certain disputes between complainants and WaSCs. The CSCs and the DGWS have duties to resolve complaints. The determination and/or resolution of such disputes and complaints is often dependent on the use of comparison between companies. This can be illustrated by the example of disputes about the charges water companies levy for connecting new properties to their water mains, as explained below, although comparisons are also relied on in resolving other disputes such as over company policies or procedures.

118. Water companies are able to recoup from owners an amount equal to the expenses reasonably incurred by them in connecting the premises to the mains. Any dispute about the amount charged may be referred to the DGWS. When considering the reasonableness of the charge, the DGWS has regard to the four elements of total costs (labour, reinstatement, materials and overheads).

119. Comparison of actual costs incurred by other companies is critical for each of those four elements, but particularly so in respect of the largest component, the connection work. In the DGWS's view reasonable costs for such work are those determined by market rates, but from the 68 disputes referred so far to the DGWS it would appear that most connections are carried out by companies' own workforces. The information on costs from the few companies which employ outside contractors (following competitive tender) has been critical in justifying determinations involving, in most cases, a reduction in the charge to the customer. For some customers the reduction has been more than 50 per cent.

Tariffs

120. The use of comparators has been and will continue to be essential in getting companies to develop their tariff structures to reflect better the costs of supplying different classes of customer. This is illustrated by the examples in the following paragraphs.

Measured and unmeasured differential

121. The difference between measured and unmeasured tariffs should be no more than the additional costs of providing a measured service. This difference is known as the measured/unmeasured differential. It is calculated by taking the average amount of water delivered by a company to an unmeasured household, applying to that amount that company's measured charge and comparing the resulting measured bill with the average unmeasured household bill for that company. In the past, the difference between measured and unmeasured tariffs has been extremely high, as shown for 1991/92 in Table 7.

122. Exercising pressure based on comparative data, the DGWS has achieved considerable success in reducing tariff differentials to the DGWS's targets of £27 in 1996/97 prices for water and sewerage (£18 for water and £9 for sewerage). This has been achieved by using estimates of the additional costs of metering incurred by the most efficient, lowest-cost, companies to persuade other high-cost companies that their costs can be reduced. In certain circumstances enforcement action has been threatened on the basis of such analysis. The DGWS has not to date had to provide to companies a detailed analysis of what they believe the additional costs of metering are. Pressure through publications has enabled the DGWS to bring company differentials into line with the DGWS's targets. Individual companies have not wanted to stand out significantly from the generality. As can be seen from Tables 7 and 8, all companies have reduced the differential between measured and unmeasured customers to within the DGWS's target of not more than £27 in 1996/97 prices.

Measured standing charges

123. Standing charges for measured household customers have also been high in the past. The DGWS has pushed companies hard to reduce these and so enable metered customers to manage their bill by paying according to the amount of water consumed. Although some companies have argued that their costs of supply are fixed and therefore standing charges should be high, companies have gradually reduced their charges in the face of comparative data and the arguments put forward by those companies who are willing to lower such charges.

Large user tariffs

124. Recently some companies have introduced tariffs for large users reflecting the lower costs which this class of customer imposes on the system and having regard to the provisions for competition for large water (and sewerage) customers. To prevent undue preference, companies have had to provide the DGWS with cost allocations to justify their tariffs, which have also been challenged by other companies making applications for inset appointments. In resolving such issues, the DGWS uses comparators to obtain a fuller understanding of the costs of supplying large users.

Impact of common control

125. A company's charging policies are influenced to a significant extent by its parent company. As between the water companies which have common ownership, similar charging policies tend to be adopted. Thus acquisitions bringing water companies under common control are likely to have an important bearing on tariff development.

TABLE 7 Difference between measured and unmeasured water bills for the years 1991/92 and 1996/97 showing the effect of tariff rebalancing, 1996/97 prices

	1991/92 £	1996/97 £
Water and sewerage		
WaSCs		
Anglian	77	7
Dŵr Cymru	151	26
North West	78	27
Northumbrian*	62	16
Severn Trent	41	27
South West	128	27
SWS	59	27
Thames	31	24
Wessex	53	24
Yorkshire	91	17
WaSC average (weighted)	**63**	**21**
Water		
WoCs		
Bournemouth & W Hampshire	25	15
Bristol	53	5
Cambridge	47	7
Chester	14	(1)
Cholderton	22	8
Essex & Suffolk	33	8
FDWS	29	9
Hartlepool	29	(9)
MKW	14	(0)
Mid Southern	39	11
North Surrey	65	16
Portsmouth	62	16
SEW	46	17
South Staffs	61	17
Sutton & East Surrey†	56	16
Tendring Hundred	31	0
Three Valleys	38	11
Wrexham	63	0
York	-	-
WoC average (weighted)	**39**	**8**
Industry average (weighted)	**47**	**10**

Source: OFWAT.

*From 1 April 1996, this company was formed by the merger of the former Northumbrian Water Ltd and North East Water plc.

†From 1 April 1996, this company was formed by the merger of East Surrey Water plc and Sutton District Water Plc.

Notes:
1. All figures are rounded to the nearest £.
2. Figures are based on company estimates of average unmeasured household consumption.

TABLE 8 Difference between measured and unmeasured bills for the years 1991/92 and 1996/97 showing the effect of tariff rebalancing, 1996/97 prices

	1991/92 £	1996/97 £
Water		
WaSCs		
Anglian	55	4
Dŵr Cymru	73	15
North West	50	25
Northumbrian*	74	9
Severn Trent	37	32
South West	50	13
SWS	32	18
Thames	15	14
Wessex	28	16
Yorkshire	20	11
WaSC average (weighted)	**36**	**17**
Industry average (weighted)	**38**	**15**
Water		
WaSCs		
Anglian	22	3
Dŵr Cymru	78	12
North West	29	3
Northumbrian	7	7
Severn Trent	5	(5)
South West	78	14
SWS	27	9
Thames	16	9
Wessex	25	7
Yorkshire	71	6
Industry average (weighted)	**27**	**4**

Source: OFWAT.

*From 1 April 1996, this company was formed by the merger of the former Northumbrian Water Ltd and North East Water plc.

Notes:
1. The total water and sewerage differential shown may not add up due to rounding.
2. All figures are rounded to the nearest £.
3. Figures are based on company estimates of average (weighted) unmeasured household consumption and metered and unmetered household supply pipe leakage.

Impact of common control

126. A company's charging policies are influenced to a significant extent by its parent company. As between the water companies which have common ownership, similar charging policies tend to be adopted. Thus acquisitions bringing water companies under common control are likely to have an important bearing on tariff development.

Financial performance

127. Regulation of the water industry is based on a system of price limits, rather than controls on profits or rates of return. But if the DGWS is to be satisfied that companies are able to finance their functions, he needs to understand the implications of price limits both for the absolute level of profit (and hence financial indicators of concern to lenders and investors) and for rates of return. Comparisons of the financial performance of companies are, therefore, of importance to the DGWS, particularly at Periodic Reviews but also on an ongoing basis.

128. Comparisons of financial parameters between companies were made in a number of areas during the Periodic Review process. These are detailed in the following paragraphs.

Dividends and dividend policy

129. The financial affairs of the water companies, under the terms of their licences, are assessed and reported upon separately from other businesses and activities of the group as if they were undertaken by a freestanding plc. This is part of the 'ring-fencing' arrangements to ensure that the appointed business has adequate access to financial resources. In a number of cases, the appointees have paid dividends to their parent companies which do not reflect the sustainable dividend that might have been paid had the appointee been a freestanding plc.

130. Comparisons were made between the dividends paid by the parent companies and those paid by appointees, on the assumption that the dividends actually paid by the parent represents the sustainable dividend. Adjustments were made to the balance sheets of certain companies where the dividends paid by the appointee exceeded those paid by the parent, to write back the cash transfers made. This was a relatively simple exercise for quoted companies but was more difficult for appointees which were subsidiaries of unquoted groups, for example subsidiaries of Lyonnaise and GU. Comparisons were also made as between companies of the levels of dividend paid. The loss of a quoted company would compound the difficulties at the next Periodic Review.

131. Although the DGWS does not control dividends, the strategy outlined above has put pressure on companies, whose policies were out of line, to normalize their dividend policy from the appointee in 1993/94 in order to reflect the adjustments made at the Periodic Review in its regulatory accounts. As an example, Northumbrian Water did not declare a dividend from its appointee for 1994/95 in order to reflect the adjustments by the DGWS in its regulatory accounts.

Financial indicators

132. In setting price limits, the DGWS has paid particular attention to the consideration of the overall return on capital. Financial indicators do, however, set constraints on this since they are of importance to providers of debt and equity finance. The key financial indicators used by the DGWS are interest cover, historic and current cost dividend covers and gearing. The levels of these indicators arising from the financial projections underpinning the price limits were reviewed and compared to ensure that they were adequate even if there were adverse changes in macro economic factors such as the RPI, interest rates or construction prices.

133. Bench-mark levels for the indicators were established by comparing levels within the sector, with practice in other countries and those contained in covenants given by companies on their borrowings.

134. The levels of indicators between companies arising from the financial modelling were also compared for consistency of approach to ensure that similar companies were treated equitably. Greater consistency can be achieved with a larger number of comparators.

Headroom

135. The price limits recognized that companies are affected to different extents by changing conditions. Investors in companies which bear greater risks can expect to earn higher returns on a continuing basis. There was no simple way to deal with such uncertainties and downside risks but the price limits allowed sufficient headroom in profits to ensure that key financial indicators were adequate in the adverse circumstances noted above.

136. It was important that the DGWS's judgments on the appropriate size of headroom should be consistent as between companies facing similar risks. The levels of returns including headroom were reviewed across companies and compared. Judgmental comparisons of this nature produce more consistent results the greater the number of observations from which to judge. With a smaller number of comparators, determining the appropriate level of headroom would be more difficult and could lead to levels which were insufficient or too generous.

Other financial comparisons

137. Financial comparisons between companies are carried out as part of routine regulation. These include comparisons of profit margins, return on capital, capital maintenance charges, average interest cost etc. Again, the greater the number of comparators, the more consistent the resulting judgment will be.

138. Further, the loss of any individual independent comparator would reduce the potential for innovative accounting and financial approaches being adopted, which may be used as examples of best practice across the industry.

Transfer pricing

Background

139. Companies regulated by the DGWS have diversified and formed themselves into groups, particularly in the case of the WaSCs. The DGWS has a duty to ensure that the appointee within such a group is financially ring-fenced and that water and sewerage customers do not cross-subsidize activities that are not connected with the supply of water and sewerage services. The Competition and Services (Utilities) Act 1992 places a duty on each of the companies to ensure that there is no cross-subsidy in respect of transactions between the appointed business and either associated companies or any non-appointed business. Amendments to Condition F of companies' licences were made in March 1993 to reflect this duty and in March 1994 the DGWS produced a Regulatory Accounting Guideline (RAG 5)—Transfer pricing in the water industry.

140. Comparative methods are used in monitoring compliance with these requirements.

Application

141. The Regulatory Accounting Guideline applies to:

— cost allocation within the appointee between the appointed and non-appointed activities;

— transfer prices for the provision of supplies, works or services between the appointed business and the associated companies; and

— transfer prices for rechargeable works where the appointee is a monopoly supplier to the associated company, for example accommodation and other shared assets.

142. The key objectives of the Guideline are to ensure that the appointed business pays a fair price for services and products received from associates and that costs should be allocated in relation to the way resources are consumed.

143. The Guideline placed a requirement on companies to report, with their Regulatory Accounts in September 1994, on the extent to which their systems complied with the Guideline and their implementation proposals for the future.

Transfer pricing review visits

144. In September 1995 OFWAT employed independent consultants to undertake a pilot study in six randomly selected WaSCs to determine how their implementation plans had been implemented in practice and the levels of compliance with the Regulatory Accounting Guideline. The pilot study was extended in January 1996 and the remaining four WaSCs were visited as were all water companies that are part of an extended group including those companies in the GU and SAUR groups.

145. Visits to companies were preceded by a questionnaire which focused on the group structure and strategy, associate companies with which the appointed business has transactions, the allocation of costs between different parts of the group and contract letting procedures. In addition specific transactions were identified both prior to and during the visit for detailed examination.

146. Responses to the questionnaire set the agenda for areas of investigation during the course of the visit. Visits on average were undertaken over a course of three or four days and involved discussions with relevant persons within the company and examination of documentation in connection with the points raised.

147. Following on from the visits the teams prepared a Statement of Facts which was agreed with the company. An additional report was provided to OFWAT describing the teams' findings which OFWAT would raise with these companies.

148. Issues had been raised as a result of the findings of the review team with each of the companies visited to date. These issues had been categorized into material issues and other issues.

149. The results of the visits to the ten WaSCs would be included in a published report. A later report would reflect OFWAT's findings in respect of companies that are part of an extended group.

Value of comparators

150. In his evidence in the Lyonnaise/Northumbrian inquiry the DGWS explained that transfer pricing was an area in which individual company performance was variable. This view has been borne out by the review team's findings. Some companies have very well-developed systems which fully reflect the Guideline, subject to the odd minor issue, and these companies provide a powerful standard against which companies with less-developed systems can be compared.

151. The Transfer Pricing Guideline was not prescriptive but provided a framework within which companies are responsible for ensuring compliance. While the Guideline relies on a high level of self-regulation, it allows the DGWS to compare and contrast the relative performance of individual companies. The extent of company compliance and the way in which the Guideline has been interpreted will lead to areas of best practice within the industry. Best practice as evidenced by individual company performance is a valuable tool in encouraging, through peer pressure applied by the DGWS, other companies to make improvements to meet their duty to operate at arm's length.

152. The duty on companies to trade at arm's length and to implement RAG 5 is still at a relatively early stage and comparative judgments provide an invaluable means of determining the extent to which individual companies can be said to operate on an arm's length basis. To lose any individual comparator is to lose an individual approach to ensuring arm's length trading.

153. Some group companies have taken a group approach to implementing the Guideline. This diminishes the ability of and extent to which individual companies within these groups can be seen to be transparent and operate at arm's length. A group-wide approach does not necessarily lend itself to the characteristics of the individual companies. If there were fewer separate entities operating and the group-wide approach was adopted more widely, this could reduce both the companies' and the DGWS's ability to demonstrate that operations were transparently at arm's length.

154. RAG 5 describes best practice for allocating costs to activities. It suggests an activity-based costing approach which would enable companies to determine more accurately what are the cost drivers of specific activities and allow them to become more efficient.

155. The Transfer Pricing Review visits have been set against the background of relative levels of compliance in individual companies as suggested by their Implementation Plans. In assessing what constitutes an issue within a company, comparisons of the way in which other companies implement the guidelines has provided a powerful standard.

156. Arising from the Transfer Pricing Review visits a discernible spectrum of compliance has been established. Companies have taken individual approaches to implementing the Guidelines with varying success. The visits have provided examples of both good and poor practice.

157. A report including the results of the Transfer Pricing Review visits will be published in July 1996. This will report on the broad findings of the visits and on individual examples of good and poor practice. The expectation is that the publication of this report will be an opportunity for companies to compare their performance with others. The teams looked only at selected areas in individual companies, but findings in other companies may guide company action in areas not looked at by the review team. Examples of best practice identified in the report will enable companies to consider their implementation.

158. The visits have identified the different strategic approaches companies have taken to placing key services including analytical services, engineering consultancy, contracting and manufacturing, information technology and waste management either in associates or retaining these services in-house. Both the GU and SAUR companies have placed these services in associates, Dynamco Limited and GU Projects Ltd respectively, which were set up to provide services to each of the companies within the group. RAG 5 stipulates that transactions with associates should be at a market price and that the best means of determining a market price is through competitive tendering. It became evident during the course of the visits that the responsibility for market testing rested with the associate and there is little evidence that anything beyond limited testing had taken place.

159. The Transfer Pricing Review visits showed that individual companies within the GU and SAUR groups tend to opt for a uniform strategy. This reduces the ability of each individual company ability to demonstrate that operations are at arm's length. The scope for the DGWS to make comparisons between companies is reduced where there is little to distinguish between individual companies within a group.

Anti-competitive practices

160. The DGWS has concurrent powers with the DGFT to investigate complaints of anti-competitive practice. A steady stream of complaints have been received and the premise underlying many of these is that the water and sewerage industry is seen as a closed world in which companies are not subject to competitive pressures. Reduction in the number of comparators and thus in the extent of comparative competition would strengthen this perception.

Use of comparators in the company inquiries

161. Upon receipt of the July Return information received by the DGWS each year an annual review of each company's performance is conducted. This has proved to be an important development in the use of comparators. As of last year's review the DGWS concluded that there were concerns about the performance of three companies, North West Water, South West Water and Yorkshire Water, and decided to carry out further inquiries. In carrying out these inquiries, and in drawing conclusions about whether the performance of each of these companies was satisfactory, considerable reliance was placed upon comparing performance with other companies.

162. Important outcomes from these inquiries included:

— setting a service standard for South West Water in respect of sewer flooding;

— imposing a price reduction for Yorkshire Water for the three years 1997/98 to 1999/2000; and

— setting service targets for Yorkshire Water in respect of unplanned supply interruptions, sewer flooding and leakage.

APPENDIX 9.1
(referred to in paragraph 9.45)

The EA's specific longer-term demand management and other proposals

Metering

— bring forward domestic metering to 80 per cent plus by end of 2004/05;

— bring forward non-domestic metering to 95 per cent plus by end of 2004/05;

— within 12 months of merging, extend free meter options to the enlarged areas;

— within 12 months of merging, extend sprinkler licences and compulsory meters for sprinkler users;

— apply appropriate demand management tariffs (encouraging metering and water conservation) within 12 months of merging.

Leakage control

— set a revised 1997/98 leakage target of 6 l/prop/h or 120 l/prop/d;

— set an 'industry-best' leakage target by 2002 in the region of 3 to 4 l/prop/h;

— offer free leakage repairs on customer supply pipes within six months of appointment;

— offer free tap washering service within six months of appointment.

Transfers

— within 12 months of merging, produce a technical review of all potential transfers of water from companies outside those held by SAUR and GU to the merged companies (for submission to the EA as part of the water resource strategic planning process) with cost benefits analysis of transfers and other options.

Alleviation of low flow situations

— voluntarily reduce (SEW) abstraction from sources affecting the Darent (sources and quantities to be identified by the EA);

— voluntarily reduce (MKW and FDWS) abstraction from sources affecting the Little Stour (sources and quantities to be identified by the EA);

— voluntarily reduce (FDWS) abstraction from sources affecting the Dour (sources and quantities to be identified by the EA).

Glossary

1991 Act	The Water Industry Act 1991.
abstraction licence	A licence granted under the Water Resources Act 1991 to abstract water from a source of supply.
appointment	The instrument by which a person is appointed under the Water Act 1989 or **1991 Act** to be the **water** or **sewerage undertaker** for the area described in that instrument.
BST	Bulk supply transfer of water. Under a BST agreement a supplier provides water (which may be either raw or treated) from a source (of which it retains the ownership) to a recipient company at a commercial rate, payable on a per cubic metre of water supplied basis.
CCA	Current cost accounting.
CGE	Compagnie Générale des Eaux SA.
chalk	The geological name for the thick, upper cretaceous formation of fine-grained, fissured, cream and white limestone which constitutes the principal aquifer of southern England.
common carriage	A proposal by the Government to increase the potential for competition by enabling persons or bodies who are not the existing undertaker for a particular area to supply customers in that area through the existing undertaker's pipe networks under commercial conditions which are agreed between the existing and incoming suppliers or, in the absence of such agreement, are determined by the **DGWS**.
comparator principle	The principle referred to in section 34(3)(a) of the **1991 Act**; that is 'the principle that the [**DGWS's**] ability in carrying out his functions by virtue of [the **1991 Act**] to make comparisons between different water enterprises should not be prejudiced'.
conjunctive use	The practice of operating a number of sources together with the objective of maximizing yield and minimizing risk by varying the output of sources so that one source can be used at maximum capacity while another is 'rested'.
CSC	Customer Service Committee. A committee appointed by the **DGWS** under section 28 of the **1991 Act** in respect of one or more **water** or **sewerage undertakers** and having the duties set out in section 29 of that Act in respect of the customers and potential customers of those undertakers.
DEA	Data envelopment analysis.
DG1–9	A series of numbered reports on levels of service which the **DGWS** requires annually from **water undertakers**, as follows: DG1 The availability of raw water DG2 The pressure of mains water DG3 Interruptions to supply DG4 Water usage restrictions DG5 Properties at risk of flooding from sewers *(this is not applicable to WoCs)* DG6 Response to written and telephoned billing enquiries

	DG7 Response to written complaints
	DG8 Response to telephone contact from customers
	DG9 Proportion of metered accounts based on actual meter readings.
DGWS	Director General of Water Services.
EA	The Environment Agency, established under the Environment Act 1995. Succeeded the **NRA** on 1 April 1996.
FDWS	Folkestone & Dover Water Services Limited, a 74 per cent owned subsidiary of **GU**.
FTA	Fair Trading Act 1973.
GU	General Utilities PLC, a subsidiary of **CGE**.
GU/Mid Kent report 1990	*General Utilities PLC and The Mid Kent Water Company: a report on the merger situation*, HMSO, Cm 1125, July 1990.
HCA	Historical cost accounting.
infrastructure assets	Underground mains and sewers, impounding and pumped raw water storage reservoirs, dams, sludge pipelines and sea outfalls. This is the definition used by **OFWAT**.
inset appointment	**Appointment** appointing a **water** or **sewerage undertaker** in respect of an area *previously* forming part of the area of supply of another undertaker.
JRC	Joint resources company proposed by **GU** and **SAUR** to hold certain water resource assets of **MKW** and to be jointly owned by **FDWS** and **SEW**.
JVA	The Joint Venture Agreement entered into by **GU** and **SAUR** on 20 December 1995.
K	The amount by which the weighted average charges for the supply of water or sewerage services are allowed to increase or decrease relative to the RPI, as determined by or under Condition B of the **appointment**. K can be positive, zero or negative.
K1	The five-year period of price regulation from 1990/91 to 1994/95.
K2	Originally, the ten-year period of price regulation from 1995/96 to 2004/05. Now a five-year period (to 1999/2000) as a result of the announcement of a **Periodic Review** for 1999.
K3	The third five-year period of price regulation (2000/01 to 2004/05).
lower greensand	A group of lower cretaceous formations that underlie the **chalk** beneath an intervening layer of (Gault) clay.
l/prop/d	Litres per property per day, a measure of leakage occurring on consumers' properties.
l/prop/h	Litres per property per hour, a measure of leakage occurring on consumers' properties; for technical reasons this is one-twentieth of the daily rate.
Lyonnaise report	*Lyonnaise des Eaux SA and Northumbrian Water Group PLC: a report on the merger situation*, HMSO, Cm 2936, July 1995.

MKH	Mid Kent Holdings plc.
MKW	Mid Kent Water plc, the 99.5 per cent owned **water undertaker** subsidiary of **MKH**.
MKEast	That part of the business of **MKW** which would be acquired by **FDWS** at **Stage 2**. (See paragraph 2.47.)
MKWest	That part of the business of **MKW** which would be acquired by **SEW** at **Stage 2**. (See paragraph 2.47.)
Ml	Megalitre (1 million litres, 1,000 cubic metres, 1,000 tonnes or 220,000 gallons).
Ml/d	Megalitres a day.
Morgan Grenfell	Morgan Grenfell & Co, Limited, a merchant bank whose ultimate holding company is Deutsche Bank AG.
NRA	National Rivers Authority. A body formed under the Water Act 1989, whose functions concern, among other things, water resources, water pollution and flood defence. Replaced by the **EA** in April 1996.
OFWAT	Office of Water Services.
outage/supply outage	The allowance made, in the assessment of overall resource capacity, for temporary loss of sources due to breakdown, pollution, alterations or repairs.
Periodic Review	The review of **K** by the **DGWS** at five- or ten-yearly intervals, as provided for by Condition B of the **appointment**.
region, the	The areas within Kent, East Sussex and West Sussex in which **FDWS**, **SEW**, **MKW** and **SWS** supply water.
regulated business	Those water or sewerage activities which are the subject of an **appointment** by the **DGWS**.
SAUR	SAUR Water Services plc, a wholly-owned subsidiary of SAUR International SA.
SAUR Group	SAUR SA and its subsidiaries including SAUR International SA.
SEW	South East Water Services plc, a wholly-owned subsidiary of **SAUR**.
sewerage undertaker	A company appointed under the Water Act 1989 or the **1991 Act** to provide sewerage services in England or Wales.
Southern Region	An administrative region of the **EA**. It includes most of Kent and Hampshire, East and West Sussex and the Isle of Wight, part of south-east London and small parts of Wiltshire, Berkshire and Surrey (see Map 2, 3 or 6).
Stage 1	The first stage of the arrangement proposed by **GU** and **SAUR** at which **GU** and **SAUR** acquire the entire issued share capital of **MKH** through a new company which is to be specially formed for the purpose of the bid.
Stage 2	The second stage of the arrangements proposed by **GU** and **SAUR** at which the business of **MKW** would be restructured dividing the water supply

	business into approximately equal halves and transferring the eastern half to **FDWS** and the western half to **SEW**; certain of the water resource assets would be transferred to the **JRC**.
Stock Exchange	International Stock Exchange, London.
supply area/area of supply	The area for which a **water undertaker** holds **appointment**.
SWC	Statutory water company, a company incorporated by an Act of Parliament for the purposes of supplying water. (Such companies were not incorporated under Companies Acts.)
SWS	Southern Water Services Limited.
WaSC	Water and sewerage company. A company appointed as a **water undertaker** and a **sewerage undertaker**.
water undertaker	A company appointed under the Water Act 1989 or the **1991 Act** to provide water services in England and Wales.
WoC	Water-only company. A company appointed as a **water undertaker** but not a **sewerage undertaker**.
yield	The reliable rate at which water can be drawn from a water source.

MAP 1
(referred to in paragraphs 5.10, 5.13 and 5.15)

Major rivers, reservoirs and surface water sources, 1996

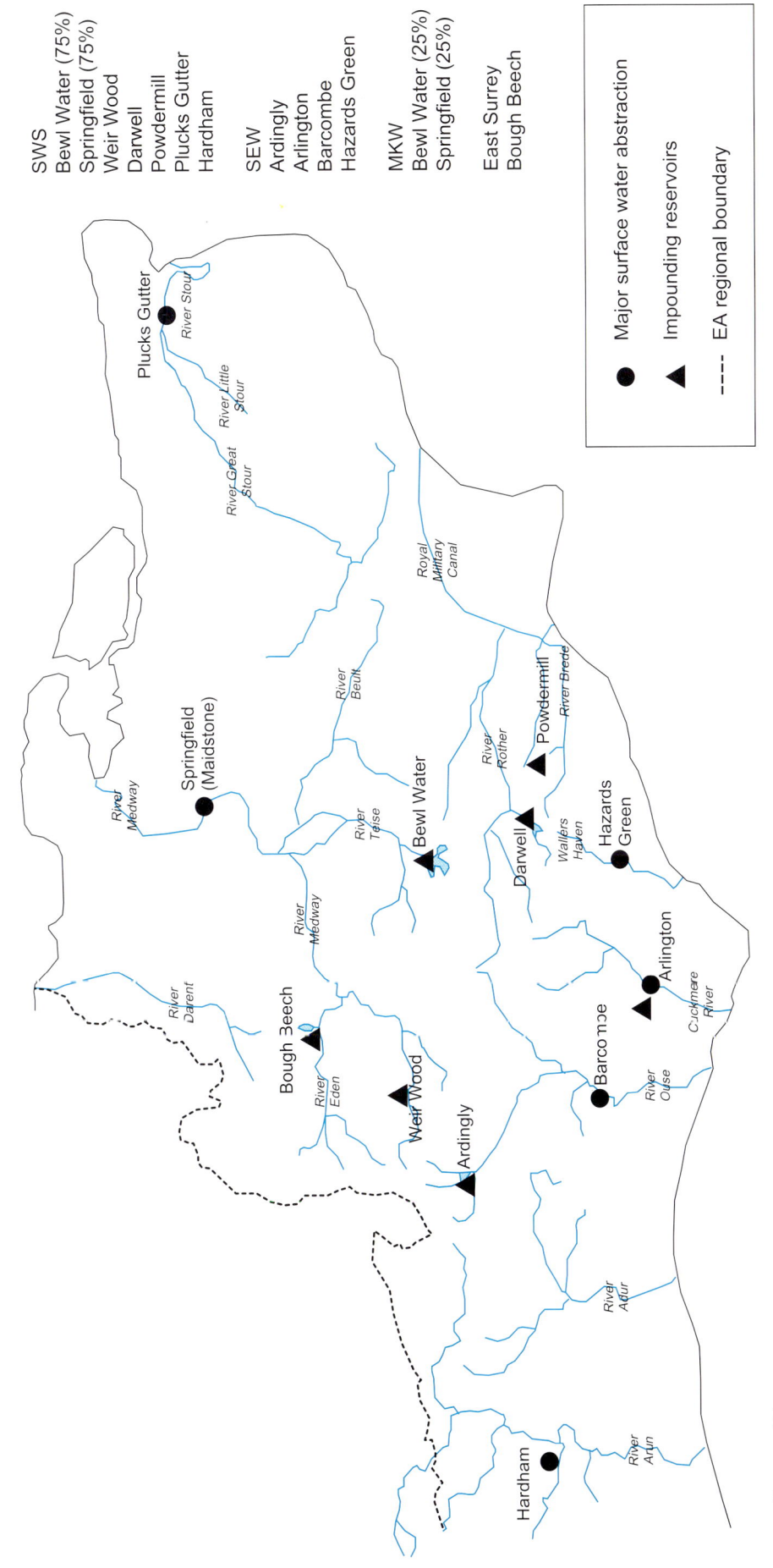

Source: EA.

MAP 2
(referred to in paragraphs 3.7, 5.7 and 5.13)

Aquifers and public water supply sources

Major aquifer—chalks and upper greensand			o	Public water supply sources
Minor aquifer—sandstones, tertiary sands and gravels			-----	EA regional boundary
Non-aquifer—clays				

Hastings beds

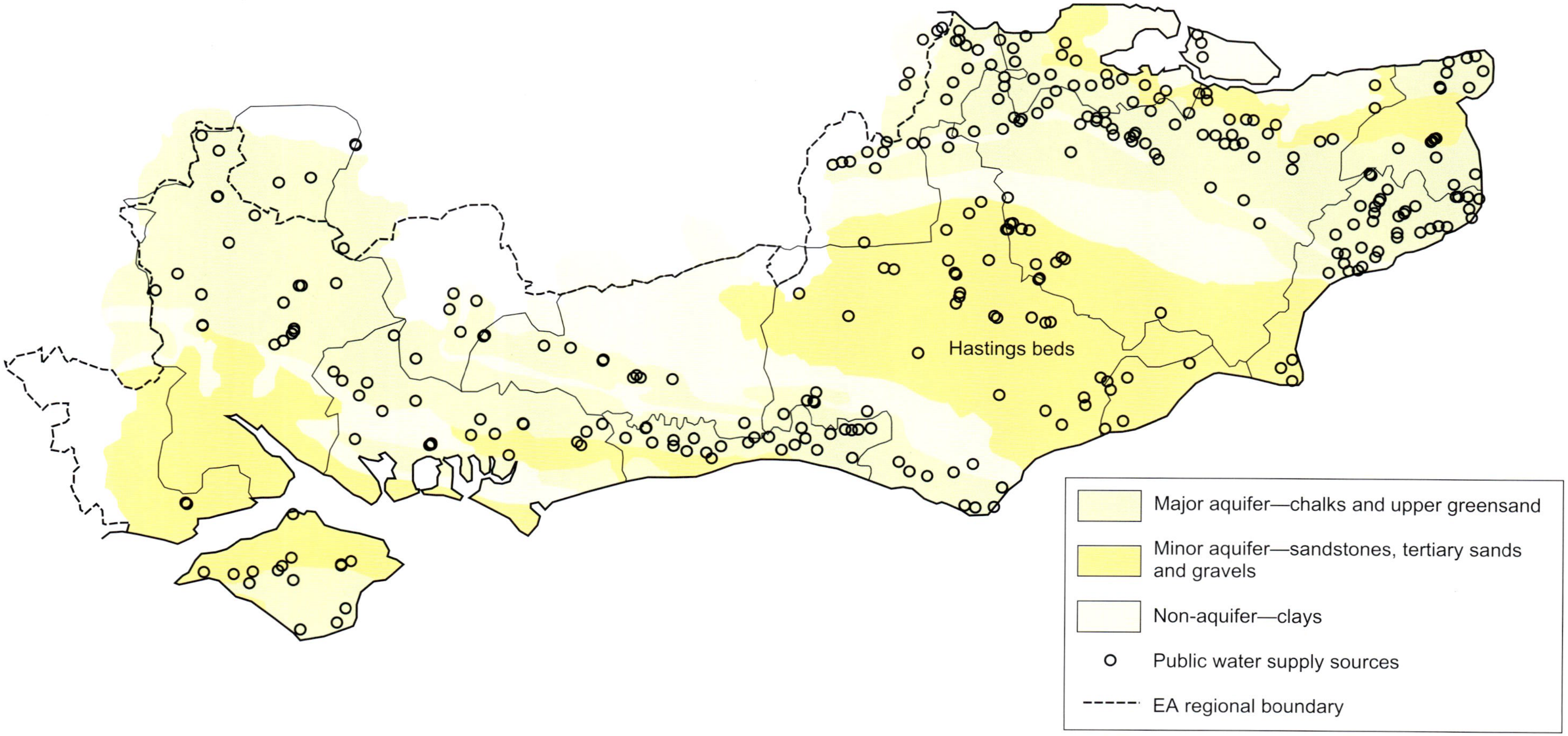

Source: EA.

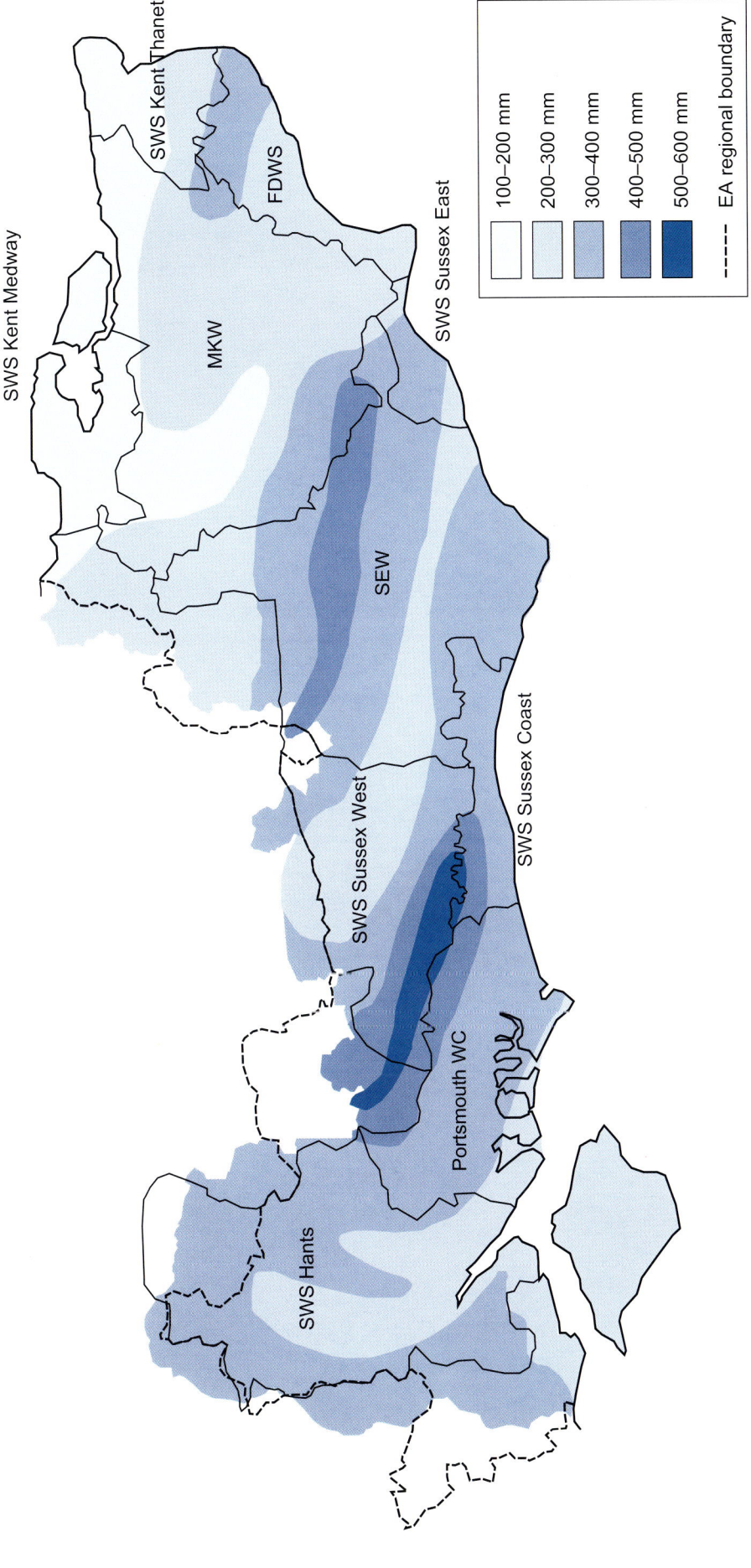

MAP 3
(referred to in paragraphs 3.7, 5.7 and 5.12)

Rainfall characteristics of Southern Region

Source: EA.

MAP 4
(referred to in paragraphs 5.57, 5.58, 6.9, 6.12, 7.31 and 9.22)

The GU and SAUR proposed primary network 'mini-grid'

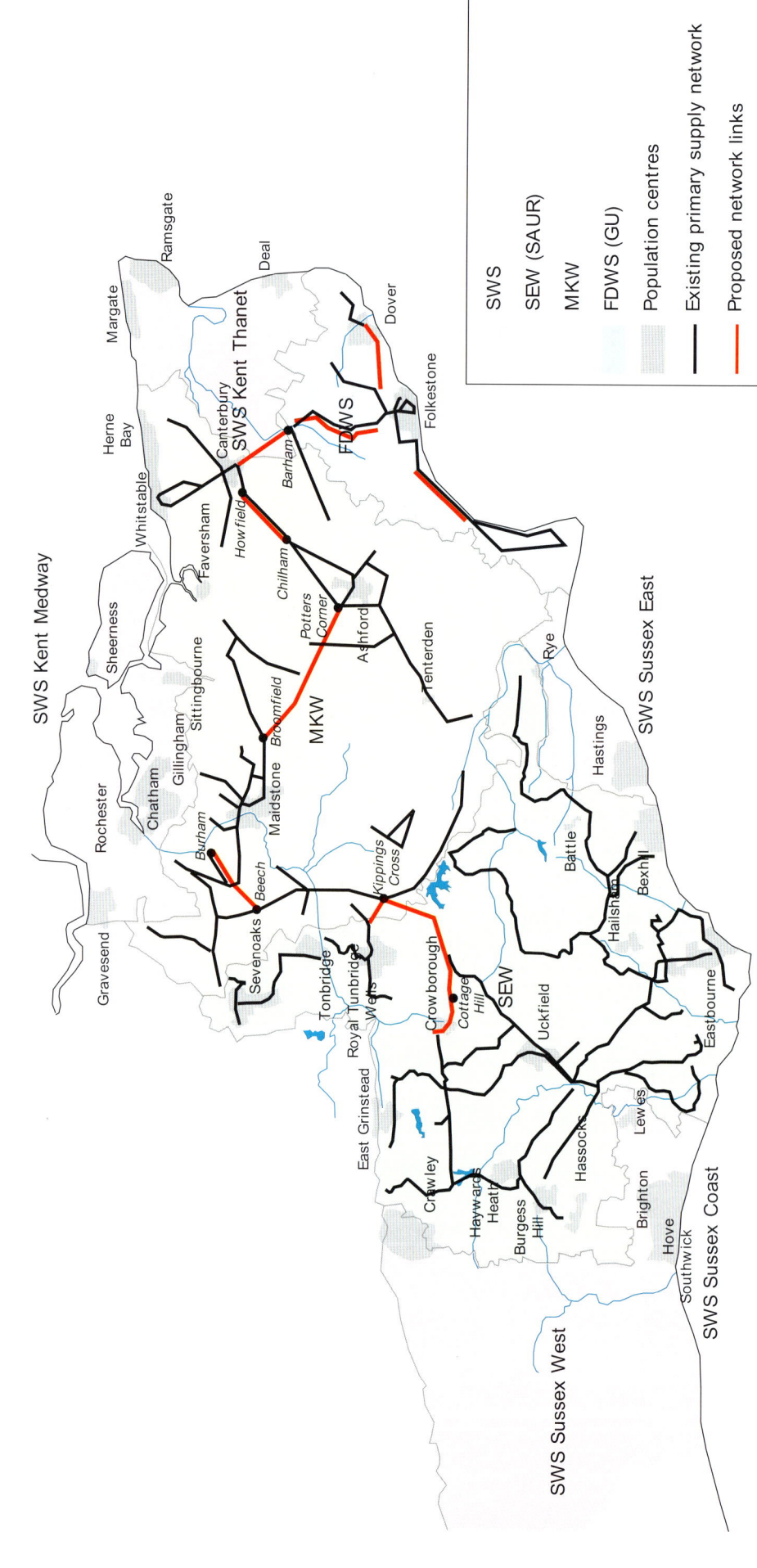

Source: GU/SAUR.

MAP 5
(referred to in paragraphs 3.71 and 7.31)

MKW existing network including primary network and proposed Strategic Business Plan (1994) mains

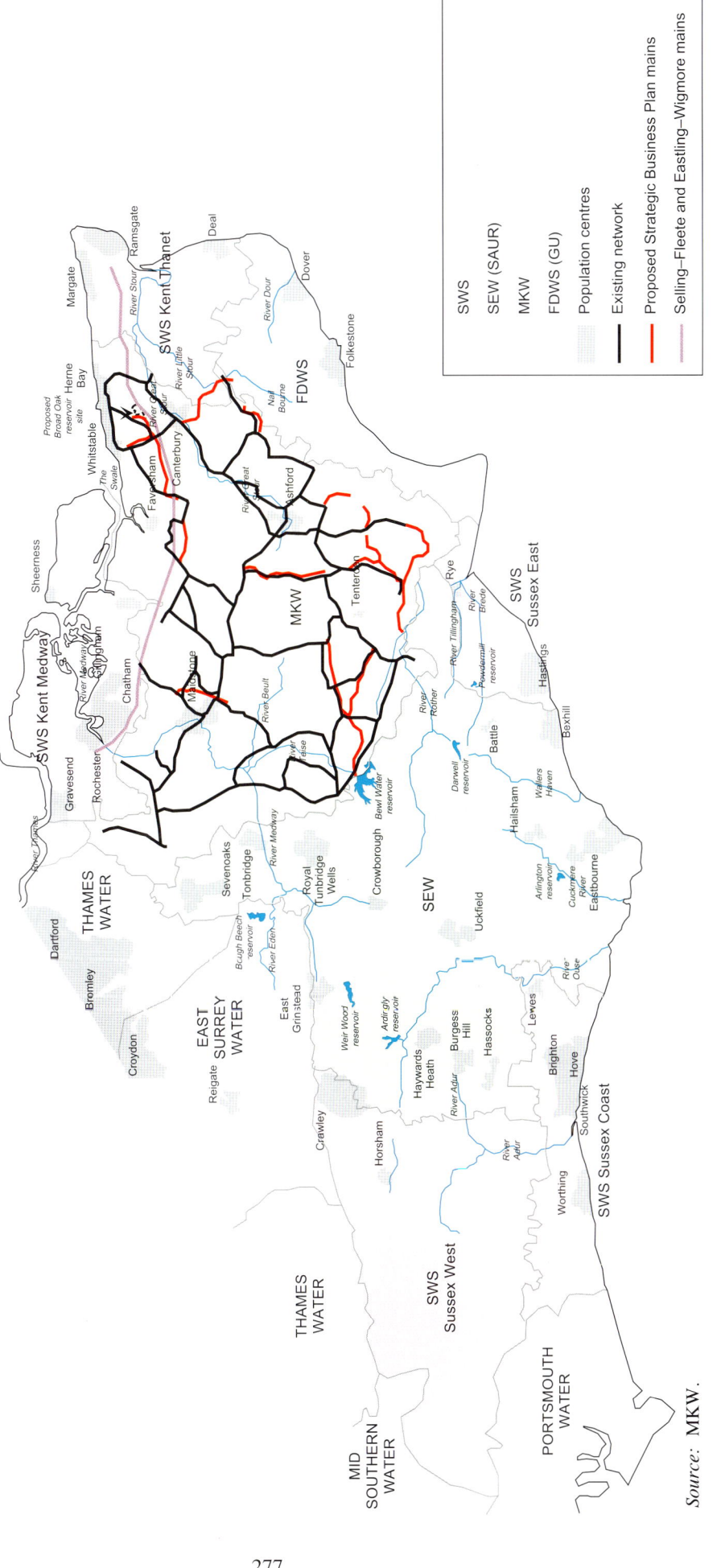

Source: MKW.

MAP 6
(referred to in paragraph 5.30)

EA resource development strategy

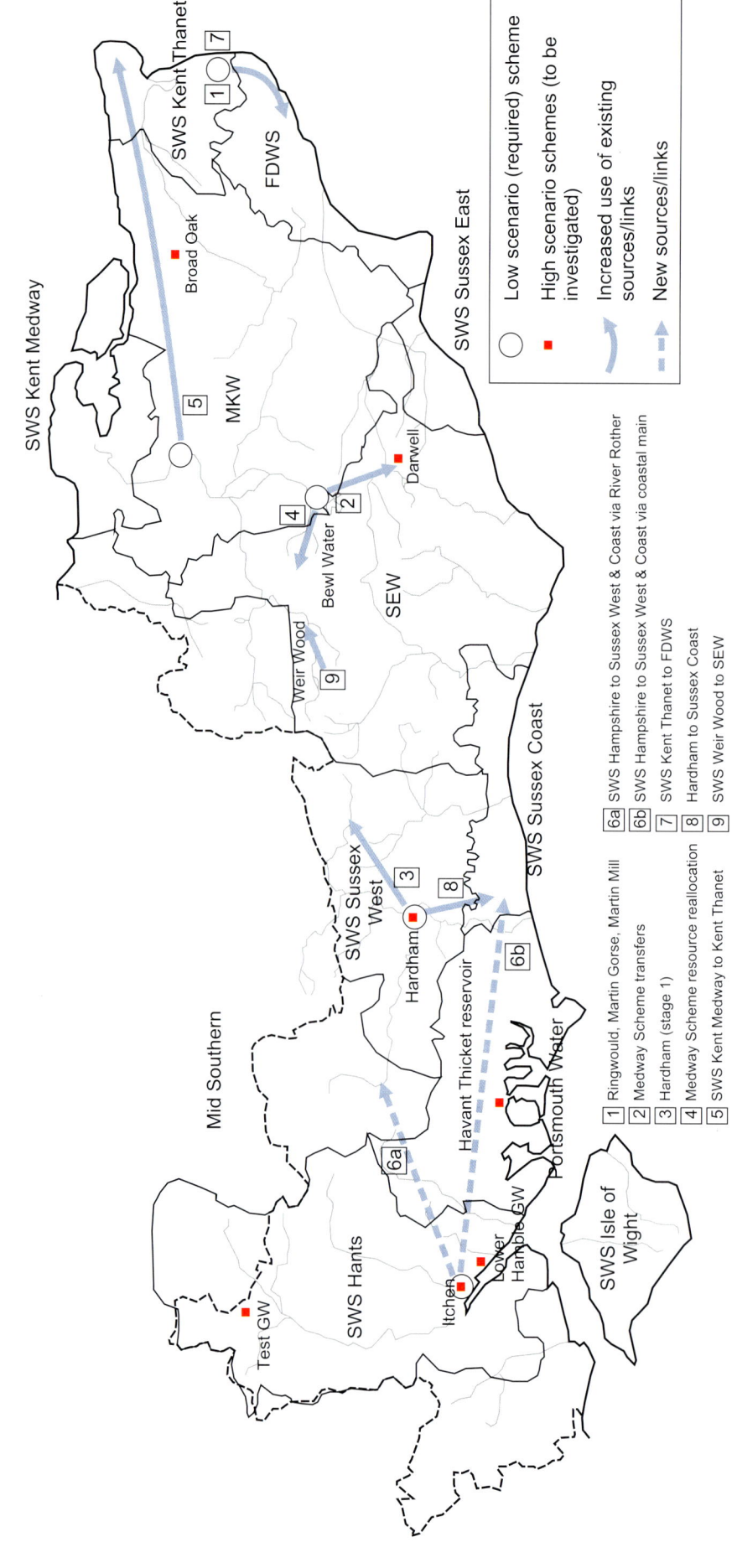

Source: EA.